CENSUS OF INDIA 1931

Owing to the antiquity and rarity of this book, certain pages are regrettably absent, and readability is compromised due to the blurring of the original text. If you possess any insights regarding the availability of these missing sections, kindly inform us. Your assistance is crucial in ensuring the completion of this significant work for the benefit of future generations.

CENSUS OF INDIA, 1931

BOOK - 38: VOLUME - XXII

GWALIOR

PART II - TABLES

RANG LAL

GYAN

Published by

Gyan Publishing House
5, Ansari Road
Daryaganj, New Delhi-110002
Phone: 011-47034999, 9811692060
E-mail: books@gyanbooks.com

Distribution Network
gyanbooks.com
India, USA, Canada, UK, Australia

ISBN: 978-81-212-7123-3 (Set) 28 Vols. In 52 Bindings

ISBN: 978-81-212-7525-5 (PB) Vol. XXII, Pt. II

First Published, 1932

2nd Impression 2024

Printed at: Gyan Press, Delhi.

CENSUS OF INDIA 1931

Census of India, 1931

VOLUME XXII

GWALIOR

PART II.—TABLES

By RANG LAL, B. A.

1932
PRINTED AT THE ALIJAH DARBAR PRESS
GWALIOR.

TABLE OF CONTENTS.

IMPERIAL TABLES.

STATE TABLES.

TABLE I.

Area, Houses and Population.

NOTE 1.—Population and area by Tehsils showing distribution by religion and literacy are given in State Table I and II at the end of this volume.

NOTE 2.—The number of villages shown in column 4 of the Table is that of inhabited villages only.

NOTE 3.—The term "Occupied Houses" means "inhabited houses" and includes dwelling shops, Sarais, Temples and Masjids, but does not include Boats and Railway trains.

NOTE 4.—In this State there are two small tracts under British Administration namely Nimach Cantonment and the Gwalior Residency Headquarters. Details of the area and population of these tracts are:—

	Area.	Persons.	Males.	Females.
1. Nimach Cantonment ...	4·11 square miles.	9,542	5,063	4,479.
2. Residency Headquarters.	1 square mile.	181	120	61.

NOTE. 5.—The area shown in column 2 of the Table is less by 16 square miles than that in Imperial Table I of 1921. The decrease is due to minor inter-statal transfer of territory and other causes fully dealt with in the Report. A list of the alterations with the reasons for them is given below:—

	Area.	Reasons.
Area in 1921 ...	26,383	Table I of 1921.
Additions.		
Indore and Dhar Darbar's. share in Sundersi.	7·9	Transferred to the Gwalior Darbar.
Larawad	3·6	
Area of some holdings which was not available in 1921.	11·9	The Area was not available in 1921. Now it is available.
	26,406·4	
Deductions.		
Pathari (Nawab) ...	29	Not Censused by Gwalior this time.
Nimrol	3	Population of this village has not been included in Gwalior State population.
Seven villages in exchange of Sundersi.	7·4	These villages have been transferred to Indore and Dhar Darbars.

TABLE I.—Area, Houses and Population.

District.	Area in Square Miles.	Towns	Villages.	OCCUPIED HOUSES. Total.	In Towns.	In Villages.	POPULATION. PERSONS. Total.	Urban.	Rural.
1	2	3	4	5	6	7	8	9	10
Gwalior State.	26,367	43	10,352	767,830	97,655	670,175	3,523,070	395,309	3,127,761
1 Gird District	1,712	6	783	83,150	32,990	50,160	364,806	131,027	233,779
2 Bhind District	1,718	2	879	86,214	3,773	82,441	418,224	15,959	402,265
3 Tonwarghar District ...	2,004	4	784	74,107	4,554	69,553	369,648	18,499	351,149
4 Sheopur District ...	2,866	1	566	30,888	1,810	29,078	137,034	6,905	130,129
5 Narwar District	3,876	5	1,300	88,161	5,986	82,175	401,586	24,382	377,204
6 Isagarh District	4,477	6	1,902	89,912	7,061	82,881	421,311	31,385	389,926
7 Bhilsa District	1,905	2	899	50,628	3,799	46,829	235,288	15,197	220,091
8 Ujjain District	2,741	6	1,133	93,233	20,468	72,765	405,961	81,914	324,047
9 Mandsaur District	1,777	5	947	62,010	10,333	51,677	272,166	41,113	231,053
10 Shajapur District	2,460	3	1,064	77,740	4,808	72,932	336,980	20,207	316,773
11 Amjhera District	1,631	3	595	31,757	2,078	29,684	160,066	8,721	151,345

District.	POPULATION. MALES. Total.	Urban.	Rural.	FEMALES. Total.	Urban.	Rural.
1	11	12	13	14	15	16
Gwalior State.	1,867,031	214,586	1,652,445	1,656,039	180,723	1,475,316
1 Gird District	197,935	72,938	124,997	166,871	58,089	108,782
2 Bhind District	228,214	8,806	219,408	190,010	7,153	182,857
3 Tonwarghar District ...	204,759	10,359	194,400	164,889	8,140	156,749
4 Sheopur District	72,925	3,558	69,367	64,109	3,347	60,762
5 Narwar District	211,555	13,068	198,487	190,031	11,314	178,717
6 Isagarh District	221,556	16,688	204,868	199,755	14,697	185,058
7 Bhilsa District	123,084	8,038	115,046	112,204	7,159	105,045
8 Ujjain District	211,274	44,874	166,400	194,687	37,040	157,647
9 Mandsaur District... ...	140,333	21,245	119,088	131,833	19,868	111,965
10 Shajapur District	174,985	10,479	164,506	161,995	9,728	152,267
11 Amjhera District	80,411	4,533	75,878	79,655	4,188	75,467

TABLE II.

Variation in Population since 1901.

NOTE 1.— The population of 1901, 1911 and 1921 given in this Table has been adjusted in conformity with the alterations made in the areas specified on the fly-leaf of Imperial Table I.

TABLE II.—Variation in Population since 1901.

District.	PERSONS.				VARIATION. INCREASE(+) DECREASE (—)		
	1931	1921	1911	1901	1921 to 1931	1911 to 1921	1901 to 1911
1	2	3	4	5	6	7	8
Gwalior State.	3,523,070	3,193,176	3,235,303	3,073,651	+ 329,894	— 42,127	+ 161,652
1 Gird District	364,806	326,466	312,339	385,104	+ 38,340	+ 14,127	— 72,765
2 Bhind District	418,224	382,179	400,159	418,175	+ 36,045	— 17,980	— 18,016
3 Tonwarghar District	369,648	336,660	379,113	376,916	+ 32,988	— 42,453	+ 2,197
4 Sheopur District	137,034	124,865	125,763	135,165	+ 12,169	— 898	— 9,402
5 Narwar District	401,586	376,715	414,328	370,111	+ 24,871	— 37,613	+ 44,217
6 Isagarh District	421,811	377,000	390,755	329,895	+ 44,811	— 13,755	+ 60,860
7 Bhilsa District	235,288	244,263	192,219	140,525	— 8,975	+ 52,044	+ 51,694
8 Ujjain Di·trict	405,961	343,370	344,314	308,631	+ 62,591	— 944	+ 35,683
9 Mandsaur District	272,166	237,745	237,128	216,977	+ 34,421	+ 617	+ 20,151
10 Shajapur District	336,980	307,393	313,409	288,565	+ 29,587	— 6,016	+ 24,844
11 Amjhera District	160,066	136,520	125,776	103,587	+ 23,546	+ 10,744	+ 22,189

District.	Net Variation during 1901 to 1931 Increase + Decrease (—)	MALES.			FEMALES.		
		1931	1921	1911	1931	1921	1911
1	9	10	11	12	13	14	15
Gwalior State.	+ 449,419	1,867,031	1,695,355	1,699,808	1,656,039	1,497,821	1,535,495
1 Gird District	— 20,298	197,935	178,371	166,946	166,871	148,095	145,393
2 Bhind District	+ 49	228,214	208,524	216,448	190,010	173,655	183,711
3 Tonwarghar District	— 7,268	204,759	186,908	207,141	164,889	149,752	171,972
4 Seopur District	+ 1,869	72,925	66,462	66,358	64,109	58,403	59,405
5 Narwar District	+ 31,475	211,555	199,212	216,828	190,031	177,503	197,500
6 Isagarh District	+ 91,416	221,556	197,720	203,774	199,755	179,280	186,981
7 Bhilsa District	+ 94,763	123,084	128,511	99,159	112,204	115,752	93,060
8 Ujjain District	+ 97,330	211,274	178,928	176,795	194,687	164,442	167,519
9 Mandsaur District	+ 55,189	140,333	122,645	122,147	131,833	115,100	114,981
10 Shajapur District	+ 48,415	174,985	159,089	161,432	161,995	148,304	151,977
11 Amjhera District	+ 56,479	80,411	68,985	62,780	79,655	67,535	62,996

TABLE III.

Towns and Villages Classified by Population.

NOTE. 1.—For definition of "Town" see fly-leaf of Table IV.

NOTE. 2.—The "Village" is the Revenue village including attached hamlets.

NOTE. 3.—In column 2 the figures 10,895 include 10,852 villages and 43 towns.

TABLE III.—Towns and Villages Classified by Population.

District	Total Number of Inhabited Towns and Villages.	Population.	Under 500 Number.	Under 500 Population.	500—1,000 Number.	500—1,000 Population.	1,000—2,000 Number.	1,000—2,000 Population.
1	2	3	4	5	6	7	8	9
Gwalior State.	10,895	3,523,070	9,331	1,703,192	1,083	742,206	371	500,370
1 Gird District ...	789	364,806	678	120,677	70	48,216	35	49,802
2 Bhind District ...	881	418,224	610	136,171	173	118,018	82	110,432
3 Tonwarghar District...	783	369,648	550	116,691	151	102,555	67	92,961
4 Sheopur District ...	567	137,034	518	78,146	32	21,609	13	16,985
5 Narwar District ...	1,305	401,586	1,110	217,547	146	101,218	43	54,199
6 Isagarh District ...	1,908	421,311	1,762	271,584	113	75,674	22	28,985
7 Bhilsa District ...	901	235,298	821	160,501	69	47,068	6	10,285
8 Ujjain District ...	1,130	405,961	991	196,142	110	74,005	25	33,386
9 Mandsaur District ...	952	272,166	840	123,910	72	51,282	28	37,594
10 Shajapur District ...	1,067	336,980	918	181,738	105	72,629	36	50,352
11 Amjhera District ...	598	160,066	538	100,085	42	27,937	12	15,389

District.	2,000—5,000 Number.	2,000—5,000 Population.	5,000—10,000 Number.	5,000—10,000 Population.	10,000—20,000 Number.	10,000—20,000 Population.	20,000—50,000 Number.	20,000—50,000 Population.	50,000—100,000 Number.	50,000—100,000 Population.	Encampments, Boat and Railway Population unclassed.
1	10	11	12	13	14	15	16	17	18	19	20
Gwalior State.	87	239,6[illegible]	13	92,964	7	80,900	1	21,999	2	132,459	9,340
1 Gird District ...	6	14,532	2	16,174	1	10,00[illegible]	1	21,999	1	78,080	4,030
2 Bhind District ...	14	[illegible]	1	5,018	1	10,311	...	...	...	...	460
3 Tonwarghar District...	13	[illegible]	1	7,210	...	...	...	...	...	...	1,213
4 Sheopur District ...	2	[illegible]	1	[illegible]	...	...	...	...	...	...	2,862
5 Narwar District ...	5	[illegible]	...		1	[illegible]	...	...	...	...	...
6 Isagarh District ...	9	[illegible]	1	[illegible]	1	[illegible]	...	...	...	...	599
7 Bhilsa District ...	3	[illegible]		...	1	[illegible]	...	...	...	...	...
8 Ujjain District ...	[illegible]	[illegible]	1	[illegible]	1	[illegible]	...	...	1	[illegible]	...
9 Mandsaur District ...	6	[illegible]	2	[illegible]	1	[illegible]		...	...	...	85
10 Shajapur District ...	[illegible]	[illegible]	[illegible]	[illegible]	...				...	...	...
11 Amjhera District ...	[illegible]	[illegible]				...	...		...	...	...

TABLE IV.

Cities and Towns Classified by Population with Variation for Fifty Years.

NOTE 1.—The term "Town" in this as well as in other Tables includes:—

(a) Every Municipality.

(b) Every Cantonment.

(c) Every other collection of houses inhabited by not less than 5,000 persons.

NOTE 2.—All the Cantonments with the exception of the one at Nimach have been included as sub-heads of the towns to which they belong.

NOTE 3.—In this Table total (A) gives the total urban population recorded in past decades and thus includes the populations of areas previously treated as towns but subsequently omitted. Total (B) gives the net urban population and has been arrived at, as will be seen from the following table, by deducting from the bare urban total (Total A) the populations of places previously treated as towns but subsequently omitted:—

	1921	1911	1901	1891	1881	Males.		Females.	
						1921	1911	1921	1911
Total A	308,383	277,789	349,771	339,543	279,647	167,234	147,812	141,149	129,977
Towns:—									
Deduct									
1. Bardu ...	...	...	...	...	6,841	...	...	...	...
2. Bhilgarh ...	...	...	...	...	6,427	...	...	...	...
3. Karahiya ...	...	...	4,969	7,182	...	...	...	...	...
4. Baroda (Sheopur).	3,988	5,078	6,881	6,760	6,767	2,067	2,592	1,921	2,481
5. Goona Station ...	4,805	5,099	6,087	...	...	2,433	2,768	2,372	2,331
6. Agar Station ...	1,110	3,487	3,990	...	...	617	1,981	493	1,506
Total ...	*9,903*	*13,659*	*21,397*	*13,912*	*20,055*	*5,117*	*7,341*	*4,786*	*6,318*
Total B ...	298,480	264,136	328,374	325,631	259,592	162,117	140,471	136,363	123,659

TABLE IV.—Cities and Towns Classified by

Serial Number.	Name of City or Town.	District.	Description of Town.	POPULATION.					
				1931	1921	1911	1901	1891	1881
1	2	3	4	5	6	7	8	9	10
	Gwalior State. Total (A)* ...			395,309	308,383	277,780	349,771	339,543	279,647
	Total (B)* ...			395,309	298,480	264,130	328,374	325,631	259,592
	Class II. 50,000 to 100,000.								
1	Lashkar City and Cantt. ...	Gird.	Municipality.	86,767	80,887	56,187	102,626	104,088	88,066
	Lashkar City Proper ...	Gird.	Municipality.	78,680	...	46,952	89,154	...	...
2	Lashkar Cantonment ...	Gird.	Cantonment.	8,087	...	9,235	13,472	...	...
3	Ujjain City and Cantt. ...	Ujjain.	Municipality.	54,650	48,908	39,295	39 892	34,691	32,932
	Ujjain City Proper ...	Ujjain.	Municipality.	53,779	...	...	...	...	...
4	Ujjain Cantonment ...	Ujjain.	Cantonment.	871	...	...	...	...	...
	Class III. 20,000 to 50,000.								
5	Gwalior	Gird.	Municipality.	21,909	13,087	14,694	16,807	...	...
	Class IV. 10,000 to 20,000.								
6	Morar and Cantt. ...	Gird.	Municipality.	18,183	20,260	13,577	19,142	24,518	24,022
	Morar Proper including Residency.	Gird.	Municipality.	10,096	...	...	...	...	...
7	Morar Cantonment ...	Gird.	Cantonment.	8,087	..	...	...	...	...
8	Mandsaur	Mandsaur.	Municipality.	15,880	16,217	16,785	20,986	25,785	22,596
9	Shivpuri	Narwar.	Municipality.	12,954	11,015	10,628	...	...	...
10	Goona...	Isagarh.	Municipality.	11,022	6,790	6,586	5,415	...	...
11	Bhilsa	Bhilsa.	Municipality.	10,570	8.801	8,427	7,481	9,670	7,070
12	Barnagar	Ujjain.	Municipality.	10,581	8,548	8,684	10 856	10,261	7,908
13	Bhind	Bhind.	Municipality.	10,341	9,619	9,183	8,032	9,188	7,412
	Class V. 5,000 to 10,000.								
14	Khachraud	Ujjain.	Municipality.	9,790	7,850	6,496	9,186	9,034	9,489
15	Nimach Cantonment ...	Mandsaur.	Cantonment.	9,542	10,490	12,318	14,024	15,291	13,069
16	Shajapur	Shajapur.	Municipality.	7,766	7,894	8,870	9,958	11,043	9,247
17	Agar	Shajapur.	Municipality.	7,815	5,079	5,784	6,452	7,692	6,193
18	Morena	Tonwarghar.	Municipality.	7,240	4,783	2,690	...	...	...
19	Sheopur	Sheopur.	Municipality.	6,905	5,898	5,581	6,712	7,600	8,403
20	Jawad...	Mandsaur.	Municipality.	6,588	6,310	6,505	8,005	8,920	...
21	Gohad...	Bhind.	Municipality.	5,618	4,845	5,189	5 848	5,878	...
22	Pachhar	Isagarh.	Municipality.	5,608	...	..	...	...	...
23	Gangapur	Mandsaur	Municipality.	5,298	..	...	...	...	5,590
24	Shujalpur	Shajapur.	Municipality.	5,126	6,072	5,938	5,731	6.669	7,186
	Class VI. under 5,000.								
25	Mungaoli	Isagarh.	Municipality.	4,957	...	...	4,797	6,158	...
26	Basoda	Bhilsa.	Municipality.	4.627	...	...	...	...	...
27	Chanderi	Isagarh.	Municipality.	4,587	4,199	2.758	4,008	5.078	...
28	Manawar	Amjhera.	Municipality.	4,311	...	...	..	...	...
29	Nimach	Mandsaur.	Municipality.	4,304	3,978	4,989	6,190	6,809	5,161
30	Sabalgarh	Tonwarghar.	Municipality.	4,248	4,424	4,985	6,089	6,111	...
31	Bhander	Gird.	Municipality.	4,078	3,912	4,817	5,183	5.967	...
32	Sonkatch	Ujjain.	Municipality.	4,068	...	...	...	...	...
33	Kolaras	Narwar.	Municipality.	4,059	..	..	...	...	5,298
34	Karera with Cantonment ...	Narwar.	Municipality.	4,024	...	...	...	...	...
	Karera Proper	Narwar.	Municipality.	3,620	...	...	...	...	...
35	Karera Cantonment ...	Narwar.	Cantonment.	404	...	...	...	...	...
36	Joura	Tawarghar.	Municipality.	3,901	...	...	...	...	...
37	Narwar	Narwar.	Municipality.	3,845	3,274	3,918	4,929	6,190	...
38	Ambah	Tonwarghar.	Municipality.	3,110	...	...	...	...	...
39	Unhel...	Ujjain.	Municipality.	2,871	...	...	...	...	...
40	Rajgarh	Amjhera.	Municipality.	2,772	...	...	...	...	...
41	Isagarh	Isagarh.	Municipality.	2,678	...	...	...	...	...
42	Bajrangarh	Isagarh.	Municipality.	2,548	...	...	...	...	...
43	Sardarpur	Amjhera.	Municipality.	1,688	...	...	...	...	...

*A and B see fly leaf

Population with Variation for Fifty Years.

Variation. Increase (+) Decrease (−) 1921 to 1931.	1911 to 1921.	1901 to 1911.	1891 to 1901.	1881 to 1891.	Variation during 1881 to 1931. Increase (+) Decrease (−).	Males 1931	Males 1921	Males 1911	Females 1931	Females 1921	Females 1911	Serial Number.
11	12	13	14	15	16	17	18	19	20	21	22	23
+ 86,926	+ 70,594	− 71,952	+ 10,228	+ 59,896	+ 115,662	214,586	167,234	147,812	180,728	141,149	129,977	
+ 96,829	34,350	− 61,244	2,743	+ 66,039	135,717	214,586	162,117	140,471	180,723	136,363	123,659	
+ 6,380	+ 24,200	− 16,430	− 1,457	− 16,017	− 1,290	47,358	44,505	30,533	39,409	35,792	25,654	1
...	...		...	...	...	42,538	...	24,245	36,142	...	22,707	
...	...		...	...	...	4,820	...	6,288	3,267	...	2,947	2
+ 10,742	+ 4,618	− 597	+ 5,201	+ 1,759	21,716	30,597	24,350	20,864	21,058	19,558	18,431	3
...	...	...	...	...	...	30,055	...	...	23,724	...	...	
...	...	...	...	...	...	542	...	...	829	...	...	4
+ 8,969	− 1,657	− 2,118	...	...	...	12,306	6,675	7,458	9,698	6,862	7,286	5
− 2,077	+ 6,683	− 5,565	− 5,376	496	5,829	11,187	12,342	8,610	6,996	7,918	4,967	6
...	...	...		..	...	5,506	...	...	4,590	...	...	
...		...		...	..	5,681	...	...	2,406	...	...	7
831	568	− 4,151	4,849	3,189	− 7,210	7,970	[illegible]	8,602	7,416	7,192	8,183	8
+ 1,033	+ 1,287					7,011	6,466	5,603	5,948	5,449	5,025	9
+ 4,232	+ 201	+ 1,171		..		6,758	3,571	3,514	5,264	3,219	3,072	10
+ 1,769	+ 374	916	2,189	+ 2,660	+ 3,501	5,569	4,709	4,428	5,001	4,082	3,999	11
+ 1,088	− 91	− 2,222	595	2,853	+ 2,623	5,567	4,502	4,431	4,964	4,041	4,200	12
+ 722	456	+ 1,101	1,156	1,776	2,929	5,801	5,396	5,081	4,540	4,283	4,052	13
+ 1,049	+ 1,354	− 2,690	+ 152	− 466	810	5,128	4,017	3,415	4,671	3,833	3,081	14
− 948	− 1,828	− 2,306	667	2,992	3,527	5,063	5,586	6,741	4,479	4,904	5,577	15
− 128	− 662	− 1,077	− 1,090	+ 1,796	− 1,461	3,993	3,971	4,410	3,773	3,923	4,466	16
+ [illegible]	655	718	1,210	+ 1,459	1,122	3,828	2,501	2,928	3,477	2,576	2,806	17
+ 2,457	+ 2,093			..	...	4,126	2,785	1,461	3,114	1,998	1,229	18
+ 1,097	867	− 1,181	688	− 803	− 1,498	3,558	3,060	2,758	3,347	2,888	2,778	19
+ 278	− 195	− 1,500	− 915		...	3,333	3,192	3,239	3,255	3,118	3,266	20
+ 773	− 294	− 204	− 35	...	...	3,005	2,534	2,659	2,613	2,311	2,480	21
...	...		...	..	...	3,095	...	...	2,513	...	...	22
...	...	...	...	...	− 297	2,786	...	...	2,557	...	...	23
− 916	+ 194	+ 207	− 928	− 467	− 2,010	2,648	3,194	3,028	2,478	2,876	2,910	24
...	...	...	− 1,361	...	...	2,781	...	...	2,226	...	...	25
...	...	...	...	..	...	2,469	...	...	2,158	...	...	26
+ 288	+ 1,446	− 1,340	− 980	...	..	2,377	2,095	1,414	2,210	2,104	1,389	27
...	...	...	...	...	...	2,161	...	...	2,150	...	...	28
+ 331	− 1,016	− 1,201	− 119	+ 1,148	− 857	2,118	2,016	2,565	2,161	1,957	2,424	29
− 176	− 561	− 1,054	− 72	...	...	2,228	2,367	2,605	2,020	2,057	2,380	30
+ 166	− 405	− 816	− 834	...	...	2,097	2,027	2,150	1,991	1,885	2,167	31
...	...	...	...	...	...	2,130	...	...	1,983	...	...	32
...	...	...	...	...	− 1,239	2,101	...	...	1,955	...	...	33
...	...	...	...	...	...	2,227	...	...	1,797	...	...	34
...	...	...	...	...	...	1,944	...	...	1,676	...	...	
...	...	...	...	...	...	283	...	...	121	...	...	35
...	...	...	...	..	...	2,167	...	...	1,784	...	...	36
+ 71	− 639	− 1,016	− 1,261	...	...	1,726	1,691	1,976	1,619	1,583	1,987	37
...	...	..	...	...	...	1,838	...	...	1,272	...	...	38
...	...	...	...	...	...	1,452	...	...	1,419	...	...	39
...	...	...	...	...	...	1,490	...	...	1,282	...	...	40
...	...	...	...	...	...	1,388	...	...	1,290	...	...	41
...	...	...	...	...	...	1,349	...	...	1,191	...	...	42
...	...	...	...	...	...	882	...	...	756	...	...	43

TABLE V.

Towns Arranged Territorially with Population by Religion.

Details of population included under other religions are :—

No.	Name of Town.	Other Religions. P.	M.	F.	Sikh. P.	M.	F.	Zoroastrian. P.	M.	F.
1	2	3	4	5	6	7	8	9	10	11
	Total ...	**492**	**257**	**235**	**269**	**167**	**102**	**223**	**90**	**133**
1	Lashkar City Municipal area ...	180	92	88	96	60	36	84	32	52
2	Morar Municipal area ...	35	21	14	32	20	12	3	1	2
3	Morar Cantonment	34	16	18	25	12	13	9	4	5
4	Bhind	1	1	...	1	1	...	...	...	...
5	Morena	4	2	2	4	2	2	...	...	...
6	Sheopur	1	1	...	1	1	...	...	...	...
7	Shivpuri	9	5	4	9	5	4	...	...	...
8	Pachhar	5	4	1	3	2	1	2	2	...
9	Mungaoli	4	3	1	4	3	1	...	...	...
10	Bhilsa	14	6	8	7	3	4	7	3	4
11	Ujjain City Municipal area ...	49	33	16	40	30	10	9	3	6
12	Barnagar	21	11	10	20	10	10	1	1	...
13	Mandsaur	17	12	5	12	9	3	5	3	2
14	Nimach	3	3	...	...	...	...	3	3	...
15	Nimach Cantonment ...	104	40	64	6	3	3	98	37	61
16	Jawad	7	5	2	5	4	1	2	1	1
17	Agar	1	...	1	1	..	1	...	...	...
18	Shujalpur	3	2	1	3	2	1	...	...	...

Civil and Military Population of Cantonments :—

Name of Cantonment.	Population. Military. Persons.	Males.	Females.	Civil. Persons.	Males.	Females.
1	2	3	4	5	6	7
Total ...	**12,382**	**8,783**	**3,599**	**14,609**	**7,606**	**7,003**
Lashkar Cantonment ...	3,934	2,579	1,355	4,153	2,241	1,912
Morar Cantonment ...	6,350	4,701	1,649	1,737	980	757
Karera Cantonment ...	404	283	121	...	...	...
Ujjain Cantonment ...	871	542	329	...	...	...
Nimach Cantonment ...	823	678	145	8,719	4,385	4,334

TABLE V.—Towns Arranged Territorially

Serial Number.	District.	Town, Municipality, Cantoment, etc.	POPULATION.			HINDU. BRAHMANIC.			HINDU. ARYA.			HINDU. HINDUISED TRIBAL.		
			Persons.	Males.	Females.	Persons.	Males.	Females	Persons.	Males.	Females.	Persons.	Males.	Females.
1	2	3	4	5	6	7	8	9	10	11	12	13	14	15
	Gwalior State.	...	395,309	214,586	180,723	285,163	155,551	129,612	435	239	196	307	147	160
	Gird District ...	...	131,027	72,938	58,089	97,901	54,753	43,148	74	51	23			
1		Lashkar City including Cantt.	86,767	47,858	39,409	64,399	35,147	29,252	43	38	5	...	...	...
		Municipal area	78,680	42,538	36,142	58,868	31,767	27,101	32	29	3	...	...	...
2		Lashkar Cantt. ...	8,087	4,820	3,267	5,531	3,380	2,151	11	9	2	...	...	...
3		Morar town including Cantt.	18,183	11,187	6,996	13,273	8,352	4,921	31	18	18	...	...	...
		Municipal area	9,915	5,386	4,529	7,597	4,155	3,442	23	10	13	...	...	...
4		Morar Cantt. ...	8,087	5,681	2,406	5,562	4,123	1,439	8	3	5	...	...	...
		Morar Residency.	181	120	61	114	74	40	...	...	...	...	...	...
5		Gwalior ...	21,999	12,306	9,693	16,778	9,481	7,297	...	...	...	...	...	...
6		Bhander ...	4,078	2,087	1,991	3,451	1,773	1,678	...	...	...	...	...	...
	Bhind District ...		15,959	8,806	7,153	12,115	6,688	5,427	3	2	1	...	...	...
7		Bhind ...	10,341	5,801	4,540	7,273	4,102	3,171	3	2	1	...	...	...
8		Gohad ...	5,618	3,005	2,613	4,842	2,586	2,256	...	...	...	...	...	...
	Tonwarghar Distt.		18,499	10,359	8,140	14,509	8,107	6,402	25	12	13	5	3	2
9		Joura ...	3,901	2,167	1,734	2,866	1,594	1,272	...	...	...	5	3	2
10		Ambah ...	3,110	1,838	1,272	2,441	1,435	1,006	...	...	...	...	...	...
11		Morena ...	7,240	4,126	3,114	5,680	3,229	2,451	25	12	13	...	...	...
12		Sabalgarh ...	4,248	2,228	2,020	3,522	1,849	1,673	...	...	...	...	...	...
	Sheopur District...		6,905	3,558	3,347	4,710	2,425	2,285	29	14	15	...	...	...
13		Sheopur ...	6,905	3,558	3,347	4,710	2,425	2,285	29	14	15	...	...	...
	Narwar District ...		24,382	13,068	11,314	18,994	10,183	8,811	23	20	3	2	2	...
14		Shivpuri ...	12,954	7,011	5,943	9,611	5,209	4,402	23	20	3	1	1	...
15		Karera including Cantt.	4,024	2,227	1,797	3,227	1,787	1,440	...	...	...	1	1	...
		Municipal area	3,620	1,944	1,676	2,941	1,578	1,363	...	...	...	1	1	...
16		Karera Cantt. ...	404	283	121	286	209	77	...	...	...	...	...	...
17		Narwar ...	3,345	1,726	1,619	2,807	1,453	1,354	...	...	...	...	...	...
18		Kolaras ...	4,059	2,104	1,955	3,349	1,734	1,615	...	...	...	...	...	...
	Isagarh District...		31,385	16,688	14,697	23,382	12,492	10,890	10	6	4	34	14	20
19		Bajrangarh ...	2,543	1,349	1,194	2,266	1,208	1,058	...	...	...	...	...	...
20		Goona ...	11,022	5,758	5,264	8,510	4,528	3,982	...	...	...	...	...	...
21		Pachhar ...	5,598	3,085	2,513	4,207	2,317	1,890	5	2	3	34	14	20
22		Isagarh ...	2,078	1,888	1,290	2,178	1,124	1,054	...	...	...	...	...	...
23		Mungaoli ...	4,957	2,731	2,226	3,327	1,818	1,509	5	4	1	...	...	...
24		Chanderi ...	4,587	2,337	2,210	2,894	1,497	1,397	...	...	...	...	...	...
	Bhilsa District ...		15,197	8,038	7,159	11,834	6,223	5,611	18	5	13	...	...	...
25		Bhilsa ...	10,570	5,569	5,001	8,253	4,315	3,938	18	5	13	...	...	...
26		Basoda ...	4,627	2,469	2,158	3,581	1,908	1,673	...	...	...	...	...	...
	Ujjain District ...		81,914	44,874	37,040	56,047	30,945	25,102	106	59	47	30	14	16
27		Ujjain city including Cantt.	54,650	30,597	24,053	37,115	21,024	16,091	86	54	32	12	5	7
		Municipal area	53,779	30,055	23,724	36,495	20,633	15,862	86	54	32	12	5	7
28		Ujjain Cantt. ...	871	542	329	620	391	229	...	...	...	...	...	...
29		Barnagar ...	10,531	5,567	4,964	7,232	3,809	3,423	20	5	15	16	8	8
30		Khachraud ...	9,799	5,128	4,671	6,566	3,444	3,122	...	...	...	2	1	1
31		Unhel ...	2,871	1,452	1,419	2,084	1,052	1,032	...	...	...	...	...	...
32		Sonkatch ...	4,063	2,130	1,933	3,050	1,616	1,434	...	...	...	...	...	...
	Mandsaur District.		41,113	21,245	19,868	26,875	13,895	12,980	54	26	28	33	21	12
33		Mandsaur ...	15,386	7,970	7,416	9,085	4,653	4,432	8	4	4	4	3	1
34		Nimach Town ...	4,304	2,143	2,161	3,050	1,508	1,512	...	...	...	7	4	3
35		Nimach Cantt ...	9,542	5,063	4,479	5,908	3,236	2,672	46	22	24	...	...	...
36		Jawad ...	6,588	3,333	3,255	4,516	2,283	2,263	...	...	...	22	14	8
37		Gangapur ...	5,293	2,736	2,557	4,286	2,215	2,071	...	...	...	...	...	...
	Shajapur District.		20,207	10,479	9,728	13,072	6,870	6,202	57	29	28	22	9	13
38		Shajapur ...	7,766	3,993	3,773	4,932	2,553	2,379	22	13	9	...	...	...
39		Agar ...	7,315	3,838	3,477	4,940	2,651	2,289	27	13	14	...	...	...
40		Shujalpur ...	5,126	2,648	2,478	3,200	1,666	1,534	8	3	5	22	9	13
	Amjhera District ..		8,721	4,533	4,188	5,724	2,970	2,751	36	15	21	181	84	97
41		Sardarpur ...	1,608	852	756	1,310	717	593	19	7	12	7	2	5
42		Rajgarh ...	2,772	1,490	1,282	1,621	877	744	...	...	...	10	1	9
43		Manawar ...	4,311	2,161	2,150	2,763	1,376	1,387	17	8	9	164	81	83

with Population by Religion.

TOTAL HINDU.			JAIN.			MUSLIM.			CHRISTIAN.			OTHERS.			Serial Number.
Persons.	Males.	Females.	Persons.	Males.	Females.	Persons.	Males.	Females.	Persons.	Males.	Females.	Persons.	Males.	Females.	
16	17	18	19	20	21	22	23	24	25	26	27	28	29	30	31
285,905	155,937	129,968	16,986	9,308	7,678	91,179	48,735	42,444	747	349	398	492	257	235	
97,975	54,804	43,171	1,682	948	734	30,876	16,930	13,946	245	127	118	249	129	120	
64,442	35,185	29,257	1,220	699	521	20,729	11,278	9,451	196	104	92	180	92	88	1
58,900	31,796	27,104	1,098	607	491	18,312	9,941	8,371	190	102	88	180	92	88	
5,542	3,389	2,153	122	92	30	2,417	1,337	1,080	6	2	4	...	...	...	2
13,304	8,365	4,939	263	140	123	4,503	2,624	1,879	44	21	23	69	37	32	3
7,620	4,165	3,455	257	137	120	1,965	1,046	919	38	17	21	35	21	14	
5,570	4,126	1,444	6	3	3	2,475	1,535	940	2	1	1	34	16	18	4
114	74	40	...	...	...	63	43	20	4	3	1	...	...	...	
16,778	9,491	7,297	192	107	85	5,024	2,716	2,308	5	2	3	...	...	...	5
3,451	1,773	1,678	7	2	5	620	312	308	...	...	...	...	...	...	6
12,118	6,690	5,428	1,230	696	534	2,605	1,416	1,189	5	3	2	1	1	...	
7,276	4,104	3,172	1,189	676	513	1,870	1,017	853	5	3	2	1	1	...	7
4,842	2,586	2,256	41	20	21	735	399	336	...	...	...	...	...	...	8
14,539	8,122	6,417	562	332	230	3,394	1,903	1,491	...	...	...	4	2	2	
2,871	1,597	1,274	115	58	57	915	512	403	...	...	...	...	...	...	9
2,441	1,435	1,006	126	80	46	543	323	220	...	...	...	...	...	...	10
5,705	3,241	2,464	321	194	127	1,210	689	521	...	...	...	4	2	2	11
3,522	1,849	1,673	...	...	...	726	379	347	...	...	...	...	...	...	12
4,739	2,439	2,300	148	78	70	2,017	1,040	977	...	...	...	1	1	...	
4,739	2,439	2,300	148	78	70	2,017	1,040	977	...	...	...	1	1	...	13
19,019	10,205	8,814	799	446	353	4,553	2,412	2,141	2	...	2	9	5	4	
9,635	5,230	4,405	340	206	134	2,968	1,570	1,398	2	...	2	9	5	4	14
3,228	1,788	1,440	75	40	35	721	399	322	...	...	...	...	...	...	15
2,942	1,579	1,363	75	40	35	603	325	278	...	...	...	...	...	...	
286	209	77	...	...	...	118	74	44	...	...	...	...	...	...	16
2,807	1,453	1,354	149	77	72	389	196	193	...	...	...	...	...	...	17
3,349	1,734	1,615	235	123	112	475	247	228	...	...	...	...	...	...	18
23,426	12,512	10,914	2,336	1,279	1,057	5,602	2,881	2,721	12	9	3	9	7	2	
2,266	1,208	1,058	159	88	71	118	53	65	...	...	...	...	...	...	19
8,510	4,528	3,982	324	182	142	2,181	1,042	1,139	7	6	1	...	...	...	20
4,246	2,333	1,913	769	430	339	573	315	258	5	3	2	5	4	1	21
2,178	1,124	1,054	91	56	35	409	208	201	...	...	...	...	...	...	22
3,332	1,822	1,510	619	329	290	1,002	577	425	...	...	...	4	3	1	23
2,894	1,497	1,397	374	194	180	1,319	686	633	...	...	...	...	...	...	24
11,852	6,228	5,624	1,006	532	474	2,319	1,269	1,050	6	3	3	14	6	8	
8,271	4,320	3,951	597	316	281	1,682	924	758	6	3	3	14	6	6	25
3,581	1,908	1,673	409	216	193	637	345	292	...	...	...	...	...	...	26
56,183	31,018	25,165	4,057	2,254	1,803	21,498	11,495	10,003	106	63	43	70	44	26	
37,218	21,088	16,130	1,906	1,080	826	15,397	8,351	7,046	85	50	35	49	33	16	27
36,593	20,692	15,901	1,906	1,080	826	15,146	8,200	6,946	85	50	35	49	33	16	
620	391	229	...	...	...	251	151	100	...	...	...	...	...	...	28
7,268	3,822	3,446	777	430	347	2,465	1,304	1,161	...	...	...	21	11	10	29
6,568	3,445	3,123	998	544	454	2,216	1,128	1,088	17	11	6	...	...	...	30
2,084	1,052	1,032	182	100	82	601	298	303	4	2	2	...	...	...	31
3,050	1,616	1,434	194	100	94	819	414	405	...	...	...	...	...	...	32
26,962	13,942	13,020	2,867	1,508	1,359	10,782	5,591	5,191	371	144	227	131	60	71	
9,097	4,660	4,437	1,377	788	589	4,889	2,557	2,332	6	3	3	17	12	5	33
3,057	1,512	1,545	250	133	117	994	495	499	...	...	...	3	3	...	34
5,954	3,258	2,696	198	97	101	2,923	1,528	1,395	363	140	223	104	40	64	35
4,568	2,297	2,271	566	295	271	1,445	735	710	2	1	1	7	5	2	36
4,286	2,215	2,071	476	245	231	531	276	255	...	...	...	...	...	...	37
13,151	6,908	6,243	1,373	730	643	5,679	2,839	2,840	...	...	...	4	2	2	
4,954	2,566	2,388	293	176	117	2,519	1,251	1,268	...	...	...	...	...	...	38
4,967	2,664	2,303	677	350	327	1,670	824	846	...	...	...	1	...	1	39
3,230	1,678	1,552	403	204	199	1,490	764	726	...	...	...	3	2	1	40
5,941	3,069	2,872	926	505	421	1,854	959	895	...	...	...	...	...	...	
1,366	726	640	3	2	1	269	154	115	...	...	...	...	...	...	41
1,631	878	753	773	422	351	368	190	178	...	...	...	...	...	...	42
2,944	1,465	1,479	150	81	69	1,217	615	602	...	...	...	...	...	...	43

TABLE VI.

Birthplace.

NOTE—This Table contains the statistics of Birthplace for the State as a whole and for each district and the cities of Lashkar and Ujjain.

TABLE VI.

District, State, Province or Country where born.	GWALIOR STATE.			DISTRICT GIRD.		
	Persons.	Males.	Females.	Persons.	Males.	Females.
1	2	3	4	5	6	7
Gwalior State.	3,523,070	1,867,031	1,656,039	364,806	197,935	166,871
A. Born in India	*3,522,870*	*1,866,888*	*1,655,982*	*364,723*	*197,891*	*166,832*
1. Districts within the State. ...	3,241,520	1,745,984	1,495,536	330,993	182,868	148,125
Gird	297,036	181,305	115,731	314,490	174,325	140,165
Bhind	408,549	226,909	181,640	5,303	2,691	2,612
Tonwarghar	358,681	251,513	107,168	4,797	2,937	1,860
Sheopur...	125,932	67,113	58,819	330	190	140
Narwar	409,235	210,828	198,407	4,806	1,979	2,827
Isagarh	402,038	212,608	189,430	403	209	194
Bhilsa	193,428	102,359	91,069	169	79	90
Ujjain	341,189	180,295	160,894	406	238	168
Mandsaur	230,817	122,875	107,942	101	64	37
Shajapur	300,505	159,555	140,950	192	142	50
Amjhera...	139,892	71,893	67,999	24	13	11
Gwalior unspecified ...	10,968	6,181	4,787	3	1	2
II. Provinces and States in India beyond Gwalior.	281,350	120,934	160,416	33,750	15,023	18,727
(a) Provinces and States adjacent to the Gwalior State.	*267,748*	*113,179*	*154,569*	*30,824*	*13,239*	*17,585*
(1) Central India Agency ...	131,333	52,053	79,280	11,978	3,476	8,502
(i) States	*127,118*	*49,952*	*77,166*	*11,918*	*3,443*	*8,475*
Ajaigarh	2	1	1	1	...	1
Alipura...	10	10	...	...	...	...
Alirajpur	501	221	280	...	...	...
Barwani	1,015	852	163	...	...	...
Bhopal	23,068	9,852	13,216	105	41	64
Bijawar	597	261	336	51	1	50
Charkhari	38	21	17	16	7	9
Chhatarpur	946	551	395	61	30	31
Datia	12,859	3,785	9,074	8,503	2,366	6,137
Dewas	9,970	4,438	5,532	73	45	28
Dhar	11,149	4,147	7,002	41	19	22
Indore	36,002	13,235	22,767	912	308	604
Jaora	5,434	1,897	3,537	13	7	6
Jhabua	1,384	618	766	...	...	...
Jobat	212	60	152	...	...	...
Khaniadhana	1,093	352	741	1	...	1
Khilchipur	481	157	324	4	4	...
Kurwai	1,670	663	1,007	...	...	...
Maihar	2	2	...	...	...	...
Narsingarh	4,103	1,728	2,375	4	...	4
Orchha	5,072	2,497	2,575	1,114	378	736
Panna	137	84	53	8	4	4
Piploda	1	...	1	...	...	...
Rajgarh	3,291	1,347	1,944	11	8	3
Ratlam	3,786	1,548	2,248	8	6	2
Rewa	315	219	96	26	9	17
Sailana	1,394	238	1,156	...	...	...
Samthar	1,234	329	905	964	210	754
Sitamau	1,292	814	478	2	...	2
(ii) British Territory	*349*	*156*	*193*	*18*	*12*	*6*
Manpur	349	156	193	18	12	6
(iii) Central India unspecified ...	*3,836*	*1,915*	*1,921*	*42*	*21*	*21*
(2) Rajputana Agency	76,480	34,872	41,608	2,824	1,521	1,303
(i) States	*73,241*	*33,547*	*39,694*	*2,737*	*1,473*	*1,264*
Alwar	1,204	711	493	170	92	78
Banswara	27	8	19	...	...	...
Bharatpur	842	495	347	294	168	181
Bikaner	195	128	67	51	30	21
Bundi	411	160	251	8	...	8
Dholpur	4,405	2,040	2,365	966	477	489
Jaipur	13,699	7,779	5,920	573	307	266
Jaisalmere	283	224	59	...	...	...
Jhalawar	3,412	929	2,483	9	1	8
Karauli	3,115	1,215	1,900	56	31	25
Kishangarh	600	335	265	91	48	43
Kotah	9,837	4,433	5,404	111	88	23
Marwar	5,785	2,847	2,938	338	173	165
Mewar	14,075	6,188	7,887	35	17	18
Partabgarh	2,971	1,276	1,695	44	31	13
Sirohi	2	2	...	...	...	...
Tonk	12,378	4,777	7,601	41	20	21

Birthplace.

WHERE ENUMERATED.

BHIND.			TONWARGHAR.			SHEOPUR.			NARWAR.		
Persons.	Males.	Females.	Persons.	Males.	Females.	Persons.	Males.	Females.	Persons.	Males.	Females.
8	9	10	11	12	13	14	15	16	17	18	19
418,224	228,214	190,010	369,648	204,759	164,889	137.034	72,925	64,109	401,586	211,555	190,031
418,224	*228,214*	*190,010*	*369,641*	*204,755*	*164,886*	*137,032*	*72,924*	*64,108*	*401,584*	*211,555*	*190,029*
403,318	224,200	179,118	359,033	201,261	157,772	126,976	68,001	58,975	392,907	208,074	184,833
1,393	432	961	3,269	1,716	1,553	346	148	198	1,480	1,142	28
398,495	222,538	175,957	3,005	615	2,390	97	48	49	116	108	8
2,698	735	1,963	318,255	196,118	122,137	1,582	933	649	258	171	87
87	49	38	1,061	486	575	122,986	66,063	56,923	965	376	589
121	60	61	455	66	389	1,795	711	1,084	385,524	204,189	181,335
63	29	34	57	28	29	102	48	54	3,577	1,438	2,139
12	5	7	25	7	18	16	6	10	53	28	25
40	16	24	467	24	443	11	9	2	20	9	11
7	5	2	12	7	5	9	7	2	8	2	6
60	47	13	35	29	6	5	3	2	16	6	10
3	3	...	12	5	7	1	...	1	9	4	5
339	281	58	2,380	2,160	220	26	20	6	931	601	330
14,906	4,014	10,892	10,608	3,494	7,114	10,056	4,923	5,133	8,677	3,481	5,196
13,988	*3,496*	*10,492*	*10,386*	*3,384*	*7,002*	*9,782*	*4,759*	*5,023*	*8,402*	*3,391*	*5,011*
2,643	657	1,986	444	34	410	1,159	677	482	3,519	1,440	2,079
2,638	*656*	*1,982*	*423*	*34*	*389*	*1,159*	*677*	*482*	*2,578*	*850*	*1,728*
...	...	...	...	...	...	...	...	...	...	...	...
...	...	...	...	...	...	...	...	...	...	...	...
...	...	...	...	...	...	...	...	...	...	...	...
...	...	...	...	...	...	...	...	...	...	...	...
15	8	12	22	11	11	35	25	10	36	18	18
...	...	...	...	...	...	397	181	216	...	...	...
...	...	...	...	...	...	4	2	2	1	...	1
...	...	...	...	...	...	431	231	200	204	107	97
2,024	547	1,477	349	7	342	63	35	28	1,070	346	724
8	1	7	...	...	...	...	...	...	2	2	...
1	...	1	6	5	1	1	...	1	6	4	2
334	61	273	10	8	2	12	5	7	26	5	21
51	1	50	...	...	...	1	1	...	...	...	...
...	...	...	...	...	...	...	...	...	1	...	1
...	...	...	...	...	...	...	...	...	...	...	...
...	...	...	...	...	...	1	1	...	1,089	382	707
...	...	...	...	...	...	...	...	...	3	...	3
...	...	...	...	...	...	...	...	...	...	...	...
...	...	...	...	...	...	...	...	...	...	...	...
1	...	1	...	...	...	...	...	...	1	1	...
6	1	5	3	1	2	38	24	14	173	28	145
3	...	3	...	...	...	2	2	...	...	...	...
...	...	...	...	...	...	...	...	...	...	...	...
3	3	...	...	...	...	6	5	1	2	...	2
3	...	3	6	...	6	2	1	1	...	...	...
15	2	13	20	...	20	166	164	2	9	4	5
...	...	...	...	...	...	...	...	...	1	1	...
174	37	137	7	2	5	...	...	...	4	2	2
...	...	...	...	...	...	...	...	...	...	...	...
...	...	...	...	...	...	...	...	...	...	...	...
...	...	...	...	...	...	...	...	...	...	...	...
5	*1*	*4*	*21*	...	*21*	...	...	...	*941*	*590*	*351*
494	262	232	3,659	1,726	1,933	8,093	3,732	4,361	2,212	1,060	1,152
482	*254*	*228*	*3,625*	*1,718*	*1,907*	*8,082*	*3,730*	*4,352*	*2,184*	*1,059*	*1,125*
52	30	22	222	136	86	17	8	9	15	8	7
...	...	...	...	...	...	...	...	...	...	...	...
7	2	5	61	36	25	27	16	11	13	9	4
1	1	...	11	11	...	18	18	...	2	1	1
8	...	8	2	2	...	113	47	66	1	...	1
162	65	97	2,804	1,175	1,629	36	12	24	134	68	66
77	62	15	154	98	56	3,184	1,627	1,557	272	177	95
15	12	3	17	10	7	1	1	..	10	10	...
...	...	...	...	...	...	5	...	5	6	2	4
9	3	6	236	200	36	867	399	468	6	6	..
...	...	...	87	2	85	8	4	4	34	34	...
4	...	4	33	18	15	3,549	1,458	2,091	1,276	487	789
58	37	21	20	9	11	107	73	34	306	203	103
83	40	43	15	10	5	28	12	16	31	17	14
3	...	3	13	11	2	2	...	2	..	...	...
...	...	...	...	...	...	...	...	...	...	...	...
3	2	1	...	...	...	125	60	65	78	37	41

TABLE VI.

District, State, Province or Country where born.	DISTRICT					
	PACHHAR.			BHILSA.		
	Persons.	Males.	Females.	Persons.	Males.	Females.
1	2	3	4	5	6	7
Gwalior State	421,311	221,556	199,755	235,289	123,081	112,201
I. *Born in India* ...	*421,2[illegible]*	*221,[illegible]*	*[illegible]*	*[illegible]*	*[illegible]*	*112,2[illegible]*
1. Districts within the State ...	405,1[illegible]	214,911	191,221	197,436	105,129	92,304
Gird	1,165	[illegible]	[illegible]	2,1[illegible]	1,2[illegible]	[illegible]
Bhind ...	[illegible]	[illegible]	[illegible]	433	[illegible]	179
Tonwarghar ...	[illegible]	[illegible]	[illegible]	459	273	186
Sheopur ...	[illegible]	[illegible]	[illegible]	110	50	60
Narwar	[illegible]	[illegible]	[illegible]	1,010	613	397
Isagarh	[illegible]	[illegible]	195,8[illegible]	2,0[illegible]	980	1,077
Bhilsa	[illegible]	[illegible]	[illegible]	151,624	101,[illegible]	50,0[illegible]
Ujjain ...	[illegible]	45	[illegible]	112	59	53
Mandsaur	44	[illegible]	16	12	8	4
Shajapur ...	[illegible]	[illegible]	43	71	22	49
Amjhera ...	370	[illegible]	7	13	4	9
Gwalior unspecified ...	1,919	991	[illegible]	1,27[illegible]	[illegible]	208
II. Provinces and States in India beyond Gwalior.	15,133	6,599	8,531	35,851	16,955	18,896
(a) *Provinces and States in India beyond Gwalior* ...	*11,116*	*[illegible]*	*[illegible]*	*31,152*	*16,201*	*18,213*
(1) Central India Agency ...	7,046	823	1,221	18,043	8,535	9,518
(i) *States*	*[illegible]*	*651*	*1,162*	*17,221*	*8,168*	*9,153*
Ajaigarh ...	...			...	...	...
Alipura ...	...	...	...	...	...	...
Alirajpur	...	...	...	...	...	...
Barwani ...	...	...	...	...	...	...
Bhopal	423	105	318	11,953	5,315	6,638
Bijawar ...	133	76	57	...	...	...
Charkhari	4	2	2	2	2	...
Chhatarpur	99	46	53	11	11	...
Datia	121	70	51	554	325	229
Dewas ...	15	8	7	13	1	12
Dhar	3	1	2	21	...	23
Indore	121	42	79	63	2[illegible]	37
Jaora	5	...	5	...	...	...
Jhabua	1	1	...	...	...	...
Jobat	...	...	...	...	...	...
Khaniadhana	46	18	28	6	1	5
Khilchipur	19	3	16	13	13	...
Kurwai	67	9	58	1,603	654	949
Maihar	...	...	...	2	2	...
Narsingarh	184	53	131	179	127	52
Orchha	9	6	3	3,217	1,766	1,451
Panna	74	49	25	25	12	13
Piploda	...	...	...	...	...	...
Rajgarh	400	12	388	114	65	49
Ratlam	14	8	6	...	...	...
Rewa	7	1	6	6	...	6
Sailana	...	...	...	...	...	...
Samthar	78	71	2	5	3	2
Sitamau	...	...	...	...	...	...
(ii) *British Territory*	...	...	...	*13*	*11*	*2*
Manpur	...	...	...	13	11	2
(iii) *Central India unspecified* ...	*216*	*164*	*52*	*219*	*158*	*91*
(2) Rajputana Agency	8,038	3,428	4,610	6,147	2,422	3,725
(i) *States*	*7,827*	*3,331*	*4,496*	*5,815*	*2,270*	*3,545*
Alwar	53	38	15	10	5	5
Banswara	...	...	...	...	...	...
Bharatpur	39	26	13	31	18	13
Bikaner	2	1	1	2	...	2
Bundi	12	6	6	...	...	...
Dholpur	96	72	24	52	38	14
Jaipur	664	351	313	331	196	185
Jaisalmere	...	...	...	...	...	...
Jhalawar	11	6	5	...	...	...
Karauli	79	61	18	1,055	7	1,048
Kishangarh	34	16	18	3	3	...
Kotah	2,322	1,211	1,111	36	12	24
Marwar	171	93	78	98	72	26
Mewar	48	29	19	96	28	8
Partabgarh	1	...	1	47	...	47
Sirohi	...	...	...	...	...	...
Tonk	4,295	1,491	2,874	4,124	1,896	2,228

Birthplace.—(*contd.*)

WHERE ENUMERATED.

UJJAIN.			MANDSAUR.			SHAJAPUR.			AMJHERA.		
Persons.	Males.	Females.	Persons.	Males.	Females.	Persons.	Males.	Females.	Persons.	Males.	Females.
8	9	10	11	12	13	14	15	16	17	18	19
405,961	211,274	194,687	272,166	140,333	131,833	336,980	174,985	161,995	160,066	80,411	79,655
405,928	*211,252*	*194,676*	*272,119*	*140,300*	*131,819*	*336,951*	*174,963*	*161,988*	*160,063*	*80,408*	*79,655*
348,308	184,662	163,646	232,232	123,471	108,761	301,828	160,423	141,405	140,321	71,952	68,369
1,465	819	646	815	512	303	444	252	192	90	61	29
491	282	209	61	27	34	147	98	49	14	9	5
151	117	34	76	37	39	136	108	28	24	19	5
103	58	45	25	18	7	38	18	20	30	9	21
179	130	49	50	34	16	119	95	24	35	24	11
702	478	224	80	60	20	472	351	121	85	64	21
294	123	171	20	12	8	291	171	120	19	8	11
335,589	178,223	157,366	952	373	579	2,809	988	1,821	684	312	372
1,454	656	798	228,487	121,681	106,806	368	163	205	315	214	101
4,656	1,889	2,767	266	129	137	295,054	157,190	137,864	50	41	9
626	338	288	35	14	21	120	67	53	138,679	71,032	67,647
2,598	1,499	1,099	1,365	574	791	1,835	927	908	296	159	137
57,620	26,590	31,030	39,887	16,829	23,058	35,123	14,540	20,583	19,742	8,456	11,286
55,318	*25,342*	*29,976*	*36,634*	*14,886*	*21,748*	*34,141*	*14,027*	*20,114*	*19,405*	*8,262*	*11,143*
37,722	15,567	22,155	12,550	4,464	8,086	24,499	9,436	15,063	16,690	6,942	9,748
36,965	*15,313*	*21,652*	*11,714*	*4,082*	*7,632*	*21,090*	*9,321*	*11,769*	*15,982*	*6,549*	*9,433*
..	...	...	...	...	...	1	1	...	...	...	...
...	...	...	...	...	...	...	...	...	10	10	...
5	1	4	4	1	3	...	...	..	492	219	273
1	1	...	4	3	1	2	...	2	1,038	878	160
3,419	1,492	1,927	90	46	44	6,910	2,736	4,174	80	40	40
2	2	...	18	...	18	1	1	...	...	...	..
...	...	...	...	...	...	11	8	3	...	...	...
75	75	...	20	11	9	13	7	6	...	...	...
116	51	65	3	3	...	25	18	7	28	17	11
6,478	3,138	3,340	721	256	465	2,551	938	1,613	109	49	60
3,988	1,611	2,377	237	177	60	97	35	62	6,747	2,295	4,452
16,236	6,349	9,887	4,925	1,466	3,459	7,688	2,672	5,016	5,675	2,293	3,382
2,194	806	1,388	2,981	980	2,001	30	16	14	159	86	73
111	3	108	108	89	19	42	33	9	1,121	492	629
...	...	...	29	22	7	...	...	...	183	38	145
..	...	...	...	...	...	...	...	...	...	...	...
12	10	2	1	...	1	429	127	302	...	...	...
...	...	...	...	...	...	...	...	...	...	...	...
...	...	...	...	...	...	...	...	...	...	...	...
178	61	117	35	21	14	3,517	1,463	2,054	4	2	2
271	148	123	5	3	2	236	142	94	...	...	...
19	12	7	3	2	1	3	3	...	...	...	...
...	...	...	1	...	1	...	...	...	...	...	...
225	132	93	10	6	4	2,455	1,088	1,367	65	28	37
2,834	1,163	1,671	663	261	402	39	14	25	217	90	127
35	25	10	8	6	2	20	5	15	3	3	...
603	204	399	754	28	726	...	...	...	36	5	31
...	...	...	1	1	...	6	3	3	...	...	...
163	99	64	1,098	700	398	14	11	3	15	4	11
260	*105*	*155*	*40*	*14*	*26*	*18*	*14*	*4*	...	...	...
260	105	155	40	14	26	18	14	4	...	...	...
497	*149*	*348*	*796*	*368*	*428*	*391*	*101*	*290*	*708*	*393*	*315*
12,869	7,001	5,868	22,625	9,501	13,124	7,723	3,369	4,354	1,796	850	946
12,318	*6,654*	*5,664*	*21,374*	*8,995*	*12,379*	*7,392*	*3,269*	*4,123*	*1,405*	*794*	*611*
315	185	130	246	156	90	85	43	42	19	10	9
7	...	7	20	8	12	...	...	...	...	...	...
227	129	98	71	53	18	70	41	29	2	2	...
60	40	20	32	24	8	21	7	14	...	...	...
85	30	55	112	42	70	9	4	5	61	29	32
89	65	24	27	16	11	72	41	31	17	11	6
5,040	2,813	2,227	1,001	914	687	1,220	849	371	550	395	155
50	13	37	18	6	12	172	172	...	...	...	...
176	75	101	1,205	345	860	2,099	500	1,599	...	...	...
584	372	212	44	22	22	169	109	60	10	5	5
229	131	98	107	55	52	32	23	9	25	19	6
927	452	475	361	161	200	1,171	523	648	44	25	19
2,193	1,188	1,005	1,433	435	998	424	240	184	607	[illegible]	[illegible]
1,574	791	783	11,769	5,018	6,751	460	231	229	...	...	[illegible]
251	120	131	2,525	1,075	1,450	64	35	29	21	4	[illegible]
...	...	...	2	2	...	...	...	...	...	...	...
511	250	261	1,771	633	1,138	1,411	448	963	19	10	[illegible]

Birthplace.—(*contd.*)

WHERE ENUMERATED.

BHIND.			TONWARGHAR.			SHEOPUR.			NARWAR.		
Persons.	Males.	Females.	Persons.	Males.	Females.	Persons.	Males.	Females.	Persons.	Males.	Females.
8	9	10	11	12	13	14	15	16	17	18	19
12	*8*	*4*	*34*	*8*	*26*	*11*	*2*	*9*	*28*	*1*	*27*
10,829	2,570	8,259	6,212	1,592	4,620	487	310	177	2,615	876	1,739
10,734	*2,516*	*8,218*	*6,047*	*1,547*	*4,500*	*483*	*306*	*177*	*2,557*	*827*	*1,730*
1,173	469	704	1,968	773	1,195	55	46	9	101	49	52
71	46	25	58	32	26	30	22	8	9	7	2
34	11	23	13	5	8	5	3	2	25	18	7
1	1	...	2	2	...	...	...	...	3	...	3
...	...	...	20	...	20	...	...	...	1	1	...
...	...	...	...	...	...	...	...	...	...	...	...
139	13	126	11	5	6	1	...	1	9	5	4
9	...	9	3	3	...	...	...	...	5	5	...
20	3	17	17	6	11	8	8	...	5	5	...
...	...	...	...	...	...	...	...	...	...	...	...
14	8	6	6	4	2	2	1	1	22	22	...
3	3	...	7	4	3	7	4	3	18	4	14
4	1	3	11	2	9	4	2	2	...	...	...
7	5	2	34	14	20	...	...	...	7	7	...
1,045	131	914	302	49	253	20	11	9	53	35	18
...	...	...	1	...	1	...	...	...	...	...	...
54	7	47	51	18	33	4	4	...	5	3	2
3,619	1,107	2,512	819	104	715	54	25	29	38	28	10
241	51	190	143	69	74	12	11	1	26	18	8
188	6	182	5	5	...	6	6	...	...	...	...
7	...	7	3	3	...	3	1	2	2	1	1
38	37	1	13	13	...	19	11	8	...	...	...
1	...	1	6	...	6	...	...	...	...	...	...
5	1	4	...	...	...	...	...	...	1	1	...
1	1	...	...	...	...	...	...	...	1	1	...
178	31	147	28	3	25	5	5	...	9	4	5
86	17	69	43	9	34	1	1	...	7	7	...
2,449	291	2,158	995	39	956	17	14	3	44	22	22
1	...	1	15	...	15	...	...	...	8	8	...
245	42	203	117	60	57	167	95	72	1,910	489	1,421
2	...	2	...	...	...	...	...	...	14	9	5
12	5	7	43	12	31	11	6	5	5	4	1
747	158	589	1,001	167	834	9	6	3	27	18	9
4	1	3	33	18	15	1	...	1	5	4	1
8	1	7	...	...	...	1	1	...	...	...	...
39	22	17	62	14	48	5	3	2	22	14	8
37	18	19	138	102	36	19	12	7	22	12	10
5	4	1	...	...	...	1	1	...	7	5	2
...	...	...	...	...	...	...	...	...	...	...	...
...	...	...	...	...	...	...	...	...	2	2	...
82	7	75	10	4	6	5	...	5	13	8	5
7	5	2	2	2	...	1	1	...	4	4	...
...	...	...	3	2	1	...	...	...	121	1	120
32	7	25	50	1	49	4	1	3	1	1	...
12	...	12	...	...	...	...	...	...	...	...	...
114	6	108	14	3	11	6	5	1	5	5	...
44	*9*	*35*	*15*	*7*	*8*	*4*	*4*	...	*27*	*18*	*9*
51	*45*	*6*	*150*	*38*	*112*	...	...	...	*31*	*31*	...
22	7	15	71	32	39	43	40	3	56	15	41
1	1	...	1	1	...	...	...	...	...	...	...
...	...	...	...	...	...	...	...	...	...	...	...
...	...	...	...	...	...	...	...	...	...	...	...
...	...	...	...	...	...	...	...	...	...	...	...
...	...	...	...	...	...	...	...	...	...	...	...
1	1	...	...	...	...	1	1	...	1	...	1
...	...	...	...	...	...	...	...	...	1	...	1
...	...	...	...	...	...	...	...	...	...	...	...
3	2	1	7	4	3	1	1	...	10	1	9
2	1	1	5	4	1	2	...	2	...	...	...
1	1	...	2	1	1	1	...	1	5	5	...
...	...	...	5	4	1	...	...	...	...	...	...
...	...	...	...	...	...	...	...	...	...	...	...
...	...	...	1	...	1	2	2	...	2	...	2
14	1	13	19	12	7	86	86	...	27	9	18
...	...	...	...	...	...	...	...	...	...	...	...
...	...	...	...	...	...	...	...	...	...	...	...
...	...	...	31	6	25	...	...	...	10	...	10

Birthplace.—(*contd.*)

WHERE ENUMERATED.

Ujjain.			Mandsaur.			Shajapur.			Amjhera.		
Persons.	Males.	Females.	Persons.	Males.	Females.	Persons.	Males.	Females.	Persons.	Males.	Females.
8	9	10	11	12	13	14	15	16	17	18	19
551	*347*	*204*	*1,251*	*506*	*745*	*331*	*100*	*231*	*391*	*56*	*335*
3,785	2,257	1,528	1,276	781	495	1,394	919	475	427	273	154
3,406	*2,063*	*1,343*	*1,088*	*687*	*407*	*1,239*	*823*	*416*	*352*	*222*	*130*
264	189	75	124	78	46	127	88	39	87	25	12
163	159	48	48	32	16	42	33	9	11	8	3
42	24	18	50	39	11	80	65	15	13	8	5
...	...	...	4	2	2	2	...	2	...	...	...
4	...	4	9	2	7	2	2	...	...	...	...
...	...	...	...	...	...	1	1	...	...	...	...
22	17	5	5	2	3	51	48	3	...	...	...
53	36	17	28	14	14	37	36	1	...	...	...
57	39	18	34	24	10	7	4	3	10	10	...
3	3	...	...	...	...	...	...	...	...	...	...
23	17	6	5	2	3	20	18	2	6	4	2
15	13	2	13	7	6	2	2	...	1	1	...
45	28	17	...	...	...	22	8	14	3	3	...
17	15	2	40	27	13	29	14	15	7	4	3
320	138	182	152	114	38	86	52	34	19	7	12
1	1	...	1	1	...	1	1	...	1	1	...
23	10	13	6	5	1	19	18	1	1	...	1
126	95	31	47	28	19	29	19	10	25	18	7
27	18	9	49	33	16	35	14	21	18	14	4
33	19	14	20	12	8	44	29	15	5	2	3
41	30	11	26	8	18	...	...	...	10	7	3
11	11	...	30	30	...	15	10	5	...	...	...
...	...	...	1	1	...	...	...	...	...	...	...
6	6	...	...	...	...	...	...	...	...	...	...
28	26	2	3	2	1	30	15	15	2	2	...
20	16	4	1	1	...	3	...	3	...	...	...
...	...	...	2	2	...	3	1	2	2	2	...
56	31	25	25	19	6	55	26	29	5	2	3
27	27	...	13	7	6	11	3	8	86	47	39
1,085	740	345	31	25	6	356	239	117	22	15	7
3	3	...	7	2	5	1	1	...	...	...	...
204	12	192	17	9	8	3	3	...	3	1	2
78	22	56	25	17	8	30	15	15	...	...	...
26	21	5	38	20	18	8	6	2	...	...	...
9	6	3	1	1	...	...	...	...	...	...	...
25	19	6	38	20	18	7	5	2	11	11	...
73	56	17	48	33	15	18	9	9	14	9	5
1	1	...	11	7	4	5	5	...	...	...	...
...	...	...	5	5	...	...	...	...	...	...	...
...	...	...	1	1	...	...	...	...	...	...	...
313	120	193	50	27	23	19	5	14	30	16	14
21	5	16	8	5	3	13	9	4	7	3	4
5	1	4	4	3	1	16	13	3	...	...	...
42	11	31	57	16	41	9	5	4	...	...	...
33	20	13	7	4	3	...	...	...	...	...	...
42	28	14	4	...	4	1	1	...	3	2	1
83	*65*	*18*	*104*	*59*	*45*	*13*	*13*	...	*17*	*4*	*13*
296	*129*	*167*	*84*	*35*	*49*	*142*	*83*	*59*	*58*	*47*	*11*
942	517	425	183	140	43	525	303	222	492	197	295
9	7	2	6	5	1	49	26	23	...	...	...
1	...	1	4	2	2	67	45	22	...	...	...
...	...	...	1	1	...	...	...	...	...	...	...
...	...	...	1	1	...	...	...	...	...	...	...
...	...	...	1	...	1	...	...	...	...	...	...
...	...	...	1	...	*1*	...	...	...	...	...	...
...	...	...	2	2	...	...	...	...	...	...	...
...	...	...	80	80	...	...	...	...	...	...	...
170	124	46	15	8	7	136	60	76	144	72	72
53	33	20	13	9	4	5	2	3	10	6	4
46	25	21	23	16	7	17	1	16	8	2	6
5	...	5	1	1	...	17	17	...	1	1	...
90	3	87	11	2	9	...	...	...	...	...	...
36	8	28	1	...	1	...	...	...	268	93	175
483	300	183	8	4	4	102	56	46	18	14	4
...	...	...	1	1	...	...	...	...	...	...	...
...	...	...	1	...	1	...	...	...	...	...	...
49	17	32	13	8	5	182	96	86	43	9	34

TABLE VI—

District, State, Province or Country where born.	DISTRICT																	
	GWALIOR STATE.			GIRD.			BHIND.			TONWARGHAR.			SHEOPUR.			NARWAR.		
	P.	M.	F.	P.	M.	F.	P.	M.	F.	P.	M.	F.	P.	M.	F.	P.	M.	F.
1	2	3	4	5	6	7	8	9	10	11	12	13	14	15	16	17	18	19
Non-contiguous Provinces and States.	11,842	7,044	4,798	2,875	1,742	1,133	694	478	216	196	110	86	270	162	108	265	89	176
(5) Ajmer-Merwara ...	2,316	1,241	1,075	152	82	70	2	...	2	6	1	5	83	63	20	13	6	7
(6) Assam ...	2	1	1	...	...	...	...	...	...	...	...	...	...	...	...	...	...	...
(7) Baluchistan ...	7	6	1	...	...	...	...	...	...	...	...	...	...	...	...	...	...	...
(8) Bengal ...	260	151	109	106	47	59	4	...	4	8	...	8	4	2	2	4	4	...
Burdwan ...	1	1	...	...	...	...	...	...	...	...	...	...	...	...	...	...	...	...
Calcutta ...	25	13	12	4	2	2	3	...	3	2	...	2	...	...	...	3	3	...
Dacca ...	4	2	2	...	...	...	...	...	...	...	...	...	...	...	...	...	...	...
Murshidabad ...	1	1	...	...	...	...	...	...	...	...	...	...	...	...	...	...	...	...
Mymensingh ...	1	1	...	1	1	...	...	...	...	...	...	...	...	...	...	...	...	...
Nadia ...	1	1	...	...	...	...	...	...	...	...	...	...	...	...	...	...	...	...
Bengal unspecified	227	132	95	101	44	57	1	...	1	6	...	6	4	2	2	1	1	...
(9) Bihar and Orissa.	102	66	36	39	22	17	5	...	5	4	...	4	2	2	...	3	3	...
Bhagalpur ...	1	1	...	...	...	...	...	...	...	...	...	...	...	...	...	...	...	...
Patna ...	2	2	...	...	...	...	...	...	...	...	...	...	...	...	...	...	...	...
Sambhalpur ...	4	4	...	...	...	...	...	...	...	...	...	...	...	...	...	...	...	...
Shahabad ...	2	2	...	...	...	...	...	...	...	...	...	...	2	2	...	...	...	...
Bihar and Orissa unspecified.	93	57	36	39	22	17	5	...	5	4	...	4	...	...	...	3	3	...
(10) Bombay ...	4,570	2,658	1,912	1,106	675	431	25	16	9	40	21	19	28	24	4	151	25	126
(i) British Districts...	*2,708*	*1,598*	*1,110*	*816*	*499*	*317*	*5*	*2*	*3*	*32*	*19*	*13*	*6*	*5*	*1*	*31*	*22*	*9*
Ahmedabad ...	320	241	79	58	37	21	1	...	1	2	2	...	...	...	...	3	3	...
Ahmednagar ...	128	53	75	37	13	24	...	...	...	3	3	...	...	...	...	8	5	3
Belgaum ...	2	2	...	...	...	...	...	...	...	...	...	...	...	...	...	...	...	...
Bijapur ...	8	5	3	...	...	...	...	...	...	...	...	...	...	...	...	...	...	...
Bombay ...	525	273	252	248	167	81	2	...	2	11	4	7	...	...	...	3	1	2
Broach ...	1	1	...	...	...	...	...	...	...	...	...	...	...	...	...	...	...	...
Dharwar ...	2	1	1	...	...	...	...	...	...	...	...	...	...	...	...	...	...	...
East Khandesh.	255	80	175	36	24	12	...	...	...	8	4	4	2	2	...	...	...	...
Hyderabad (Sind)	2	1	1	...	...	...	...	...	...	...	...	...	...	...	...	...	...	...
Kaira ...	3	2	1	...	...	...	...	...	...	...	...	...	...	...	...	...	...	...
Kanara ...	23	21	2	...	...	...	...	...	...	...	...	...	...	...	...	2	2	...
Karachi ...	3	3	...	...	...	...	...	...	...	...	...	...	...	...	...	...	...	...
Kolaba ...	1	1	...	...	...	...	...	...	...	...	...	...	...	...	...	9	9	...
Nasik ...	85	46	39	19	9	10	...	...	...	...	...	...	...	...	...	...	...	...
Panch Mahals.	6	4	2	5	3	2	...	...	...	4	3	1	4	3	1	4	1	3
Poona ...	358	165	193	154	85	69	1	1	...	...	...	...	...	...	...	...	...	...
Ratnagiri ...	449	318	131	107	68	39	1	1	...	1	...	1	...	...	...	2	1	1
Satara ...	464	339	125	134	80	54	...	...	...	...	...	...	...	...	...	...	...	...
Sholapur ...	41	24	17	15	11	4	...	...	...	3	3	...	...	...	...	...	...	...
Surat ...	28	16	12	3	2	1	...	...	...	...	...	...	...	...	...	...	...	...
Thana ...	4	2	2	...	...	...	...	...	...	...	...	...	...	...	...	...	...	...
States ...	*520*	*411*	*109*	*143*	*92*	*51*	*5*	*4*	*1*	*4*	*2*	*2*	*12*	*12*	...	...	...	...
Bhavnagar ...	4	4	...	...	...	...	...	...	...	1	1	...	...	...	...	...	...	...
Bhor ...	5	...	5	...	...	...	...	...	...	...	...	...	...	...	...	...	...	...
Cambay ...	1	1	...	...	...	...	...	...	...	2	...	2	...	...	...	...	...	...
Cutch ...	27	25	2	...	...	...	...	...	...	...	...	...	11	11	...	...	...	...
Jamnagar ...	11	11	...	...	...	...	...	...	...	...	...	...	...	...	...	...	...	...
Jath ...	1	1	...	...	...	...	...	...	...	...	...	...	...	...	...	...	...	...
Kolhapur ...	129	108	21	40	24	16	4	4	...	...	...	...	...	...	...	...	...	...
Lunavada ...	3	2	1	...	...	...	...	...	...	...	...	...	...	...	...	...	...	...
Miraj ...	1	1	...	1	1	...	...	...	...	...	...	...	...	...	...	...	...	...
Palanpur ...	1	1	...	...	...	...	...	...	...	...	...	...	...	...	...	...	...	...
Rajkot ...	312	233	79	102	67	35	1	...	1	1	1	...	1	1	...	...	...	...
Sangli ...	1	1	...	...	...	...	...	...	...	...	...	...	...	...	...	...	...	...
Savantwadi ...	24	23	1	...	...	...	...	...	...	...	...	...	...	...	...	...	...	...
(iii) Bombay unspecified	*1,312*	*619*	*693*	*147*	*84*	*63*	*15*	*10*	*5*	*4*	...	*4*	*10*	*7*	*3*	*120*	*3*	*117*
(11) Burma ...	4	4	...	3	3	...	...	...	...	22	10	12	8	6	2	7	2	5
(12) Delhi ...	662	416	246	422	252	170	...	...	...	...	...	...	...	...	...	3	3	...
(13) Madras ...	85	52	33	20	14	6	...	...	...	...	...	...	...	...	...	...	...	...
Arcot (North) ...	1	1	...	...	...	...	...	...	...	...	...	...	...	...	...	...	...	...
Guntur ...	3	3	...	...	...	...	...	...	...	...	...	...	...	...	...	...	...	...
Kurnool ...	3	3	...	...	...	...	...	...	...	...	...	...	...	...	...	...	...	...
Madras ...	29	17	12	...	...	...	...	...	...	...	...	...	...	...	...	...	...	...
Vizagapatam ...	1	1	...	...	...	...	...	...	...	...	...	...	...	...	...	3	3	...
Madras unspecified	48	27	21	20	14	6	...	...	...	...	...	...	...	...	...	...	...	...

Birthplace.—(*contd*).

WHERE ENUMERATED.

ISAGARH.			BHILSA.			UJJAIN.			MANDSAUR.			SHAJAPUR.			AMJHERA.		
P.	M.	F.	P.	M.	F.	P.	M.	F.	P.	M.	F.	P.	M.	F.	P.	M.	F.
20	21	22	23	24	25	26	27	28	29	30	31	32	33	34	35	36	37
637	386	251	508	335	173	2,191	1,224	880	3,094	1,859	1,235	862	465	397	337	194	143
31	18	13	14	12	2	273	164	109	1,669	852	817	62	43	19	11	...	11
..	...	...	...	...	...	...	...	...	2	1	1	...	...	...	...	...	...
...	...	...	..	...	...	...	...	...	6	6	...	1	...	1	...	...	...
3	3	...	14	9	5	77	61	16	21	11	10	14	9	5	5	5	...
...	...	...	...	...	...	...	...	...	1	1	...	...	...	...	...	...	...
1	1	...	8	3	5	...	...	...	3	3	...	...	...	...	1	1	...
...	...	...	...	...	...	...	...	...	4	2	2	...	...	...	...	...	...
...	...	...	...	...	...	...	...	...	1	1	...	...	...	...	...	...	...
...	...	...	...	...	...	...	...	...	...	...	...	...	...	...	...	...	...
...	...	...	...	...	...	...	...	...	1	1	...	...	...	...	...	...	...
2	2	...	6	6	...	77	61	16	11	8	8	14	9	5	4	4	...
10	7	3	7	7	...	3	3	...	28	22	6	1	...	1	...	...	...
...	...	...	...	...	...	...	...	...	1	1	...	...	...	...	...	...	...
...	...	...	...	...	...	...	...	...	2	2	...	...	...	...	...	...	...
...	...	...	...	...	...	..	...	...	4	4	...	...	...	..	...	...	...
...	...	...	...	...	...	...	...	...	...	...	...	...	...	...	...	...	...
10	7	3	7	7	...	8	8	...	21	15	6	1	...	1	...	...	...
239	126	113	323	205	118	1,118	621	497	788	589	199	507	221	286	245	135	110
140	*68*	*72*	*130*	*85*	*45*	*538*	*337*	*201*	*560*	*422*	*138*	*298*	*86*	*212*	*152*	*53*	*99*
...	...	...	...	...	...	176	162	14	34	10	24	32	19	13	14	8	6
...	...	...	8	8	...	13	2	11	28	13	15	14	4	10	17	5	12
...	...	...	2	2	...	...	...	...	...	...	...	...	...	...	...	...	...
...	...	...	...	...	...	...	...	...	8	5	3	...	...	...	...	...	...
27	5	22	31	9	22	167	72	95	30	15	15	6	...	6	...	...	...
...	...	...	...	...	...	...	..	...	1	1	...	...	...	...	...	...	...
...	...	...	...	...	...	...	...	...	2	1	1	...	...	...	...	...	...
3	1	2	2	2	...	52	35	17	22	5	17	130	7	123	...	...	...
...	...	...	...	...	...	...	...	...	2	1	1	...	...	...	...	...	...
...	...	...	...	...	...	...	...	...	3	2	1	...	...	...	...	...	...
...	...	...	...	...	...	...	...	...	23	21	2	...	...	...	...	...	...
...	...	...	...	...	...	...	...	...	1	1	...	...	...	...	...	...	...
...	...	...	...	...	...	1	1	...	...	...	...	...	...	...	...	...	...
33	18	15	...	...	...	7	5	2	6	1	5	8	4	4	8	...	8
...	...	...	...	...	...	...	...	...	1	1	...	...	...	...	...	...	...
11	7	4	5	5	...	43	18	25	35	25	10	9	7	2	88	10	78
5	3	2	25	10	15	3	2	1	261	233	28	47	1	46	...	...	...
59	34	25	57	49	8	61	38	23	80	74	6	44	37	7	26	26	...
1	...	1	...	...	...	6	...	6	11	5	6	5	5	...	3	3	...
1	...	1	...	...	...	9	2	7	8	6	2	3	2	1	1	1	...
...	...	...	...	...	...	...	...	...	4	2	2	...	...	...	...	...	...
59	*37*	*22*	*106*	*96*	*10*	*33*	*21*	*12*	*113*	*102*	*11*	*42*	*42*	...	*3*	*3*	...
...	...	...	...	...	...	3	3	...	...	...	...	...	...	...	...	...	...
...	...	...	...	...	...	...	...	...	5	...	5	...	...	...	...	...	...
...	...	...	...	...	...	...	...	...	1	1	...	...	...	...	...	...	...
...	...	...	25	25	...	...	...	...	...	...	...	...	...	...	...	...	...
...	...	...	...	...	...	...	...	...	...	...	...	...	...	...	...	...	...
...	..	...	...	...	...	...	...	...	1	1	...	...	...	...	...	...	...
...	...	...	5	5	...	...	...	...	79	74	5	...	...	...	1	1	...
...	...	...	...	...	...	...	...	...	3	2	1	...	...	...	...	...	...
...	...	...	...	...	...	...	...	...	...	...	...	...	...	...	...	...	...
...	...	...	...	...	...	...	...	...	...	...	...	...	...	...	1	1	...
59	37	22	70	61	9	30	18	12	5	5	...	42	42	...	1	1	...
...	...	...	...	...	...	...	...	...	1	1	...	...	...	...	...	...	...
...	...	...	6	5	1	...	...	...	18	18	...	...	...	...	...	...	...
40	*21*	*19*	*84*	*21*	*63*	*547*	*263*	*284*	*115*	*65*	*50*	*167*	*93*	*74*	*90*	*79*	*11*
...	...	...	...	...	...	...	...	...	1	1	...	...	...	...	...	...	...
24	16	8	...	...	...	71	50	21	48	24	24	60	56	4	...	...	...
2	2	...	1	...	1	6	4	2	50	29	21	3	...	3	...	...	...
...	...	...	...	...	...	...	..	...	1	1	...	...	...	...	...	...	...
...	...	...	...	...	...	...	...	...	8	8	...	...	...	...	...	...	...
...	...	...	..	...	...	...	...	...	8	8	...	...	...	...	...	...	...
...	...	...	...	...	...	...	...	...	29	17	12	...	...	...	...	...	...
...	...	...	...	...	...	...	...	...	1	1	..	...	...	...	...	...	...
2	2	...	1	...	1	6	4	2	13	4	9	3	...	3	...	...	...

TABLE VI—

District, State, Province or Country where born.	GWALIOR STATE.			DISTRICT GIRD.			BHIND.			TONWARGHAR.			SHEOPUR.			NARWAR.		
	P.	M.	F.	P.	M.	F.	P.	M.	F.	P.	M.	F.	P.	M.	F.	P.	M.	F.
1	2	3	4	5	6	7	8	9	10	11	12	13	14	15	16	17	18	19
(14) N. W. F. Province...	144	102	42	10	7	3	...	...	...	...	...	...	3	3	...	...	...	...
Peshawar ...	46	38	8	...	...	...	...	...	...	...	...	...	3	3	...	...	...	...
N. W. F. unspecified.	98	64	34	10	7	3	...	...	...	...	...	...	...	...	...	...	...	...
(15) Punjab ...	2,896	1,912	984	865	567	298	658	462	196	95	59	36	78	50	28	82	46	36
(i) *British Districts* ...	*2,576*	*1,721*	*852*	*697*	*476*	*221*	*635*	*449*	*186*	*77*	*45*	*32*	*68*	*42*	*26*	*78*	*44*	*34*
Ambala ...	34	9	25	12	3	9	1	...	1	3	2	1	...	...	...	1	...	1
Amritsar ...	381	315	66	17	11	6	174	164	10	9	3	6	...	...	...	...	...	...
Gujranwala ...	6	6	...	...	...	...	2	2	...	...	...	...	...	...	...	...	...	...
Gurdaspur ...	176	104	72	1	1	...	184	77	57	...	...	...	5	2	3	...	...	...
Gurgaon ...	257	153	104	142	89	53	18	7	11	2	1	1	11	8	3	5	4	1
Hissar ...	12	8	4	1	...	1	1	...	1	...	...	...	...	...	...	6	6	...
Hoshiarpur ...	15	11	4	1	1	...	12	8	4	...	...	...	...	...	...	...	...	...
Jhelum ...	8	8	...	...	...	...	8	8	...	...	...	...	...	...	...	...	...	...
Jullunder ...	158	108	50	5	4	1	113	76	37	12	10	2	2	1	1	3	...	3
Karnal ...	33	25	8	18	17	1	...	...	...	8	8	...	...	...	...	...	...	...
Lahore ...	114	83	31	33	21	12	17	14	3	1	1	...	1	1	...	...	...	...
Ludhiana ...	74	52	22	31	21	10	5	3	2	4	2	2	...	...	...	7	6	1
Multan ...	13	11	2	4	2	2	...	...	...	...	...	...	...	...	...	...	...	...
Rawalpindi ...	41	30	11	7	5	2	16	11	5	...	...	...	1	1	...	...	...	...
Rohtak ...	269	211	58	158	138	20	44	19	25	2	1	1	2	1	1	6	5	1
Shahpur ...	2	1	1	1	1	...	...	...	...	...	...	...	...	...	...	...	...	...
Sialkot ...	54	29	25	3	2	1	10	4	6	...	...	...	...	...	...	...	...	...
Simla ...	5	5	...	...	...	...	...	...	...	...	...	...	...	...	...	...	...	...
Punjab unspecified	934	565	369	268	160	108	85	61	24	41	22	19	46	28	18	50	23	27
(ii) *States.* ...	*320*	*188*	*132*	*168*	*91*	*77*	*23*	*13*	*10*	*18*	*14*	*4*	*10*	*8*	*2*	*4*	*2*	*2*
Bilaspur ...	1	1	...	...	...	...	...	...	...	...	...	...	...	...	...	...	...	...
Jind ...	4	4	...	...	...	...	...	...	...	3	3	...	...	...	...	...	...	...
Kapurthala ...	10	5	5	1	...	1	1	...	1	...	...	...	3	1	2	...	...	...
Nabha ...	24	12	12	7	2	5	2	1	1	...	...	...	...	...	...	...	...	...
Pataudi ...	1	...	1	...	...	...	...	...	...	...	...	...	...	...	...	...	...	...
Patiala ...	280	166	114	160	89	71	20	12	8	15	11	4	7	7	...	4	2	2
(16) Baroda State ...	492	230	262	68	29	39	...	...	...	19	19	...	64	12	52	2	...	2
(17) Hyderabad State ...	232	157	75	58	28	30	...	...	...	2	...	2	...	...	...	...	...	...
(18) Kashmir State ...	39	30	9	22	14	8	...	...	...	...	...	...	...	...	...	...	...	...
(19) Mysore State ...	31	18	13	4	2	2	...	...	...	...	...	...	...	...	...	...	...	...
(c) India unspecified	1,743	669	1,074	40	35	5	224	40	184	26	...	26	4	2	2	10	1	9
(d) French & Portuguese Settlements—																		
Goa ...	16	11	5	10	6	4	...	...	...	...	...	...	...	...	...	...	...	...
Chandarnagar	1	1	...	1	1	...	...	...	...	...	...	...	...	...	...	...	...	...
(B) Born in other Asiatic countries.	124	99	25	42	33	9	...	...	...	4	1	3	2	1	1	1	...	1
(i) Within British Dominions—																		
Ceylon ...	2	1	1	1	1	...	...	...	...	...	...	...	...	...	...	...	...	...
Straits Settlement.	1	1	...	...	...	...	...	...	...	...	...	...	...	...	...	...	...	...
(ii) Outside British Dominions—																		
Afghanistan	52	43	9	10	7	3	...	...	...	...	...	...	1	1	...	...	...	...
Arabia ...	4	3	1	...	...	...	...	...	...	...	...	...	...	...	...	...	...	...
Nepal ...	56	44	12	27	22	5	...	...	...	4	1	3	1	...	1	1	...	1
Persia ...	3	3	...	1	1	...	...	...	...	...	...	...	...	...	...	...	...	...
Tibet ..	1	1	...	1	1	...	...	...	...	...	...	...	...	...	...	...	...	...
Turkey in Asia	3	2	1	...	...	...	...	...	...	...	...	...	...	...	...	...	...	...
(iii) Asia unspecified...	2	1	1	2	1	1	...	...	...	...	...	...	...	...	...	...	...	...
(C) Born in Europe ...	56	37	19	19	11	8	...	...	...	3	3	...	...	...	...	1	...	1
(i) Within British Dominions—																		
England & Wales..	36	27	9	14	8	6	...	...	...	2	2	...	...	...	...	...	...	...
Irish Free State..	5	3	2	...	...	...	...	...	...	...	...	...	...	...	...	...	...	...
Scotland ...	7	4	3	2	1	1	...	...	...	1	1	...	...	...	...	...	...	...
(ii) Continental Europe																		
Belgium ...	3	1	2	...	...	...	...	...	...	...	...	...	...	...	...	...	...	...
[illegible] ...	1	...	1	1	...	1	...	...	...	...	...	...	...	...	...	1	...	1
Germany ...	1	...	1	...	...	...	...	...	...	...	...	...	...	...	...	...	...	...
Italy ...	1	1	...	1	1	...	...	...	...	...	...	...	...	...	...	...	...	...
Russia [illegible]	1	1	...	1	1	...	...	...	...	...	...	...	...	...	...	...	...	...
[illegible]	1	...	1	...	...	...	...	...	...	...	...	...	...	...	...	...	...	...
(D) Born in America	19	7	12	2	...	2	...	...	...	...	...	...	...	...	...	...	...	...
[illegible]																		
[illegible] ...	16	7	9	...	...	...	...	...	...	...	...	...	...	...	...	...	...	...
[illegible]	3	...	3	2	...	2	...	...	...	...	...	...	...	...	...	...	...	...
(E) Born at sea ...	1	...	1	...	...	...	...	...	...	...	...	...	...	...	...	...	...	...

Birthplace—(*concld.*)

WHERE ENUMERATED.

ISAGARH.			BHILSA.			UJJAIN.			MANDSAUR.			SHAJAPUR.			AMJHERA.		
P.	M.	F.	P.	M.	F.	P.	M.	F.	P.	M.	F.	P.	M.	F.	P.	M.	F.
20	21	22	23	24	25	26	27	28	29	30	31	32	33	34	35	36	37
...	...	...	4	3	1	46	29	17	39	32	7	42	28	14	...	...	...
...	...	...	4	3	1	...	...	...	39	32	7	...	...	...	...	...	...
...	...	...	...	...	...	46	29	17	...	...	...	42	28	14	...	...	...
318	208	110	118	81	37	260	166	94	266	162	104	114	69	45	42	42	...
312	*203*	*109*	*96*	*75*	*21*	*243*	*152*	*91*	*234*	*143*	*91*	*98*	*57*	*41*	*38*	*38*	...
2	2	...	...	...	...	1	1	...	14	1	13	...	...	...	...	...	...
98	62	36	17	12	5	34	34	...	12	10	2	1	...	1	19	19	...
2	2	...	2	2	...	...	...	...	...	...	...	...	...	...	...	...	...
36	24	12	...	...	...	...	...	...	...	...	...	...	...	...	...	...	...
1	1	...	...	...	...	31	12	19	44	31	13	3	...	3	...	...	...
...	...	...	...	...	...	2	...	2	1	1	...	...	...	...	1	1	...
...	...	...	...	...	...	2	2	...	...	...	...	...	...	...	...	...	...
...	...	...	...	...	...	...	...	...	...	...	...	...	...	...	...	...	...
3	1	2	1	1	...	9	9	...	5	1	4	...	...	...	...	...	...
1	1	...	...	...	...	...	...	...	9	2	7	2	2	...	...	...	...
17	15	2	13	8	5	4	4	...	25	18	7	2	...	2	1	1	...
8	2	6	...	...	...	11	11	...	6	5	1	...	...	...	2	2	...
...	...	...	...	...	...	9	9	...	...	...	...	...	...	...	...	...	...
...	...	...	...	...	...	1	1	...	13	9	4	3	3	...	...	...	...
9	8	1	13	9	4	2	2	...	32	27	5	1	1	...	...	...	...
...	...	...	...	...	...	1	...	1	...	...	...	...	...	...	...	...	...
27	16	11	...	...	...	3	3	...	8	1	7	...	...	...	8	8	...
...	...	...	...	...	...	...	...	...	5	5	...	...	...	...	...	...	...
108	69	39	50	48	7	133	64	69	60	32	28	86	51	35	12	12	...
6	*5*	*1*	*22*	*6*	*16*	*17*	*14*	*3*	*32*	*19*	*13*	*16*	*12*	*4*	*4*	*4*	...
...	...	...	...	...	...	...	...	...	1	1	...	...	...	...	...	...	...
1	1	...	...	...	...	...	...	...	...	...	...	...	...	...	...	...	...
3	2	1	...	...	...	...	...	...	1	1	...	1	1	...	...	...	...
...	...	...	...	...	...	2	...	2	6	3	3	7	6	1	...	...	...
...	...	...	...	...	...	...	...	...	1	...	1	...	...	...	...	...	...
2	2	...	22	6	16	15	14	1	23	14	9	8	5	3	4	4	...
10	6	4	...	...	...	217	101	116	37	24	13	43	28	15	32	11	21
...	...	...	22	13	9	15	11	4	120	94	26	15	11	4	...	...	...
...	...	...	5	5	...	10	10	...	2	1	1	...	...	...	...	...	...
...	...	...	...	...	...	8	4	4	17	11	6	...	...	...	2	1	1
77	24	53	891	416	475	197	24	173	154	79	75	120	48	72	...	...	...
...	...	...	...	...	...	1	...	1	5	5	...	...	...	...	...	...	...
...	...	...	...	...	...	...	...	...	...	...	...	...	...	...	...	...	...
10	10	...	1	1	...	18	15	3	14	13	1	29	22	7	3	3	...
...	...	...	...	...	...	1	...	1	...	...	...	...	...	...	...	...	...
...	...	...	...	...	...	1	1	...	...	...	...	...	...	...	...	...	...
4	4	...	1	1	...	7	6	1	8	8	...	21	16	5	...	...	...
...	...	...	...	...	...	2	1	1	2	2	...	...	...	...	...	...	...
6	6	...	...	...	...	5	5	...	1	1	...	8	6	2	8	8	...
...	...	...	...	...	...	2	2	...	...	...	...	...	...	...	...	...	...
...	...	...	...	...	...	...	...	...	...	...	...	...	...	...	...	...	...
...	...	...	...	...	...	...	...	...	3	2	1	...	...	...	...	...	...
...	...	...	...	...	...	...	...	...	...	...	...	...	...	...	...	...	...
2	2	...	...	...	...	3	3	...	28	18	10	...	...	...	...	...	...
2	2	...	...	...	...	8	8	...	15	12	3	...	...	...	...	...	...
...	...	...	...	...	...	...	...	...	5	3	2	...	...	...	...	...	...
...	...	...	...	...	...	...	...	...	4	2	2	...	...	...	...	...	...
...	...	...	...	...	...	...	...	...	3	1	2	...	...	...	...	...	...
...	...	...	...	...	...	...	...	...	...	...	...	...	...	...	...	...	...
...	...	...	...	...	...	...	...	...	...	...	...	...	...	...	...	...	...
...	...	...	...	...	...	...	...	...	...	...	...	...	...	...	...	...	...
...	...	...	...	...	...	...	...	...	...	...	...	...	...	...	...	...	...
...	...	...	...	...	...	...	...	...	1	...	1	...	...	...	...	...	...
1	1	...	...	...	...	11	4	7	5	2	3	...	...	...	...	...	...
1	1	...	...	...	...	10	4	6	5	2	3	...	...	...	...	...	...
...	...	...	...	...	...	1	...	1	...	...	...	...	...	...	...	...	...
...	...	...	...	...	...	1	...	1	...	...	...	...	...	...	...	...	...

TABLE VII.

Age, Sex and Civil Condition.

NOTE 1.—This Table is divided into three parts. Part I shows the distribution for the State as a whole of the total population and of each religion by age, sex and civil condition. Part II shows the distribution in districts of the total population and of the main religions by age, sex and civil condition. Part III gives similar details for Cities.

NOTE 2.—The age recorded at this census was the age nearest birthday and not the number of years completed as at the last census. The numbers recorded were grouped into tenary and septenary groups and then re-distributed in the ordinary quinary groups. This re-distribution was first effected for the districts and the smoothed figures were then consolidated for the State.

TABLE VII.—Age, Sex and Civil Condition. *Part I—State Summary.*

Age.	POPULATION.			UNMARRIED.			MARRIED.			WIDOWED.		
	Persons.	Males.	Females.	Persons.	Males.	Females.	Persons.	Males.	Females.	Persons.	Males.	Females.
1	2	3	4	5	6	7	8	9	10	11	12	13
All Religions ...	3,523,070	1,867,031	1,656,039	1,416,646	874,082	542,564	1,683,673	851,956	831,717	422,751	140,993	281,758
0—1	111,641	56,593	55,048	110,807	56,828	54.484	698	288	465	186	87	99
1—2	97,046	48,321	48,725	95.902	47,937	47.965	1,031	349	682	118	35	78
2—3	99,993	49,075	50,918	98.386	48,529	49,807	1.511	505	1,006	146	41	105
3—4	101,288	50,660	50,628	98,580	49,788	48,792	2,325	757	1,568	383	115	268
4—5	99,046	50,974	48,072	95,716	49,961	45,755	2,837	871	1,966	493	142	351
Total 0—5	509,014	255,623	253,391	499,341	252,538	246,803	8,402	2,715	5,687	1,271	370	901
5—10	448,541	239,108	209,433	386,386	222,280	164,106	59,126	15,872	43,254	8,079	1,006	2,073
10—15	431,207	233,911	197 296	296,712	192,292	104,420	128,988	39,553	89,480	5,512	2,066	3,446
15—20	352,983	186,671	166,312	97,806	85,022	12,784	243,540	96 912	146,628	11,687	4,787	6,900
20—25	353,248	185,484	167,764	56,918	51,785	5 133	278,795	126,554	152,241	17,535	7,145	10,390
25—30	303,758	162,907	140,851	24,674	22,268	2,406	251,309	130,222	121,087	27,775	10,417	17,358
30—35	267,031	145,826	121,205	16,944	15,147	1,797	215,674	118,055	97,619	34,413	12,624	21,789
35—40	222,880	121,433	101,447	11 177	9,962	1,215	161,842	94,772	67,070	49 861	16,699	33,162
40—45	188,838	102,652	86,186	8,858	7,846	1,012	125,249	76,935	48,314	54,731	17,871	36,860
45—50	143,771	78,451	65,320	6,015	5,313	702	80,818	55,039	25,779	56,938	18,099	38,839
50—55	109,023	58,716	50,307	4,342	3,810	532	56 173	39,408	16,765	48,508	15,498	33,010
55—60	75,312	38,595	36,717	2,636	2,147	489	31,776	23,932	7,844	40,900	12,516	28,384
60—65	61,307	30,206	31,101	2,150	1,635	515	23,622	18,139	5,483	35,535	10,432	25,103
65—70	23,221	11,489	11,732	1,054	772	282	7,941	5,983	1,958	14,226	4,784	9,492
70 & Over.	32,936	15,959	16,977	1,683	1,315	368	10,423	7,865	2,558	20,830	6,779	14,051
Hindu (Brahmanic)	3,255,977	1,724,311	1,531,666	1,303,777	806 255	497,522	559,428	787,735	771,693	392,772	130,321	262,451
0—1	103,288	52,424	50,864	102 551	52,175	50,376	635	215	420	102	34	68
1—2	89,597	44,627	44,970	88 560	44,272	44,288	952	327	625	85	28	57
2—3	92,297	45,311	46,986	90,790	44 813	45,977	1,383	464	919	124	34	90
3—4	93,415	46,750	46,665	90,951	45 974	44,977	2,110	668	1,442	354	108	246
4—5	91,544	47,168	44,376	88,464	46,240	42,224	2,629	796	1,833	451	132	319
Total 0—5	470,141	236,280	233,861	461,316	233,474	227,842	7,709	2,470	5,239	1,116	336	780
5—10	415,505	221,727	193,778	356,512	205,725	150,787	56 111	15,067	41,044	2,882	935	1,947
10—15	399,255	217,222	182,733	272,923	177,651	95,272	121,867	37,645	84,222	5,165	1,926	3,239
15—20	327,086	172 284	154 052	88 895	77,636	11 259	227,244	90,901	136,343	10,897	4,447	6,450
20—25	326,228	171,208	155,020	51,382	46,934	4,448	258,415	117,597	140,818	16,431	6,677	9,754
25—30	280,874	150,445	130,429	22,410	20,371	2,039	232,478	120,412	112,066	25,986	9,662	16,324
30—35	247,136	134.727	112,409	15,435	13,936	1,499	199,601	109,109	90,492	32,100	11,682	20,418
35—40	206,073	112,115	93 958	10,233	9,225	1 008	149,278	87,379	61,899	46,562	15,511	31,051
40—45	174,530	94,678	79,852	8 161	7,314	847	115,223	70,747	44,476	51,146	16,617	34,529
45—50	132,563	72,071	60,492	5,574	4,989	585	78,937	50,288	28,649	53,052	16,794	36,258
50—55	100,212	53,715	46,497	4,006	3,560	446	51,176	35,823	15,353	45,030	14,332	30,698
55—60	68,922	35,081	33,841	2,395	1,969	426	28,755	21,646	7,110	37,772	11,467	26,305
60—65	56,084	27,422	28.662	1,984	1,511	473	21,876	16,884	4,992	32,724	9,527	23,197
65—70	21,038	10,824	10,714	984	726	258	7,059	5 307	1,752	12,995	4,291	8,704
70 & Over.	29,680	14,312	15,368	1,557	1 234	333	9,199	6,961	2,238	18,914	6,117	12,797
Arya	1,308	688	620	597	327	270	584	310	274	127	51	76
0—1	49	23	26	47	22	25	2	1	1	...	...	...
1—2	42	17	25	40	16	24	...	...	...	2	...	1
2—3	35	14	21	34	14	20	1	...	1	...	...	...
3—4	45	15	30	42	15	27	1	...	1	2	...	2
4—5	37	18	19	37	18	19	...	...	...	...	...	...
Total 0—5	208	87	121	200	85	115	4	1	3	4	1	3
5—10	168	88	80	153	84	69	11	2	9	4	2	2
10—15	167	92	75	137	81	56	27	9	18	8	2	1
15—20	131	66	65	53	37	16	71	26	45	7	3	4
20—25	117	48	69	21	16	5	88	30	58	8	2	6
25—30	93	43	50	6	4	2	79	36	43	8	3	5
30—35	93	52	41	8	6	2	70	40	30	15	6	9
35—40	75	45	30	4	3	1	53	33	20	18	9	9
40—45	63	38	25	5	4	1	44	26	18	14	8	6
45—50	60	37	23	4	2	2	47	33	14	9	2	7
50—55	41	28	13	3	2	1	29	23	6	9	3	6
55—60	34	27	7	1	1	...	26	22	4	7	4	3
60—65	22	14	8	1	1	...	13	12	1	8	1	7
65—70	15	9	6	...	...	...	11	8	3	4	1	3
70 & Over.	21	14	7	1	1	...	11	9	2	9	4	5

TABLE VII.—Age, Sex and Civil Condition. *Part I—State Summary.—(contd.)*

Age.	POPULATION.			UNMARRIED.			MARRIED.			WIDOWED.		
	Persons.	Males.	Females.	Persons.	Males.	Females.	Persons.	Males.	Females.	Persons.	Males.	Females.
1	2	3	4	5	6	7	8	9	10	11	12	13
Hinduised Tribal.	14,291	7,248	7,043	6,827	3,730	3,097	6,377	3,155	3,222	1,087	363	724
0—1	518	270	248	507	266	241	7	4	3	4	...	4
1—2	496	233	263	492	231	261	4	2	2	...	...	...
2—3	567	264	303	557	259	298	8	3	5	2	2	...
3—4	593	301	292	574	288	286	16	11	5	3	2	1
4—5	508	251	257	499	246	253	9	5	4	...	...	...
Total 0—5	2,682	1,319	1,363	2,629	1·290	1,339	44	25	19	9	4	5
5—10	2,044	1,012	1,032	1,898	986	912	167	50	117	9	6	3
10—15	1,919	965	954	1,438	814	624	465	140	325	16	11	5
15—20	1,399	705	694	410	304	106	948	386	562	41	15	26
20—25	1,310	667	643	210	168	42	1,054	479	575	46	20	26
25—30	985	491	494	68	52	16	863	414	449	54	25	29
30—35	885	451	434	62	47	15	745	373	372	78	31	47
35—40	806	440	366	47	36	11	657	372	285	102	32	70
40—45	684	360	324	30	18	12	521	306	215	133	36	97
45—50	516	260	256	18	5	13	355	214	141	143	41	102
50—55	379	196	183	8	4	4	237	156	81	134	36	98
55—60	263	140	123	5	3	2	140	99	41	118	38	80
60—65	203	109	94	2	2	...	96	75	21	105	32	73
65—70	93	38	55	...	...	...	36	25	11	57	13	44
70 & Over	93	65	28	2	1	1	49	41	8	42	23	19
Muslim	204,297	109,412	94,885	85,996	51,546	34,450	96,719	50,133	46,586	21,582	7,733	13,849
0—1	6,407	3,178	3,229	6,336	3,165	3,171	46	11	35	25	2	23
1—2	5,740	2,849	2,891	5,657	2,829	2,828	62	15	47	21	5	16
2—3	5,914	2,906	3,008	5,800	2,870	2,930	97	31	66	17	5	12
3—4	6,002	2,985	3,017	5,815	2,916	2,899	171	67	104	16	2	14
4—5	5,776	2,943	2,833	5,569	2,878	2,691	172	57	115	35	8	27
Total 0—5	29,839	14,861	14,978	29,177	14,658	14,519	548	181	367	114	22	92
5—10	25,459	13,430	12,029	22,878	12,757	10,121	2,424	620	1,804	157	53	104
10—15	23,920	12,769	11,151	18,188	11,199	6,989	5,532	1,466	4,066	260	104	156
15—20	20,078	10,613	9,465	6,942	5,725	1,217	12,607	4,663	7,944	529	225	304
20—25	21,047	11,209	9,838	4,330	3,789	541	15,909	7,042	8,867	808	378	430
25—30	17,688	9,735	7,953	1,650	1,362	288	14,753	7,777	6,976	1,285	596	689
30—35	15,138	8,498	6,640	1,018	782	236	12,512	7,005	5,507	1,608	711	897
35—40	12,736	7,052	5,684	605	429	176	9,756	5,732	4,024	2,375	891	1,484
40—45	10,744	6,005	4,739	417	293	124	7,785	4,817	2,968	2,542	895	1,647
45—50	8,326	4,770	3,556	242	165	77	5,328	3,728	1,600	2,761	882	1,879
50—55	6,483	3,685	2,798	205	138	67	3,830	2,766	1,064	2,448	781	1,667
55—60	4,691	2,585	2,106	161	108	53	2,300	1,742	558	2,230	735	1,495
60—65	3,936	2,083	1,853	109	71	38	1,766	1,364	402	2,061	648	1,413
65—70	1,595	839	756	52	29	23	674	509	165	869	301	568
70 & Over	2,617	1,278	1,339	72	41	31	1,010	726	284	1,535	511	1,024
Jain	45,079	24,238	20,841	18,324	11,629	6,695	19,726	10,148	9,578	7,029	2,461	4,568
0—1	1,319	672	647	1,306	669	637	8	2	6	5	1	4
1—2	1,118	571	547	1,100	565	535	13	5	8	5	1	4
2—3	1,120	550	570	1,095	543	552	22	7	15	3	...	3
3—4	1,154	573	581	1,119	559	560	27	11	16	8	3	5
4—5	1,116	564	552	1,083	550	533	26	12	14	7	2	5
Total 0—5	5,827	2,930	2,897	5,703	2,886	2,817	96	37	59	28	7	21
5—10	5,099	2,695	2,404	4,665	2,554	2,111	408	131	277	26	10	16
10—15	5,022	2,746	2,276	3,863	2,434	1,429	1,093	291	802	66	21	45
15—20	4,147	2,225	1,922	1,382	1,256	126	2,605	923	1,682	160	46	114
20—25	4,358	2,258	2,100	883	819	64	3,232	1,368	1,864	238	66	172
25—30	3,944	2,094	1,850	490	448	42	3,020	1,520	1,500	434	126	308
30—35	3,593	1,990	1,603	385	355	30	2,610	1,447	1,163	598	188	410
35—40	3,043	1,693	1,350	274	260	14	1,980	1,184	796	789	249	540
40—45	2,692	1,489	1,203	232	210	22	1,579	972	607	881	307	574
45—50	2,216	1,258	958	168	146	22	1,096	740	356	952	372	580
50—55	1,817	1,039	778	105	97	8	846	604	242	866	338	528
55—60	1,337	723	614	67	62	5	513	393	120	757	268	489
60—65	1,020	552	468	50	48	2	346	285	61	624	219	405
65—70	467	272	195	18	17	1	155	129	26	294	126	168
70 & Over	502	279	223	39	37	2	147	124	23	316	118	198

TABLE VII.—Age, Sex and Civil Condition. *Part I—State Summary—(concld.)*

Age.	POPULATION.			UNMARRIED.			MARRIED.			WIDOWED.		
	Persons.	Males.	Females.	Persons.	Males.	Females.	Persons.	Males.	Females.	Persons.	Males.	Females.
1	2	3	4	5	6	7	8	9	10	11	12	13
Christian ...	**1,198**	**592**	**606**	**650**	**299**	**351**	**478**	**267**	**211**	**70**	**26**	**44**
0—1	34	12	22	34	12	22	...	...	...	...	...	...
1—2	31	13	18	31	13	18	...	...	...	...	...	...
2—3	33	16	17	33	16	17	...	...	...	...	...	...
3—4	49	22	27	49	22	27	...	...	...	...	...	...
4—5	42	19	23	41	18	23	1	1	...	...	...	...
Total 0—5	189	82	107	188	81	107	1	1	...	...	...	...
5—10	146	65	81	141	63	78	5	2	3	...	...	...
10—15	131	59	72	127	57	70	4	2	2	...	...	...
15—20	112	42	70	77	35	42	34	7	27	1	...	1
20—25	108	48	60	52	29	23	53	18	35	3	1	2
25—30	93	53	40	26	16	10	63	35	28	4	2	2
30—35	104	60	44	18	9	9	79	47	32	7	4	3
35—40	81	46	35	5	2	3	72	41	31	4	3	1
40—45	69	42	27	5	2	3	56	36	20	8	4	4
45—50	47	28	19	3	2	1	35	24	11	9	2	7
50—55	45	24	21	5	2	3	30	19	11	10	3	7
55—60	33	20	13	2	1	1	23	17	6	8	2	6
60—65	22	15	7	1	...	1	16	13	3	5	2	3
65—70	8	4	4	...	...	...	4	3	1	4	1	3
70 & Over.	10	4	6	...	...	...	3	2	1	7	2	5
Sikh ...	**681**	**446**	**235**	**338**	**249**	**89**	**278**	**164**	**114**	**65**	**33**	**32**
0—1	21	13	8	21	13	8	...	...	...	...	...	...
1—2	19	11	8	19	11	8	...	...	...	...	...	...
2—3	20	12	8	20	12	8	...	...	...	...	...	...
3—4	21	12	9	21	12	9	...	...	...	...	...	...
4—5	19	10	9	19	10	9	...	...	...	...	...	...
Total 0—5	100	58	42	100	58	42	...	...	...	...	...	...
5—10	71	53	18	70	53	17	...	...	...	1	...	1
10—15	75	51	24	68	49	19	5	...	5	2	2	...
15—20	61	31	30	32	24	8	27	6	21	2	1	1
20—25	61	43	18	26	26	...	34	16	18	1	1	...
25—30	60	38	22	13	12	1	43	23	20	4	3	1
30—35	55	36	19	9	8	1	41	26	15	5	2	3
35—40	47	33	14	5	5	...	33	24	9	9	4	5
40—45	44	33	11	4	3	1	35	27	8	5	3	2
45—50	28	20	8	3	3	...	17	13	4	8	4	4
50—55	35	24	11	6	6	...	22	14	8	7	4	3
55—60	22	13	9	1	1	...	14	10	4	7	2	5
60—65	9	6	3	...	...	...	3	3	...	6	3	3
65—70	4	2	2	...	...	...	1	1	...	3	1	2
70 & Over.	9	5	4	1	1	...	3	1	2	5	3	2
Zoroastrian ...	**239**	**96**	**143**	**137**	**47**	**90**	**83**	**44**	**39**	**19**	**5**	**14**
0—1	5	1	4	5	1	4	...	...	...	...	...	...
1—2	3	...	3	3	...	3	...	...	...	...	...	...
2—3	7	2	5	7	2	5	...	...	...	...	...	...
3—4	9	2	7	9	2	7	...	...	...	...	...	...
4—5	4	1	3	4	1	3	...	...	...	...	...	...
Total 0—5	28	6	22	28	6	22	...	...	...	...	...	...
5—10	19	8	11	19	8	11	...	...	...	...	...	...
10—15	18	7	11	18	7	11	...	...	...	...	...	...
15—20	19	5	14	15	5	10	4	...	4	...	...	...
20—25	24	8	16	14	4	10	10	4	6	...	...	...
25—30	21	8	13	11	3	8	10	5	5	...	...	...
30—35	27	12	15	9	4	5	16	8	8	2	...	2
35—40	19	9	10	4	2	2	13	7	6	2	...	2
40—45	12	7	5	4	2	2	6	4	2	2	1	1
45—50	15	7	8	3	1	2	8	4	4	4	2	2
50—55	11	5	6	4	1	3	3	3	...	4	1	3
55—60	10	6	4	4	2	2	5	4	1	1	...	1
60—65	11	5	6	3	2	1	6	3	3	2	...	2
65—70	1	1	...	...	...	...	1	1	...	...	...	...
70 & Over.	4	2	2	1	...	1	1	1	...	2	1	1

TABLE VII.

Age, Sex and Civil Condition.

PART II.

Details by Districts.

TABLE VII.—Age, Sex and Civil Condition. *Part II.—Details by Districts.*

Age.	POPULATION.			UNMARRIED.			MARRIED.			WIDOWED.		
	Persons.	Males.	Females	Persons.	Males.	Females.	Persons.	Males.	Females.	Persons.	Males.	Females
1	2	3	4	5	6	7	8	9	10	11	12	13
							District Gird.					
All Religions ...	364,806	197,935	166,871	140,174	86,604	53,570	175,946	93,406	82,540	48,686	17,925	30,761
0—1	10,476	5,038	5,438	10,415	5,006	5,409	59	31	28	2	1	1
1—2	9,456	4,480	4,976	9,361	4,433	4,928	93	46	47	2	1	1
2—3	9,479	4,553	4,926	9,373	4,514	4,859	87	38	49	19	1	18
3—4	9,391	4,663	4,728	9,230	4,590	4,640	129	64	65	32	9	23
4—5	9,101	4,603	4,498	8,921	4,513	4,408	153	80	73	27	10	17
Total 0—5	47,903	23,337	24,566	47,300	23,056	24,244	521	259	262	82	22	60
5—10	42,068	22,622	19,446	36,989	20,971	16,018	4,888	1,556	3,332	191	95	96
10—15	42,166	23,304	18,862	29,468	19,127	10,341	12,214	3,906	8,308	484	271	213
15—20	37,887	20,527	17,360	11,128	9,718	1,410	25,227	10,039	15,188	1,532	720	812
20—25	38,366	20,865	17,501	6,887	6,267	620	29,092	13,442	15,650	2,387	1,156	1,231
25—30	33,669	19,067	14,602	2,960	2,719	241	27,373	14,790	12,583	3,336	1,558	1,778
30—35	30,044	17,698	12,346	1,898	1,709	189	24,089	14,127	9,962	4,057	1,862	2,195
35—40	24,798	14,510	10,288	1,094	952	142	18,027	11,373	6,654	5,677	2,185	3,492
40—45	20,600	11,726	8,874	817	711	106	13,698	8,799	4,899	6,085	2,216	3,869
45—50	15,771	8,535	7,236	547	479	68	8,353	5,822	2,531	6,871	2,234	4,637
50—55	12,012	6,329	5,683	416	364	52	5,666	4,040	1,626	5,930	1,925	4,005
55—60	7,704	3,873	3,831	229	187	42	2,966	2,238	728	4,509	1,448	3,061
60—65	6,068	2,853	3,215	173	141	32	2,173	1,682	491	3,722	1,030	2,692
65—70	2,259	1,125	1,134	105	83	22	704	541	163	1,450	501	949
70 & Over.	3,491	1,564	1,927	163	120	43	955	742	213	2,373	702	1,671
Hindu (Brahmanic).	322,345	174,591	147,754	122,743	75,779	46,964	155,700	82,720	72,980	43,902	16,092	27,810
0—1	9,236	4,451	4,785	9,179	4,421	4,758	55	29	26	2	1	1
1—2	8,369	3,958	4,411	8,281	3,912	4,369	86	45	41	2	1	1
2—3	8,878	4,021	4,857	8,287	3,986	4,301	73	34	39	18	1	17
3—4	8,273	4,101	4,172	8,134	4,037	4,097	107	55	52	32	9	23
4—5	8,022	4,039	3,983	7,865	3,958	3,907	135	72	63	22	9	13
Total 0—5	42,278	20,570	21,708	41,746	20,314	21,432	456	235	221	76	21	55
5—10	37,290	20,033	17,257	32,574	18,478	14,096	4,538	1,465	3,073	178	90	88
10—15	37,574	20,799	16,775	25,860	16,857	9,003	11,253	3,682	7,571	461	260	201
15—20	33,539	18,219	15,320	9,500	8,321	1,179	22,605	9,216	13,389	1,434	682	752
20—25	33,742	18,346	15,396	5,769	5,240	528	25,745	12,019	13,726	2,228	1,081	1,147
25—30	29,781	16,815	12,966	2,529	2,331	198	24,199	13,076	11,123	3,053	1,408	1,645
30—35	26,734	15,743	10,991	1,648	1,498	150	21,410	12,593	8,817	3,676	1,652	2,024
35—40	22,038	12,888	9,150	958	854	104	15,928	10,084	5,844	5,152	1,950	3,202
40—45	18,230	10,331	7,899	714	636	78	11,955	7,682	4,273	5,561	2,013	3,548
45—50	13,896	7,430	6,466	493	437	56	7,157	4,976	2,181	6,246	2,017	4,229
50—55	10,534	5,474	5,060	370	329	41	4,814	3,410	1,404	5,350	1,735	3,615
55—60	6,645	3,305	3,340	196	165	31	2,481	1,857	624	3,968	1,283	2,685
60—65	5,191	2,391	2,800	149	127	22	1,803	1,382	421	3,239	882	2,357
65—70	1,939	950	989	94	77	17	581	443	138	1,264	430	834
70 & Over	2,934	1,297	1,637	143	109	34	775	600	175	2,016	588	1,428
Muslim ...	39,232	21,575	17,657	16,211	10,049	6,162	18,766	9,884	8,882	4,255	1,642	2,613
0—1	1,163	552	611	1,159	550	609	4	2	2	...	...	...
1—2	1,018	487	531	1,011	486	525	7	1	6	...	...	...
2—3	1,035	499	536	1,021	495	526	13	4	9	1	...	1
3—4	1,010	527	513	1,020	518	502	20	9	11	...	...	...
4—5	1,008	528	480	985	519	466	18	8	10	5	1	4
Total 0—5	5,264	2,593	2,671	5,196	2,568	2,628	62	24	38	6	1	5
5—10	4,489	2,436	2,053	4,149	2,346	1,803	327	85	242	13	5	8
10—15	4,276	2,340	1,936	3,372	2,126	1,246	892	201	678	22	10	12
15—20	4,012	2,140	1,872	1,513	1,305	208	2,413	799	1,614	86	36	50
20—25	4,279	2,359	1,919	1,037	913	87	3,107	1,316	1,791	142	71	71
25—30	3,576	2,065	1,511	377	341	36	2,953	1,585	1,368	246	139	107
30—35	3,026	1,787	1,239	211	178	33	2,486	1,415	1,071	326	144	182
35—40	2,521	1,484	1,037	113	77	36	1,951	1,194	757	457	213	244
40—45	2,171	1,332	839	88	61	27	1,626	1,045	581	451	176	275
45—50	1,712	1,013	699	47	35	12	1,110	792	318	555	186	369
50—55	1,317	750	567	38	28	10	783	582	201	526	170	356
55—60	925	512	413	26	16	10	412	318	94	487	148	339
60—65	702	411	291	19	10	9	339	273	66	431	128	303
65—70	280	155	125	10	5	5	109	86	23	166	59	107
70 & Over	527	252	275	19	10	9	173	136	37	335	106	229

TABLE VII.—Age, Sex and Civil Condition. *Part II.—Details by Districts.—(contd.)*

Age.	POPULATION.			UNMARRIED.			MARRIED.			WIDOWED.		
	Persons.	Males.	Females.	Persons.	Males.	Females.	Persons.	Males.	Females.	Persons.	Males	Females.
1	2	3	4	5	6	7	8	9	10	11	12	13
District Gird—(concld.)												
Jain ...	2,569	1,405	1,164	916	606	310	1,179	631	548	474	168	306
0—1	61	29	32	61	29	32	...	...	...	...	...	...
1—2	55	30	25	55	30	25	...	...	...	...	...	...
2—3	52	26	26	51	26	25	1	...	1	...	...	...
3—4	57	27	30	55	27	28	2	...	2	...	...	...
4—5	54	29	25	54	29	25	...	...	...	...	...	...
Total 0—5	279	141	138	276	141	135	3	...	3	...	...	...
5—10	236	128	108	213	122	91	23	6	17	...	...	...
10—15	261	137	124	185	116	69	75	20	55	1	1	...
15—20	260	131	129	72	64	8	177	65	112	11	2	9
20—25	270	145	125	54	51	3	200	90	110	16	4	12
25—30	249	146	103	37	34	3	178	102	76	34	10	24
30—35	224	131	93	26	25	1	150	92	58	48	14	34
35—40	186	105	81	18	18	...	108	69	39	60	18	42
40—45	168	90	78	12	12	...	86	54	32	65	24	41
45—50	134	78	56	6	6	...	65	43	22	63	29	34
50—55	101	58	43	5	5	...	49	35	14	47	18	29
55—60	83	42	41	6	6	...	29	22	7	48	14	34
60—65	69	40	29	4	4	...	20	18	2	45	18	27
65—70	28	20	8	1	1	...	10	9	1	17	10	7
70 & Over.	26	13	13	1	1	...	6	6	...	19	6	13
District Bhind.												
All Religions. ...	418,224	228,214	190,010	171,808	112,525	59,283	189,075	95,100	93,975	57,341	20,589	36,752
0—1	14,073	7,573	6,500	13,975	7,535	6,440	88	36	52	10	2	8
1—2	10,925	5,696	5,229	10,840	5,665	5,175	79	29	50	6	2	4
2—3	11,029	5,482	5,547	10,927	5,453	5,474	89	26	63	13	3	10
3—4	11,702	5,943	5,759	11,546	5,888	5,658	127	43	84	29	12	17
4—5	11,995	6,310	5,685	11,794	6,235	5,559	156	55	101	45	20	25
Total 0—5	59,724	31,004	28,720	59,082	30,776	28,306	539	189	350	103	39	64
5—10	52,380	28,962	23,418	45,584	27,073	18,511	6,517	1,771	4,746	279	118	161
10—15	49,307	27,870	21,437	38,850	28,258	10,592	14,958	4,420	10,538	499	192	307
15—20	40,163	21,799	18,364	11,395	10,696	699	27,375	10,573	16,802	1,393	530	863
20—25	40,349	21,226	19,123	7,236	6,853	383	30,772	13,526	17,246	2,341	847	1,494
25—30	37,576	20,336	17,240	4,067	3,854	213	29,524	15,068	14,456	3,985	1,414	2,571
30—35	34,021	19,142	14,879	3,349	3,180	169	25,780	14,147	11,633	4,892	1,815	3,077
35—40	26,510	15,256	11,254	2,219	2,108	111	17,868	10,713	7,155	6,423	2,435	3,988
40—45	22,388	12,931	9,457	1,701	1,596	105	13,615	8,685	4,930	7,072	2,650	4,422
45—50	17,448	9,931	7,517	1,166	1,105	61	8,731	6,049	2,682	7,551	2,777	4,774
50—55	13,712	7,627	6,085	856	823	33	6,081	4,323	1,758	6,775	2,481	4,294
55—60	9,831	4,968	4,863	547	513	34	3,264	2,465	799	6,020	1,990	4,030
60—65	7,713	3,767	3,946	398	367	31	2,302	1,796	506	5,013	1,604	3,409
65—70	3,190	1,530	1,660	153	141	12	841	643	198	2,196	741	1,455
70 & Over.	3,912	1,865	2,047	205	182	23	908	727	181	2,799	956	1,843
Hindu (Brahmanic)	398,110	217,360	180,750	163,158	107,180	55,978	180,144	90,603	89,541	54,808	19,577	35,231
0—1	13,425	7,251	6,174	13,331	7,215	6,116	85	35	50	9	1	8
1—2	10,414	5,442	4,972	10,334	5,413	4,921	75	28	47	5	1	4
2—3	10,487	5,218	5,269	10,390	5,190	5,200	85	26	59	12	2	10
3—4	11,105	5,656	5,449	10,958	5,601	5,357	118	43	75	29	12	17
4—5	11,417	6,024	5,393	11,237	5,955	5,282	141	51	90	39	18	21
Total 0—5	56,848	29,591	27,257	56,250	29,374	26,876	504	183	321	94	34	60
5—10	49,934	27,625	22,309	43,389	25,798	17,591	6,277	1,714	4,563	268	113	155
10—15	46,979	26,528	20,451	32,123	22,095	10,028	14,373	4,250	10,123	483	183	300
15—20	38,177	20,721	17,456	10,735	10,141	594	26,103	10,070	16,033	1,339	510	829
20—25	38,271	20,153	18,118	6,792	6,493	299	29,245	12,859	16,386	2,234	806	1,428
25—30	35,754	19,400	16,354	3,817	3,667	150	28,135	14,389	13,746	3,802	1,344	2,458
30—35	32,458	18,291	14,167	3,172	3,048	124	24,608	13,509	11,099	4,678	1,734	2,944
35—40	25,291	14,556	10,735	2,118	2,028	90	17,027	10,213	6,814	6,146	2,315	3,831
40—45	21,369	12,361	9,008	1,627	1,543	84	12,965	8,296	4,669	6,777	2,522	4,255
45—50	16,642	9,459	7,183	1,106	1,059	47	8,295	5,753	2,542	7,241	2,647	4,594
50—55	13,035	7,219	5,816	811	788	23	5,744	4,077	1,667	6,480	2,354	4,126
55—60	9,311	4,682	4,629	509	487	22	3,054	2,307	747	5,748	1,888	3,860
60—65	7,328	3,570	3,758	371	348	23	2,170	1,695	475	4,782	1,527	3,255
65—70	3,019	1,438	1,581	142	135	7	788	603	185	2,089	700	1,389
70 & Over.	3,699	1,761	1,938	196	176	20	856	685	171	2,647	900	1,747

TABLE VII.—Age, Sex and Civil Condition. *Part II—Details by Districts.—(contd.)*

Age.	POPULATION.			UNMARRIED.			MARRIED.			WIDOWED.		
	Persons.	Males.	Females.	Persons.	Males.	Females.	Persons.	Males.	Females.	Persons.	Males.	Females.
1	2	3	4	5	6	7	8	9	10	11	12	13
District Bhind—(concld.)												
Muslim ...	12,652	6,837	5,812	5,559	3,399	2,190	5,759	2,949	2,810	1,341	539	802
0—1	410	211	199	408	210	198	2	1	1	...	...	...
1—2	328	163	165	325	162	163	3	1	2	...	...	...
2—3	347	168	179	344	167	177	2	...	2	1	1	...
3—4	386	189	197	379	189	190	7	...	7	...	...	...
4—5	369	189	180	358	188	170	9	1	8	2	...	2
Total 0—5	1,840	920	920	1,814	916	898	23	3	20	3	1	2
5—10	1,590	879	711	1,418	840	578	168	88	180	4	1	3
10—15	1,549	901	648	1,185	775	360	408	123	285	6	3	3
15—20	1,329	740	589	474	386	88	825	344	481	30	10	20
20—25	1,357	709	648	310	231	79	981	450	531	66	28	38
25—30	1,161	594	567	158	95	58	901	458	448	107	46	61
30—35	947	508	439	93	51	42	749	412	337	105	45	60
35—40	723	418	305	47	27	20	530	319	211	146	72	74
40—45	621	348	273	39	21	18	417	249	168	165	78	87
45—50	473	277	196	26	15	11	284	197	87	163	65	98
50—55	384	237	148	25	15	10	218	164	49	146	58	88
55—60	282	152	130	25	13	12	124	92	32	133	47	86
60—65	215	104	111	16	8	8	75	56	19	124	40	84
65—70	95	47	48	8	3	5	30	26	4	57	18	39
70 & Over.	123	53	70	6	3	3	31	23	8	86	27	59
Jain ...	6,554	3,442	3,112	2,618	1,666	952	2,799	1,349	1,450	1,107	427	680
0—1	214	95	119	212	94	118	1	...	1	1	1	...
1—2	158	76	82	156	75	81	1	...	1	1	1	...
2—3	169	80	89	167	80	87	2	...	2	...	...	...
3—4	181	82	99	179	82	97	2	...	2	...	...	...
4—5	152	65	97	172	80	92	6	3	3	4	2	2
Total 0—5	914	418	496	886	411	475	12	3	9	6	4	2
5—10	759	405	354	696	393	303	66	18	48	7	4	3
10—15	[illegible]	393	300	522	346	176	166	46	120	10	6	4
15—20	592	308	291	161	152	9	408	147	261	23	9	14
20—25	[illegible]	[illegible]	328	115	111	4	493	197	296	40	12	28
25—30	549	256	292	80	75	5	486	199	237	72	22	50
30—35	531	283	249	69	57	3	370	194	176	101	32	69
35—40	427	234	193	31	31	1	259	156	113	124	45	79
40—45	354	194	159	30	27	3	201	120	81	122	47	75
45—50	[illegible]	[illegible]	125	30	27	3	128	83	45	135	58	77
50—55	257	147	110	16	16	...	103	69	34	128	62	76
55—60	[illegible]	121	94	12	12	...	65	50	15	129	47	79
60—65	123	50	73	11	11	...	44	35	9	93	34	64
65—70	47	20	23	3	3	...	20	16	4	44	20	24
70 & Over.	79	41	38	2	2	...	18	16	2	59	23	36

District Tonwarghar.

TABLE VII.—Age, Sex and Civil Condition. *Part II.—Details by Districts.—(contd.)*

Age.	POPULATION.			UNMARRIED.			MARRIED.			WIDOWED.		
	Persons.	Males.	Females.	Persons.	Males.	Females.	Persons.	Males.	Females.	Persons.	Males.	Females.
1	2	3	4	5	6	7	8	9	10	11	12	13
District Tonwarghar.—(concld.)												
Hindu (Brahmanic.)	356,721	197,628	159,093	155,981	99,105	56,876	158,384	80,428	77,956	42,356	18,095	24,261
0—1	11,675	6.254	5,421	11,644	6,234	5,410	26	15	11	5	5	...
1—2	9,298	4.856	4.437	9,261	4,839	4,422	29	15	14	3	2	1
2—3	9.988	5,098	4 890	9 988	5,072	4,866	40	18	22	5	3	2
3—4	10,221	5.361	4,860	10,125	5,317	4 808	72	31	41	24	13	11
4—5	10,090	5,455	4,635	9,963	5,398	4,565	97	42	55	30	15	15
Total 0—5	51,262	27,019	24,243	50.931	26,860	24,071	261	121	143	67	38	29
5—10	46,364	26,190	20,174	41.304	24,247	17,057	4.768	1.789	2 999	272	154	118
10—15	45 200	26.118	19.082	32.968	21.246	11,722	11,608	4,596	7,072	564	276	288
15—20	35 164	19.984	15,280	11.608	9.511	2,092	22.368	9 908	12,460	1,198	520	678
20—25	34,770	19,201	15,569	6 855	6,091	764	26.163	12,303	13.860	1,752	807	945
25—30	30,753	16,834	13.919	3,788	3,418	370	24,077	12,182	11,895	2,888	1,234	1,654
30—35	26,826	14,932	11,894	2,708	2 446	262	20.525	10 942	9,583	3,593	1,544	2,049
35—40	22,046	12 321	9,725	1,741	1,586	155	15 403	8,601	6 802	4 902	2,134	2,768
40—45	18,706	10,556	8,150	1 399	1,247	152	11,981	6.986	5 045	5,326	2 373	2 953
45—50	14,388	8.158	6,230	918	809	109	7.988	4,903	3.085	5,532	2,446	3,086
50—55	10,926	6,075	4,851	684	625	59	5.513	3.391	2 122	4 729	2,059	2,670
55—60	7,749	4,069	3.680	440	403	37	3,254	2.048	1,206	4,055	1,618	2,437
60—65	6,252	3 115	3.137	330	316	14	2,379	1 497	882	3,543	1,302	2,241
65—70	3,321	1,896	1,425	149	145	4	990	566	424	1,682	685	997
70 & Over.	3,494	1,710	1,784	163	155	8	1,078	650	428	2,253	905	1,348
Muslim ...	10,732	5,949	4,783	4,728	2,888	1,840	4,948	2,573	2,375	1,056	488	568
0—1	302	167	135	300	167	133	2	...	2	...	...	...
1—2	270	138	132	268	137	131	2	1	1	...	...	...
2—3	291	154	137	290	154	136	1	...	1	...	...	...
3—4	304	158	146	300	158	142	4	...	4	...	...	...
4—5	299	157	142	289	151	138	9	5	4	1	1	...
Total 0—5	1,466	774	692	1,447	767	680	18	6	12	1	1	...
5—10	1,321	742	579	1,228	709	519	90	31	59	3	2	1
10—15	1,283	708	575	1,012	629	383	267	77	190	4	2	2
15—20	1,104	597	507	447	342	105	636	245	391	21	10	11
20—25	1,160	651	509	306	249	57	821	333	488	33	19	14
25—30	978	542	436	108	78	30	812	429	383	58	35	23
30—35	817	457	360	55	37	18	681	373	308	81	47	34
35—40	679	387	292	38	23	15	512	297	215	129	67	62
40—45	575	341	234	32	19	13	405	254	151	138	68	70
45—50	416	251	165	20	13	7	265	180	85	131	58	73
50—55	315	180	135	14	9	5	180	123	57	121	48	73
55—60	225	124	101	9	6	3	110	73	37	106	45	61
60—65	189	99	90	7	5	2	83	55	28	99	39	60
65—70	92	43	49	3	1	2	29	20	9	60	22	38
70 & Over.	112	53	59	2	1	1	39	27	12	71	25	46
Jain ...	2,081	1,122	959	901	546	355	844	423	421	336	153	183
0—1	51	25	26	51	25	26	...	...	...	...	...	...
1—2	41	17	24	41	17	24	...	...	...	...	...	...
2—3	52	21	31	51	20	31	1	1	...	...	...	...
3—4	55	25	30	55	25	30	...	...	...	...	...	...
4—5	59	28	31	58	28	30	1	...	1	...	...	...
Total 0—5	258	116	142	256	115	141	2	1	1	...	...	...
5—10	251	116	135	230	111	119	20	4	16	1	1	...
10—15	257	136	121	198	117	81	54	17	37	5	2	3
15—20	199	117	82	67	59	8	121	53	68	11	5	6
20—25	205	110	95	85	82	3	155	72	83	15	6	9
25—30	175	96	79	29	27	2	126	61	65	20	8	12
30—35	154	93	61	27	26	1	101	56	45	26	11	15
35—40	147	90	57	18	18	...	90	54	36	39	18	21
40—45	129	78	51	17	17	...	71	42	29	41	19	22
45—50	96	54	42	9	9	...	40	24	16	47	21	26
50—55	73	44	29	6	6	...	24	15	9	43	23	20
55—60	52	29	23	3	3	...	16	10	6	33	16	17
60—65	38	19	19	2	2	...	10	6	4	26	11	15
65—70	19	12	7	1	1	...	5	4	1	13	7	6
70 & Over.	28	12	16	3	3	...	9	4	5	16	5	11

TABLE VII.—Age, Sex and Civil Condition. *Part II.—Details by Districts.—(contd)*

Age.	POPULATION.			UNMARRIED.			MARRIED.			WIDOWED.		
	Persons.	Males.	Females.	Persons.	Males.	Females.	Persons.	Males.	Females.	Persons.	Males.	Females.
1	2	3	4	5	6	7	8	9	10	11	12	13
District Sheopur.												
All Religions ...	137,034	72,925	64,109	59,681	36,331	23,350	63,210	31,441	31,769	14,143	5,153	8,990
0—1	4,321	2,233	2,088	4,319	2,233	2,086	1	...	1	1	...	1
1—2	3,893	2,000	1,893	3,879	1,995	1,884	13	5	8	1	...	1
2—3	4,138	2,062	2,076	4,112	2,052	2,060	25	10	15	1	...	1
3—4	4,181	2,101	2,080	4,136	2,082	2,054	42	19	23	3	...	3
4—5	4,032	2,042	1,990	3,975	2,014	1,961	46	23	23	11	5	6
Total 0—5	20,565	10,438	10,127	20,421	10,376	10,045	127	57	70	17	5	12
5—10	18,534	9,945	8,589	16,946	9,472	7,474	1,556	464	1,092	32	9	23
10—15	17,324	9,380	7,944	13,145	8,195	4,950	4,081	1,147	2,934	98	38	60
15—20	12,308	6,470	5,838	3,871	3,346	525	8,110	2,958	5,152	327	166	161
20—25	13,058	7,178	5,880	2,268	2,108	160	10,288	4,807	5,476	507	263	244
25—30	13,392	7,107	6,285	1,056	981	75	11,425	5,723	5,702	911	403	508
30—35	11,429	5,865	5,564	681	640	41	9,576	4,748	4,833	1,172	482	690
35—40	8,583	4,630	3,953	890	867	23	6,371	3,623	2,748	1,822	640	1,182
40—45	7,118	3,838	3,280	316	297	19	4,787	2,916	1,871	2,010	670	1,340
45—50	5,097	2,877	2,220	194	184	10	2,870	1,961	909	2,033	732	1,301
50—55	3,836	2,156	1,680	126	121	5	1,944	1,393	551	1,766	642	1,124
55—60	2,426	1,288	1,138	117	108	9	974	772	202	1,335	408	927
60—65	1,820	952	868	103	95	8	654	528	126	1,063	329	734
65—70	647	318	329	25	23	2	190	149	41	432	146	286
70 & Over.	902	438	464	22	18	4	262	200	62	618	220	398
Hindu (Brahmanic)	130,378	69,396	60,982	56,776	34,620	22,156	60,147	29,860	30,287	13,455	4,916	8,539
0—1	4,125	2,137	1,988	4,123	2,137	1,986	1	...	1	1	...	1
1—2	3,708	1,896	1,812	3,694	1,891	1,803	13	5	8	1	...	1
2—3	3,931	1,955	1,976	3,906	1,946	1,960	24	9	15	1	...	1
3—4	3,969	1,993	1,978	3,924	1,977	1,947	42	19	23	3	...	3
4—5	3,831	1,944	1,887	3,774	1,916	1,858	46	23	23	11	5	6
Total 0—5	19,564	9,928	9,636	19,421	9,867	9,554	126	56	70	17	5	12
5—10	17,676	9,494	8,182	16,134	9,031	7,103	1,510	454	1,056	32	9	23
10—15	16,564	8,968	7,596	12,509	7,812	4,697	3,959	1,118	2,841	96	38	58
15—20	11,696	6,170	5,526	3,670	3,184	486	7,722	2,829	4,893	304	157	147
20—25	12,370	6,843	5,527	2,143	2,003	140	9,751	4,591	5,160	476	249	227
25—30	12,782	6,779	6,004	1,001	938	62	10,914	5,454	5,460	869	387	482
30—35	10,915	5,580	5,335	654	616	38	9,136	4,500	4,636	1,125	464	661
35—40	8,175	4,414	3,761	880	860	20	6,049	3,442	2,607	1,746	612	1,134
40—45	6,770	3,703	3,067	311	292	19	4,543	2,767	1,776	1,916	644	1,272
45—50	4,829	2,729	2,100	186	177	9	2,710	1,847	863	1,933	705	1,228
50—55	3,624	2,030	1,594	121	116	5	1,821	1,300	521	1,682	614	1,068
55—60	2,280	1,193	1,084	112	103	9	900	711	189	1,268	382	886
60—65	1,692	874	818	95	87	8	599	483	116	998	304	694
65—70	584	277	307	19	17	2	162	125	37	403	135	268
70 & Over.	856	411	445	21	17	4	245	183	62	590	211	379
Muslim ...	5,765	3,064	2,701	2,479	1,471	1,008	2,677	1,390	1,287	609	233	406
0—1	161	76	85	161	76	85	...	...	...	...	...	...
1—2	156	88	68	156	88	68	...	...	...	...	...	...
2—3	173	94	79	172	93	79	1	1	...	...	...	...
3—4	178	90	88	178	90	88	...	...	...	...	...	...
4—5	177	88	89	177	88	89	...	...	...	...	...	...
Total 0—5	845	436	409	844	435	409	1	1	...	...	...	...
5—10	754	400	354	711	392	319	43	8	35	...	...	...
10—15	649	360	289	544	333	211	103	27	76	2	...	2
15—20	517	255	262	166	135	31	333	113	220	18	7	11
20—25	600	287	313	104	85	19	469	189	280	27	13	14
25—30	512	291	251	51	38	13	455	239	217	35	14	21
30—35	453	255	194	25	22	3	386	218	168	39	16	23
35—40	353	189	164	8	5	3	276	159	117	69	25	44
40—45	294	151	143	3	3	...	209	127	82	82	21	61
45—50	238	134	104	4	4	...	145	106	39	89	24	65
50—55	188	110	78	3	3	...	109	82	27	76	25	51
55—60	127	76	51	3	3	...	62	49	13	62	24	38
60—65	118	68	50	7	7	...	50	40	10	61	21	40
65—70	53	33	20	5	5	...	22	19	3	23	6	17
70 & Over.	40	21	19	1	1	...	18	18	...	20	7	19

TABLE VII.—Age, Sex and Civil Condition. *Part II.—Details by Districts.—(contd.)*

Age.	Population.			Unmarried.			Married.			Widowed.		
	Persons.	Males.	Females.	Persons.	Males.	Females.	Persons.	Males.	Females.	Persons.	Males.	Females.
1	2	3	4	5	6	7	8	9	10	11	12	13
District Sheopur.—(concld.)												
Jain ...	238	137	101	92	70	22	99	47	52	47	20	27
0—1	5	4	1	5	4	1	...	...	...	...	...	...
1—2	5	5	...	5	5	...	...	...	...	...	...	...
2—3	4	2	2	4	2	2	...	..	...	...	...	...
3—4	2	1	1	2	1	1	...	...	...	...	...	...
4—5	5	2	3	5	2	3	...	...	...	...	...	...
Total 0—5	21	14	7	21	14	7	...	...	...	...	...	...
5—10	21	12	9	20	11	9	1	1	...	...	...	...
10—15	27	14	13	19	13	6	8	1	7	...	...	...
15—20	21	11	10	8	8	...	11	3	8	2	...	2
20—25	23	15	8	8	8	...	14	7	7	1	...	1
25—30	23	13	10	4	4	...	15	8	7	4	1	3
30—35	20	8	12	...	...	...	13	6	7	7	2	5
35—40	18	7	11	1	1	...	11	4	7	6	2	4
40—45	20	11	9	2	2	...	11	6	5	7	3	4
45—50	17	10	7	3	3	...	8	5	3	6	2	4
50—55	11	8	3	2	2	...	4	3	1	5	3	2
55—60	5	4	1	2	2	...	1	1	...	2	1	1
60—65	3	3	...	1	1	...	...	...	...	2	2	...
65—70	6	5	1	1	1	..	1	1	...	4	3	1
70 & Over.	2	2	...	...	...	...	1	1	...	1	1	...
District Narwar.												
All Religions ...	431,585	211,555	193,031	167,338	105,592	61,746	191,107	95,919	95,158	43,141	13,014	30,127
0—1	11,560	5,855	5,705	11,523	5,842	5,681	39	15	24	1	1	...
1—2	11,001	5,477	5,524	10,938	5,457	5,481	61	19	42	2	1	1
2—3	11,999	5,882	6,117	11,890	5,844	6,046	106	37	69	3	1	2
3—4	12,116	6,078	6,038	11,937	6,012	5,925	157	61	96	22	5	17
4—5	11,832	6,145	5,687	11,617	6,060	5,557	183	77	106	32	8	42
Total 0—5	58,508	29,437	29,071	57,902	29,212	28,690	546	209	337	60	16	44
5—10	53,032	28,226	24,806	47,510	27,054	20,456	5,240	1,113	4,127	302	79	223
10—15	50,632	27,615	23,017	36,538	23,418	13,120	13,606	4,026	9,580	488	141	347
15—20	40,730	21,884	18,846	11,467	10,103	1,364	28,182	11,388	16,794	1,081	393	688
20—25	40,468	21,271	19,197	6,563	6,096	467	31,846	14,482	17,364	2,059	693	1,366
25—30	36,092	19,200	16,892	2,739	2,547	192	30,031	15,528	14,503	3,322	1,125	2,197
30—35	31,236	16,626	14,610	1,667	1,526	141	25,887	13,823	12,064	3,682	1,277	2,405
35—40	25,846	13,502	12,344	1,013	[illegible]43	103	19,191	10,879	8,312	5,612	1,680	3,932
40—45	21,573	11,288	10,285	799	720	79	14,841	8,822	6,019	5,930	1,743	4,187
45—50	15,229	8,109	7,120	440	391	49	8,952	6,023	2,929	5,827	1,695	4,132
50—55	11,648	6,273	5,375	311	271	40	6,374	4,600	1,774	4,963	1,402	3,561
55—60	6,933	3,537	3,396	139	120	19	3,080	2,421	659	3,714	996	2,718
60—65	5,522	2,708	2,814	98	83	15	2,121	1,693	428	3,303	932	2,371
65—70	1,807	810	997	32	28	4	520	411	109	1,285	401	884
70 & Over.	2,250	1,019	1,231	60	50	10	680	531	149	1,510	438	1,072
Hindu (Brahmanic).	388,074	204,258	183,816	161,435	98,912	62,523	183,141	90,838	92,303	41,498	12,508	28,990
0—1	11,140	5,649	5,491	11,106	5,934	5,172	36	14	22	1	1	...
1—2	10,650	5,291	5,359	10,559	5,248	5,311	59	18	41	2	1	1
2—3	11,618	5,692	5,926	11,514	5,656	5,858	101	35	66	3	1	2
3—4	11,724	5,890	5,834	11,551	5,825	5,726	152	60	92	21	5	16
4—5	11,447	5,943	5,504	11,242	5,865	5,377	178	70	108	32	8	24
Total 0—5	56,582	28,468	28,114	56,002	28,255	27,747	521	197	324	59	16	43
5—10	51,446	27,389	24,057	46,011	26,229	19,782	5,147	1,091	4,056	295	76	219
10—15	49,078	26,715	22,363	35,286	22,629	12,657	13,823	3,949	9,874	469	137	332
15—20	39,402	21,139	18,263	10,953	9,657	1,296	27,413	11,102	16,311	1,036	380	656
20—25	39,058	20,515	18,543	6,241	5,804	437	30,830	14,043	16,787	1,987	668	1,319
25—30	34,873	18,543	16,330	2,614	2,436	178	29,053	15,022	14,031	3,206	1,085	2,121
30—35	30,188	16,041	14,147	1,587	1,457	130	25,055	13,957	11,098	3,526	1,207	2,319
35—40	24,951	13,019	11,942	989	897	92	18,553	10,506	8,047	5,419	1,616	3,803
40—45	20,832	10,879	9,953	756	681	75	14,351	8,519	5,832	5,725	1,679	4,046
45—50	14,662	7,786	6,876	411	363	48	8,629	5,793	2,836	5,622	1,630	3,992
50—55	11,197	6,022	5,175	286	250	36	6,134	4,427	1,707	4,777	1,345	3,432
55—60	6,631	3,374	3,257	125	108	17	2,954	2,318	636	3,552	948	2,604
60—65	5,294	2,595	2,699	91	77	14	2,037	1,621	416	3,166	897	2,269
65—70	1,736	797	939	31	27	4	490	386	104	1,215	334	881
70 & Over.	2,134	976	1,158	59	49	10	651	507	144	1,424	420	1,004

TABLE VII—Age, Sex and Civil Condition. *Part II.—Details by Districts—(contd.)*

Age.	POPULATION.			UNMARRIED.			MARRIED.			WIDOWED.		
	Persons.	Males.	Females.	Persons.	Males.	Females.	Persons.	Males.	Females.	Persons.	Males.	Females.
1	2	3	4	5	6	7	8	9	10	11	12	13
District Narwar.—(concld.)												
Muslim ...	9,237	5,001	4,236	4,007	2,448	1,559	4,206	2,220	1,986	1,024	333	691
0—1	288	146	142	285	145	140	3	1	2	...	...	...
1—2	235	127	108	233	126	107	2	1	1	...	...	...
2—3	251	119	132	251	119	132	...	...	...	...	...	...
3—4	258	120	138	258	120	138	...	...	...	...	...	...
4—5	262	136	126	254	131	123	8	5	3	...	...	...
Total 0—5	1,294	648	646	1,281	641	640	13	7	6	...	...	...
5—10	1,124	601	523	1,057	585	472	61	13	48	6	3	3
10—15	1,046	582	464	858	529	329	176	50	126	12	3	9
15—20	902	506	396	356	300	56	519	196	323	27	10	17
20—25	998	538	460	226	202	24	724	315	409	48	21	27
25—30	860	465	395	81	68	13	703	368	335	76	29	47
30—35	735	406	329	49	39	10	597	337	260	89	30	59
35—40	612	334	278	33	28	5	457	268	189	122	38	84
40—45	495	274	221	27	24	3	347	213	134	121	37	84
45—50	385	225	160	17	16	1	242	169	73	126	40	86
50—55	308	179	129	14	11	3	180	130	50	114	38	76
55—60	194	108	86	6	4	2	90	73	17	98	31	67
60—65	145	74	71	1	...	1	57	48	9	87	26	61
65—70	58	27	31	...	...	...	20	15	5	38	12	26
70 & Over.	81	34	47	1	1	...	20	18	2	60	15	45
Jain ...	3,610	1,937	1,673	1,584	1,046	538	1,444	728	716	582	163	419
0—1	106	51	55	106	51	55	...	...	...	...	...	...
1—2	97	49	48	97	49	48	...	...	...	...	...	...
2—3	103	56	47	99	55	44	4	1	3	...	...	...
3—4	103	51	52	98	50	48	4	1	3	1	...	1
4—5	96	49	47	95	48	47	1	1	...	...	...	...
Total 0—5	505	256	249	495	253	242	9	3	6	1	...	1
5—10	417	230	187	394	225	169	22	5	17	1	...	1
10—15	411	234	177	331	220	111	73	13	60	7	1	6
15—20	340	189	151	187	128	9	188	58	130	15	3	12
20—25	345	179	166	86	82	4	235	93	142	24	4	20
25—30	311	168	143	42	41	1	230	117	113	39	10	29
30—35	278	161	117	29	28	1	202	113	89	47	20	27
35—40	241	132	109	18	18	...	154	89	65	69	25	44
40—45	222	122	100	14	14	...	124	79	45	84	29	55
45—50	167	91	76	12	12	...	80	55	25	75	24	51
50—55	128	66	62	11	10	1	52	38	14	65	18	47
55—60	98	50	48	8	8	...	32	27	5	58	15	43
60—65	74	35	39	6	6	...	24	22	2	44	7	37
65—70	40	15	25	1	1	...	10	10	...	29	4	25
70 & Over.	33	9	24	...	...	...	9	6	3	24	3	21
District Isagarh.												
All Religions ...	421,311	221,556	199,755	180,162	109,207	70,955	194,805	98,057	96,748	46,344	14,292	32,052
0—1	12,975	6,528	6,447	12,868	6,503	6,365	76	21	55	31	4	27
1—2	11,753	5,880	5,873	11,587	5,845	5,742	133	32	101	33	3	30
2—3	12,339	6,053	6,286	12,085	5,995	6,090	220	52	168	34	6	28
3—4	12,923	6,325	6,598	12,501	6,229	6,272	325	82	244	96	14	82
4—5	12,861	6,399	6,462	12,546	6,288	6,058	391	98	293	124	13	111
Total 0—5	62,851	31,185	31,666	61,387	30,860	30,527	1,146	285	861	318	40	278
5—10	57,365	30,304	27,061	50,758	28,923	21,835	5,923	1,289	4,634	684	92	592
10—15	55,860	30,393	25,467	39,814	25,793	14,021	14,919	4,318	10,601	1,127	282	845
15—20	43,199	22,822	20,377	12,674	10,922	1,752	29,043	11,347	17,696	1,482	553	929
20—25	41,883	21,972	19,911	6,683	5,964	719	33,191	15,191	18,000	2,009	817	1,192
25—30	35,884	19,223	16,661	2,575	2,173	402	29,855	15,801	14,054	3,454	1,249	2,205
30—35	30,021	16,082	13,939	1,500	1,226	274	24,579	13,541	11,038	3,942	1,315	2,627
35—40	24,623	12,993	11,630	940	759	181	18,147	10,567	7,580	5,536	1,667	3,869
40—45	21,431	11,574	9,857	812	663	149	14,309	9,022	5,287	6,310	1,889	4,421
45—50	16,115	9,011	7,104	780	657	123	9,334	6,519	2,815	6,001	1,835	4,166
50—55	11,669	6,336	5,303	554	446	108	6,264	4,404	1,860	4,851	1,516	3,335
55—60	8,256	4,027	4,229	333	138	195	3,711	2,653	1,058	4,212	1,236	2,976
60—65	6,595	2,953	3,642	400	99	301	2,618	1,890	728	3,577	964	2,613
65—70	2,302	1,028	1,274	318	142	176	787	572	215	1,197	314	883
70 & Over.	3,257	1,623	1,634	634	442	192	979	658	321	1,644	523	1,121

TABLE VII.—Age, Sex and Civil Condition. *Part II.—Details by Districts.—(contd.)*

Age.	POPULATION.			UNMARRIED.			MARRIED.			WIDOWED.		
	Persons.	Males.	Females.	Persons.	Males.	Females.	Persons.	Males.	Females.	Persons.	Males.	Females.
1	2	3	4	5	6	7	8	9	10	11	12	13
District Isagàrh—(concld.)												
Hindu (Brahmanic)	**397,956**	**209,130**	**188,826**	**169,694**	**102,825**	**66,869**	**184 581**	**92,919**	**91,662**	**43,681**	**13,386**	**30,295**
0—1	12,226	6,151	6,075	12,142	6,120	6,018	68	18	45	21	4	17
1—2	11,088	5,547	5,541	10,944	5,514	5,430	120	31	89	24	2	22
2—3	11,666	5,742	5,924	11,439	5,687	5,752	199	49	150	28	6	22
3—4	12,228	5,986	6,242	11,886	5,899	5,987	307	74	233	85	13	72
4—5	12,172	6,049	6,123	11,686	5,949	5,737	371	87	284	115	13	102
Total 0—5	59,380	29,475	29,905	58,047	29,178	28,869	1,060	259	801	273	38	235
5—10	54,331	28,716	25,615	47,991	27,420	20,571	5,693	1,208	4,485	647	88	559
10—15	53,040	28,851	24,189	37,579	24,422	13,157	14,374	4,153	10,221	1,087	276	811
15—20	40,963	21,599	19,364	11,810	10,173	1,637	27,731	10 891	16,840	1,422	535	887
20—25	39,523	20,720	18,803	6,115	5,451	664	31,498	14,490	17,008	1,910	779	1,131
25—30	33,844	18,119	157,25	2,352	1,974	378	28,183	14,954	13,229	3,309	1,191	2,118
30—35	28,288	15 135	13,153	1,363	1,109	254	23,171	12,779	10,392	3,754	1,247	2,507
35—40	23,274	12,268	11,011	848	684	164	17,164	10,006	7,158	5,262	1 573	3,689
40—45	20,251	10,922	9,329	732	603	129	13,515	8,546	4,969	6,004	1,773	4,231
45—50	15,157	8,459	6,698	728	623	105	8,782	6,131	2,651	5,647	1,705	3,942
50—55	10,913	5,939	4,974	519	424	95	5,867	4,116	1,751	4,527	1,399	3,128
55—60	7,735	3,761	3,974	312	122	190	3,485	2,497	988	3,938	1,142	2,796
60—65	6,176	2,742	3,434	383	86	297	2,452	1,768	684	3,341	888	2,453
65—70	2,104	938	1,166	318	140	178	706	518	188	1,085	280	805
70 & Over.	2,977	1,491	1,486	602	416	186	900	603	297	1,475	472	1,003
Muslim ...	**15,834**	**8,355**	**7,509**	**7,153**	**4,334**	**2,819**	**7,019**	**3,482**	**3,537**	**1,692**	**539**	**1,153**
0—1	516	252	204	500	251	249	9	1	8	7	...	7
1—2	444	214	230	431	213	218	9	1	8	4	...	4
2—3	475	214	261	458	212	246	14	2	12	3	...	3
3—4	477	226	251	457	221	236	14	5	9	6	...	6
4—5	467	235	232	444	228	216	14	7	7	9	...	9
Total 0—5	2,379	1,141	1,238	2,290	1,125	1,165	60	16	44	29	...	29
5—10	2,045	1,059	986	1,857	1,013	844	157	44	113	31	2	29
10—15	1,893	1,018	874	1,496	920	576	364	96	268	32	2	30
15—20	1,548	863	685	637	551	86	872	300	572	39	12	27
20—25	1,651	897	754	437	392	45	1.150	476	674	64	29	35
25—30	1,377	765	612	154	136	18	1,133	589	544	90	40	50
30—35	1,148	636	512	86	72	14	949	524	425	113	40	73
35—40	922	473	449	55	41	14	694	376	318	173	56	117
40—45	803	425	378	44	29	15	567	330	237	192	66	126
45—50	633	354	279	29	16	13	381	266	115	223	72	151
50—55	492	270	222	22	11	11	278	194	84	192	65	127
55—60	361	188	173	17	12	5	180	121	59	164	55	109
60—65	284	138	146	14	10	4	120	83	37	150	45	105
65—70	139	54	85	5	2	3	59	34	25	75	18	57
70 & Over.	190	74	116	10	4	6	55	33	22	125	37	88
Jain ...	**6,512**	**3,554**	**2,958**	**2,833**	**1,776**	**1,057**	**2,777**	**1,437**	**1,340**	**902**	**341**	**561**
0—1	202	108	94	198	108	90	1	...	1	3	...	3
1—2	185	101	84	178	101	77	4	...	4	3	...	3
2—3	157	79	78	148	78	70	6	1	5	3	...	3
3—4	164	88	76	158	85	73	3	2	1	3	1	2
4—5	186	97	89	180	93	87	6	4	2	...	...	...
Total 0—5	894	473	421	862	465	397	20	7	13	12	1	11
5—10	852	457	395	782	420	362	68	37	31	2	...	2
10—15	802	450	352	635	386	249	161	62	99	6	2	4
15—20	600	315	285	199	177	22	384	134	250	17	4	13
20—25	620	308	312	120	110	10	466	189	277	34	9	25
25—30	587	299	288	63	59	4	469	222	247	55	18	37
30—35	515	279	236	44	41	3	401	213	188	70	25	45
35—40	374	228	146	34	32	2	242	159	83	98	37	61
40—45	333	197	136	33	29	4	190	121	69	110	47	63
45—50	289	176	113	20	17	3	145	104	41	124	55	69
50—55	237	141	96	12	11	1	105	82	23	120	48	72
55—60	143	71	75	4	4	...	40	30	10	102	37	65
60—65	127	70	57	3	3	...	44	37	7	80	30	50
65—70	56	36	20	...	...	...	22	20	2	34	16	18
70 & Over.	80	54	26	22	22	...	20	20	...	38	12	26

TABLE VII.—Age, Sex and Civil Condition. *Part II Details by Districts.—(contd.)*

Age.	Population.			Unmarried.			Married.			Widowed.		
	Persons.	Males.	Females.	Persons.	Males.	Females.	Persons.	Males.	Females.	Persons.	Males.	Females.
1	2	3	4	5	6	7	8	9	10	11	12	13
						District Bhilsa.						
All Religions ...	235,288	123,084	112,204	98,628	59,813	38,815	110,190	54,971	55,219	26,470	8,300	18,170
0—1	8,027	4,016	4,011	7,939	3,991	3,948	61	16	45	27	9	18
1—2	6,610	3,218	3,392	6,527	3,186	3,341	62	23	39	21	9	12
2—3	6,869	3,315	3,554	6,760	3,270	3,490	85	34	51	24	11	13
3—4	7,290	3,605	3,685	7,138	3,541	3,597	113	49	64	39	15	24
4—5	7,064	3,563	3,501	6,912	3,506	3,406	111	44	67	41	13	28
Total 0—5	35,860	17,717	18,143	35,276	17,494	17,782	432	166	266	152	57	95
5—10	30,670	16,261	14,409	27,519	15,690	11,829	2,941	504	2,437	210	67	143
10—15	29,188	15,817	13,371	21,281	13,850	7,431	7,596	1,868	5,728	311	99	212
15—20	24,908	12,746	12,162	7,272	6,289	983	16,879	6,132	10,747	757	325	432
20—25	25,071	12,711	12,360	3,879	3,537	342	19,948	8,593	11,355	1,244	581	663
25—30	20,590	10,855	9,735	1,282	1,147	135	17,487	8,950	8,537	1,821	758	1,063
30—35	17,425	9,396	8,029	761	656	105	14,497	7,907	6,590	2,167	773	1,394
35—40	14,199	7,876	6,323	434	377	57	10,599	6,519	4,080	3,166	980	2,186
40—45	11,767	6,631	5,136	332	292	40	8,021	5,273	2,748	3,414	1,066	2,348
45—50	8,584	4,763	3,821	212	182	30	4,864	3,544	1,320	3,508	1,037	2,471
50—55	6,343	3,398	2,945	155	131	24	3,219	2,421	798	2,969	846	2,123
55—60	4,464	2,085	2,379	95	75	20	1,697	1,368	329	2,672	642	2,030
60—65	3,696	1,616	2,080	71	52	19	1,218	992	226	2,407	572	1,835
65—70	1,151	557	594	21	14	7	357	305	52	773	238	535
70 & Over	1,372	655	717	38	27	11	435	369	66	899	259	640
Hindu (Brahmanic	219,968	114,901	105,067	91,900	55,785	36,115	103,206	51,386	51,820	24,862	7,730	17,132
0—1	7,501	3,750	3,751	7,416	3,726	3,690	59	15	44	26	9	17
1—2	6,159	3,006	3,153	6,080	2,975	3,105	59	22	37	20	9	11
2—3	6,394	3,101	3,293	6,291	3,057	3,234	80	33	47	23	11	12
3—4	6,795	3,370	3,425	6,662	3,314	3,348	94	41	53	39	15	24
4—5	6,589	3,329	3,260	6,445	3,272	3,173	104	44	60	40	13	27
Total 0—5	33,438	16,556	16,882	32,894	16,344	16,550	396	155	241	148	57	91
5—10	28,708	15,228	13,480	25,691	14,682	11,009	2,816	482	2,334	201	64	137
10—15	27,408	14,853	12,555	19,853	12,951	6,902	7,258	1,807	5,451	297	95	202
15—20	23,447	11,996	11,451	6,743	5,826	917	15,982	5,857	10,125	722	313	409
20—25	23,506	11,905	11,601	3,569	3,249	320	18,758	8,101	10,657	1,179	555	624
25—30	19,229	10,123	9,106	1,177	1,053	124	16,337	8,357	7,980	1,715	713	1,002
30—35	16,281	8,770	7,511	708	610	98	13,540	7,439	6,101	2,033	721	1,311
35—40	13,260	7,348	5,912	407	353	54	9,883	6,078	3,805	2,970	917	2,053
40—45	10,972	6,170	4,802	305	269	36	7,463	4,908	2,555	3,204	993	2,211
45—50	7,995	4,412	3,583	193	166	27	4,508	3,285	1,223	3,294	961	2,333
50—55	5,875	3,120	2,755	146	123	23	2,950	2,217	733	2,779	780	1,999
55—60	4,141	1,885	2,256	91	71	20	1,523	1,221	302	2,527	593	1,934
60—65	3,436	1,460	1,976	69	50	19	1,091	882	209	2,276	528	1,748
65—70	1,047	498	549	19	13	6	320	272	48	708	213	495
70 & Over.	1,225	577	648	35	25	10	381	325	56	809	227	582
Muslim ...	12,422	6,651	5,771	5,597	3,314	2,283	5,636	2,907	2,729	1,189	430	759
0—1	428	211	217	425	210	215	2	1	1	1	...	1
1—2	368	169	199	364	168	196	3	1	2	1	...	1
2—3	393	175	218	387	174	213	5	1	4	1	...	1
3—4	421	199	222	403	191	212	18	8	10	...	...	...
4—5	402	198	204	394	198	196	7	...	7	1	...	1
Total 0—5	2,012	952	1,060	1,973	941	1,032	35	11	24	4	...	4
5—10	1,643	867	776	1,540	849	69	94	15	79	9	3	6
10—15	1,458	786	672	1,187	738	449	260	44	216	11	4	7
15—20	1,170	592	578	431	369	62	717	214	503	22	9	13
20—25	1,255	644	611	258	236	22	943	385	558	54	23	31
25—30	1,090	591	499	89	78	11	919	475	444	82	38	44
30—35	915	503	412	42	36	6	777	427	350	96	40	56
35—40	750	428	322	21	18	3	583	361	222	146	49	97
40—45	640	387	253	22	20	2	465	308	157	153	59	94
45—50	474	293	181	16	14	2	298	220	78	160	59	101
50—55	367	220	147	8	7	1	220	167	53	139	46	93
55—60	244	156	88	3	3	...	139	120	19	102	33	69
60—65	205	126	79	2	2	...	107	94	13	96	30	66
65—70	88	49	39	2	1	1	34	30	4	52	18	34
70 & Over.	111	57	54	3	2	1	45	36	9	63	19	44

TABLE VII.—Age, Sex and Civil Condition. *Part II.—Details by Districts (contd.)*

Age.	POPULATION.			UNMARRIED.			MARRIED.			WIDOWED.		
	Persons.	Males.	Females.	Persons.	Males.	Females.	Persons.	Males.	Females.	Persons.	Males	Females.
1	2	3	4	5	6	7	8	9	10	11	12	13
District Bhilsa (contd.)												
Jain ...	2,489	1,329	1,160	979	620	359	135	578	557	375	131	244
0—1	81	45	36	81	45	36	...	...	...	...	...	...
1—2	74	40	31	74	40	34	...	...	...	...	...	...
2—3	72	34	38	72	34	38	...	...	...	...	...	...
3—4	65	29	36	64	29	35	1	...	1	...	...	...
4—5	63	31	32	63	31	32	...	...	...	...	...	...
Total 0—5	355	179	176	354	179	175	1	...	1	...	...	...
5—10	277	143	134	240	136	113	28	7	21	...	...	...
10—15	277	153	124	205	138	67	69	15	54	8	...	8
15—20	245	139	107	86	84	2	149	52	97	10	2	8
20—25	265	140	125	45	45	...	210	93	117	10	2	8
25—30	239	126	113	16	16	...	200	104	96	23	6	17
30—35	200	111	89	11	10	1	154	90	64	35	11	24
35—40	156	82	74	5	5	...	106	64	42	45	13	32
40—45	127	62	65	3	3	...	73	45	28	51	14	37
45—50	97	50	47	3	2	1	46	31	15	48	17	31
50—55	83	48	35	1	1	...	38	28	10	44	19	25
55—60	70	40	30	1	1	...	30	23	7	39	16	23
60—65	49	27	22	...	...	...	19	15	4	30	12	18
65—70	15	10	5	...	...	...	3	3	...	12	7	5
70 & Over	34	20	14	...	...	...	9	8	1	25	12	13
District Ujjain.												
All Religions —	405,961	211,274	194,687	147,594	91,533	56,061	206 051	104,151	101,900	52,316	15,590	36,726
0—1	13,293	6,595	6,698	13,193	6,566	6,627	88	24	64	12	5	7
1—2	11,355	5,604	5,751	11,212	5 565	5,647	134	37	97	9	2	7
2—3	11,384	5 533	5,851	11,169	5,469	5,700	205	62	143	10	2	8
3—4	11,053	5 488	5,565	10,635	5,374	5 261	378	101	277	40	13	27
4—5	10,334	5 418	4,916	9,778	5,283	4,495	500	119	381	56	16	40
Total 0—5	57,419	28,638	28,781	55,987	28 257	27,730	1,305	343	962	127	38	89
5—10	48 937	25,468	23,469	38 870	22,960	15,910	9,654	2,372	7,282	413	136	277
10—15	47,202	24 366	22 836	29,164	19,238	9,926	17,346	4,859	12,487	692	269	423
15—20	41,350	21,239	20,111	9,740	8,657	1,083	30,261	12,021	18,240	1 349	561	788
20—25	42,431	22,156	20 275	5 997	5 565	432	34,601	15,838	18 763	1 833	753	1,080
25—30	34,077	18,286	15 791	2 301	2,057	244	28,641	15,187	13,454	3,135	1,042	2,093
30—35	29 971	16,425	13 546	1,635	1,428	207	24,175	13,610	10 565	4 161	1,387	2,774
35—40	26,290	14,020	12,270	1,192	1,072	120	18,728	11,098	7,630	6,370	1,850	4,520
40—45	22,060	11,652	10,408	944	860	84	14,411	8 946	5,465	6,705	1,846	4,859
45—50	17,024	9,089	7,935	629	530	99	9,562	6,707	2,855	6,833	1 852	4 981
50—55	13,264	6,918	6,346	472	368	104	6,928	4,962	1,966	5,864	1,588	4,276
55—60	9,438	4 835	4,603	263	211	52	4,090	3,200	890	5,085	1,424	3,661
60—65	8,260	4,101	4,159	193	160	33	3,371	2,677	694	4,696	1,264	3,432
65—70	3,111	1,568	1,543	75	61	14	1,177	930	247	1,859	577	1,282
70 & Over.	5,127	2,513	2,614	132	109	23	1,801	1,401	400	3,194	1,003	2,191
Hindu (Brahmanic).	357,911	85,6381	172,273	128,074	79,907	48,167	182,601	91,909	90,692	47,236	13,822	33,414
0—1	11,882	5 877	6,005	11,792	5,850	5,942	80	22	58	10	5	5
1—2	10,044	4,928	5,116	9,915	4 894	5,021	122	32	90	7	2	5
2—3	10,030	4,845	5,185	9,838	4,789	5,049	185	55	130	7	1	6
3—4	9,696	4,801	4 895	9,320	4,704	4,616	339	85	254	37	12	25
4—5	9,093	4,789	4,304	8 577	4,667	3,910	463	106	357	53	16	3
Total 0—5	50,745	25,240	25,505	49,442	24,904	24,538	1,189	300	889	114	36	78
5—10	43,208	22,489	20,719	33,708	20,166	13 627	9,043	2,201	6,842	572	122	250
10—15	41,727	21,519	20,208	25,027	16,768	8,259	16,065	4,501	11,564	635	250	385
15—20	36,643	18,785	17 858	8,197	7,460	737	27,215	10 818	16 397	1,231	507	724
20—25	37,455	19,507	17,948	5,065	4,765	300	30 746	14,083	16 663	1,644	659	985
25—30	29,965	16,027	13,938	1 888	1,711	177	25,263	13,411	11,852	2,814	905	1,909
30—35	26,389	14,419	11,970	1 328	1 184	144	21,300	12 003	9,297	3,761	1 232	2 529
35—40	23 117	12 282	10,835	984	911	73	16,361	9,719	6,642	5 772	1,652	4,123
40—45	19,418	10 194	9 224	819	761	58	12 515	7,798	4 722	6,084	1,640	4,444
45—50	15,024	7,975	7,049	567	489	78	8 272	5 841	2 431	6 185	1,645	4 540
50—55	11,692	6,048	5,644	407	323	84	5,986	4,314	1,672	5,299	1,411	3,868
55—60	8 270	4,187	4,083	212	172	40	3,465	2 737	728	4 593	1 278	3 315
60—65	7,228	3,543	3,685	166	140	26	2 834	2,276	558	4,228	1,127	3,101
65—70	2,689	1,831	1,858	68	58	10	957	775	182	1,669	508	1,166
70 & Over	4,341	2,092	2,249	116	100	16	1,390	1,137	253	2,835	855	1,980

TABLE VII.—Age, Sex and Civil Condition. *Part II.—Details by Districts.—(contd.)*

Age.	POPULATION.			UNMARRIED.			MARRIED.			WIDOWED.		
	Persons.	Males.	Females.	Persons.	Males.	Females.	Persons.	Males.	Females.	Persons.	Males.	Females.
1	2	3	4	5	6	7	8	9	10	11	12	13
District Ujjain.—(concld).												
Muslim ...	40,346	21,426	18,920	16,420	9,666	6,754	19,820	10,352	9,468	4,106	1,408	2,698
0—1	1,229	624	605	1,221	622	599	7	2	5	1	...	1
1—2	1,141	586	555	1,128	582	546	11	4	7	2	...	2
2—3	1,172	598	574	1,150	591	559	19	6	13	3	1	2
3—4	1,164	590	574	1,130	577	553	32	13	19	2	...	2
4—5	1,079	542	537	1,043	529	514	33	13	20	3	...	3
Total 0—5	5,785	2,940	2,845	5,672	2,901	2,771	102	38	64	11	1	10
5—10	4,887	2,535	2,352	4,318	2,371	1,947	535	152	383	34	12	22
10—15	4,552	2,361	2,191	3,441	2,044	1,397	1,064	300	764	47	17	30
15—20	3,939	2,040	1,899	1,249	951	298	2,593	1,042	1,551	97	47	50
20—25	4,208	2,244	1,964	748	643	105	3,303	1,519	1,784	157	82	75
25—30	3,400	1,868	1,532	332	277	55	2,817	1,479	1,338	251	112	139
30—35	2,952	1,645	1,307	243	187	56	2,899	1,833	1,066	310	125	185
35—40	2,658	1,444	1,214	159	116	43	2,013	1,170	843	486	158	328
40—45	2,195	1,204	991	85	63	22	1,608	980	628	507	161	346
45—50	1,629	903	726	40	24	16	1,077	725	352	512	154	358
50—55	1,271	695	576	49	33	16	777	530	247	445	132	313
55—60	974	534	440	43	32	11	525	386	139	406	116	290
60—65	875	466	409	22	15	7	465	343	122	388	108	280
65—70	340	188	152	9	5	4	182	127	55	149	56	93
70 & Over.	681	359	322	10	4	6	365	228	137	306	127	179
Jain ...	6,149	3,398	2,751	2,359	1,541	818	2,962	1,560	1,402	828	297	531
0—1	135	74	61	133	74	59	1	...	1	1	...	1
1—2	128	71	57	127	70	57	1	1	...	...	...	...
2—3	145	73	72	144	72	72	1	1	...	...	...	...
3—4	143	72	71	137	69	68	5	2	3	1	1	...
4—5	121	65	56	117	65	52	4	...	4	...	...	...
Total 0—5	672	355	317	658	350	308	12	4	8	2	1	1
5—10	638	330	308	573	315	258	61	14	47	4	1	3
10—15	686	351	335	510	314	196	169	36	133	7	1	6
15—20	594	326	268	221	199	22	361	123	238	12	4	8
20—25	624	343	281	144	131	13	461	204	257	19	8	11
25—30	591	336	255	65	58	7	472	260	212	54	18	36
30—35	520	312	208	57	53	4	392	236	156	71	28	43
35—40	429	249	180	46	43	3	294	177	117	89	29	60
40—45	371	210	161	35	32	3	240	142	98	96	36	60
45—50	311	179	132	20	17	3	169	114	55	122	48	74
50—55	257	150	107	12	11	1	134	98	36	111	41	70
55—60	172	99	73	6	6	...	85	66	19	81	27	54
60—65	138	77	61	5	5	...	57	45	12	76	27	49
65—70	68	38	30	3	3	...	27	19	8	38	16	22
70 & Over.	78	43	35	4	4	...	28	22	6	46	17	29
District Mandsaur.												
All Religions ...	272,166	140,333	131,833	99,953	60,334	39,619	139,075	70,198	68,877	33,138	9,801	23,337
0—1	8,651	4,250	4,401	8,540	4,226	4,314	100	22	78	11	2	9
1—2	7,869	3,872	3,997	7,623	3,797	3,826	231	65	166	15	10	5
2—3	7,888	3,930	3,958	7,524	3,805	3,719	348	117	231	16	8	8
3—4	7,776	3,902	3,874	7,256	3,740	3,516	460	151	309	30	11	19
4—5	7,405	3,761	3,644	6,836	3,590	3,246	535	157	378	34	14	20
Total 0—5	39,589	19,715	19,874	37,809	19,158	18,651	1,674	512	1,162	106	45	61
5—10	34,291	17,684	16,607	27,288	15,475	11,813	6,770	2,110	4,660	233	99	134
10—15	33,103	17,336	15,767	20,618	13,170	7,448	12,054	3,966	8,088	431	200	231
15—20	28,374	14,488	13,886	6,363	5,625	738	21,179	8,494	12,685	1,060	369	463
20—25	27,280	14,055	13,225	3,430	3,077	353	22,700	10,545	12,245	1,060	433	627
25—30	20,361	10,961	9,400	1,218	1,026	192	17,611	9,402	8,209	1,532	533	999
30—35	18,916	10,033	8,886	888	769	119	15,748	8,547	7,201	2,280	714	1,566
35—40	17,164	9,000	8,164	689	615	74	12,639	7,812	5,827	3,636	1,073	2,563
40—45	15,333	8,033	7,300	604	511	68	10,387	6,259	4,128	4,544	1,210	3,334
45—50	12,803	6,455	6,348	415	359	56	7,095	4,771	2,324	5,293	1,825	3,468
50—55	9,282	4,724	4,558	257	221	36	4,818	3,351	1,467	4,212	1,152	3,060
55—60	6,175	3,299	2,978	126	103	23	2,715	2,115	600	3,827	977	2,850
60—65	4,978	2,573	2,405	111	92	19	2,010	1,639	371	2,857	842	2,015
65—70	1,843	963	880	56	45	11	647	564	83	1,140	354	786
70 & Over.	2,471	1,146	1,325	73	60	13	743	611	132	1,655	475	1,180

TABLE VII.—Age, Sex and Civil Condition. *Part II.—Details by Districts.—(contd.)*

Age.	POPULATION.			UNMARRIED.			MARRIED.			WIDOWED.		
	Persons.	Males.	Females.	Persons.	Males.	Females.	Persons.	Males.	Females.	Persons.	Males.	Females.
1	2	3	4	5	6	7	8	9	10	11	12	13
District Mandsaur.—(concld.)												
Hindu (Brahmanic)	237,040	122,062	114,978	85,400	51,792	33,608	122,560	61,811	60,749	29,080	8,459	20,621
0—1	7,520	3,656	3,864	7,419	3,634	3,785	92	20	72	9	2	7
1—2	6,828	3,355	3,473	6,601	3,287	3,314	215	61	154	12	7	5
2—3	6,854	3,426	3,428	6,516	3,312	3,204	325	108	217	13	6	7
3—4	6,741	3,392	3,349	6,286	3,245	3,041	428	137	291	27	10	17
4—5	6,442	3,289	3,153	5,906	3,127	2,779	503	149	354	33	13	20
Total 0—5	34,385	17,118	17,267	32,728	16,605	16,123	1,563	475	1,088	94	38	56
5—10	29,878	15,425	14,453	23,349	13,351	9,995	6,313	1,980	4,333	216	91	125
10—15	28,914	15,145	13,769	17,465	11,280	6,185	11,086	3,708	7,378	363	157	206
15—20	24,986	12,778	12,208	5,295	4,758	537	18,972	7,708	11,264	719	312	407
20—25	23,903	12,353	11,550	2,852	2,574	278	20,118	9,392	10,726	933	387	546
25—30	17,573	9,500	8,073	1,008	850	158	15,250	8,194	7,056	1,315	456	859
30—35	16,360	8,658	7,702	718	626	92	13,659	7,416	6,243	1,983	616	1,367
35—40	14,952	7,814	7,138	583	522	61	11,148	6,339	4,809	3,221	953	2,268
40—45	13,584	6,960	6,624	518	466	52	9,009	5,425	3,584	4,057	1,069	2,988
45—50	11,229	5,588	5,641	355	315	40	6,122	4,107	2,015	4,752	1,166	3,586
50—55	8,038	4,045	3,993	219	191	28	4,089	2,847	1,242	3,730	1,007	2,723
55—60	5,283	2,722	2,561	109	88	21	2,317	1,815	502	2,857	819	2,038
60—65	4,263	2,181	2,082	89	73	16	1,738	1,417	321	2,436	691	1,745
65—70	1,557	798	759	48	38	10	540	467	73	969	293	676
70 & Over.	2,135	977	1,158	64	52	12	636	521	115	1,435	404	1,031
Muslim ...	24,525	12,800	11,725	10,117	5,908	4,209	11,830	6,026	5,824	2,558	866	1,692
0—1	773	415	358	765	413	352	7	2	5	1	...	1
1—2	747	379	368	732	374	358	12	2	10	3	3	...
2—3	752	369	383	730	358	372	19	9	10	3	2	1
3—4	741	359	382	714	347	367	27	12	15	...	...	...
4—5	697	333	364	669	325	344	27	7	20	1	1	...
Total 0—5	3,710	1,855	1,855	3,610	1,817	1,793	92	32	60	8	6	2
5—10	3,190	1,638	1,552	2,814	1,521	1,293	364	111	253	12	6	6
10—15	3,006	1,593	1,413	2,229	1,348	881	732	210	522	45	35	10
15—20	2,429	1,231	1,198	758	617	141	1,597	568	1,029	74	46	28
20—25	2,395	1,213	1,182	393	351	42	1,926	830	1,096	76	32	44
25—30	1,952	1,036	916	111	95	16	1,708	884	824	133	57	76
30—35	1,748	953	795	83	69	14	1,488	815	673	177	69	108
35—40	1,492	808	684	45	36	9	1,190	686	504	257	86	171
40—45	1,290	686	604	23	18	5	974	585	389	293	83	210
45—50	1,028	566	462	14	9	5	684	474	210	330	83	247
50—55	794	432	362	10	7	3	490	346	144	294	79	215
55—60	567	300	267	11	7	4	257	194	63	299	99	200
60—65	479	260	219	8	6	2	195	158	37	276	96	180
65—70	182	102	80	3	2	1	74	67	7	105	33	72
70 & Over	263	127	136	5	5	...	79	66	13	179	56	123
Jain ...	8,139	4,297	3,842	.1	2,079	1,231	3,523	1,790	1,733	1,306	428	878
0—1	269	138	131	268	138	130	1	...	1	...	...	...
1—2	219	106	113	217	105	112	2	1	1	...	...	...
2—3	203	99	104	201	99	102	2	...	2	...	...	...
3—4	208	107	101	202	106	96	4	1	3	2	...	2
4—5	191	100	91	188	100	88	3	...	3	...	...	...
Total 0—5	1,090	559	540	1,076	548	528	12	2	10	2	...	2
5—10	904	472	432	848	461	387	52	9	43	4	2	2
10—15	866	460	406	691	430	261	156	25	131	19	5	14
15—20	715	373	342	219	205	14	462	159	303	34	9	25
20—25	738	373	365	134	124	10	562	238	324	42	11	31
25—30	640	332	308	76	70	6	489	245	244	75	17	58
30—35	687	328	359	66	63	3	460	240	220	111	25	86
35—40	581	303	278	51	49	2	388	222	166	142	32	110
40—45	539	296	243	54	45	9	317	198	119	108	53	115
45—50	454	260	194	42	34	8	229	154	75	183	72	111
50—55	375	214	161	23	21	2	190	133	57	162	60	102
55—60	270	146	124	12	11	1	107	82	25	151	53	98
60—65	188	102	86	10	10	...	52	43	9	126	49	77
65—70	85	53	32	5	5	...	25	22	3	55	26	29
70 & Over	57	35	22	3	3	...	22	18	4	32	14	18

TABLE VII.—Age Sex, and Civil Condition. *Part II.—Details by Districts.—(contd.)*

Age.	POPULATION.			UNMARRIED.			MARRIED.			WIDOWED.		
	Persons.	Males.	Females.	Persons.	Males.	Females.	Persons.	Males.	Females.	Persons.	Males.	Females.
1	2	3	4	5	6	7	8	9	10	11	12	13
						District Shajapur.						
All Religions ...	**336,980**	**174,985**	**161,995**	**117,777**	**72,356**	**45,421**	**177,441**	**89,423**	**88,018**	**41,762**	**13,206**	**28,556**
0—1	10,930	5,428	5,507	10,776	5,378	5,408	126	44	82	28	6	22
1—2	9,281	4,491	4,790	9,118	4,425	4,688	150	62	88	18	4	14
2—3	8,917	4 312	4 605	8,674	4 224	4,450	226	83	143	17	5	12
3—4	8,695	4,274	4 421	8,253	4,158	4,098	389	101	288	50	15	35
4—5	8,788	4,412	4,326	8,182	4,271	3,861	537	122	415	69	19	50
Total 0—5	**46,561**	**22,912**	**23,649**	**44,951**	**22,451**	**22,500**	**1,428**	**412**	**1,016**	**182**	**49**	**133**
5—10	40,829	21,118	19,711	31,665	18 643	13,022	8,774	2,342	6,432	390	133	257
10—15	38,994	20,523	18,471	23,129	15 382	7,747	15 194	4,891	10,303	671	250	421
15—20	32,008	16,394	15 614	7,110	6 228	882	23 734	9,745	13,989	1,164	421	743
20—25	33,087	16,588	16,499	4,351	3,900	451	27,321	12,163	15,058	1,515	525	990
25—30	27,484	14,038	13,446	1,717	1,509	208	23,577	11,777	11,800	2,190	752	1,438
30—35	25,283	13 518	11,765	1,317	1,124	193	20,935	11,400	9 535	3,031	994	2,037
35—40	22,612	12,050	10 562	1,036	908	128	16,793	9,698	7,095	4,783	1,444	3,339
40—45	18,822	9 838	8 984	792	708	84	12 787	7,554	5 233	5,243	1,576	3,667
45—50	14,913	8,033	6,880	555	496	59	9,040	5,987	3,053	5,318	1,550	3,768
50—55	11,465	6,235	5 230	402	355	47	6,518	4 532	1,986	4 545	1,348	3,197
55—60	8,915	4,976	3 939	272	239	33	4 380	3,443	946	4 254	1,294	2,960
60—65	7,687	4,231	3,453	227	199	28	3 590	2,826	764	3,870	1,206	2,664
65—70	3,066	1,720	1 346	93	78	15	1,861	1 030	331	1,612	612	1,000
70 & Over.	5,254	2,811	2,443	160	136	24	2,100	1,623	477	2,994	1,052	1,942
Hindu (Brahmanic)	**304,304**	**157,723**	**146,581**	**104,628**	**64,586**	**40,042**	**161,957**	**81,334**	**80,623**	**37,719**	**11,803**	**25,916**
0—1	9 856	4 916	4,940	9,727	4,870	4,857	116	42	74	13	4	9
1—2	8,307	4,022	4,285	8,161	3,962	4,199	139	58	81	7	2	5
2—3	7,953	3,826	4,127	7,738	3,749	3,989	204	74	130	11	3	8
3—4	7,723	3,771	3 952	7,329	3,673	3,656	352	85	267	42	13	29
4—5	7,771	3,901	3,870	7,221	3,778	3,443	493	107	336	57	16	41
Total 0—5	**41,610**	**20,436**	**21,174**	**40,176**	**20,032**	**20,144**	**1,304**	**366**	**938**	**130**	**38**	**92**
5—10	36,550	18 905	17,645	28,058	16 593	11,445	8,174	2,200	5,974	338	112	226
10—15	34 948	18 429	16 519	20,582	13 686	6,693	13,931	4 522	9,459	585	221	364
15—20	29,111	14 824	14 287	6,2.5	5,525	740	21 803	8,912	12 891	1,043	387	656
20—25	30,098	14 991	15 107	3,859	3 473	386	24,880	11,053	13,827	1,359	465	894
25—30	24,823	12,623	12,200	1,515	1,352	163	21,344	10,608	10,736	1,954	663	1,301
30—35	22,936	12,242	10,694	1,172	1,025	147	19,028	10,332	8,696	2,736	885	1,851
35—40	20,548	10,966	9 582	924	881	93	15,265	8,827	6,438	4,359	1,308	3,051
40—45	17,110	8,926	8 184	725	661	64	11,621	6,849	4,772	4,764	1,416	3,348
45—50	13,546	7,277	6,269	515	469	46	8,215	5,420	2,795	4,816	1,388	3,428
50—55	10,390	5 625	4 765	369	332	37	5 907	4 089	1,818	4,114	1,204	2,910
55—60	8,074	4 497	3,577	248	223	25	3,981	3,164	847	3 845	1,140	2,705
60—65	7,010	3,869	3 141	211	188	23	3 296	2,597	699	3,508	1,084	2,419
65—70	2,783	1,561	1,222	86	72	14	1,241	943	298	1,456	546	910
& Over.	4,767	2,552	2,215	143	124	19	1,917	1,482	435	2,707	946	1,761
...	**27,005**	**14,276**	**12,729**	**10,952**	**6,444**	**4,508**	**12,916**	**6,740**	**6,176**	**3,137**	**1,092**	**2,045**
0—1	931	417	484	890	415	495	6	...	6	15	2	13
1—2	883	401	482	816	398	418	6	1	5	11	2	9
2—3	821	417	404	800	410	390	16	6	10	5	1	4
3—4	820	421	399	782	409	373	30	10	20	8	2	6
4—5	822	438	384	773	424	349	40	11	29	9	3	6
0—5	**4,197**	**2,094**	**2,103**	**4,051**	**2,056**	**1,995**	**98**	**23**	**70**	**48**	**10**	**38**
5—10	3,631	1,860	1,771	3 068	1,784	1,529	523	107	416	45	19	26
10—15	3,413	1 740	1,673	2,292	1,411	881	1,045	303	742	76	26	50
15—20	2,431	1,325	1,106	698	586	112	1,636	712	924	97	27	70
20—25	2,493	1,351	1,142	393	345	51	1,977	957	1,020	120	49	71
25—30	2,221	1,199	1,022	147	115	32	1,896	1,011	885	178	73	105
30—35	1,934	1,058	876	100	67	33	1,606	905	701	228	86	142
35—40	1,661	850	781	76	48	28	1,259	725	534	326	107	219
40—45	1,347	727	620	45	28	17	938	575	363	364	124	240
45—50	1,068	592	476	23	14	9	660	459	201	395	119	266
50—55	833	477	356	18	11	7	487	360	127	328	106	222
55—60	634	366	268	14	9	5	312	239	73	303	118	190
60—65	519	278	241	11	7	4	228	175	53	290	96	194
65—70	215	119	93	5	4	1	91	64	27	119	51	68
70 & Over.	403	210	193	13	9	4	160	120	40	285	81	164

TABLE VII.—Age, Sex and Civil Condition. *Part II.—Details by Districts.—(contd.)*

Age.	POPULATION.			UNMARRIED.			MARRIED.			WIDOWED.		
	Persons.	Males.	Females.	Persons.	Males.	Females.	Persons.	Males.	Females.	Persons.	Males.	Females
1	2	3	4	5	6	7	8	9	10	11	12	13
District Shajapur.—(concld.)												
Jain ...	4,831	2,579	2,252	1,884	1,148	736	2,136	1,151	985	811	280	531
0—1	141	80	61	137	78	59	4	2	2	...	...	...
1—2	113	56	57	108	53	55	5	3	2	...	...	...
2—3	116	56	60	111	53	58	5	3	2	...	...	...
3—4	125	65	60	120	61	59	5	4	1	...	...	...
4—5	119	59	60	112	55	57	4	4	...	3	...	3
Total 0—5	614	316	298	588	300	288	23	16	7	3	...	3
5—10	547	298	249	481	268	213	60	28	32	6	2	4
10—15	539	301	238	399	249	150	133	50	83	7	2	5
15—20	382	205	177	135	109	26	226	89	137	21	7	14
20—25	409	205	201	86	74	12	291	121	170	32	10	22
25—30	384	193	191	52	39	13	288	140	148	44	14	30
30—35	356	197	159	44	31	13	253	145	108	59	21	38
35—40	343	180	163	34	28	6	221	127	94	88	25	63
40—45	314	161	153	20	17	3	193	115	78	101	29	72
45—50	264	143	121	15	11	4	143	91	50	106	39	67
50—55	217	121	96	13	10	3	111	74	37	93	37	56
55—60	186	102	84	8	5	3	87	64	23	91	33	58
60—65	143	77	66	4	3	1	61	50	11	78	24	54
65—70	62	36	26	2	2	...	26	20	6	34	14	20
70 & Over.	71	44	27	3	2	1	20	19	1	48	23	25
District Amjhera.												
All Religions ...	160,066	80,411	79,655	71,867	40,220	31,647	72,539	35,804	36,735	15,660	4,387	11,273
0—1	5,301	2,634	2,667	5,261	2,623	2,638	32	9	23	8	2	6
1—2	5,294	2,590	2,701	5,247	2,574	2,673	44	15	29	3	1	2
2—3	5,622	2,663	2,959	5,540	2,655	2,885	78	27	51	4	1	3
3—4	5,579	2,737	2,842	5,433	2,674	2,759	128	55	73	18	8	10
4—5	5,234	2,681	2,553	5,093	2,624	2,469	118	49	69	23	8	15
Total 0—5	27,030	13,325	13,705	26,574	13,150	13,424	400	155	245	56	20	36
5—10	22,435	11,415	11,020	20,402	10,867	9,535	1,954	527	1,427	69	21	48
10—15	20,684	10,372	10,312	15,518	8,864	6,654	5,028	1,464	3,564	138	44	94
15—20	15,576	7,647	7,929	4,665	3,523	1,142	10,420	3,959	6,461	491	165	326
20—25	15,112	7,498	7,614	2,427	2,046	381	11,805	5,207	6,598	780	245	535
25—30	12,724	6,360	6,364	833	731	103	10,766	5,321	5,445	1,125	308	817
30—35	10,880	5,555	5,325	457	379	78	9,095	4,774	4,321	1,328	402	926
35—40	9,374	4,793	4,581	343	234	109	7,265	4,033	3,232	1,766	526	1,240
40—45	8,131	4,145	3,986	295	182	113	5,927	3,422	2,505	1,909	541	1,368
45—50	5,880	3,180	2,700	128	97	31	3,758	2,545	1,213	1,994	538	1,456
50—55	4,471	2,386	2,085	86	67	19	2,645	1,851	794	1,740	468	1,272
55—60	3,135	1,580	1,555	52	35	17	1,506	1,123	383	1,577	422	1,155
60—65	2,487	1,218	1,269	36	23	13	1,093	858	235	1,358	337	1,021
65—70	881	387	494	23	10	13	333	243	90	525	134	391
70 & Over.	1,266	550	716	28	12	16	431	322	109	804	216	588
Hindu (Brahmanic).	143,170	71,624	71,546	63,988	35,764	28,224	65,007	31,927	33,080	14,175	3,933	10,242
0—1	4,699	2,332	2,367	4,672	2,325	2,347	22	5	17	5	2	3
1—2	4,737	2,323	2,414	4,700	2,310	2,390	35	12	23	2	1	1
2—3	5,003	2,392	2,611	4,933	2,369	2,564	67	23	44	3	...	3
3—4	4,940	2,426	2,514	4,826	2,382	2,444	99	38	61	15	6	9
4—5	4,670	2,406	2,264	4,548	2,355	2,193	103	45	58	19	6	13
Total 0—5	24,049	11,879	12,170	23,679	11,741	11,938	326	123	203	44	15	29
5—10	20,120	10,233	9,887	18,245	9,734	8,511	1,812	483	1,329	63	16	47
10—15	18,523	9,297	9,226	13,871	7,905	5,966	4,527	1,359	3,168	125	33	92
15—20	13,908	6,819	7,089	4,124	3,080	1,044	9,335	3,595	5,740	449	144	305
20—25	13,532	6,669	6,863	2,122	1,785	337	10,681	4,663	6,018	729	221	508
25—30	11,496	5,682	5,814	722	641	81	9,723	4,765	4,958	1,051	276	775
30—35	9,761	4,916	4,845	377	317	60	8,169	4,289	3,880	1,215	360	855
35—40	8,411	4,244	4,167	301	199	102	6,497	3,564	2,933	1,613	481	1,132
40—45	7,288	3,676	3,612	255	155	100	5,305	3,026	2,279	1,728	495	1,233
45—50	5,195	2,798	2,397	103	83	20	3,309	2,232	1,077	1,784	484	1,300
50—55	3,988	2,118	1,870	74	59	15	2,351	1,635	716	1,563	424	1,139
55—60	2,803	1,403	1,400	41	27	14	1,341	1,000	341	1,421	376	1,045
60—65	2,219	1,032	1,187	30	19	11	977	766	211	1,212	297	915
65—70	759	340	419	20	9	11	284	209	75	455	122	333
70 & Over.	1,118	468	650	25	11	14	370	268	102	723	189	534

TABLE VII.—Age, Sex and Civil Condition. *Part II.—Details by Districts.*—(*concld.*)

Age.	POPULATION. Persons.	Males.	Females.	UNMARRIED. Persons.	Males.	Females.	MARRIED. Persons.	Males.	Females.	WIDOWED. Persons.	Males.	Females
1	2	3	4	5	6	7	8	9	10	11	12	13
						District Amjhera.—(*concld.*)						
Hinduized Tribal.	8,443	4,292	4,151	4,296	2,288	2,008	3,548	1,798	1,750	599	206	393
0—1	309	170	139	300	167	133	6	3	3	3	...	3
1—2	313	150	163	311	149	162	2	1	1	...	...	...
2—3	368	168	200	363	165	198	4	2	2	1	1	...
3—4	375	179	196	364	172	192	9	6	3	2	1	1
4—5	329	157	172	322	153	169	7	4	3	...	...	...
Total 0—5	1,694	824	870	1,660	806	854	28	16	12	6	2	4
5—10	1,327	662	665	1,239	631	608	83	26	57	5	5	...
10—15	1,160	581	579	903	506	397	248	67	181	9	8	1
15—20	768	390	378	248	187	61	496	194	302	19	9	10
20—25	717	367	350	126	97	29	567	257	310	24	13	11
25—30	532	265	267	38	24	14	465	226	239	29	15	14
30—35	486	258	228	29	16	13	412	223	189	45	19	26
35—40	454	257	197	17	10	7	378	227	151	59	20	39
40—45	404	217	187	18	7	11	314	192	122	72	18	54
45—50	319	169	150	12	2	10	228	143	85	79	24	55
50—55	221	121	100	4	1	3	145	99	46	72	21	51
55—60	153	79	74	2	1	1	85	58	27	66	20	46
60—65	113	55	58	...	...	...	53	39	14	60	16	44
65—70	50	11	39	...	...	...	18	8	10	32	3	29
70 & Over.	50	36	14	...	...	...	28	23	5	22	13	9
Muslim ...	6,480	3,428	3,052	2,743	1,625	1,118	3,122	1,610	1,512	615	193	422
0—1	236	107	129	232	106	126	4	1	3	...	...	...
1—2	200	97	103	193	95	98	7	2	5	...	...	...
2—3	204	99	105	197	97	100	7	2	5	...	...	...
3—4	213	106	107	194	96	98	19	10	9	...	...	...
4—5	194	99	95	183	97	86	7	...	7	4	2	2
Total 0—5	1,047	508	539	999	491	508	44	15	29	4	2	2
5—10	785	413	372	723	397	326	62	16	46	...	...	...
10—15	796	380	416	572	346	226	221	32	189	3	2	1
15—20	697	324	373	213	183	30	466	130	336	18	11	7
20—25	651	345	306	122	112	10	508	222	286	21	11	10
25—30	533	321	212	47	41	6	455	265	190	31	15	16
30—35	466	289	177	28	24	4	394	246	148	44	19	25
35—40	365	207	158	10	10	...	291	177	114	64	20	44
40—45	313	180	133	9	7	2	231	151	80	73	22	51
45—50	270	162	108	6	5	1	177	135	42	87	22	65
50—55	184	105	79	4	3	1	113	88	25	67	14	53
55—60	128	69	59	4	3	1	59	47	12	65	19	46
60—65	115	59	56	2	1	1	47	39	8	66	19	47
65—70	49	28	21	2	1	1	24	21	3	23	6	17
70 & Over.	81	38	43	2	1	1	30	26	4	49	11	38
Jain ...	1,907	1,038	869	818	531	287	828	454	374	261	53	208
0—1	54	23	31	54	23	31	...	...	...	...	...	...
1—2	43	20	23	42	20	22	...	...	...	1	...	1
2—3	47	24	23	47	24	23	...	...	...	...	...	...
3—4	51	26	25	49	24	25	1	1	...	1	1	...
4—5	40	19	21	39	19	20	1	...	1	...	...	...
Total 0—5	235	112	123	231	110	121	2	1	1	2	1	1
5—10	197	104	93	189	102	87	7	2	5	1	...	1
10—15	198	112	86	168	105	63	29	6	23	1	1	...
15—20	199	112	87	77	71	6	118	40	78	4	1	3
20—25	206	115	91	56	51	5	145	64	81	5	...	5
25—30	157	89	68	26	25	1	117	62	55	14	2	12
30—35	159	87	71	21	21	...	114	62	52	23	4	19
35—40	141	83	58	15	15	...	97	63	34	29	5	24
40—45	121	68	53	12	12	...	73	50	23	36	6	30
45—50	94	47	45	8	8	...	43	34	9	43	7	36
50—55	78	42	36	4	4	...	36	29	7	38	9	29
55—60	50	29	21	5	4	1	21	18	3	24	7	17
60—65	38	22	16	4	3	1	15	14	1	19	5	14
65—70	21	8	13	1	...	1	6	5	1	14	3	11
70 & Over.	14	6	8	1	...	1	5	4	1	8	2	6

TABLE VII.

Age, Sex and Civil Condition.

Part III.

Cities.

TABLE VII.—Age, Sex and Civil Condition. *Part III.—Cities.*

Age.	POPULATION.			UNMARRIED.			MARRIED.			WIDOWED.		
	Persons.	Males.	Females.	Persons.	Males.	Females.	Persons.	Males.	Females.	Persons.	Males.	Females.
1	2	3	4	5	6	7	8	9	10	11	12	13
						Lashkar City.						
All Religions ...	86,767	47,358	39,409	32,178	20,542	11,636	42,147	22,173	19,974	12,442	4,643	7,799
0—1	2,467	1,230	1,237	2,465	1,229	1,236	2	1	1	...	...	...
1—2	2,091	1,085	1,006	2,084	1,081	1,003	7	4	3	...	...	...
2—3	2,013	1,042	971	2,003	1,038	965	9	4	5	1	...	1
3—4	1,959	1,020	939	1,948	1,018	930	14	7	7	2	...	2
4—5	2,037	1,022	1,015	2,005	1,007	998	28	13	15	4	2	2
Total 0—5	10,567	5,399	5,168	10,500	5,368	5,132	60	29	31	7	2	5
5—10	8,824	4,863	3,961	8,052	4,670	3,382	743	184	559	29	9	20
10—15	8,917	4,813	4,104	6,718	4,230	2,488	2,134	500	1,634	70	33	37
15—20	8,945	4,729	4,216	2,948	2,590	358	5,740	2,018	3,722	262	121	141
20—25	9,610	5,143	4,467	2,010	1,877	133	7,113	3,044	4,069	487	222	265
25—30	8,139	4,597	3,542	765	718	47	6,568	3,055	3,063	806	374	432
30—35	7,000	4,140	2,860	460	420	40	5,568	3,228	2,340	972	492	480
35—40	5,926	3,438	2,488	235	204	31	4,312	2,660	1,652	1,379	574	805
40—45	5,101	2,911	2,190	170	146	24	3,482	2,226	1,256	1,449	539	910
45—50	4,105	2,337	1,768	97	81	16	2,357	1,669	688	1,651	587	1,064
50—55	3,359	1,890	1,469	86	73	13	1,758	1,281	477	1,515	536	979
55—60	2,400	1,227	1,173	58	47	11	1,001	779	222	1,341	401	940
60—65	1,936	950	986	47	38	9	746	598	148	1,143	314	829
65—70	704	367	337	21	16	5	241	192	49	442	159	283
70 & Over.	1,234	554	680	21	14	7	324	260	64	889	280	609
Hindu (Brahmanic).	64,399	35,147	29,252	23,011	14,876	8,135	31,588	16,701	14,887	9,800	3,570	6,230
0—1	1,831	922	909	1,830	922	908	1	...	1	...	...	...
1—2	1,509	792	717	1,505	790	715	4	2	2	...	...	...
2—3	1,430	756	674	1,425	754	671	4	2	2	1	...	1
3—4	1,395	735	660	1,385	730	655	8	5	3	2	...	2
4—5	1,357	726	631	1,339	715	624	16	10	6	2	1	1
Total 0—5	7,522	3,931	3,591	7,484	3,911	3,573	33	19	14	5	1	4
5—10	6,461	3,522	2,939	5,868	3,376	2,492	569	139	430	24	7	17
10—15	6,519	3,531	2,988	4,801	3,101	1,700	1,659	403	1,256	59	27	32
15—20	6,686	3,552	3,134	2,072	1,861	211	4,406	1,592	2,814	208	99	109
20—25	7,192	3,855	3,337	1,419	1,343	76	5,376	2,330	3,046	397	182	215
25—30	6,135	3,464	2,671	539	519	20	4,935	2,650	2,285	661	295	366
30—35	5,332	3,168	2,164	330	312	18	4,237	2,498	1,739	765	358	407
35—40	4,487	2,604	1,883	161	146	15	3,256	2,038	1,218	1,070	420	650
40—45	3,843	2,173	1,670	112	100	12	2,570	1,650	920	1,161	423	738
45—50	3,072	1,726	1,346	69	63	6	1,690	1,197	493	1,313	466	847
50—55	2,505	1,393	1,112	63	59	4	1,257	912	345	1,185	422	763
55—60	1,795	896	899	40	36	4	710	552	158	1,045	308	737
60—65	1,431	680	751	30	27	3	518	417	101	883	236	647
65—70	518	266	252	13	13	...	163	132	31	342	121	221
70 & Over.	901	386	515	10	9	1	209	172	37	682	205	477
Muslim ...	20,729	11,278	9,451	8,564	5,272	3,292	9,799	5,037	4,762	2,366	969	1,397
0—1	599	293	306	598	292	306	1	1	...	...	...	...
1—2	550	276	274	547	274	273	3	2	1	...	...	...
2—3	554	270	284	549	268	281	5	2	3	...	...	...
3—4	539	272	267	533	270	263	6	2	4	...	...	...
4—5	644	274	370	630	270	360	12	3	9	2	1	1
Total 0—5	2,886	1,385	1,501	2,857	1,374	1,483	27	10	17	2	1	1
5—10	2,243	1,273	970	2,071	1,228	843	167	43	124	5	2	3
10—15	2,230	1,207	1,023	1,803	1,112	691	417	90	327	10	5	5
15—20	2,073	1,062	1,011	808	680	128	1,216	361	855	49	21	28
20—25	2,260	1,195	1,065	540	493	47	1,635	662	973	85	40	45
25—30	1,837	1,035	802	190	171	19	1,516	789	727	131	75	56
30—35	1,509	871	638	103	84	19	1,222	662	560	184	125	59
35—40	1,314	756	558	58	43	15	977	569	408	279	144	135
40—45	1,112	672	440	45	35	10	846	534	312	221	103	118
45—50	887	549	338	24	16	8	606	429	177	257	104	153
50—55	736	455	281	18	11	7	460	342	118	258	102	156
55—60	556	339	217	16	9	7	325	267	58	215	63	152
60—65	451	239	212	13	8	5	206	164	42	232	67	165
65—70	165	86	79	7	3	4	71	54	17	87	29	58
70 & Over.	310	154	156	11	5	6	108	81	27	191	68	123

TABLE VII.—Age, Sex and Civil Condition. *Part III.—Cities.—(contd.)*

Age.	POPULATION.			UNMARRIED.			MARRIED.			WIDOWED.		
	Persons.	Males.	Females.	Persons.	Males.	Females.	Persons.	Males.	Females.	Persons.	Males.	Females.
1	2	3	4	5	6	7	8	9	10	11	12	13
						Lashkar City,—(concld.).						
Jain ...	1,220	699	521	406	286	120	567	323	244	247	90	157
0—1	27	11	16	27	11	16	...	...	...	...	...	...
1—2	20	13	7	20	13	7	...	...	...	...	...	...
2—3	21	13	8	21	13	8	...	...	...	...	...	...
3—4	19	10	9	19	10	9	...	...	...	...	...	...
4—5	27	17	10	27	17	10	...	...	...	...	...	...
Total 0—5	114	64	50	114	64	50	...	...	...	...	...	...
5—10	92	52	40	85	50	35	7	2	5	...	...	...
10—15	110	61	49	82	53	29	27	7	20	1	1	...
15—20	116	64	52	36	33	3	75	30	45	5	1	4
20—25	116	65	51	25	24	1	86	41	45	5	...	5
25—30	120	72	48	20	18	2	87	50	37	13	4	9
30—35	118	75	43	16	16	...	80	50	30	22	9	13
35—40	95	57	38	12	12	...	55	36	19	28	9	19
40—45	86	47	39	8	8	...	44	28	16	34	11	23
45—50	72	40	32	1	1	...	36	25	11	35	14	21
50—55	59	32	27	2	2	...	29	20	9	28	10	18
55—60	46	22	24	2	2	...	16	12	4	28	8	20
60—65	43	26	17	3	3	...	14	12	2	26	11	15
65—70	19	14	5	...	...	...	7	6	1	12	8	4
70 & Over.	14	8	6	...	...	...	4	4	...	10	4	6
Christian ...	196	104	92	95	48	47	86	50	36	15	6	9
0—1	4	1	3	4	1	3	...	...	...	...	...	...
1—2	5	2	3	5	2	3	...	...	...	...	...	...
2—3	3	2	1	3	2	1	...	...	...	...	...	...
3—4	3	2	1	3	2	1	...	...	...	...	...	...
4—5	3	2	1	3	2	1	...	...	...	...	...	...
Total 0—5	18	9	9	18	9	9	...	...	...	...	...	...
5—10	9	6	3	9	6	3	...	...	...	...	...	...
10—15	9	3	6	9	3	6	...	...	...	...	...	...
15—20	13	7	6	12	6	6	1	1	...	...	...	...
20—25	21	10	11	13	8	5	8	2	6	...	...	...
25—30	25	12	13	13	7	6	12	5	7	...	...	...
30—35	20	13	7	8	5	3	12	8	4	...	...	...
35—40	12	7	5	2	1	1	9	6	3	1	...	1
40—45	15	8	7	3	1	2	11	6	5	1	1	...
45—50	16	8	8	3	1	2	10	6	4	3	1	2
50—55	13	7	6	3	1	2	7	5	2	3	1	2
55—60	9	6	3	...	...	...	7	5	2	2	1	1
60—65	8	3	5	1	...	1	6	3	3	1	...	1
65—70	1	...	1	1	...	1	...	...	...	...	...	...
70 & Over.	7	5	2	...	...	...	3	3	...	4	2	2
Others ...	223	130	93	102	60	42	107	62	45	14	8	6
0—1	6	3	3	6	3	3	...	...	...	...	...	...
1—2	7	2	5	7	2	5	...	...	...	...	...	...
2—3	5	1	4	5	1	4	...	...	...	...	...	...
3—4	3	1	2	3	1	2	...	...	...	...	...	...
4—5	6	3	3	6	3	3	...	...	...	...	...	...
Total 0—5	27	10	17	27	10	17	...	...	...	...	...	...
5—10	19	10	9	19	10	9	...	...	...	...	...	...
10—15	19	11	8	18	11	7	1	...	1	...	...	...
15—20	27	14	13	15	10	5	12	4	8	...	...	...
20—25	31	18	13	13	9	4	18	9	9	...	...	...
25—30	22	14	8	3	3	...	18	11	7	1	...	1
30—35	21	13	8	3	3	...	17	10	7	1	...	1
35—40	18	14	4	2	2	...	15	11	4	1	1	...
40—45	15	11	4	2	2	...	11	8	3	2	1	1
45—50	8	4	4	...	...	...	5	2	3	3	2	1
50—55	6	3	3	...	...	...	5	2	3	1	1	...
55—60	4	4	...	...	...	...	3	3	...	1	1	...
60—65	3	2	1	...	...	...	2	2	...	1	...	1
65—70	1	1	...	...	...	...	...	...	...	1	1	...
70 & Over.	2	1	1	...	...	...	...	...	...	2	1	1

TABLE VII.—Age, Sex and Civil Condition. *Part III.—Cities.—(contd.)*

Age.	POPULATION.			UNMARRIED.			MARRIED.			WIDOWED.		
	Persons.	Males.	Females.	Persons.	Males.	Females.	Persons.	Males.	Females.	Persons.	Males.	Females.
1	2	3	4	5	6	7	8	9	10	11	12	13
						Ujjain City.						
All Religions ...	54,650	30,597	24,053	21,534	13,902	7,632	26,646	14,180	12,466	6,470	2,515	3,955
0—1	1,385	759	626	1,373	759	614	10	...	10	2	...	2
1—2	1,320	683	637	1,307	681	626	12	2	10	1	...	1
2—3	1,374	703	671	1,349	694	655	25	9	16	...	...	...
3—4	1,281	706	575	1,244	694	550	35	11	24	2	1	1
4—5	1,696	958	738	1,624	939	685	68	16	47	9	3	6
Total 0—5	7,056	3,809	3,247	6,897	3,767	3,130	145	38	107	14	4	10
5—10	5,199	2,772	2,427	4,431	2,588	1,843	747	176	571	21	8	13
10—15	6,025	3,107	2,918	4,341	2,672	1,669	1,626	407	1,219	58	28	30
15—20	6,083	3,489	2,594	2,153	1,759	394	3,722	1,607	2,115	208	123	85
20—25	6,332	3,757	2,575	1,512	1,323	189	4,517	2,257	2,260	303	177	126
25—30	4,892	2,804	2,088	659	531	128	3,787	2,075	1,712	446	198	248
30—35	4,225	2,469	1,756	472	398	74	3,193	1,818	1,375	560	253	307
35—40	3,683	2,243	1,440	337	306	31	2,588	1,619	969	758	318	440
40—45	3,005	1,883	1,122	225	214	11	2,046	1,388	658	734	281	453
45—50	2,308	1,294	1,014	157	105	52	1,419	956	463	732	233	499
50—55	1,955	975	980	138	75	63	1,146	702	444	671	198	473
55—60	1,392	689	703	100	73	27	670	418	252	622	198	424
60—65	1,170	585	585	63	49	14	507	341	166	600	195	405
65—70	515	252	263	14	12	2	223	125	98	278	115	163
70 & Over.	810	469	341	35	30	5	310	253	57	465	186	279
Hindu (Brahmanic).	37,115	21,024	16,091	14,468	9,792	4,676	17,795	9,355	8,440	4,852	1,877	2,975
0—1	928	521	407	919	521	398	7	...	7	2	...	2
1—2	901	471	430	890	470	420	10	1	9	1	...	1
2—3	929	472	457	910	466	444	19	6	13	...	...	...
3—4	842	472	370	812	464	348	28	7	21	2	1	1
4—5	1,091	641	450	1,033	630	403	51	9	42	7	2	5
Total 0—5	4,691	2,577	2,114	4,564	2,551	2,013	115	23	92	12	3	9
5—10	3,446	1,884	1,562	2,840	1,753	1,087	588	123	465	18	8	10
10—15	4,140	2,173	1,967	2,795	1,836	959	1,235	312	983	50	25	25
15—20	4,261	2,502	1,759	1,488	1,270	218	2,599	1,125	1,474	174	107	67
20—25	4,350	2,645	1,705	1,100	966	134	3,016	1,536	1,480	234	143	91
25—30	3,371	1,923	1,448	486	397	89	2,557	1,382	1,175	328	144	184
30—35	2,898	1,686	1,212	343	310	33	2,135	1,188	947	420	188	232
35—40	2,429	1,547	882	262	258	4	1,624	1,059	565	543	230	313
40—45	1,933	1,274	659	195	191	4	1,220	888	332	518	195	323
45—50	1,558	874	684	135	90	45	888	620	268	535	164	371
50—55	1,410	677	733	104	48	56	792	479	313	514	150	364
55—60	977	458	519	68	47	21	429	256	173	480	155	325
60—65	797	380	417	51	41	10	282	186	96	464	153	311
65—70	359	154	205	9	8	1	119	55	64	231	91	140
70 & Over.	495	270	225	28	26	2	136	123	13	331	121	210
Muslim ...	15,397	8,351	7,046	6,345	3,683	2,662	7,613	4,099	3,514	1,439	569	870
0—1	421	221	200	418	221	197	3	...	3	...	...	...
1—2	385	195	190	383	194	189	2	1	1	...	...	...
2—3	401	207	194	395	204	191	6	3	3	...	...	...
3—4	391	209	182	385	206	179	6	3	3	...	...	...
4—5	548	286	262	536	279	257	10	6	4	2	1	1
Total 0—5	2,146	1,118	1,028	2,117	1,104	1,013	27	13	14	2	1	1
5—10	1,555	800	755	1,424	758	666	128	42	86	3	...	3
10—15	1,647	831	816	1,385	755	630	254	73	181	8	3	5
15—20	[illegible]	875	723	594	427	167	972	433	539	32	15	17
20—25	1,729	965	764	363	314	49	1,300	619	691	66	32	34
25—30	[illegible]	724	558	154	118	36	1,023	557	466	105	49	56
30—35	1,141	661	480	118	77	41	901	528	373	122	56	66
35—40	1,109	[illegible]	512	65	84	27	839	478	366	196	77	119
40—45	[illegible]	518	420	23	16	7	719	424	295	196	78	118
45—50	[illegible]	[illegible]	293	19	13	6	468	291	177	169	59	110
50—55	[illegible]	[illegible]	224	31	25	6	309	185	124	136	42	94
55—60	[illegible]	[illegible]	166	30	24	6	213	140	73	125	38	87
60—65	[illegible]	[illegible]	133	11	7	4	204	138	66	119	56	63
65—70	[illegible]	[illegible]	53	5	4	1	94	61	33	39	20	19
70 & Over.	[illegible]	[illegible]	102	6	3	3	162	121	41	121	63	58

TABLE VII.—Age, Sex and Civil Condition. *Part III.—Cities.—(concld).*

Age.		POPULATION.			UNMARRIED.			MARRIED.			WIDOWED.		
		Persons.	Males.	Females.	Persons.	Males.	Females.	Persons.	Males.	Females.	Persons.	Males.	Females.
1		2	3	4	5	6	7	8	9	10	11	12	13
Ujjain City.—(concld.)													
Jain	...	1,906	1,080	826	585	346	239	1,152	670	482	169	64	105
	0—1	29	14	15	29	14	15	...	...	...	...	...	...
	1—2	29	14	15	29	14	15	...	...	...	...	...	...
	2—3	39	21	18	39	21	18	...	...	...	...	...	...
	3—4	38	21	17	37	20	17	1	1	...	...	...	...
	4—5	44	23	21	42	22	20	2	1	1	...	...	...
Total	0—5	179	93	86	176	91	85	3	2	1	...	...	...
	5—10	167	71	96	137	60	77	30	11	19	...	...	...
	10—15	208	86	122	132	64	68	76	22	54	...	...	...
	15—20	206	99	107	56	51	5	148	47	101	2	1	1
	20—25	233	137	96	40	39	1	190	96	94	3	2	1
	25—30	219	145	74	13	12	1	193	128	65	13	5	8
	30—35	169	109	60	8	8	...	143	92	51	18	9	9
	35—40	140	97	43	9	9	...	113	78	35	18	10	8
	40—45	122	83	39	6	6	...	98	69	29	18	8	10
	45—50	87	52	35	2	1	1	58	42	16	27	9	18
	50—55	61	39	22	2	1	1	39	33	6	20	5	15
	55—60	41	25	16	2	2	...	23	19	4	16	4	12
	60—65	36	21	15	1	1	...	18	14	4	17	6	11
	65—70	17	12	5	...	...	...	10	9	1	7	3	4
	70 & Over.	21	11	10	1	1	...	10	8	2	10	2	8
Christian	...	85	50	35	49	30	19	34	19	15	2	1	1
	0—1	2	1	1	2	1	1	...	...	...	...	...	...
	1—2	1	1	...	1	1	...	...	...	...	...	...	...
	2—3	2	1	1	2	1	1	...	...	...	...	...	...
	3—4	3	1	2	3	1	2	...	...	...	...	...	...
	4—5	4	3	1	4	3	1	...	...	...	...	...	...
Total	0—5	12	7	5	12	7	5	...	...	...	...	...	...
	5—10	12	8	4	12	8	4	...	...	...	...	...	...
	10—15	12	7	5	12	7	5	...	...	...	...	...	...
	15—20	6	4	2	6	4	2	...	...	...	...	...	...
	20—25	4	2	2	4	2	2	...	...	...	...	...	...
	25—30	4	2	2	2	1	1	2	1	1	...	...	...
	30—35	6	3	3	1	1	...	5	2	3	...	...	...
	35—40	6	3	3	...	...	...	6	3	3	...	...	...
	40—45	6	4	2	...	...	...	5	3	2	1	1	...
	45—50	7	4	3	...	...	...	6	4	2	1	...	1
	50—55	4	2	2	...	...	...	4	2	2	...	...	...
	55—60	3	2	1	...	...	...	3	2	1	...	...	...
	60—65	2	1	1	...	...	...	2	1	1	...	...	...
	65—70	1	1	...	...	...	...	1	1	...	...	...	...
Hinduized Tribal		12	5	7	9	3	6	3	2	1	...	...	...
	1—2	1	...	1	1	...	1	...	...	...	...	...	...
	4—5	1	1	...	1	1	...	...	...	...	...	...	...
Total	0—5	2	1	1	2	1	1	...	...	...	...	...	...
	5—10	3	1	2	3	1	2	...	...	...	...	...	...
	10—15	3	1	2	3	1	2	...	...	...	...	...	...
	20—25	3	1	2	1	...	1	2	1	1	...	...	...
	40—45	1	1	...	...	...	...	1	1	...	...	...	...
Others	...	135	87	48	78	48	30	49	35	14	8	4	4
	0—1	5	2	3	5	2	3	...	...	...	...	...	...
	1—2	3	2	1	3	2	1	...	...	...	...	...	...
	2—3	3	2	1	3	2	1	...	...	...	...	...	...
	3—4	7	3	4	7	3	4	...	...	...	...	...	...
	4—5	8	4	4	8	4	4	...	...	...	...	...	...
Total	0—5	26	13	13	26	13	13	...	...	...	...	...	...
	5—10	16	8	8	15	8	7	1	...	1	...	...	...
	10—15	15	9	6	14	9	5	1	...	1	...	...	...
	15—20	12	9	3	9	7	2	3	2	1	...	...	...
	20—25	11	6	5	4	2	2	7	4	3	...	...	...
	25—30	13	9	4	4	3	1	9	6	3	...	...	...
	30—35	10	9	1	2	2	...	8	[illegible]	1	[illegible]	[illegible]	[illegible]
	35—40	8	7	1	1	1	...	7	[illegible]	1	[illegible]	[illegible]	[illegible]
	40—45	4	3	1	1	1	...	2	[illegible]	...	[illegible]	[illegible]	[illegible]
	45—50	3	3	...	1	1	...	[illegible]	[illegible]	...	[illegible]	[illegible]	[illegible]
	50—55	5	5	...	1	1	...	[illegible]	[illegible]	...	[illegible]	[illegible]	[illegible]
	55—60	4	3	1	...	...	...	[illegible]	2	[illegible]	[illegible]	[illegible]	[illegible]
	60—65	2	1	1	...	...	...	[illegible]	1	[illegible]	[illegible]	[illegible]	[illegible]
	65—70	1	1	...	...	...	...	...	...	[illegible]	[illegible]	[illegible]	[illegible]
	70 & Over.	5	1	4	...	...	...	[illegible]	1	[illegible]	[illegible]	[illegible]	[illegible]

TABLE VIII.

Civil Condition by Age for Selected Castes.

NOTE.—This Table does not deal with the whole population but with certain selected castes which are considered of local importance.

TABLE VIII.—Civil Condition by Age

Caste.	Locality.	Sex.	Population Dealt with.	UNMARRIED. Total.	0—6	7—13	14—16	17—23	24—43	44 & over.
1	2	3	4	5	6	7	8	9	10	11
Hindu.										
1 Ahir. ...	Narwar and Isagarh.	Male	70,208	33,812	12,832	11,435	3,788	2,830	1,961	976
		Female	60,474	20,526	11,788	6,944	1,068	292	257	177
2 Balai. ...	Ujjain and Shajapur.	Male	49,031	19,455	8,277	6,119	2,557	1,241	976	285
		Female	48,797	16,115	9,872	4,823	1,035	181	129	75
3 Pasis. ...	Gird and Ujjain.	Male	48,011	21,182	6,862	5,853	2,687	2,352	2,594	894
		Female	39,739	11,928	7,105	4,251	390	148	83	41
4 Beragi. ...	Ujjain and Mandsaur.	Male	16,177	7,318	2,756	2,107	884	574	655	342
		Female	14,026	4,870	2,400	1,814	414	149	57	36
5 Bhil. ...	Amjhera.	Male	39,430	16,491	6,989	5,450	1,820	1,427	658	147
		Female	38,849	14,331	6,877	4,745	422	140	69	78
6 Bhilala. ...	Amjhera.	Male	18,205	8,891	3,227	3,089	874	1,064	539	98
		Female	17,931	8,486	4,505	3,302	336	199	60	34
7 Brahmin. ... (except Dakshini).	State.	Male	159,411	73,872	24,956	20,210	8,022	8,114	9,212	3,358
		Female	123,457	39,151	22,006	13,245	1,815	622	524	339
8 Brahmin Dakshini. ...	Gird and Ujjain.	Male	6,826	3,423	929	774	608	512	338	262
		Female	6,325	2,151	1,195	857	61	26	10	2
9 Chamar. ...	Isagarh & Narwar.	Male	212,626	92,510	38,783	30,395	10,718	6,877	4,010	1,727
		Female	203,324	72,892	44,560	24,216	2,069	1,183	547	317
10 Gadariya. ...	Bhind and Narwar.	Male	45,433	19,844	7,508	6,155	2,030	1,447	1,180	524
		Female	42,308	16,123	9,930	5,231	457	275	183	47
11 Gujar. ...	Tonwarghar and Shajapur.	Male	60,816	28,231	10,410	9,098	3,176	2,618	2,232	707
		Female	58,498	22,145	12,748	7,384	1,480	344	117	72
12 Kachhi. ...	Gird and Bhind.	Male	91,891	39,664	16,990	12,905	4,108	3,039	2,092	530
		Female	79,723	29,451	18,041	8,977	1,105	678	366	284
13 Kayastha. ...	Gird and Shajapur.	Male	18,866	9,335	2,887	2,307	1,431	1,495	946	269
		Female	15,060	5,671	3,070	2,215	211	101	49	25
14 Kirar. ...	Tonwarghar and Narwar.	Male	40,981	18,872	7,459	6,033	2,494	1,417	1,231	238
		Female	34,916	13,069	7,333	4,257	723	294	232	180
15 Koli. ...	Gird & Tonwarghar.	Male	41,043	18,857	6,846	5,597	2,593	1,543	983	850
		Female	34,309	12,090	7,072	4,230	374	247	126	41
16 Kumhar. ...	Gird and Ujjain.	Male	32,836	13,243	6,230	4,067	1,260	972	518	196
		Female	29,649	10,070	6,642	2,816	223	129	93	67
17 Lodhi. ...	Narwar & Isagarh.	Male	48,903	21,097	8,746	6,488	2,813	1,857	1,380	273
		Female	42,870	13,266	8,201	4,018	637	169	143	48
18 Maratha. ...	Gird and Ujjain.	Male	7,823	3,451	1,003	943	414	678	333	80
		Female	6,828	2,029	1,070	720	97	67	61	14
19 Mina. ...	Sheopur & Isagarh.	Male	34,376	15,493	5,491	5,065	2,169	1,423	998	352
		Female	32,749	12,031	6,717	4,552	844	189	174	106
20 M[illegible]. ...	Gird and Bhilsa.	Male	6,669	3,166	1,159	1,129	357	279	174	69
		Female	6,244	2,633	1,496	970	86	53	16	7
21 Nai. ...	State.	Male	28,877	12,601	4,709	4,093	1,479	1,277	767	299
		Female	25,496	8,272	4,925	2,462	376	251	148	90
22 Rajput [illegible]	Bhilsa.	Male	11,379	5,160	1,759	1,299	626	682	412	214
		Female	7,217	2,049	990	597	149	112	103	61
23 Rajput [illegible]	Gird and Ujjain.	Male	12,542	6,334	1,975	1,575	649	753	879	213
		Female	11,927	3,294	1,579	1,026	215	241	169	84
24 Rajput Kachhwaha.	Bhind & Tonwarghar.	Male	9,641	3,447	1,025	957	449	463	471	191
		Female	6,425	2,215	[illegible]	831	215	17[illegible]	26	41
25 Rajput [illegible]	Isagarh and Bhilsa.	Male	11,[illegible]	6,0[illegible]	2,[illegible]	1,870	570	747	4[illegible]	197
		Female	11,1[illegible]	3,[illegible]47	2,849	1,0[illegible]	297	154	81	4[illegible]
26 Rajput [illegible]	Tonwarghar.	Male	[illegible]	10,144	2,737	2,[illegible]	[illegible]	1,212	[illegible]	45[illegible]
		Female	14,[illegible]	4,[illegible]	2,124	1,600	21[illegible]	2[illegible]	[illegible]	15[illegible]
27 [illegible]	Narwar & Isagarh.	Male	[illegible]	[illegible]	[illegible]	[illegible]	1,[illegible]	1,1[illegible]	[illegible]	12[illegible]
		Female	[illegible]	15,[illegible]	9,93[illegible]	5,[illegible]	[illegible]	[illegible]	[illegible]	[illegible]
28 [illegible]	[illegible]	Male	[illegible]	[illegible]	2,[illegible]	1,[illegible]	[illegible]	[illegible]	[illegible]	[illegible]
		Female	[illegible]	[illegible]	2,[illegible]	1,4[illegible]	[illegible]	141	[illegible]	[illegible]
29 [illegible]	State.	Male	[illegible]	[illegible]	[illegible]	4,195	1,[illegible]	1,0[illegible]	[illegible]	[illegible]
		Female	[illegible]	[illegible]	[illegible]	[illegible]	[illegible]	[illegible]	[illegible]	[illegible]

for Selected Castes.

MARRIED.							WIDOWED.						
Total.	0—6	7—13	14—16	17—23	24—43	44 & over	Total.	0—6	7—13	14—16	17—23	24—43	44 & over.
12	13	14	15	16	17	18	19	20	21	22	23	24	25
29,604	160	1,540	1,875	5,493	14,276	6,260	6,792	55	205	241	888	2,358	3,550
29,714	442	2,248	3,618	7,878	12,652	2,881	10,234	69	253	202	859	3,071	6,280
25,401	280	2,298	2,915	4 823	10,069	5,016	4,175	43	115	166	283	1,050	2,568
25,520	481	3,137	4,485	5,589	8,682	3,146	7,162	40	122	165	520	1,885	4,430
20,230	100	674	1,565	3,720	9,320	4,851	6,599	21	44	115	304	2,174	3,941
18,991	109	1,498	2,557	4,719	7,541	2,567	8,820	11	56	122	308	2,729	5,599
7,196	142	338	524	1,164	3,817	1,711	1,663	7	16	39	118	590	893
6,745	196	593	781	1,727	2,601	847	2,411	11	35	69	175	918	1,208
21,150	143	825	1,486	3,949	9,149	5,648	1,789	16	20	87	128	675	913
20,381	203	1,207	2,940	5,243	9,084	1,704	3,628	12	29	56	138	1,328	2,065
8,768	100	425	763	1,839	4,390	1,251	546	1	2	3	34	189	317
7,555	64	300	608	1,816	3,989	778	1,890	8	21	26	42	584	1,209
66,761	504	2,614	4,967	12,613	27.822	18,241	18,778	61	93	163	497	6,756	11,203
57,551	649	4,723	6,834	14,441	23,622	7,277	26,785	128	150	324	612	9,311	16,260
2,543	7	17	144	462	1,169	744	860	1	2	16	26	198	617
2,758	17	194	420	632	1,070	425	1,416	11	30	22	62	410	881
99,862	1,893	5,418	8,874	20,101	46 536	17,540	20,254	112	192	504	829	6,687	11,930
100,195	1,081	10,961	12,942	21,276	42,080	11,855	30,237	150	204	596	1,272	10.309	17,706
22,365	159	1,340	1,817	4,718	10,071	4,260	4,224	48	43	160	201	1,437	2.340
20,917	364	2,374	2,713	4 508	8,075	2,883	5,268	66	78	110	396	1,767	2,856
26,003	248	1,180	2,141	3,900	12,326	6,208	6,582	28	97	107	239	2,516	3,595
26,494	374	2,298	3,462	6,095	10,064	4,201	9,859	113	94	144	294	3,885	5.378
44,066	402	1,899	3,291	8 155	21,292	9,027	8 161	55	114	184	218	3,119	4,471
38,283	430	3,409	4,948	8,910	15,875	4,666	12,039	108	159	235	394	4,094	7.049
7,458	28	180	585	966	4,028	1,671	2,083	2	18	52	97	430	1,484
6,788	79	360	609	1,529	2,979	1,232	2,601	29	27	54	172	833	1,486
18,271	71	877	1,600	3,814	8,478	3,481	3,838	21	59	119	218	1,544	1,877
17,108	100	1,262	2,088	4,796	6,948	1,914	4,739	19	47	65	288	1,616	2,704
18,940	155	728	1,275	3 886	8,420	4 476	3,746	27	35	84	175	1,483	1,992
17,132	196	1,616	2,122	4,395	6,984	1,869	5,086	53	50	128	229	1,671	2,955
16,261	155	976	1,339	2,909	7 052	3,830	3,332	24	85	109	169	1,374	1,571
15.469	210	1,461	1,540	3,166	6,425	2,667	4,110	39	79	111	159	1,348	2,374
23,797	111	887	1,679	4,234	12,388	4,498	4,019	20	51	102	347	1,813	1,686
23,004	340	2,194	2,801	5,377	10,125	2,167	6,600	35	59	84	169	2,453	3,800
3,511	29	98	205	692	1,682	855	861	1	3	19	28	329	481
2,920	59	264	256	669	1,198	476	1,379	5	9	15	51	449	850
15,728	122	686	1,067	2.967	7,789	3,147	3,165	41	42	70	108	1,133	1,771
16,226	544	1,890	1,806	3,977	6,107	1,902	4,491	25	40	126	196	1,087	2,417
3,082	39	130	178	505	1,570	665	621	10	14	16	47	235	299
2,649	39	186	394	665	1,042	323	1,002	1	11	26	50	384	580
13,147	93	538	845	2,347	6,491	2.833	3,126	21	37	47	96	1,114	1,811
12,984	185	1,135	1,567	2,833	5,403	1,861	4,240	50	119	164	252	1,276	2,379
4,873	69	208	392	1,075	2,039	1,090	1,346	10	14	24	46	462	790
3,848	76	281	465	836	1,406	784	1,320	26	67	70	131	448	578
5,908	26	220	536	1,243	2,262	1,616	1,601	...	19	40	61	454	1,027
5,810	64	592	632	1,340	2,094	1,088	2,713	28	44	78	121	820	1,022
4,632	30	180	214	779	2,191	1,238	922	6	9	16	39	302	550
3,060	6	154	349	812	1,223	516	1,090	2	28	30	90	383	557
4,806	49	163	282	722	2,578	1,017	969	...	9	11	30	341	578
5,075	156	468	666	1,301	2,088	451	2,272	23	40	61	105	782	1,261
7.292	53	253	673	1,981	2,941	1,391	2,732	6	58	57	124	934	1,553
5,345	73	335	633	1,044	2,177	1,033	2,508	5	26	78	119	919	1,861
17,428	251	641	1,172	3,519	9,009	2,836	1,392	3	5	14	55	541	774
17,578	338	1,602	2,735	4,783	6,788	1,282	3,401	44	36	57	105	1,282	1,877
5,898	30	265	460	889	2,811	1,443	907	2	10	18	30	236	611
6,060	101	747	850	1,403	2,067	892	2,095	12	40	186	197	659	1,051
14,172	209	620	1,101	2,821	6,407	3.014	2,709	35	55	68	104	946	1.501
13,582	198	1,888	1,622	2,919	5,988	1,472	4,040	59	61	187	152	1,304	2,327

TABLE IX.

Infirmities.

NOTE 1.—This Table is divided into two parts. Part I shows the distribution of the persons afflicted by age, and Part II the distribution by Districts

NOTE 2.—No person suffering from more than one infirmity has been returned in this State.

TABLE IX.—Infirmities. *Part I.—Distribution by Age.*

Age.		POPULATION AFFLICTED.			INSANE.			DEAF-MUTES.			BLIND.			LEPERS.		
		Persons.	Males.	Females.	P.	M.	F.	P.	M.	F.	P.	M.	F.	P.	M.	F.
1		2	3	4	5	6	7	8	9	10	11	12	13	14	15	16
Total	...	8,593	3,728	4,865	453	292	161	1,306	739	567	6,409	2,425	3,984	425	272	153
	0—1	17	8	9	...	...	...	...	...	...	17	8	9	...	...	...
	1—2	18	10	8	...	...	...	2	1	1	16	9	7	...	...	...
	2—3	19	11	8	...	...	...	3	1	2	16	10	6	...	...	...
	3—4	36	21	15	...	...	...	6	3	3	30	18	12	...	...	...
	4—5	59	31	28	3	2	1	16	9	7	39	20	19	1	...	1
Total	0—5	149	81	68	3	2	1	27	14	13	118	65	53	1	...	1
	5—10	248	133	115	22	14	8	80	47	33	138	69	69	8	3	5
	10—15	251	147	104	26	18	8	81	52	29	136	71	65	8	6	2
	15—20	283	152	131	36	22	14	76	47	29	153	70	83	18	13	5
	20—25	303	156	147	41	28	13	82	50	32	163	64	99	17	14	3
	25—30	360	166	194	36	23	13	91	50	41	210	78	132	23	15	8
	30—35	441	196	245	31	21	10	94	51	43	285	104	181	31	20	11
	35—40	545	247	298	40	26	14	98	59	39	367	135	232	40	27	13
	40—45	590	253	337	44	28	16	92	57	35	413	141	272	41	27	14
	45—50	717	300	417	42	29	13	105	60	45	527	183	344	43	28	15
	50—55	793	340	453	29	19	10	102	59	43	615	232	383	47	30	17
	55—60	1,082	440	642	26	16	10	110	64	46	898	330	568	48	30	18
	60—65	1,120	443	677	31	20	11	107	53	54	935	343	592	47	27	20
	65—70	753	311	442	27	14	13	67	34	33	629	244	385	30	19	11
	70 & Over.	958	363	595	19	12	7	94	42	52	822	296	526	28	18	10

TABLE IX.—Infirmities. *Part II.—Distribution by Districts.*

District.		POPULATION AFFLICTED.			INSANE.			DEAF-MUTES.			BLIND.			LEPERS.		
		Persons.	Males.	Females.	P.	M.	F.	P.	M.	F.	P.	M.	F.	P.	M.	F.
1		2	3	4	5	6	7	8	9	10	11	12	13	14	15	16
Gwalior State.	...	8,593	3,728	4,865	453	292	161	1,306	739	567	6,409	2,425	3,984	425	272	153
Gird District	...	1,017	403	614	92	60	32	201	104	97	694	218	476	30	21	9
Bhind District	...	1,106	514	592	60	40	20	262	143	119	800	281	519	65	41	24
Tonwarghar District	...	778	372	406	31	19	12	149	89	60	558	240	318	41	24	17
Sheopur District	...	414	188	226	17	12	5	80	50	30	310	122	188	7	4	3
Narwar District	...	1,057	422	635	48	26	22	129	62	67	885	342	543	25	22	3
Isagarh District	...	903	306	597	38	24	14	[illegible]	58	81	835	294	541	31	20	11
Bhilsa District	...	419	[illegible]	229	[illegible]	12	6	83	45	38	307	125	182	10	7	3
[illegible] District	...	[illegible]	282	501	40	23	17	85	46	39	675	257	418	63	56	27
[illegible] District	...	557	245	312	40	23	17	82	49	33	382	142	240	53	31	22
[illegible] District	...	[illegible]	[illegible]	[illegible]	45	34	11	103	64	39	751	317	434	57	33	24
[illegible] District	...	284	129	155	15	10	5	44	29	15	212	87	125	23	13	10

TABLE X.

Occupation or Means of Livelihood.

NOTE 1.—This Table is divided into two Parts. Part I shows the statistics for the State as a whole and for each District and Part II shows figures for the cities of Lashkar and Ujjain.

NOTE 2.—Groups and Orders against which there were no entries have not been shown.

TABLE X.—Occupation or Means of

Group No.	Occupation.	GWALIOR STATE. Total earners ... 1,535,701; Total working dependents ... 201,152; Total non-working dependents... 1,786,217; Total population ... 3,523,070 — Total following occupation.	As principal occupation. Males.	As principal occupation. Females.	As working dependents. Males.	As working dependents. Females.	As subsidiary to other occupation. Males.	As subsidiary to other occupation. Females.
1	2	3	4	5	6	7	8	9
	Total ...	**1,921,997**	**1,209,935**	**325,766**	**69,463**	**131,689**	**156,452**	**28,692**
	A. Production of raw materials	*1,369,105*	*876,117*	*229,759*	*51,635*	*106,492*	*91,338*	*13,761*
	I. Exploitation of animals and vegetation ...	*1,366,004*	*874,530*	*229,122*	*51,495*	*106,377*	*90,779*	*13,701*
	1. Pasture and Agriculture	**1,365,306**	**874,105**	**229,070**	**51,484**	**106,343**	**90,627**	**13,677**
	(a) Cultivation	*1,305,498*	*839,674*	*223,663*	*42,864*	*104,649*	*82,412*	*12,226*
1	Non-cultivating proprietors taking rent in money or kind.	54,092	39,699	4,085	975	993	7,691	844
2	Estate agents and managers of owners ...	218	24	2	...	...	192	...
4	Rent collectors, clerks, etc.	11	10	1	...	...	...	...
5	Cultivating owners	187,058	146,091	20,078	2,839	2,430	14,398	1,217
6	Tenant cultivators	772,886	556,415	118,229	18,485	33,205	41,160	4,892
7	Agricultural labourers	291,778	98,485	80,668	20,615	68,016	18,771	5,273
	(b) Cultivation of special crops, fruit, etc., (Planters, managers, clerks and labourers).	*1,515*	*1,018*	*91*	*28*	*21*	*200*	*154*
16	Market gardeners, flower and fruit growers ...	1,515	1,018	91	28	24	200	154
	(c) Forestry	*4,098*	*1,614*	*1,406*	*139*	*352*	*404*	*153*
17	Forest of officers, rangers, guards, etc. ...	115	102	...	1	...	12	...
18	Wood cutters and charcoal burners ...	796	254	360	8	41	113	20
19	Collectors of forest produce	3,181	1,282	1,046	130	311	279	133
20	Collectors of lac	6	6	...	...	...	...	...
	(d) Stock raising	*54,196*	*3,1761*	*3,910*	*8,453*	*1,318*	*7,611*	*1,143*
21	Cattle and buffalo breeders and keepers ...	9,146	5,686	459	1,226	250	1,462	43
22	Breeders of transport animals	1	1	...	...	...	...	...
23	Herdsmen, shepherds and breeders of other animals.	45,049	26,074	3,451	7,227	1,068	6,129	1,100
	(e) Raising of small animals and insects ...	*9*	*8*	...	...	...	...	*1*
24	Birds, bees, etc.	9	8	...	...	...	...	1
	2. Fishing and Hunting	698	425	52	11	34	152	24
27	Fishing and pearling	636	390	45	11	34	139	17
28	Hunting	62	35	7	...	...	13	7
	II. Exploitation of minerals	*3,101*	*1,587*	*637*	*140*	*115*	*559*	*63*
	4. Non-Metallic Minerals	3,101	1,587	637	140	115	559	63
37	Building materials (including stone, materials for cement manufacture and clays).	2,785	1,363	599	111	114	548	60
33	Mica	5	...	5	...	...	...	...
40	Salt, saltpetre and other saline substances ...	196	129	43	9	1	11	3
41	Other non-metallic minerals	115	95	...	20	...	...	...

Livelihood. *Part I.—District Details.*

GIRD.							BHIND.						
Total earners ... 169,979							Total earners ... [illegible],022						
Total working dependents ... 16,515							Total working dependents ... 9,217						
Total non-working dependents ... 178,382							Total non-working dependents ... 223,985						
Total population ... 364,876							Total population ... 418,224						
Total following occupation.	As principal occupation.		As working dependents.		As subsidiary to other occupation.		Total following occupation.	As principal occupation.		As working dependents.		As subsidiary to other occupation.	
	M.	F.	M.	F.	M.	F.		M.	F.	M.	F.	M.	F.
10	11	12	13	14	15	16	17	18	19	20	21	22	23
201 275	136 897	33.012	6.793	9,723	15,176	2,675	227,505	148,440	36,552	4,264	4,953	27,769	5,506
107,839	68,455	19,410	3,679	6,675	8,503	1,105	178,322	121,727	29,398	3,155	2,805	18,139	3,098
106,764	67,661	19,270	3,563	6,573	8,217	1,078	178,243	121,673	29,382	3,155	2,804	18,133	3,096
106,508	67,822	19,258	3,565	6,573	8,213	1,077	178 212	121,647	29,380	3,155	2 803	18,131	3,096
103,474	64,338	18,675	2,933	6,300	7,222	1,016	174,376	120,034	29,042	2,692	2,737	17,153	2,715
3,242	2 276	345	49	91	604	7	11 892	8,851	928	157	214	1,427	810
...	...	...	...	...	...	...	2	...	...	...	...	2	...
...	...	...	...	...	...	...	...	...	...	...	...	...	...
9,777	6,115	2 164	103	104	1 226	46	28,751	22,265	2,778	181	...	3,299	258
63,180	50 659	11,233	1,126	1,841	3,754	542	120,606	84,159	22,309	1,910	1,450	10,027	1,011
18,216	5,288	4,591	1 640	4 032	1,721	421	12,875	4,739	3,032	497	1,078	2,398	1'136
219	176	43	17	2	1	...	197	...	7	...	...	44	146
219	156	43	17	2	1	...	197	...	7	...	...	44	146
138	128	...	8	...	21	1	19	4	...	...	...	15	...
56	55	...	1	...	...	...	...	...	...	...	...	...	...
18	...	...	...	...	17	1	...	...	...	...	...	...	...
84	73	...	7	...	4	...	19	4	...	...	...	15	...
...	...	...	...	...	...	...	...	...	...	...	...	...	...
3,651	3,195	540	617	271	969	59	3,620	1,609	331	460	66	919	235
1,328	439	...	78	...	607	4	172	135	2	13	5	6	31
...	...	...	...	...	...	...	...	...	...	...	...	...	...
4,323	2,856	540	539	271	962	55	3,484	1,474	329	447	61	913	224
6	5	...	...	...	...	1	...	...	...	...	...	...	...
6	5	...	...	...	...	1	...	...	...	...	...	...	...
56	39	12	...	...	4	1	31	26	2	...	1	2	...
45	30	12	...	...	2	1	28	25	2	...	1	...	...
11	9	...	...	...	2	...	8	1	...	...	...	2	...
1,275	594	140	114	112	288	27	79	54	16	...	1	6	2
1,275	594	140	114	112	288	27	79	54	16	...	1	6	2
1,211	511	140	105	112	286	27	26	22	4	...	...	...	...
...	...	...	...	...	...	...	...	...	...	...	...	...	...
64	58	...	9	...	2	...	58	32	12	...	1	6	2
...	...	...	...	...	...	...	...	...	...	...	...	...	...

TABLE X.—Occupation or Means of

Group No.	Occupation	TONWARGHAR. Total following occupation	As principal occupation. Males.	As principal occupation. Females.	As working dependents. Males.	As working dependents. Females.	As subsidiary to other occupation. Males.	As subsidiary to other occupation. Females.
		Total earners ... 176,579; Total working dependents ... 19,923; Total non-working dependents ... 173,146; Total population ... 369,648						
1	2	24	25	26	27	28	29	30
	Total ...	223,924	143,969	32,610	7,572	12,351	22,924	4,498
	A. Production of raw materials	*180,639*	*122,296*	*26,747*	*6,338*	*10,037*	*13,086*	*2,135*
	I. Exploitation of animals and vegetation ...	*179,348*	*121,547*	*26,304*	*6,318*	*10,035*	*13,010*	*2,134*
	1. Pasture and Agriculture	179,330	121,545	26,304	6,318	10,035	13,001	2,127
	(a) Cultivation	*175,682*	*120,134*	*26,262*	*5,172*	*10,029*	*12,041*	*2,044*
1	Non cultivating proprietors taking rent in money or kind.	7,651	5,655	406	106	38	1,342	109
2	Estate agents and managers of owners ...	...	...	...	...	...	...	...
4	Rent collectors, clerks, etc.	...	...	...	...	...	...	...
5	Cultivating owners	24,839	19,727	2,861	388	151	1,607	155
6	Tenant cultivators	128,851	92,487	20,176	2,970	4,443	7,750	1,026
7	Agricultural labourers	14,341	2,265	2,819	1,758	5,403	1,342	754
	(b) Cultivation of special crops, fruit, etc. (Planters, managers, clerks and labourers).	*94*	...	...	...	...	*94*	...
10	Market gardeners, flower and fruit growers ...	94	...	...	...	...	94	...
	(c) Forestry	*15*	*13*	...	...	...	*2*	...
17	Forest officers, rangers, guards, etc. ...	15	13	...	...	...	2	...
18	Wood-cutters and charcoal burners	...	...	...	...	...	...	...
19	Collectors of forest produce	...	...	...	...	...	...	...
20	Collectors of lac	...	...	...	...	...	...	...
	(d) Stock raising	*3,539*	*1,398*	*42*	*1,146*	*6*	*861*	*83*
21	Cattle and buffalo breeders and keepers ...	520	104	16	38	2	346	14
22	Breeders of transport animals	1	1	...	...	...	...	...
23	Herdsmen, shepherds, goatherds and breeders of other animals.	3,018	1,293	26	1,108	4	518	69
	(e) Raising of small animals and insects ...	...	...	...	...	...	...	...
24	[illegible]	...	...	...	...	...	...	...
	2. Fishing and Hunting	18	2	...	...	...	9	7
[illegible]	[illegible]	5	1	...	...	...	4	...
[illegible]	[illegible]	13	1	...	...	...	5	7
	[illegible]	*1,2?1*	*719*	*443*	*2?*	*2*	*76*	*1*
	4. [illegible] minerals	1,2?1	719	443	20	2	76	1
[illegible]	[illegible]	1,0?2	610	407	...	2	73	...
[illegible]	[illegible]	[illegible]	...	5	...	...	...	...
[illegible]	[illegible]	[illegible]	41	31	...	...	3	1
[illegible]	[illegible] ...	[illegible]	[illegible]	...	20	...	...	...

Livelihood. *Part I.—District Details.—(contd.)*

SHEOPUR.							NARWAR.						
Total earners ... 81,609							Total earners ... 173,635						
Total working dependents ... 12,584							Total working dependents ... 29,087						
Total non-working dependents ... 62,841							Total non-working dependents ... 198,864						
Total population ... 137,034							Total population ... 401,586						
Total following occupation.	As principal occupation.		As working dependents.		As subsidiary to other occupation.		Total following occupation.	As principal occupation.		As working dependents.		As subsidiary to other occupation.	
	M.	F.	M.	F.	M.	F.		M.	F.	M.	F.	M.	F.
31	32	33	34	35	36	37	38	39	40	41	42	43	44
81,045	48,566	13,043	4,177	8,407	5,871	981	228,754	141,060	32,575	7,851	21,233	23,404	2,628
57,121	*34,672*	*8,692*	*3,233*	*6,758*	*3,193*	*523*	*170,633*	*107,840*	*21,088*	*6,234*	*17,825*	*16,051*	*1,595*
57,059	*34,607*	*8,692*	*3,283*	*6,758*	*3,196*	*523*	*170,568*	*107,818*	*21,088*	*6,234*	*17,825*	*16,040*	*1,563*
57,058	34,606	8,692	3,283	6,758	3,196	523	170,443	107,739	21,088	6,233	17,825	15,995	1,563
51,250	*31,342*	*7,711*	*2,673*	*6,335*	*2,541*	*448*	*161,292*	*102,449*	*20,141*	*5,342*	*17,636*	*14,326*	*1,398*
1,310	1,076	94	19	1	111	16	7,863	4,318	296	155	70	2,721	303
...	...	...	...	...	...	...	1	1	...	...	...	...	...
...	...	...	...	...	...	...	...	...	...	...	...	...	...
5,892	4,597	303	90	9	288	15	24,183	18,747	1,088	450	404	3,317	182
29,585	21,456	8,701	871	1,828	1,450	279	93,683	69,746	10,784	2,128	5,416	5,170	444
14,644	4,213	3,413	1,093	4,097	692	136	35,557	9,637	7,973	2,614	11,746	3,118	469
13	*13*	...	...	...	...	...	*2*	*2*	...	...	...	...	...
13	13	...	...	...	...	...	2	2	...	...	...	...	...
1,790	*706*	*680*	*61*	*167*	*145*	*31*	*802*	*292*	*362*	*24*	*56*	*53*	*15*
15	15	...	...	...	...	...	24	14	...	...	...	10	...
373	...	331	...	41	...	...	61	53	...	8	...	...	...
1,396	685	318	61	126	145	31	717	225	362	16	56	43	15
6	6	...	...	...	...	...	...	...	...	...	...	...	...
4,005	*2,513*	*301*	*549*	*56*	*510*	*44*	*8,344*	*4,993*	*585*	*861*	*133*	*1,616*	*150*
590	350	...	133	...	116	11	159	66	33	7	24	40	...
...	...	...	...	...	...	...	...	...	...	...	...	...	...
3,415	2,215	301	416	56	394	33	8,185	4,927	563	860	109	1,576	150
...	...	...	...	...	...	...	*3*	*3*	...	...	...	...	...
...	...	...	...	...	...	...	3	3	...	...	...	...	...
1	1	...	...	...	...	...	125	79	...	1	...	45	...
1	1	...	...	...	...	...	125	79	...	1	...	45	...
...	...	...	...	...	...	...	...	...	...	...	...	...	...
65	*65*	...	...	...	...	...	*65*	*22*	...	...	...	*11*	*32*
65	65	...	...	...	...	...	65	22	...	...	...	11	32
65	65	...	...	...	...	...	65	22	...	...	...	11	32
...	...	...	...	...	...	...	...	...	...	...	...	...	...
...	...	...	...	...	...	...	...	...	...	...	...	...	...
...	...	...	...	...	...	...	...	...	...	...	...	...	...

TABLE X.—Occupation or Means of

ISAGARH.

Total earners	...	...	...	190,923
Total working dependents	...	...	...	17,319
Total non working dependents	...	...	...	213,069
Total population	...	...	...	421,311

Group No.	Occupation.	Total following occupation.	As principal occupation. Males.	As principal occupation. Females.	As working dependents. Males.	As working dependents. Females.	As subsidiary to other occupation. Males.	As subsidiary to other occupation. Females.
1	2	45	46	47	48	49	50	51
	Total ...	**230,073**	**152,189**	**38,734**	**7,049**	**10,270**	**18,214**	**3,617**
	A. Production of raw materials	*162,322*	*111,402*	*25,184*	*4,867*	*7,260*	*11,954*	*1,655*
	I. Exploitation of animals and vegetation ...	*162,322*	*111,402*	*25,184*	*4,867*	*7,260*	*11,954*	*1,6[illegible]*
	1. Pasture and Agriculture	**162,202**	**111,332**	**25,176**	**4,862**	**7,260**	**11,920**	**1,652**
	(a) Cultivation	*155,157*	*106,533*	*24,[illegible]*	*4,403*	*7,185*	*10,898*	*1,517*
1	Non-cultivating proprietors taking rent in money or kind.	4,800	6,412	210	58	48	519	58
2	Estate agents and managers of owners ...	...	...	...	...	...	...	...
4	Rent collectors, clerks, etc.	...	...	...	...	...	...	...
5	Cultivating owners	12,904	10,562	946	876	811	780	69
6	Tenant cultivators	102,921	80,097	12,040	2,122	2,597	5,884	781
7	Agricultural labourers	34,942	12,462	11,425	1,847	4,229	4,815	664
	(b) Cultivation of special crops, fruit, etc. (Planters, managers, clerks and labourers).	*220*	*211*	*6*	...	*1*	*2*	...
16	Market gardeners, flower and fruit growers ...	220	211	6	...	1	2	...
	(c) Forestry	*529*	*285*	*107*	*31*	*53*	*73*	*80*
17	Forest officers, rangers, guards, etc.	8	8	...	...	...	...	...
18	Wood cutters and charcoal burners	260	190	28	...	...	33	...
19	Collectors of forest produce	366	88	79	81	58	40	80
20	Collectors of lac	...	...	...	...	...	...	...
	(d) Stock raising	*6,196*	*4,303*	*442*	*428*	*21*	*947*	*55*
21	Cattle and buffalo breeders and keepers ...	640	517	6	37	...	80	...
22	Breeders of transport animals	...	...	...	...	...	...	...
23	Herdsmen, shepherds and breeders of other animals.	5,556	3,786	436	391	21	867	55
	(e) Raising of small animals & insects...	...	...	...	...	...	...	...
24	Birds, bees, etc.	...	...	...	...	...	...	...
	2. Fishing and Hunting	120	70	8	5	...	34	3
27	Fishing and pearling	105	58	5	5	...	34	3
28	Hunting	15	12	3	...	...	...	...
	II. Exploitation of minerals	...	...	...	...	...	...	...
	4. Non-Metallic Minerals	...	...	...	...	...	...	...
37	Building materials (including stone, materials for cement manufacture and clays).	...	...	...	...	...	...	...
38	Mica	...	...	...	...	...	...	...
40	Salt, saltpetre and other saline substances ...	...	...	...	...	...	...	...
41	Other non-metallic minerals	...	...	...	...	...	...	...

Livelihood, *Part I—District Details.—(contd.)*

BHILSA.							UJJAIN						
Total earners ... 102,524 Total working dependents ... 10,002 Total non-working dependents... 122,762 Total population ... 235,288							Total earners ... 169,780 Total working dependents ... 18,308 Total non-working dependents ... 217,873 Total population ... 405,961						
Total following occupation.	As principal occupation.		As working dependents.		As subsidiary to other occupation.		Total following occupation.	As principal occupation.		As working dependents.		As subsidiary to other occupation.	
	M.	F.	M.	F.	M.	F.		M.	F.	M.	F.	M.	F.
52	53	54	55	56	57	58	59	60	61	62	63	64	65
122,592	81,862	20,662	4,633	5,369	8,679	1,387	199,880	122,429	47,351	7,117	11,191	9,068	2,724
85,507	*58,861*	*14,051*	*3,577*	*3,740*	*4,705*	*567*	*131,763*	*81,305*	*32,693*	*4,493*	*9,120*	*3,357*	*800*
85,460	*58,855*	*14,041*	*3,577*	*3,740*	*4,680*	*567*	*131,727*	*81,261*	*32,693*	*4,493*	*9,120*	*3,357*	*800*
85,384	58,812	14,040	3,574	3,740	4,652	566	131,655	81,241	32,689	4,492	9,095	3,338	800
80,692	*55,436*	*13,923*	*2,637*	*3,708*	*4,389*	*549*	*121,121*	*76,768*	*31,601*	*3,555*	*8,850*	*2,832*	*518*
2,555	2,159	121	31	21	218	10	5,604	4,096	1,090	68	206	129	15
28	6	1	...	...	21	...	...	...	...	...	...	...	...
4	3	1	...	...	...	...	...	...	...	...	...	...	...
10,921	9,395	645	197	88	535	81	20,080	18,586	4,928	382	771	488	25
33,841	29,105	6,283	750	593	2,005	155	57,848	43,397	9,579	1,521	1,929	1,229	198
28,313	14,768	6,922	1,709	3,006	1,585	353	40,592	15,789	16,004	1,694	5,944	986	285
133	*92*	*2*	*3*	...	*28*	*8*	*576*	*505*	*14*	*5*	*21*	*31*	...
133	92	2	3	...	28	8	576	505	14	5	21	31	...
93	*13*	*41*	...	*1*	*31*	*7*	*138*	*4*	*115*	...	*18*	*1*	...
1	1	...	...	...	...	...	...	...	...	...	...	...	...
...	...	...	...	...	...	...	...	...	...	...	...	...	...
92	12	41	...	1	31	7	138	4	115	...	18	1	...
...	...	...	...	...	...	...	...	...	...	...	...	...	...
4,466	*3,271*	*74*	*884*	*31*	*201*	*2*	*6,817*	*3,961*	*959*	*932*	*206*	*474*	*282*
3,915	3,081	1	825	...	7	1	556	400	74	2	12	68	...
...	...	...	...	...	...	...	...	...	...	...	...	...	...
551	*190*	*73*	*59*	*31*	*197*	*1*	*6,261*	*3,564*	*885*	*930*	*194*	*406*	*282*
...	...	...	...	...	...	...	...	...	...	...	...	...	...
...	...	...	...	...	...	...	...	...	...	...	...	...	...
76	43	1	3	...	28	1	72	23	4	1	25	19	...
63	31	1	3	...	27	1	72	23	4	1	25	19	...
13	12	...	...	...	1	...	...	...	...	...	...	...	...
47	*9*	*13*	...	...	*25*	...	*41*	*41*	...	...	...	...	...
47	9	13	...	...	25	...	41	41	...	...	...	...	...
47	9	13	...	...	25	...	41	41	...	...	...	...	...
...	...	...	...	...	...	...	...	...	...	...	...	...	...
...	...	...	...	...	...	...	...	...	...	...	...	...	...
...	...	...	...	...	...	...	...	...	...	...	...	...	...

TABLE X.—Occupation or Means of

Group No.	Occupation.	MANDSAUR. Total earners ... 103,937; Total working dependents ... 26,456; Total non-working dependents ... 141,773; Total population ... 272,166						
		Total following occupation.	As principal occupation.		As working dependents.		As subsidiary to other occupation.	
			Males.	Females.	Males.	Famales.	Males.	Females.
1	2	66	67	68	69	70	71	72
	Total ...	146,556	74,419	29,518	7,492	18,964	13,895	2,263
	A. Production of raw materials	*93,920*	*44,675*	*20,040*	*5,157*	*15,436*	*7,679*	*933*
	I. Exploitation of animals and vegetation ...	*93,835*	*44,622*	*20,015*	*5,151*	*15,436*	*7,679*	*932*
	1. Pasture and Agriculture	93,828	44,619	20,011	5,151	15,436	7,679	932
	(*a*) *Cultivation*	*89,277*	*41,918*	*19,633*	*4,609*	*15,271*	*6,968*	*878*
1	Non-cultivating proprietors taking rent in money or kind.	7,070	5,109	680	286	241	743	11
2	Estate agents and managers of owners ...	6	6	...	...	...	...	...
4	Rent collectors, clerks, etc.	7	7	...	...	...	...	...
5	Cultivating owners	15,246	10 958	1,860	171	256	1,864	142
6	Tenant cultivators	38,758	20,141	9,075	2,478	3,515	2,694	255
7	Agricultural labourers	28,190	5,702	7,418	1,674	11,259	1,067	470
	(*b*) *Cultivation of special crops, fruit, etc. (Planters, managers, clerks and labourers).*	*9*	*7*	...	*2*	...	...	...
16	Market gardeners, flower and fruit growers ...	9	7	...	2	...	...	...
	(*c*) *Forestry*	*319*	*198*	*85*	*14*	*6*	...	*16*
17	Forest officers, rangers, guards, etc.... ...	1	1	...	...	...	...	...
18	Wood cutt rs and charcoal burners	18	2	...	...	...	...	16
19	Collectors of forest produce	300	195	85	14	6	...	...
20	Collectors of lac	...	...	...	...	...	...	...
	(*d*) *Stock raising*	*4,223*	*2,496*	*293*	*526*	*159*	*711*	*38*
21	Cattle and buffalo breeders and keepers ...	577	5	282	...	152	189	...
22	Breeders of transport animals	...	...	...	...	...	...	...
23	Herdsmen, shepherds and breeders of other animals.	3,646	2,491	61	526	7	523	38
	(*e*) *Raising of small animals and insects* ...	...	...	...	...	...	...	...
24	Birds, bees, etc.	...	...	...	...	...	...	...
	2. Fishing and Hunting	7	3	4	...	...	...	...
25	Fishing and pearling	3	3	...	...	...	...	...
26	Hunting	4	...	4	...	...	...	...
	II. Exploitation of minerals	*83*	*53*	*27*		...	...	*7*
	4. Non-Metallic Minerals	83	53	23	6	...	...	1
[illegible]	[illegible] materials (including stones and clays).	83	53	25	6	...	...	1
[illegible]	[illegible]	...	...	...	...	...	...	...
[illegible]	[illegible] ...	...	...	...	...	...	...	...
[illegible]	[illegible]	...	...	...	...	...	...	...

Livelihood. *Part I.—District Details.—(contd.)*

SHAJAPUR.							AMJHERA.						
Total earners ... ... 143,813 Total working dependents ... ... 18,916 Total non-working dependents ... ... 174,251 Total population 336,980							Total earners ... ... 57,970 Total working dependents ... ... 22,825 Total non-working dependents ... ... 79,271 Total population 160,066						
Total following occupation.	As principal occupation.		As working dependents.		As subsidiary to other occupation.		Total following occupation.	As principal occupation.		As working dependents.		As subsidiary to other occupation.	
	M.	F.	M.	F.	M.	F.		M.	F.	M.	F.	M.	F.
73	74	75	76	77	78	79	80	81	82	83	84	85	86
172,948	112,126	31,687	6,509	12,407	8,423	1,796	84,445	47,978	9,992	6,006	16,819	3,038	612
131,180	*86,256*	*24,299*	*5,558*	*10,982*	*3,080*	*1,005*	*69,851*	*38,625*	*8,154*	*5,294*	*15,844*	*1,526*	*348*
131,027	*86,256*	*24,299*	*5,538*	*10,982*	*2,927*	*1,003*	*69,851*	*38,625*	*8,154*	*5,294*	*15,844*	*1,526*	*348*
130,945	86,211	24,288	5,558	10,977	2,918	993	69,741	38,531	8,144	5,293	15,841	1,584	348
125,431	*82,819*	*23,984*	*4,337*	*10,792*	*2,629*	*870*	*67,733*	*37,903*	*8,070*	*4,468*	*15,606*	*1,413*	*273*
2,300	1,527	467	43	142	113	8	306	220	13	3	1	69	...
148	...	...	...	...	148	...	33	11	1	...	...	21	...
...	...	...	...	...	...	...	...	...	...	...	...	...	...
24,370	21,116	1,826	355	283	547	243	10,365	9,058	477	291	51	457	51
54,848	42,901	8,144	928	1,516	1,147	207	36,931	22,267	4,355	1,636	8,078	596	49
43,770	17,275	13,547	3,011	8,851	674	412	20,028	6,847	3,224	2,538	7,476	270	172
52	*32*	*19*	*1*	...	...	...	...	...	...	...	...	...	...
52	32	19	1	...	...	...	...	...	...	...	...	...	...
92	*1*	*16*	*1*	*51*	*23*	...	*43*	...	...	...	...	*40*	*3*
...	...	...	...	...	...	...	...	...	...	...	...	...	...
23	...	...	...	...	23	...	43	...	...	...	...	40	3
69	1	16	1	51	...	...	...	...	...	...	...	...	...
...	...	...	...	...	...	...	...	...	...	...	...	...	...
5,370	*3,359*	*269*	*1,219*	*134*	*266*	*123*	*1,965*	*623*	*74*	*825*	*235*	*131*	*72*
549	345	77	83	18	24	2	140	64	29	10	37	...	...
...	...	...	...	...	...	...	...	...	...	...	...	...	...
4,821	3,014	192	1,136	116	242	121	1,825	504	45	815	198	131	72
...	...	...	...	...	...	...	...	...	...	...	...	...	...
...	...	...	...	...	...	...	...	...	...	...	...	...	...
82	45	11	...	5	9	12	110	94	10	1	3	2	...
81	45	11	...	5	8	12	108	94	10	1	3	...	...
1	...	...	...	...	1	...	2	...	...	...	...	2	...
153	...	...	...	...	*153*	...	...	...	...	...	...	...	...
153	...	...	...	...	153	...	...	...	...	...	...	...	...
153	...	...	...	...	153	...	...	...	...	...	...	...	...
...	...	...	...	...	...	...	...	...	...	...	...	...	...
...	...	...	...	...	...	...	...	...	...	...	...	...	...
...	...	...	...	...	...	...	...	...	...	...	...	...	...

TABLE X.—Occupation or Means of

Groupe. No.	Occupation.	GWALIOR STATE,						
		Total following occup-tion.	As principal occupation.		As working dependents.		As subsidiary to other occupation.	
			Males.	Females.	Males.	Females.	Males.	Females.
1	2	3	4	5	6	7	8	9
	B. Preparation & supply of material substances.	*238,818*	*183,576*	*42,108*	*8,001*	*11,981*	*35,987*	*7,163*
	III. Industry	*126,830*	*122,071*	*23,017*	*5,033*	*8,390*	*19,581*	*3,738*
	5. Textiles	39,635	28,324	4,957	899	1,834	2,932	698
42	Cotton ginning, cleaning and pressing ...	3,078	2,066	440	86	117	289	80
43	Cotton spinning, sizing and weaving ...	31,510	22,994	3,787	711	1,305	2,164	549
45	Rope, twine, string and other fibres ...	120	43	40	...	19	17	1
46	Wool carding, spinning and weaving. ...	784	383	114	8	38	241	...
49	Dyeing, bleaching, printing, preparation and sponging of textiles.	3,978	2,774	545	64	351	173	51
50	Lace, crepe, embroideries, fringes, etc., and insufficiently described textile industries.	165	64	31	1	4	48	17
	6. Hides, Skins and Hard Materials from the Animal Kingdom.	9,620	5,552	1,764	224	483	1,463	134
51	Working in leather	9,616	5,550	1,764	223	483	1,462	134
53	Bone, ivory, horn, shell, etc., workers (except buttons).	4	2	...	1	...	1	...
	7. Wood.	19,284	12,033	2,933	515	886	2,451	466
54	Sawyers	3	3	...	...	...	...	...
55	Carpenters, turners and joiners, etc. ...	11,266	8,604	352	334	81	1,738	157
56	Basket makers and other industries of woody materials, including leaves and thatchers and builders working with bamboo, reeds or similar materials.	8,015	3 426	2,591	181	805	713	309
	8. Metals	8,187	5,252	733	221	329	1,562	87
58	Makers of arms, guns, etc.	71	41	...	3	...	27	...
59	Blacksmiths, other workers in iron, makers of implements.	6,154	4,094	603	168	306	963	20
60	Workers in brass, copper and bell metal ...	1,616	778	129	47	28	572	67
61	Workers in other metals (except precious metals).	346	339	4	3	...	...	...
	9. Ceramics	15,948	9,788	2,961	530	1,090	1,325	254
63	Potters and makers of earthenware	14,868	9,186	2,722	500	1,049	1,249	207
64	Brick and tile makers	517	294	113	11	22	75	2
65	Other workers in ceramics	568	358	126	19	19	1	45
	10. Chemical products Properly so called and analogous.	10,858	7,030	1,413	272	439	1,434	220
66	Manufacture of matches, fireworks and other explosives.	662	400	56	7	51	137	11
67	Manufacture of ærated and mineral waters and ice.	161	147	4	...	...	5	5
68	Manufacture and refining of vegetable oils ...	10,020	6,528	1,343	265	388	1,292	204
70	Others	15	5	10	...	...	...	...
	11. Food Industries...	7,350	2,996	2,628	86	693	329	6 8
71	Rice pounders and huskers and flour grinders ...	3,784	225	2,333	14	645	157	410
72	Grain parchers, etc.	848	361	172	14	31	79	191
73	Butchers	389	378	5	1	...	3	2
75	Sweetmeat and condiment makers	2,080	1,874	77	45	9	75	...
76	Toddy drawers	2	2	...	...	...	...	...
78	Manufacturers of tobacco	106	27	41	...	8	15	15
81	Others	141	129	...	12	...	...	...

Livelihood. *Part I—District Details.—(contd.)*

GIRD.							BHIND.						
Total following occupation.	As principal occupation.		As working dependents.		As subsidiary to other occupation.		Total following occupation.	As principal occupation.		As working dependents.		As subsidiary to other occupation.	
	M.	F.	M.	F.	M.	F.		M.	F.	M.	F	M.	F.
10	11	12	13	14	15	16	17	18	19	20	21	22	23
49,090	*35,703*	*6,370*	*1,043*	*1,480*	*3,831*	*663*	*31,826*	*18,192*	*5,287*	*842*	*1,640*	*4,797*	*1,068*
34,355	*26,283*	*4,184*	*707*	*919*	*1,988*	*274*	*21,495*	*12,491*	*4,095*	*584*	*1,213*	*2,470*	*642*
15,732	13,729	873	157	195	695	103	3,943	2,230	713	93	315	394	198
663	483	157	24	39	10	...	476	329	48	22	5	52	25
14,591	12,927	678	115	145	629	102	3,101	1,647	605	70	286	328	165
36	33	...	...	...	3	...	...	...	...	...	...	...	...
4	4	...	...	...	...	...	32	18	14	...	...	...	...
433	320	32	18	11	52	...	320	225	51	1	24	14	5
25	12	11	...	...	1	1	14	11	...	...	...	...	3
1,254	695	211	46	48	248	6	1,501	1,120	139	12	112	118	...
1,254	695	211	46	48	248	6	1,501	1,120	139	12	112	118	...
...	...	...	...	...	...	...	...	...	...	...	...	...	...
2,023	1,174	459	66	87	214	23	1,936	1,310	218	70	28	286	24
...	...	...	...	...	...	...	...	...	...	...	...	...	...
1,166	854	95	17	17	176	7	1,282	968	10	60	5	171	18
857	320	364	49	70	38	16	704	342	208	10	28	115	6
784	579	57	31	16	101	...	862	329	148	32	25	267	61
2	2	...	...	...	...	...	8	...	...	...	...	8	...
592	438	57	80	16	51	...	105	...	78	...	13	14	5
172	121	...	1	...	50	...	628	203	75	32	12	250	55
18	18	...	...	...	...	...	126	126	...	...	...	...	...
1,806	989	485	45	118	156	13	1,604	1,154	285	56	78	29	2
1,679	944	412	42	112	156	13	1,498	1,062	285	46	78	25	2
50	45	1	3	1	...	...	32	29	...	...	...	3	...
77	...	72	...	5	...	...	74	63	...	10	...	1	...
1,531	1,411	11	29	48	3	29	2,407	1,135	573	66	160	398	75
79	70	...	3	...	1	5	275	178	17	...	6	68	6
37	37	...	...	...	...	...	...	...	...	...	...	...	...
1,412	1,301	11	26	48	2	24	2,182	957	556	66	154	380	69
3	3	...	...	...	...	...	...	...	...	...	...	...	...
1,472	1,031	279	33	57	21	51	1,445	440	586	9	237	56	117
401	37	264	4	52	3	51	848	29	498	...	213	2	111
107	67	15	6	4	15	...	388	156	93	5	24	54	6
120	120	...	...	...	...	...	68	68	...	...	...	...	...
699	686	...	11	...	2	...	191	187	...	4	...	...	...
...	...	...	...	...	...	...	...	...	...	...	...	...	...
18	11	...	...	1	1	...	...	...	...	...	...	...	...
133	120	...	12	...	...	...	...	...	...	...	...	...	...

TABLE X.—Occupation or Means of

Group No.	Occupation.	TONWARGHAR.						
		Total following occupation.	As principal occupation.		As working dependents.		As subsidiary to other occupation.	
			Males.	Females.	Males.	Females.	Males.	Females.
1	2	24	25	26	27	28	29	30
	B. Preparation and supply of material substances	*26,050*	*13,508*	*3,255*	*692*	*1,279*	*6,146*	*1,260*
	III. Industry	*16,890*	*8,382*	*2,426*	*400*	*895*	*3,996*	*791*
	5. Textiles	**3,484**	**1,485**	**538**	**129**	**276**	**851**	**185**
42	Cotton ginning, cleaning and pressing ...	337	168	16	8	2	129	14
43	Cotton spinning, sizing and weaving ...	2,712	1,108	464	111	257	629	148
45	Rope, twine, string and other fibres ...	2	...	1	...	...	1	...
46	Wool carding, spinning and weaving ...	8	...	...	...	...	8	...
49	Dyeing, bleaching, printing, preparation and sponging of textiles.	344	201	40	9	16	56	22
50	Lace, crepe, embroideries, fringes, etc., and insufficiently described textile industries.	61	13	17	1	1	28	1
	6. Hides, Skins and Hard Materials from the Animal Kingdom.	**481**	**214**	**27**	**3**	**21**	**189**	**27**
51	Working in leather	481	214	27	3	21	189	27
53	Bone, ivory, horn, shell, etc., workers (except buttons).	...	...	...	...	...	...	...
	7. Wood	**1,493**	**771**	**81**	**29**	**67**	**501**	**44**
54	Sawyers	...	...	...	...	...	...	...
55	Carpenters, turners and joiners, etc.... ...	1,047	674	15	12	8	336	2
56	Basket makers and other industries of woody materials, including leaves and thatchers and builders working with bamboo, reeds or similar materials.	446	97	66	17	59	165	42
	8. Metals	**370**	**209**	**31**	**6**	**10**	**110**	**4**
58	Makers of arms, guns, etc.	5	...	...	...	...	5	...
59	Blacksmiths, other workers in iron, makers of implements.	140	110	1	3	3	22	1
60	Workers in brass, copper and bell metal ...	214	89	30	2	7	88	3
61	Workers in other metals (except precious metals).	11	10	...	1	...	...	...
	9. Ceramics	**1,510**	**746**	**242**	**48**	**69**	**319**	**86**
63	Potters and makers of earthenware... ...	1,493	730	242	47	69	319	86
64	Brick and tile makers	7	7	...	...	...	...	...
65	Other workers in ceramics	10	9	...	1	...	...	...
	10. Chemical Products properly so-called and analogous.	**1,655**	**748**	**311**	**22**	**67**	**460**	**47**
66	Manufacture of matches, fireworks and other explosives.	58	30	12	1	3	12	...
67	Manufacture of aerated and mineral waters and ice.	...	...	...	...	...	...	...
68	Manufacture and refining of vegetable oils ...	1,597	718	299	21	64	448	47
70	Others	...	...	...	...	...	...	...
	11. Food Industries	**758**	**138**	**249**	**2**	**169**	**28**	**232**
71	Rice pounders and huskers and flour grinders ...	399	4	237	...	103	2	48
72	Grain parchers, etc.	220	22	9	1	1	3	181
73	Butchers	55	52	2	...	...	1	...
75	Sweetmeat and condiment makers	81	60	1	1	...	22	...
76	Toddy drawers	...	...	...	...	...	...	...
77	Manufacturers of tobacco	...	...	...	...	...	...	...
81	Others	...	...	...	...	...	...	...

Livelihood. *Part I.—District Details.—(contd.)*

SHEOPUR.							NARWAR.						
Total following occupation.	As principal occupation.		As working dependents.		As subsidiary to other occupation.		Total following occupation.	As principal occupation.		As working dependents.		As subsidiary to other occupation.	
	M.	F.	M.	F.	M.	F.		M.	F.	M.	F.	M.	F.
31	32	33	34	35	36	37	38	39	40	41	42	43	44
12,687	*7,752*	*1,803*	*553*	*818*	*1,523*	*238*	*32,247*	*18,888*	*5,911*	*828*	*1,461*	*4,599*	*560*
6,606	*4,385*	*887*	*199*	*437*	*570*	*123*	*20,719*	*12,913*	*3,273*	*607*	*1,081*	*2,694*	*151*
1,257	684	241	41	165	95	31	3,007	1,860	710	59	219	141	18
90	78	10	2	5	...	...	77	52	13	5	8	...	4
1,005	496	208	34	146	92	29	2,159	1,425	517	49	154	1	18
...	...	...	...	...	...	...	11	4	...	...	...	7	...
...	...	...	...	...	...	...	286	9	76	...	82	119	...
156	111	23	5	12	3	2	524	370	104	5	80	14	1
6	4	...	...	2	...	...	...	...	...	...	...	...	...
246	...	10	...	2	218	16	770	435	212	15	61	47	...
246	...	10	...	2	218	16	770	435	212	15	61	47	...
...	...	...	...	...	...	...	...	...	...	...	...	...	...
590	443	53	12	12	63	7	2,970	1,832	556	63	159	334	26
...	...	...	...	...	...	...	...	...	...	...	...	...	...
428	373	3	12	2	32	6	1,401	952	117	85	28	269	...
162	70	50	...	10	31	1	1,569	880	489	28	181	65	26
348	234	13	7	42	52	...	1,028	621	77	28	5	297	...
...	...	...	...	...	...	...	1	1	...	...	...	...	...
318	209	8	7	42	52	...	1,011	605	77	27	5	297	...
18	13	5	...	...	...	...	7	7	...	...	...	...	...
12	12	...	...	...	...	...	9	8	...	1	...	...	...
566	372	85	29	65	6	9	1,694	985	264	123	137	171	14
566	372	85	29	65	6	9	1,685	976	264	123	137	171	14
...	...	...	...	...	...	...	9	9	...	...	...	...	...
...	...	...	...	...	...	...	...	...	...	...	...	...	...
553	409	112	3	14	5	10	1,405	733	179	56	66	323	48
8	8	...	...	..	...	...	16	9	2	1	4	...	...
...	...	...	...	...	...	...	...	...	...	...	...	...	...
545	401	112	8	14	5	10	1,389	724	177	55	62	323	48
...	...	...	...	...	...	...	...	...	...	...	...	...	...
185	61	101	...	4	10	6	492	207	181	4	94	6	...
116	2	98	...	4	8	4	279	3	173	3	94	6	...
5	5	...	...	...	...	...	7	6	...	1	...	...	...
64	57	8	...	...	2	2	38	38	...	...	...	...	...
...	...	...	..	...	...	...	168	160	8	...	...	...	...
...	...	...	...	...	...	...	...	...	...	...	...	...	...
...	...	...	...	...	...	...	...	...	...	...	...	...	...
...	...	...	...	...	...	...	...	...	...	...	...	...	...

TABLE X.—Occupation or Means of

Group No.	Occupation.	ISAGARH.						
		Total following occupation.	As principal occupation.		As working dependents.		As subsidiary to other occupation.	
			Males.	Females.	Males.	Famales.	Males.	Females.
1	2	45	46	47	48	49	50	51
	B. Preparation and supply of material substances.	*31,434*	*21,065*	*4,791*	*1,081*	*1,011*	*2,748*	*705*
	III. Industry	*20,270*	*14,482*	*2,610*	*715*	*581*	*1,544*	*308*
	5. Textiles	2,410	1,670	424	82	59	149	17
42	Cotton ginning, cleaning and pressing ...	255	198	20	8	8	20	1
43	Cotton spinning, sizing and weaving ...	1,825	1,280	341	72	45	71	16
45	Rope, twine, string and other fibres... ...	13	1	12	...	...	...	...
46	Wool carding, spinning and weaving ...	98	86	16	1	5	40	...
49	Dyeing, bleaching, printing, preparation and sponging of textiles.	214	164	34	1	1	14	...
50	Lace, crepe, embroideries, fringes, etc., and insufficiently described textile industries.	5	...	1	...	...	4	...
	6. Hides, Skins and Hard Materials from the Animal Kingdom.	610	420	103	38	9	27	13
51	Working in leather	610	420	103	88	9	27	13
53	Bone, ivory, horn, shell, etc., workers (except buttons).	...	...	...	...	...	...	...
	7. Wood	2,188	1,534	278	46	96	217	17
54	Sawyers	...	...	...	...	...	...	...
55	Carpenters, turners and joiners, etc., ...	1,871	1,149	26	25	5	166	...
56	Basket makers and other industries of woody materials, including leaves and thatchers and builders working with bamboo, reeds or similar materials.	817	385	252	21	91	51	17
	8. Metals	728	621	28	34	6	38	1
58	Makers of arms, guns, etc.	...	...	...	...	...	...	...
59	Blacksmiths, other workers in iron, makers of implements.	678	574	25	34	6	38	1
60	Workers in brass, copper and bell metals ...	43	41	2	...	...	...	...
61	Workers in other metals (except precious metals).	7	6	1	...	...	...	...
	9. Ceramics	1,947	1,287	377	75	73	108	27
63	Potters and makers of earthenware	1,944	1,286	376	75	73	107	27
64	Brick and tile makers	2	1	...	...	...	1	...
65	Other workers in ceramics	1	...	1	...	...	...	...
	10. Chemical Products properly so-called and analogous.	1,134	1,074	1	45	1	9	4
66	Manufacture of matches, fireworks and other explosives.	15	10	1	...	1	8	...
67	Manufacture of aerated and mineral waters and ice.	40	40	...	...	...	...	...
68	Manufacture and refining of vegetable oils ...	1,079	1,024	...	45	...	6	4
70	Others	...	...	...	...	...	...	...
	11. Food Industries	377	124	185	6	37	2	23
71	Rice pounders and huskers and flour grinders ...	284	5	169	1	37	...	22
72	Grain parchers, etc.	36	31	8	...	...	1	1
73	Butchers	...	...	...	...	...	...	...
75	Sweetmeat and condiment makers	102	88	8	5	...	1	...
76	Toddy drawers...	...	...	...	...	...	...	...
78	Manufacturers of tobacco	5	...	5	...	...	...	...
81	Others	...	...	...	...	...	...	...

Livelihood. *Part I.—District Details.—(contd.)*

BHILSA.							UJJAIN						
Total following occupation.	As principal occupation.		As working dependents.		As subsidiary to other occupation.		Total following occupation.	As principal occupation.		As working dependents.		As subsidiary to other occupation.	
	M.	F.	M.	F.	M.	F.		M.	F.	M.	F.	M.	F.
52	53	54	55	56	57	58	59	60	61	62	63	64	65
17,160	*10,800*	*2,610*	*351*	*748*	*2,171*	*480*	*33,379*	*22,100*	*5,000*	*1,200*	*687*	*3,306*	*1,086*
11,389	*7,740*	*1,761*	*251*	*496*	*990*	*151*	*21,143*	*14,294*	*3,511*	*734*	*492*	*1,402*	*710*
923	657	92	19	26	124	5	4,936	3,815	566	233	92	167	63
293	208	22	...	4	59	...	418	245	122	8	43	...	...
428	206	53	14	19	31	5	3,877	2,971	436	216	40	167	47
1	...	...	...	...	1	...	17	...	8	...	9	...	...
44	16	...	2	...	26	...	30	30	...	...	...	...	...
144	117	16	3	3	5	...	594	569	...	9	...	...	16
13	10	1	...	...	2	...	...	...	...	...	...	...	...
751	336	159	6	46	214	30	1,837	976	635	58	82	86	...
791	335	159	6	46	214	30	1,837	976	695	58	82	86	...
...	...	...	...	...	...	...	...	...	...	...	...	...	...
1,840	1,225	316	35	127	115	22	2,595	1,576	378	108	67	257	209
8	3	...	...	...	...	...	...	...	...	...	...	...	...
894	804	6	22	8	54	...	1,659	1,233	...	96	...	206	124
943	418	310	13	119	61	22	986	848	378	12	67	51	85
366	288	20	9	5	44	...	1,125	937	...	3	...	134	21
...	...	...	...	...	...	...	88	88	...	...	...	...	...
316	260	4	8	1	43	...	866	692	...	29	...	132	13
41	22	13	1	4	1	...	103	90	...	3	...	2	8
9	6	3	...	...	...	...	118	117	...	1	...	...	...
1,109	760	144	37	55	104	9	1,610	.196	143	43	28	162	38
1,035	783	137	33	51	104	7	1,427	1,086	90	41	14	158	38
44	27	7	4	4	...	2	168	95	53	2	14	4	...
...	...	...	...	...	...	...	15	15	...	...	...	...	...
541	418	83	7	31	2	...	450	321	38	16	2	68	5
32	28	1	...	3	...	...	70	15	...	2	...	53	...
26	26	...	...	...	...	...	40	26	4	...	...	5	5
483	364	82	7	28	2	...	330	280	24	14	2	10	...
...	...	...	...	...	...	...	10	...	10	...	...	...	...
360	42	208	2	53	1	54	1,220	472	577	9	55	16	91
344	32	207	...	51	...	54	780	55	544	...	46	...	91
3	3	...	...	...	...	...	70	56	11	1	2	...	...
5	5	...	...	...	...	...	21	20	...	1	...	...	...
6	...	1	2	2	1	...	364	341	...	7	...	16	...
...	...	...	...	...	...	...	...	...	...	...	...	...	...
2	2	...	...	...	...	...	29	...	22	...	7	...	...
...	...	...	...	...	...	...	...	...	...	...	...	...	...

TABLE X.—Occupation or Means of

Group No.	Occupation.	MANDSAUR. Total following occupation.	As principal occupation. Males.	As principal occupation. Females.	As working dependents. Males.	As working dependents. Females.	As subsidiary to other occupation. Males.	As subsidiary to other occupation. Females.
1	2	66	67	68	69	70	71	72
	B. Preparation and supply of material substances.	*26,045*	*16,364*	*3,705*	*821*	*1,633*	*2,972*	*547*
	III. Industry	*15,424*	*8,950*	*2,751*	*374*	*1,299*	*1,706*	*344*
	5. Textiles	1,997	1,059	440	47	298	130	23
42	Cotton ginning, cleaning and pressing ...	178	160	13	5	...	...	...
43	Cotton spinning, sizing and weaving ...	638	181	208	18	91	118	22
45	Rope, twine, string and other fibres	27	...	17	...	10	...	...
46	Wool carding, spinning and weaving ...	240	221	2	5	...	12	...
49	Dyeing, bleaching, printing, preparation and sponging of textiles.	912	495	200	19	197	...	1
50	Lace, crepe, embroideries, fringes, etc., and insufficiently described textile industries.	2	2	...	...	...	...	...
	6. Hides, Skins and Hard Materials from the Animal Kingdom.	1,192	661	263	22	97	148	1
51	Working in leather	1,188	659	263	21	97	147	1
53	Bone, ivory, horn, shell, etc., workers (except buttons).	4	2	...	1	...	1	...
	7. Wood	1,281	710	208	46	92	144	81
54	Sawyers	...	...	...	...	...	...	...
55	Carpenters, turners and joiners, etc. ...	598	489	...	19	...	90	...
56	Basket makers and other industries of woody materials, ncluding leaves and thatchers and builders working with bamboo, reeds or similar materials.	683	221	208	27	92	54	81
	8. Metals	1,499	578	322	16	219	364	...
58	Makers of arms, guns, etc.	6	...	...	3	...	3	...
59	Blacksmiths, other workers in iron, makers of implements.	1,269	468	319	11	219	252	...
60	Workers in brass, copper and bell metal ...	208	94	3	2	...	109	...
61	Workers in other metals (except precious metals).	16	16	...	...	...	...	...
	9. Ceramics	1,998	1,069	482	37	267	90	53
63	Potters and makers of earthenware	1,580	783	451	29	258	51	8
64	Brick and tile makers	65	16	10	...	...	39	...
65	Other workers in ceramics	353	270	21	8	9	...	45
	10. Chemical Products properly so-called and analogous.	328	217	...	12	...	97	2
66	Manufacture of matches, fireworks and other explosives.	13	13	...	...	...	...	...
67	Manufacture of aerated and mineral waters and ice.	18	18	...	...	...	...	...
68	Manufacture and refining of vegetable oils ...	296	185	...	12	...	97	2
70	Others	1	1	...	...	...	...	...
	11. Food Industries	408	203	133	10	25	1	36
71	Rice pounders and huskers and flour grinders ...	172	43	85	1	21	1	21
72	Grain parchers, etc.	4	1	3	...	...	...	...
73	Butchers	1	1	...	...	...	...	...
[illegible]	Sweetmeat and condiment makers	178	134	31	9	4	...	...
[illegible]	Toddy drawers	2	2	...	...	...	...	...
[illegible]	Manufacturers of tobacco	42	13	14	...	...	...	15
[illegible]	Others	9	9	...	...	..	...	...

Livelihood. *Part I.—District Details.—(contd.)*

SHAJAPUR.							AMJHERA.						
Total following occupation.	As principal occupation.		As working dependents.		As subsidiary to other occupation.		Total following occupation.	As principal occupation.		As working dependents.		As subsidiary to other occupation.	
	M.	F.	M.	F.	M.	F.		M.	F.	M.	F.	M.	F.
73	74	75	76	77	78	79	80	81	82	83	84	85	86
22,037	*14,507*	*2,750*	*440*	*727*	*3,248*	*365*	*6,863*	*7,697*	*623*	*237*	*467*	*646*	*193*
14,473	*9,341*	*2,041*	*336*	*636*	*1,950*	*169*	*4,066*	*2,810*	*448*	*126*	*341*	*271*	*70*
1,357	739	259	19	120	174	46	589	387	101	11	69	12	9
243	175	13	4	...	19	82	48	25	11	...	8	...	4
845	420	221	11	95	96	2	329	238	61	1	27	2	...
10	3	2	...	...	5	...	3	2	...	...	...	...	1
59	16	6	...	1	36	...	33	33	...	...	...	...	...
171	122	16	4	24	5	...	166	80	29	10	33	10	4
29	3	1	...	...	13	12	10	9	...	...	1	...	...
764	541	5	16	4	162	36	174	154	...	8	1	6	5
764	541	5	16	4	162	36	174	154	...	8	1	6	5
...	...	...	...	...	...	...	...	...	...	...	...	...	...
2,087	1,303	356	29	121	270	8	281	155	30	11	30	50	5
...	...	...	...	...	...	...	...	...	...	...	...	...	...
1,298	989	80	27	8	194	...	172	119	...	9	...	44	...
789	314	276	2	113	76	8	109	36	30	2	30	6	5
831	640	38	15	...	138	...	246	216	2	10	1	17	...
...	...	...	...	...	...	...	16	...	...	...	...	16	...
704	591	37	14	...	62	...	155	147	2	5	1	...	...
111	83	1	1	...	76	...	71	65	...	5	...	1	...
16	16	...	...	...	...	...	4	4	...	...	...	...	...
1,749	1,011	379	30	154	172	3	355	219	75	7	46	8	...
1,596	962	303	28	148	147	8	330	202	72	7	44	5	...
116	49	39	2	1	25	...	24	16	3	...	2	3	...
37	...	32	...	5	...	...	1	1	...	...	...	...	...
564	424	82	9	17	32	...	290	190	23	7	33	37	...
89	88	...	...	1	...	...	57	1	23	...	33	...	...
...	...	...	...	...	...	...	...	...	...	...	...	...	...
524	385	82	9	16	32	...	233	189	...	7	...	37	...
1	1	...	...	...	...	...	...	...	...	...	...	...	...
454	162	81	10	17	182	2	179	113	48	1	5	6	6
230	23	49	5	16	135	2	25	2	14	...	8	...	6
29	7	22	...	...	...	...	29	7	16	...	...	6	...
2	2	...	...	...	...	...	15	15	...	...	...	...	...
178	129	10	5	1	38	...	110	89	18	1	2	...	...
...	...	...	...	...	...	...	...	...	...	...	...	...	...
15	1	...	...	...	14	...	...	...	...	...	...	...	...
...	...	...	...	...	...	...	...	...	...	...	...	...	...

Livelihood. *Part I—District Details.—(contd.)*

GIRD.							BHIND.						
Total following occupation.	As principal occupation.		As working dependents.		As subsidiary to other occupation.		Total following occupation.	As principal occupation.		As working dependents.		As subsidiary to other occupation.	
	M.	F.	M.	F.	M.	F.		M.	F.	M.	F	M.	F.
10	11	12	13	14	15	16	17	18	19	20	21	22	23
5,751	3,928	1,018	181	236	344	41	5,733	3,489	883	209	201	848	103
1,711	1,292	245	67	35	72	...	1,318	938	...	73	...	251	56
923	592	212	17	52	48	2	642	379	119	24	17	84	19
2	2	...	...	...	...	...	...	...	...	...	...	...	...
1,851	958	561	57	149	107	30	2,140	914	689	89	178	262	28
1,260	1,100	...	43	...	117	...	1,638	1,233	75	73	6	251	...
4	4	...	...	...	...	...	...	...	...	...	...	...	...
77	64	...	1	...	12	...	...	...	...	...	...	...	...
77	64	...	1	...	12	...	...	...	...	...	...	...	...
...	...	...	...	...	...	...	...	...	...	...	...	...	...
1,557	1,244	139	44	32	90	8	381	325	21	...	...	24	11
1,557	1,244	139	44	32	90	8	381	325	21	...	...	24	11
...	...	...	...	...	...	...	4	4	...	...	...	...	...
...	...	...	...	...	...	...	4	4	...	...	...	...	...
...	...	...	...	...	...	...	...	...	...	...	...	...	...
43	11	...	...	...	32	...	...	...	...	...	...	...	...
43	11	...	...	...	32	...	...	...	...	...	...	...	...
2,305	1,428	652	71	82	72	...	1,679	955	529	37	57	50	51
300	300	...	...	...	...	...	...	...	...	...	...	...	...
26	1	...	...	...	25	...	...	...	...	...	...	...	...
4	4	...	...	...	...	...	...	...	...	...	...	...	...
378	260	40	39	21	18	...	274	223	...	9	...	42	...
44	42	...	...	...	2	...	33	27	2	...	...	4	...
1,558	821	612	32	61	32	...	1,372	705	527	28	57	4	51
1,636	*1,132*	*75*	*42*	*8*	*402*	*37*	*1,254*	*1,007*	*4*	*15*	...	*227*	*1*
4	4	...	...	...	...	...	43	31	...	...	...	12	...
...	...	...	...	...	...	...	43	31	...	..	...	12	...
...	...	...	...	...	...	...	...	...	...	...	...	...	...
4	4	...	...	...	...	...	...	...	...	...	...	...	...

TABLE X.—Occupation or Means of

Group. No.	Occupation.	TONWARGHAR.						
		Total following occupation.	As principal occupation.		As working dependents.		As subsidiary to other occupation.	
			Males.	Females.	Males.	Females.	Males.	Females.
1	2	24	25	26	27	28	29	30
	B. Preparation and supply of material substances—(contd.)							
	III. Industry—(contd.)							
	12. Industries of Dress and the Toilet ...	5,444	2,948	659	107	195	1,379	156
82	Boot, shoe, sandal and clog makers	1,388	719	147	35	25	427	30
83	Tailors, milliners, dress-makers and darners ...	769	289	56	10	31	379	4
84	Embroiderers, hat-makers and makers of other articles of wear.	4	4	...	...	...	...	...
85	Washing and cleaning	1,590	847	430	32	186	32	118
86	Barbers, hair-dressers and wig-makers ...	1,697	1,069	25	30	8	541	9
87	Other industries connected with the toilet ...	1	...	1	...	...	...	...
	13. Furniture Industries	1	1	...	...	...	...	...
88	Cabinet-makers, carriage painters, etc. ...	..	...	...	...	...	...	...
89	Upholsterers, tent-makers, etc.	1	1	...	...	...	...	...
	14. Building Industries	270	171	10	12	3	73	1
90	Lime burners, cement workers; Excavators and well sinkers; Stone cutters and dressers; Brick layers and masons; Builders (other than buildings made of bamboo or similar materials), painters, decorators of houses, tilers, plumbers, etc.	270	171	10	12	3	73	1
	15. Construction of Means of Transport ...	...	...	...	...	...	...	...
91	Persons engaged in making, assembling or repairing motor vehicles or cycles.	...	...	...	...	...	...	...
92	Carriage, cart, palki, etc., makers and wheel wrights.	...	...	...	...	...	...	...
	16. Production and Transmission of Physical Force.	...	...	...	..	...	...	...
94	Heat, light, electricity, motive power, etc. Gas works and electric light and power.	...	...	...	...	...	...	...
	17. Miscellaneous and undefined Industries.	1,444	951	278	42	78	86	9
95	Printers, engravers, book-binders, etc. ...	1	1	...	...	...	...	...
96	Makers of musical instruments	3	2	1	...	...	...	...
97	Makers of clocks and surgical or scientific instruments, etc.	1	...	...	...	...	1	...
98	Makers of jewellery and ornaments ...	374	349	3	9	1	9	3
99	Other miscellaneous and undefined industries (toy-making, taxidermy, etc.).	15	13	1	1	...	...	...
100	Scavenging	1,050	586	273	32	77	76	6
	IV. Transport	*770*	*417*	*11*	*9*	*8*	*316*	*9*
	19. Transport by Water	62	15	...	...	...	44	3
101	Ship-owners, boat-owners and their employees, officers, mariners, etc. Ship brokers, boatmen and towmen.	57	10	...	...	...	44	3
102	Persons (other than labourers) employed in harbours, docks, rivers and canals, including pilots.	...	...	...	...	...	...	...
103	Labourers employed on harbours, docks, rivers and canals.	5	5	...	...	...	...	...

Livelihood. *Part I.—District Details.—(contd.)*

SHEOPUR.							NARWAR.						
Total following occupation.	As principal occupation.		As working dependents.		As subsidiary to other occupation.		Total following occupation.	As principal occupation.		As working dependents.		As subsidiary to other occupation.	
	M.	F.	M.	F.	M.	F.		M.	F.	M.	F.	M.	F.
31	32	33	34	35	36	37	38	39	40	41	42	43	44
2,122	1,628	139	83	67	87	46	8,151	5,622	759	238	231	1,261	40
1,144	1,020	81	29	7	7	...	4,343	3,085	160	99	11	970	18
153	113	19	2	2	17	...	615	541	20	8	35	6	5
...	...	...	...	...	...	...	...	...	...	...	...	...	...
402	392	69	6	[illegible]	24	44	1,897	927	459	52	173	274	22
[illegible]	[illegible]	...	14	...	41	2	1,410	1,229	53	108	9	11	...
...	...		...	...	...	...	10	...	7	...	3	...	...
...	...	...	...	...	...	...	6	6	...	...	...	...	...
...	...	...	...	...	...	...	6	6	...	...	...	...	...
...	...	...	...	...	...	...	...	...	...	...	...	...	...
106	61	5	7	...	33	...	287	138	27	...	17	103	2
107	63	[illegible]	7	...	31	...	287	138	27	...	17	103	2
...	...	...	...	...	...	...	...	...	...	...	...	...	...
...	...	...	...	...	...	...	...	...	...	...	...	...	...
...	...	...	...	...	...	...	...	...	...	...	...	...	...
...	...	...	...	...	...	...	...	...	...	...	...	...	...
...	...	...	...	...	...	...	...	...	...	...	...	...	...
633	420	125	17	66	2	3	909	474	308	21	92	11	3
...	...	...	...	...	...	...	...	...	...	...	...	...	...
10	...	6	...	4	...	...	3	3	...	...	...	...	...
6	6	...	...	...	...	...	1	1	...	...	...	...	...
151	149	...	2	...	...	...	2	2	...	...	...	...	...
...	...	...	...	...	...	...	12	3	9	...	...	...	...
466	265	119	15	62	2	3	891	465	299	21	92	11	3
1,292	*748*	*257*	*31*	*14*	*212*	*30*	*249*	*145*	*6*	*1*	*6*	*91*	...
26	4	1	...	...	21	...	...	...	...	...	...	...	...
6	4	1	...	...	...	...	...	...	...	...	...	...	...
21	...	...	...	...	21	...	...	...	...	...	...	...	...
...	...	...	...	...	...	...	...	...	...	...	...	...	...

TABLE X.—Occupation or Means of

Group No.	Occupation.	ISAGARH.						
		Total following occupation.	As principal occupation.		As working dependents.		As subsidiary to other occupation.	
			Males.	Females.	Males.	Females.	Males.	Females.
1	2	45	46	47	48	49	50	51
	B. Preparation and supply of material substances—(contd.)							
	III. Industry—(contd.)							
	12 Industries of Dress and the Toilet ...	8,198	5,890	685	323	189	950	170
82	Boot, shoe, sandal and clog makers	3,998	2,852	129	178	54	685	105
83	Tailors, milliners, dress-makers and darners ...	826	612	117	88	10	80	19
84	Embroiderers, hat-makers and makers of other articles of wear.	...	...	...	...	...	...	...
85	Washing and cleaning	1,526	800	400	47	101	132	46
86	Barbers, hair-dressers and wig-makers ...	1,848	1,626	89	65	15	108	...
87	Other industries connected with the toilet ...	...	...	...	...	...	...	...
	13. Furniture Industries...	...	...	...	...	...	...	...
88	Cabinet makers, carriage painters, etc. ...	...	...	...	...	...	...	...
89	Upholsterers, tent-makers, etc.	...	...	...	...	...	...	...
	14. Building Industries	536	413	77	1	...	13	32
90	Lime burners, cement workers; Excavators and well sinkers; Stone cutters and dressers; Brick layers and masons; Builders (other than buildings made of bamboo or similar materials), painters, decorators of houses, tilers, plumbers, etc.	536	413	77	1	...	13	32
	15. Construction of Means of Transport ...	...	...	...	...	...	...	...
91	Persons engaged in making, assembling or repairing motor vehicles or cycles.	...	...	...	...	...	...	...
92	Carriage, cart, palki, etc., makers and wheel wrights.	...	...	...	...	...	...	...
	16. Production and Transmission of Physical Force.	...	...	...	...	...	...	...
94	Heat, light, electricity, motive power, etc. Gas works and electric light and power.	...	...	...	...	...	...	...
	17. Miscellaneous and undefined Industries ...	2,142	1,440	482	65	120	31	4
95	Printers, engravers, book-binders, etc. ...	1	...	1	...	...	...	...
96	Makers of musical instruments	...	...	...	...	...	...	...
97	Makers of clocks and surgical or scientific instruments, etc.	1	1	...	...	...	...	...
98	Makers of jewellery and ornaments	647	613	13	14	2	5	...
99	Other miscellaneous and undefined industries ([illegible], taxidermy, etc.).	16	12	...	4	...	...	...
100	[illegible]	1,477	811	463	47	118	26	4
	IV. Transport	866	554	44	12	4	250	2
	17. Transport by Water	...	...	...	...	...	...	...
[illegible]	[illegible]	...	...	...	...	...	...	...
[illegible]	[illegible]	...	...	...	...	...	...	...
[illegible]	[illegible]	...	...	...	...	...	...	...

Livelihood. *Part I.—District Details.—(contd.)*

BHILSA.							UJJAIN						
Total following occupation.	As principal occupation.		As working dependents.		As subsidiary to other occupation.		Total following occupation.	As principal occupation.		As working dependents.		As subsidiary to other occupation.	
	M.	F.	M.	F.	M.	F.		M.	F.	M.	F.	M.	F.
52	53	54	55	56	57	58	59	60	61	62	63	64	65
[illegible]	3,175	[illegible]	109	[illegible]	[illegible]	6	5,619	3,866	791	166	113	420	260
[illegible]		[illegible]	[illegible]	31	[illegible]	...	1,411	[illegible]	...	49	...	65	...
[illegible]	[illegible]	[illegible]	[illegible]	[illegible]	31	1	[illegible]	[illegible]	[illegible]	41	57	211	248
[illegible]	.	[illegible]		2	..	.	..	...	...	...	...	...	...
[illegible]	[illegible]	[illegible]	35	61	72	5	[illegible]	702	473	32	40	70	17
[illegible]	[illegible]	[illegible]	[illegible]	[illegible]	[illegible]	...	[illegible]	[illegible]	2	15	7	64	...
	..	.	...	...		.	...	...	...	...	...	...	...
..				.	..		22	5	14	...	3	...	...
...	..	..	.	..	...	..	22	5	14	...	3	...	...
...	.	.	..	...	..	..	...		...	...	...	...	...
[illegible]	244	[illegible]	3	...	20	...	491	436	5	13	...	23	14
[illegible]	[illegible]	[illegible]	3	...	[illegible]	...	491	[illegible]	5	13	...	23	14
...	...		..		...	...	...	...	...	...	...	...	...
...	...		...	...	..	...	...	..	...	...	...	...	...
...	...	...	...	...	...	...	...	...	...	...	...	...	...
...	.	.	..	...	...	...	...	...	...	...	...	...	...
.	..	..	...	...	...	...	...	...	...	...	...	...	...
[illegible]	[illegible]	[illegible]	24	[illegible]	31	[illegible]	1,238	691	361	55	50	69	9
2	2	...	..	...	...	..	...	...	...	...	...	...	...
...	.	...	..	...	...	...	227	14	167	2	44	...	...
1	1	...	..	...	...	...	10	10	...	...	...	...	...
[illegible]	[illegible]	1	4	4	25	...	211	208	...	3	...	...	...
7	2	3	...	2	...	...	...	...	...	...	...	...	...
[illegible]	[illegible]	[illegible]	20	20	6	25	[illegible]	[illegible]	191	50	6	69	9
563	[illegible]	21	9	6	179	47	719	703	...	28	...	18	...
...	...	...	...	...	...	...	...	...	...	...	...	...	...
...	...	...	...	...	...	...	...	...	...	...	...	...	...
...	...	...	...	...	...	...	...	...	...	...	...	...	...
...	...	...	...	...	...	...	...	...	...	...	...	...	...

TABLE X.—Occupation or Means of

Group No.	Occupation.	MANDSAUR.						
		Total following occupation.	As principal occupation.		As working dependents.		As subsidiary to other occupation.	
			Males.	Females.	Males.	Females.	Males.	Females.
1	2	66	67	68	69	70	71	72
	[illegible] ([illegible])							
	[illegible]							
	12. Industries of Dress and the Toilet ...	4,166	2,556	614	119	188	589	100
[illegible]	[illegible] clog makers	1,453	956	118	8 5	55	218	76
[illegible]	Tailors [illegible] dress makers and darners ...	1,877	712	263	28	73	291	10
[illegible]	[illegible] hat makers and makers of other articles of wear.	...	...	...	...	...	...	...
[illegible]	[illegible]	480	228	183	15	49	...	5
[illegible]	[illegible] hair dressers and wig makers ...	856	660	70	41	11	85	9
[illegible]	[illegible] connected with the toilet ...	...	...	...	...	...	...	...
	13. Furniture Industries	...	...	...	...	...	...	...
[illegible]	[illegible] carriage painters, etc. ...	...	...	...	...	...	...	...
[illegible]	[illegible]	...	...	...	...	...	...	...
	14. Building Industries	818	653	64	26	67	1	7
[illegible]	[illegible] workers. Excavators and [illegible] dressers. Brick [illegible] materials), [illegible] tilers, plu[illegible]	818	653	64	26	67	1	7
	15. Construction of Means of Transport ...	50	5	...	...	...	45	...
[illegible]	[illegible]	5	5	...	...	...	...	...
[illegible]	[illegible] and wheel[illegible]	45	...	...	...	...	45	...
	16. Production and transmission of Physical Force	...	...	...	...	...	...	...
[illegible]	[illegible]	...	...	...	...	...	...	...
	17. [illegible] Industries ...	1,[illegible]	1,239	225	30	46	97	41
	[illegible]	13	17	...	...	...	...	...
	[illegible]	...	...	...	...	...	...	...
	[illegible]	2	1	...	...	...	1	[illegible]
	[illegible]	[illegible]	[illegible]	7	[illegible]	5	[illegible]	...
	[illegible]	[illegible]	[illegible]	...	1	[illegible]	...	2
	[illegible]	[illegible]	[illegible]	[illegible]	[illegible]	41	[illegible]	[illegible]
	[illegible]	[illegible]	[illegible]	[illegible]	[illegible]	[illegible]	[illegible]	
	[illegible] ...	...						
	[illegible]							

Livelihood. *Part I.—District Details.—(contd.)*

SHAJAPUR. Total following occupation.	As principal occupation. M.	F.	As working dependents. M.	F.	As subsidiary to other occupation. M.	F.	AMJHERA. Total following occupation.	As principal occupation. M.	F.	As working dependents. M.	F.	As subsidiary to other occupation. M.	F.
[illegible]	[illegible]	[illegible]	[illegible]	[illegible]	[illegible]	[illegible]	80	81	82	83	84	85	86
[illegible]	[illegible]	[illegible]	126	162	413	77	1,376	928	141	56	127	79	45
[illegible]	[illegible]	[illegible]	[illegible]	[illegible]	[illegible]	[illegible]	659	270	71	[illegible]	73	73	42
[illegible]	[illegible]	[illegible]	45	47	[illegible]	...	[illegible]	240	20	6	44	3	3
...			...			...	..	...	...	...	...	...	...
[illegible]		9		[illegible]	[illegible]		172	74	40	6	10	...	...
[illegible]	[illegible]	[illegible]	[illegible]	[illegible]	[illegible]		[illegible]	[illegible]	...	3	...	3	...
...			..				...	...	...	...	...	...	...
11	.	1	...	10	.	.	...	...	...	...	...	..	...
11	..	1	..	10	..	..	...	...	...	...	...	..	...
...				.	..	...	..	...	...	...	...	...	...
[illegible]	[illegible]	[illegible]	[illegible]	1	[illegible]	2	188	112	11	4	7	31	...
[illegible]	[illegible]	[illegible]	[illegible]	1	[illegible]	5	[illegible]	112	11	4	7	64	...
..			.		.	...	...	...	...	...	...	...	...
...		.	...	...	.	.	...	...	...	...	...	...	...
...	.			.			...	...	...	...	...	...	...
.		..		..		..	...	...	...	...	...	...	...
..		.		...			...	...	...	...	...	...	...
739	295	[illegible]	7	[illegible]	[illegible]	47	[illegible]	336	17	11	22	2	...
2	2		...	...	...	...	15	15	...	...	...	...	...
...	..	...	.	...	...	..	3	3	...	...	...	...	...
[illegible]	[illegible]	2	2	...	...	...	...	...	...	...	...	...	...
[illegible]	25	[illegible]	...	1	73	47	237	[illegible]	6	7	2	...	...
6	...	...	...	...	6	...	...	...	...	...	...	...	...
[illegible]	[illegible]	201	5	[illegible]	[illegible]	...	133	96	11	4	20	2	...
[illegible]	[illegible]	[illegible]	..	8	[illegible]	3	230	175	7	9	1	36	2
2	...	...	...	...	...	2	...	...	...	...	...	...	...
2	..	...	...	...	...	2	...	...	...	...	...	...	...
...	...	...	...	...	...	...	...	...	...	...	...	...	...
...	...	...	...	...	...	...	...	...	...	...	...		

TABLE X.—Occupation or Means of

Group No.	Occupation.	GWALIOR STATE. Total following occupation.	As principal occupation. Males.	As principal occupation. Females.	As working dependents. Males.	As working dependents. Famales.	As subsidiary to other occupation. Males.	As subsidiary to other occupation. Females.
1	2	3	4	5	6	7	8	9
	B. Preparation and supply of material substances.—(contd.).							
	IV. Transport.—(concld.).							
	20. Transport by Road.	6,955	4,247	420	174	87	1,901	126
105	Persons (other than labourers) employed on the construction and maintenance of roads and bridges.	27	26	...	...	1	...	...
106	Labourers employed on roads and bridges ...	2,207	1,718	141	34	16	191	107
107	Owners, managers and employees (excluding personal servants) connected with mechanically driven vehicles (including trams).	565	351	189	5	18	2	...
108	Owners, managers and employees (excluding personal servants) connected with other vehicles.	3,716	1,894	74	115	45	1,572	16
109	Palki, etc., bearers and owners	69	69	...	...	...	...	...
110	Pack elephant, camel, mule, ass and bullock owners and drivers.	302	121	15	20	7	136	3
111	Porters and messengers	69	68	1	...	...	...	...
	21. Transport by Rail	2,410	2,084	196	18	42	70	...
112	Railway employees of all kinds other than coolies.	1,345	1,201	52	17	41	34	...
113	Labourers employed on railway construction and maintenance and coolies and porters employed on railway premises.	1,065	883	144	1	1	36	...
	22. Post Office, Telegraph and Telephone services.	480	474	...	3	...	3	...
114	Post Office, Telegraph and Telephone services ...	480	474	...	3	...	3	...
	V. Trade	*92,006*	*54,646*	*13,474*	*2,773*	*3,462*	*14,355*	*3,296*
	23. Banks, establishments of credit, exchange and insurance.	7,285	3,365	429	296	51	2,955	189
115	Bank managers, money lenders, exchange and insurance agents, money changers and brokers and their employees.	7,285	3,365	429	296	51	2,955	189
	24. Brokerage, commission and export ...	1,323	726	1	28	1	545	22
116	Brokers, commission agents, commercial travellers, warehouse owners and employees.	1,323	726	1	28	1	545	22
	25. Trade in textiles...	3,288	2,767	101	93	23	214	90
117	Trade in piece-goods, wool, cotton, silk, hair and other textiles.	3,288	2,767	101	93	23	214	90
	26. Trade in skins, leather and furs ...	356	285	36	22	4	3	6
118	Trade in skins, leather, furs, feathers, horn, etc., and the articles made from these.	356	285	36	22	4	3	6
	27. Trade in wood	396	334	1	61	...	...	...
119	Trade in wood (not firewood)	389	327	1	60	...	...	...
120	Trade in bamboos and canes	8	7	..	1	...	...	...
	28. Trade in metals	248	116	1	...	...	127	4
121	Trade in metals, machinery, knives, tools, etc. ...	248	116	1	...	...	127	4
	30. Trade in chemical products	202	177	6	3	15	1	...
122	Drugs, dyes, paints, petroleum, explosives, etc.	202	177	6	3	15	1	...
	31. Hotels, cafes, restaurants etc. ...	1,550	1,059	107	41	21	282	2
123	[illegible]	850	742	67	23	16	150	1
124	Owners and managers of hotels, cookshops, sarais, etc., and their employees.	190	100	1	1	...	84	1
125	[illegible] ...	504	417	2[illegible]	17	2	56	...

TABLE X.—Occupation or Means of

Group No.	Occupation.	TONWARGHAR. Total following occupation.	As principal occupation. Males.	As principal occupation. Females.	As working dependents. Males.	As working dependents. Females.	As subsidiary to other occupation. Males.	As subsidiary to other occupation. Females.
1	2	24	25	26	27	28	29	30
	B. Preparation and supply of material substances—(concld.)							
	IV. Transport.—(contd.)							
	20. Transport by Road	398	114	11	8	8	251	6
105	Persons (other than labourers) employed on the construction and maintenance of roads and bridges.	...	...	...	...	...	...	...
106	Labourers employed on roads and bridges ...	55	28	1	...	1	24	1
107	Owners, managers and employees (excluding personal servants) connected with mechanically driven vehicles (including trams).	10	10	...	...	...	...	...
108	Owners, managers and employees (excluding personal servants) connected with other vehicles	298	59	8	6	...	226	6
109	Palki, etc., bearers and owners	...	...	...	...	...	...	...
110	Pack elephant, camel, mule, ass and bullock owners and drivers.	86	17	7	8	7	1	...
111	Porters and messengers	...	...	...	...	...	...	...
	21. Transport by Rail	277	255	...	1	...	21	...
112	Railway employees of all kinds other than coolies.	270	250	...	1	...	19	...
113	Labourers employed on railway construction and maintenance and coolies and porters employed on railway premises.	7	5	...	...	...	2	...
	22. Post Office, Telegraph and Telephone services.	33	33	...	...	...	...	...
114	Post Office, Telegraph and Telephone services ...	33	33	...	...	...	...	...
	V. Trade	*8,390*	*4,709*	*818*	*193*	*376*	*1,834*	*460*
	23. Banks, establishments of credit, exchange and insurance.	922	244	27	9	2	632	8
115	Bank managers, money lenders, exchange and insurance agents, money changers and brokers and their employees.	922	244	27	9	2	632	8
	24. Brokerage commission and export ...	92	75	1	2	1	8	5
116	Brokers, commission agents, commercial travellers, warehouse owners and employees.	92	75	1	2	1	8	5
	25. Trade in textiles	293	255	14	5	...	19	...
117	Trade in piece-goods, wool, cotton, silk, hair and other textiles.	293	255	14	5	...	19	...
	26. Trade in skins, leather and furs ...	2	2	...	...	...	...	...
118	Trade in skins, leather, furs, feathers, horn, etc. and the articles made from these.	2	2	...	...	...	...	...
	27. Trade in wood	5	5	...	...	...	...	...
119	Trade in wood (not fire-wood)	5	5	...	...	...	...	...
121	Trade in bamboos and canes	...	...	...	...	...	...	...
	28. Trade in metals	47	4	...	...	...	48	...
123	Trade in metals, machinery, knives, tools, etc. ...	47	4	...	...	...	48	...
	30. Trade in chemical products ...	4	4	...	...	...	...	...
125	Drugs, dyes, paints, petroleum, explosives, etc.	4	4	...	...	...	...	...
	31. Hotels, cafes, restaurants, etc. ...	107	51	...	2	...	54	...
126	Vendors of wine, liquors, aerated waters and ice.	5	4	...	...	...	1	...
127	Owners and managers of hotels, cook shops, sarais, etc. (and employees).	53	...	...	...	...	53	...
128	Hawkers of drink and food stuffs	49	47	...	2	...	...	...

Livelihood. *Part I.—District Details.—(contd.)*

SHEOPUR.							NARWAR.						
Total following occupation.	As principal occupation.		As working dependents.		As subsidiary to other occupation.		Total following occupation.	As principal occupation.		As working dependents.		As subsidiary to other occupation.	
	M.	F.	M.	F.	M.	F.		M.	F.	M.	F.	M.	F.
31	32	33	34	35	36	37	38	39	40	41	42	43	44
1,194	686	239	34	14	191	30	186	82	6	1	6	91	...
...	...	...	...	...	...	...	...	...	...	...	...	...	...
504	396	94	...	8	45	26	46	39	1	...	6	...	...
320	167	145	3	11	...	...	...	...	...	...	...	...	...
289	111	...	31	...	143	4	140	43	5	1	...	91	...
...	...	...	...	...	...	...	...	...	...	...	...	...	...
15	12	...	...	...	3	...	...	...	...	...	...	...	...
...	...	...	...	...	...	...	...	...	...	...	...	...	...
55	38	17	...	...	...	...	30	30	...	...	...	...	...
55	38	17	...	...	...	...	27	27	...	...	...	...	...
...	...	...	...	...	...	...	3	3	...	...	...	...	...
20	20	...	...	...	...	...	33	33	...	...	...	...	...
20	20	...	...	...	...	...	33	33	...	...	...	...	...
4,756	*2,619*	*659*	*320*	*367*	*741*	*80*	*11,279*	*5,830*	*2,632*	*220*	*374*	*1,814*	*409*
354	68	14	168	...	14	30	988	585	80	11	5	302	5
354	68	14	168	...	74	30	988	585	80	11	5	302	5
22	1	...	...	...	21	...	24	...	...	...	...	24	...
22	1	...	...	...	21	...	24	...	...	...	...	24	...
123	102	5	6	5	5	...	208	185	7	2	...	14	...
123	102	5	6	5	5	...	208	185	7	2	...	14	...
...	...	...	...	...	...	...	...	...	...	...	...	...	...
...	...	...	...	...	...	...	...	...	...	...	...	...	...
93	62	...	31	...	...	...	...	...	...	...	...	...	...
93	62	...	31	...	...	...	...	...	...	...	...	...	...
...	...	...	...	...	...	...	...	...	...	...	...	...	...
...	...	...	...	...	...	...	4	4	...	...	...	...	...
...	...	...	...	...	...	...	4	4	...	...	...	...	...
...	...	...	...	...	...	...	2	2	...	...	...	...	...
...	...	...	...	...	...	...	2	2	...	...	...	...	...
37	18	2	...	15	2	...	64	53	11	...	...	...	...
31	13	2	...	15	2	...	42	41	1	...	...	...	...
...	...	...	...	...	...	...	7	7	...	...	...	...	...
6	6	...	...	...	...	...	15	5	10	...	...	...	...

TABLE X.—Occupation or Means of

Group No.	Occupation.	ISAGARH.						
		Total following occupation.	As principal occupation.		As working dependents.		As subsidiary to other occupation.	
			Males.	Females.	Males.	Females.	Males.	Females.
1	2	45	46	47	48	49	50	51
	B. Preparation and supply of material substances.—(contd.)							
	IV. Transport.—(concld.)							
	20. Transport by Road	760	461	44	8	4	241	2
105	Persons (other than labourers) employed on the construction and maintenance of roads and bridges.	...	...	...	...	...	...	...
106	Labourers employed on roads and bridges ...	240	223	10	4	...	2	1
107	Owners, managers and employees (excluding personal servants) connected with mechanically driven vehicles including trams).	12	12	...	...	...	...	...
108	Owners, managers and employees (excluding personal servants) connected with other vehicles.	402	220	28	4	4	146	...
109	Palki, etc., bearers and owners	...	...	...	...	...	...	...
110	Pack elephant, camel, mule, ass and bullock owners and drivers.	106	6	6	...	...	93	1
111	Porters and messengers	...	...	...	...	...	...	...
	21. Transport by Rail	84	71	...	4	...	9	...
112	Railway employees of all kinds other than coolies.	57	45	...	3	...	9	...
113	Labourers employed on railway construction and maintenance and coolies and porters employed on railway premises.	27	26	...	1	...	...	...
	22. Post Office, Telegraph and Telephone services.	22	22	...	...	...	...	...
114	Post Office, Telegraph and Telephone services ...	22	22	...	...	...	...	...
	V. Trade	*10,298*	*6,029*	*2,110*	*354*	*456*	*954*	*395*
	23. Banks, establishments of credit, exchange and insurance.	530	362	18	15	8	122	5
115	Bank managers, money lenders, exchange and insurance agents, money changers and brokers and their employees.	530	362	18	15	8	122	5
	24. Brokerage commission and export ...	8	8	...	...	...	...	...
116	Brokers, commission agents, commercial travellers, warehouse owners and employees.	8	8	...	...	...	...	...
	25. Trade in textiles	378	318	3	13	2	42	...
117	Trade in piece-goods, wool, cotton, silk, hair and other textiles.	378	318	3	13	2	42	...
	26. Trade in skins, leather and furs ...	38	29	...	...	...	3	6
118	Trade in skins, leather, furs, feathers, horn, etc., and the articles made from these.	38	29	...	...	...	3	6
	27. Trade in wood	8	7	...	1	...	...	...
119	Trade in wood (not firewood)	...	...	...	...	...	...	...
121	Trade in bamboos and canes	8	7	...	1	...	...	...
	29. Trade in metals	...	...	...	...	...	...	...
[illegible]	Trade in metals, machinery, knives, tools, etc. ...	...	...	...	...	...	...	...
	[illegible] Trade in chemical products ...	...	...	...	...	...	...	...
[illegible]	[illegible] drugs, paints, [illegible], explosives, etc. ...	...	...	...	...	...	...	...
	31. Hotels cafes, restaurants, etc. ...	58	37	...	5	1	14	1
[illegible]	Vendors of wine, [illegible] aerated waters and ice ...	[illegible]	19	...	1	1	14	1
[illegible]	[illegible]	...	...	...	...	...	...	...
[illegible]	[illegible]	21	[illegible]	...	4	...	...	...

Livelihood. *Part I.—District Details.—(contd.)*

BHILSA.							UJJAIN.						
Total following occupation.	As principal occupation.		As working dependents.		As subsidiary to other occupation.		Total following occupation.	As principal occupation.		As working dependents.		As subsidiary to other occupation.	
	M.	F.	M.	F.	M.	F.		M.	F.	M.	F.	M.	F.
52	53	54	55	56	57	58	59	60	61	62	63	64	65
417	163	23	6	6	172	47	471	425	...	28	...	18	...
...	...	...	...	...	...	...	...	...	...	...	...	...	...
222	96	20	5	5	50	46	82	67	...	8	...	12	...
14	14	...	...	...	...	...	55	55	...	...	...	...	...
181	53	3	1	1	122	1	288	279	...	8	...	1	...
...	...	...	...	...	...	...	...	...	...	...	...	...	...
...	...	...	...	...	...	...	46	24	...	17	...	5	...
...	...	...	...	...	...	...	...	...	...	...	...	...	...
134	127	1	...	..	6	...	194	194	...	...	...	...	...
18	12	...	...	...	6	...	88	88	...	...	...	...	...
116	115	1	...	...	...	...	106	106	...	...	...	...	...
14	10	...	3	...	1	...	84	84	...	...	...	...	...
14	10	...	3	...	1	...	84	84	...	...	...	...	...
5,206	*2,760*	*825*	*91*	*246*	*1,002*	*282*	*11,487*	*7,103*	*1,489*	*438*	*195*	*1,886*	*376*
366	126	24	4	1	202	9	1,000	268	23	16	18	664	11
366	126	24	4	1	202	9	1,000	268	23	16	18	664	11
20	20	...	...	...	...	...	225	214	...	11	...	...	...
20	20	...	...	...	...	...	225	214	...	11	...	...	...
121	95	4	10	5	7	...	519	448	...	18	...	29	24
121	95	4	10	5	7	...	519	448	...	18	...	29	24
106	87	15	1	3	...	...	...	...	...	...	...	...	...
106	87	15	1	3	...	...	...	...	...	...	...	...	...
2	1	1	...	...	...	...	...	...	...	...	...	...	...
2	1	1	...	...	...	...	...	...	...	...	...	...	...
...	...	...	...	...	...	...	...	...	...	...	...	...	...
20	19	1	...	...	...	...	...	...	...	...	...	...	...
20	19	1	...	...	...	...	...	...	...	...	...	...	...
55	36	4	...	15	...	...	50	49	...	1	...	...	...
55	36	4	...	15	...	...	50	49	...	1	...	...	...
82	78	4	...	...	...	...	402	293	52	13	1	43	...
8	5	3	...	...	...	...	229	126	52	7	1	43	...
1	1	...	...	...	...	...	8	8	...	...	...	...	...
73	72	1	...	...	...	...	170	164	...	6	...	...	

TABLE X.—Occupation or Means of

Group No.	Occupation.	MANDSAUR.						
		Total following occupation.	As principal occupation.		As working dependents.		As subsidiary to other occupation.	
			Males.	Females.	Males.	Females.	Males.	Females.
1	2	66	67	68	69	70	71	72
	B. Preparation and supply of material substances—(contd.)							
	IV. Transport.—(concld.)							
	20. Transport by Road	717	499	25	24	33	136	...
105	Persons (other than labourers) employed on the construction and maintenance of roads and bridges.	2	1	...	...	1	...	...
106	Labourers employed on roads and bridges ..	7	4	8	...	...	...	...
107	Owners, managers and employees (excluding personal servants) connected with mechanically driven vehicles (including trams).	25	21	...	2	...	2	...
108	Owners, managers and employees (excluding personal servants) connected with other vehicles.	605	808	19	22	82	134	...
109	Palki, etc., bearers and owners	...	...	...	...	...	...	...
110	Pack elephant, camel, mule, ass and bullock owners and drivers.	9	7	2	...	...	...	...
111	Porters and messengers	69	68	1	...	...	...	...
	21. Transport by Rail	444	354	33	12	41	4	...
112	Railway employees of all kinds other than coolies.	428	842	83	12	41	...	...
113	Labourers employed on railway construction and maintenance and coolies and porters employed on railway premises.	16	12	...	...	...	4	...
	22. Post Office, Telegraph and Telephone services.	51	51	...	...	...	...	...
114	Post Office, Telegraph and Telephone services ...	51	51	...	...	...	...	...
	V. Trade...	*9,409*	*6,510*	*896*	*414*	*260*	*1,126*	*203*
	23. Banks, establishments of credit, exchange and insurance.	594	368	80	23	7	111	5
115	Bank managers, money lenders, exchange and insurance agents, money changers and brokers and their employees.	594	868	80	28	7	111	5
	24. Brokerage commission and export ...	373	294	...	8	...	71	...
116	Brokers, commission agents, commercial travellers, warehouse owners and employees.	878	294	...	8	...	71	...
	25. Trade in textiles	609	551	25	10	4	...	19
117	Trade in piece-goods, wool, cotton, silk, hair and other textiles.	609	551	25	10	4	...	19
	26. Trade in skins, leather and furs ...	37	29	6	1	1	...	...
118	Trade in skins, leather, furs, feathers, horn, etc., and the articles made from these.	87	29	6	1	1	...	...
	27. Trade in wood	1	1	...	...	...	...	...
119	Trade in wood (not fire-wood)	1	1	...	...	...	...	...
121	Trade in bamboos and canes	...	...	...	...	...	...	...
	28. Trade in metals	11	11	...	...	...	...	...
123	Trade in metals, machinery, knives, tools, etc. ...	11	11	...	...	...	...	...
	30. Trade in chemical products ...	10	7	1	1	...	1	...
125	Drugs, dyes, paints, petroleum, explosives, etc. ...	10	7	1	1	...	1	...
	31. Hotels, cafes, restaurants, etc. ...	140	134	1	3	...	2	...
126	Vendors of wine, liquors, aerated waters and ice.	109	106	...	2	...	1	...
127	Owners and managers of hotels, cook shops, sarais, etc. (and employees).	8	5	1	1	...	1	...
128	Hawkers of drink and food stuffs	28	28	...	...	...	...	...

Livelihood. Part I.—District Details.—(contd.)

SHAJAPUR.							AMJHERA.						
Total following occupation.	As principal occupation.		As working dependents.		As subsidiary to other occupations.		Total following occupation.	As principal occupation.		As working dependents.		As subsidiary to other occupation.	
	M.	F.	M.	F.	M.	F.		M.	F.	M.	F.	M.	F.
[illegible]	54	55	56	57	58	59	60	61	62	83	84	85	86
226	[illegible]	48	...	7	[illegible]	1	205	150	7	9	1	36	2
...	...	.	...	...		..	...	.	...	...	...	...	...
233	[illegible]	1	...	...	8	...	72	63	7	1	1	...	...
52		44		7		.	...	...	...	...	...	...	...
[illegible]	[illegible]	2			102	...	121	85	...	8	...	26	2
[illegible]	33			..		2	2	2	...	...	..	...	...
...	.	.	.	...	...	..	...	...	...	..	...	.	...
235	[illegible]	143		1	[illegible]	..	3	3	...	...	...	...	...
[illegible]	[illegible]			.	..	..	1	1	...	...	...	...	...
[illegible]	[illegible]	142		1	[illegible]	..	2	2	...	...	..	...	...
28	28	...	..	..		..	22	22	...	...	...	...	...
[illegible]	[illegible]		.	.	.		22	22	...	...	...	...	...
[illegible]	[illegible]	[illegible]	[illegible]	[illegible]	[illegible]	[illegible]	[illegible]	1,212	165	102	125	339	121
819	280	68	9		[illegible]	55	409	252	23	17	4	21	22
[illegible]	[illegible]	[illegible]	9	..	[illegible]	55	409	252	23	17	4	21	22
128	17	..	7	...	104	...	4	4	...	...	...	...	...
[illegible]	17	...	7	...	104	.	4	4	...	...	...	...	...
233	118	23	3	..	44	45	136	116	2	13	...	5	...
[illegible]	[illegible]	20	3	...	44	45	136	116	2	13	...	5	...
...	...	...	...	...	...	...	...	...	...	...	...	...	...
...	...	...	...	...	..	...	...	...	...	...	...	...	...
...	...	...	...	...	...	..	3	3	...	...	...	...	...
..	...	...	...	...	...	...	3	3	...	...	...	...	...
...	...	...	...	...	...	...	...	...	...	...	...	...	...
...	...	...	...	...	...	...	...	...	...	...	...	...	...
...	...	...	...	...	...	...	...	...	...	...	...	...	...
8	7	1	...	...	...	...	...	...	...	...	...	...	...
6	7	1	...	...	...	...	...	...	...	...	...	...	...
105	91	1	6	...	7	...	95	41	4	1	1	48	...
82	73	...	2	...	7	...	95	41	4	1	1	48	...
...	...	...	...	...	...	...	...	...	...	...	...	...	...
23	18	1	4	...	...	...	...	...	...	...	...	...	...

TABLE X.—Occupation or Means of

Group No.	Occupation.	GWALIOR STATE.						
		Total following occupation.	As principal occupation.		As working dependents.		As subsidiary to other occupation.	
			Males.	Females.	Males.	Famales.	Males.	Females.
1	2	3	4	5	6	7	8	9
	B. Preparation and supply of material substances—(contd).							
	V. Trade—(contd.).							
	32. Other trade in food stuffs	36,821	19,529	7,200	952	2,001	5,357	1,752
129	Grain and pulse dealers	2,864	1,890	105	99	12	239	19
130	Dealers in sweetmeats, sugar and spices ...	721	652	47	10	1	14	...
131	Dealers in dairy product, eggs and poultry ...	5,133	2,210	809	134	319	1,801	360
132	Dealers in animals for food	218	...	...	...	...	181	37
133	Dealers in fodder for animals	6,742	2,321	2,206	192	513	601	459
134	Dealers in other food stuffs	21,221	12 175	3,830	504	1,122	2,749	845
135	Dealers in tobacco	130	49	4	1	2	72	2
136	Dealers in opium	46	20	3	1	...	22	...
137	Dealers in ganja	210	212	6	11	2	9	...
	33. Trade in clothing and toilet articles ...	.,427	1,351	11	29	...	6	30
138	Trade in ready-made clothing and other articles of dress and the toilet (hats, umbrellas, socks, ready-made shoes, perfumes, etc.).	1,427	1,351	11	29	...	6	30
	34. Trade in furniture	6	4	2	...	...	...	...
140	Hardware, cooking utensils, porcelain, crokery, glassware, bottles, articles for gardening, etc.	6	4	2	...	...	...	...
	35. Trade in building matarials ...	16	13	...	...	2	1	...
141	Trade in building materials (other than bricks, tiles and woody materials).	16	13	...	...	2	1	...
	36. Trade in means of transport ...	982	498	1	26	...	403	54
142.	Dealers and hirers in mechanical transport, motors, cycles, etc.	4	...	...	...	...	4	...
143	Dealers and hirers in other carriages, carts, boats, etc.	8	6	...	...	...	2	...
144	Dealers and hirers of elephants, camels, horses, cattle, asses, mules, etc.	970	492	1	26	...	397	54
	37. Trade in fuel...	7,569	2,176	2 984	192	701	796	720
145	Dealers in firewood, charcoal, coal, cowdung, etc.	7,569	2,176	2,984	192	701	796	720
	38. Trade in articles of luxury and those pertaining to letters and the arts and sciences.	4,357	3,054	804	104	206	154	25
146	Dealers in precious stones, jewellery (real and imitation), clocks, optical instruments, etc.	1,300	1,211	14	45	...	30	...
147	Dealers in common bangles, bead, necklaces, fans, small articles, toys, hunting and fishing tackle, flowers, etc.	3,022	1,819	790	59	206	123	25
148	Publishers, book-sellers, stationers, dealers in music, pictures, musical instruments and curiosities.	25	24	...	...	...	1	...

Livelihood. *Part I—District Details.—(contd.)*

GIRD.							BHIND.						
Total following occupation.	As principal occupation.		As working dependents.		As subsidiary to other occupation.		Total following occupation.	As principal occupation.		As working dependents.		As subsidiary to other occupation.	
	M.	F.	M.	F.	M.	F.		M.	F.	M.	F.	M.	F.
10	11	12	13	14	15	16	17	18	19	20	21	22	23
5,431	2,858	1,323	179	323	595	211	3,6[illegible]	1,639	741	98	345	522	264
147	134	1	1	...	11	...	303	188	53	81	3	18	10
[illegible]	292	[illegible]	...	...	14	...	12	...	12	...	...	...	...
873	[illegible]	160	15	57	209	90	252	111	45	15	5	56	20
34	...	...	...	...	..	34	...	...	...	...	...	..	...
1[illegible]9	23	127	...	19	...	...	2[illegible]7	108	27	19	27	87	19
[illegible]	2,027	1,023	91	257	262	78	2,767	1,202	603	33	310	404	215
[illegible]	37	...	1	...	...	...	7	...	...	...	...	7	...
13	12	...	1	...	...	...	...	...	...	...	...	...	...
...	...		...	...	...	...	22	21	1	...	...	...	...
[illegible]	599	...	5	...	1	...	43	41	...	...	...	3	...
[illegible]	599	...	5	...	1	...	13	40	...	...	...	8	...
3	3	...	...	...	...	...	...	...	...	...	...	...	...
3	3	...	...	...	...	...	...	...	...	...	...	...	...
5	5	...	..	...	..	...	...	...	...	...	...	...	...
5	5	...	...	...	...	...	...	...	...	...	...	...	...
61	...	...	...	...	61	...	...	...	...	...	...	...	...
4	...	...	...	...	4	...	...	...	...	...	...	...	...
2	...	...	...	...	2	...	...	...	...	...	...	...	...
54	...	...	...	...	54	...	...	...	...	...	...	...	...
708	126	390	14	97	5	76	407	104	118	...	24	118	43
708	126	390	14	97	5	76	407	104	118	...	24	118	43
356	252	71	17	11	5	...	715	471	125	20	23	53	23
83	[illegible]	...	1	...	...	...	204	185	1	6	...	12	...
312	209	71	16	11	5	...	510	285	121	14	28	41	23
11	11	...	...	...	...	...	1	1	...	...	...	...	...

TABLE X.—Occupation or Means of

Group No.	Occupation.	TONWARGHAR. Total following occupation.	As principal occupation. Males.	Females.	As working dependents. Males.	Females.	As subsidiary to other occupation. Males.	Females.
1	2	24	25	26	27	28	29	30
	B. Preparation and supply of material substances (contd.).							
	V. Trade.—(contd.).							
	32. Other trade in food stuffs... ...	3,367	1,523	440	56	270	783	293
129	Grain and pulse dealers	163	103	3	8	1	55	1
130	Dealers in sweetmeats, sugar and spices ...	2	2	...	...	...	...	...
131	Dealers in dairy product, eggs and poultry ...	397	217	22	...	21	64	23
132	Dealers in animals for food	3	...	...	...	...	...	3
133	Dealers in fodder for animals	519	167	85	26	68	139	43
134	Dealers in other food stuffs	2,249	1,008	328	27	160	503	228
135	Dealers in tobacco	2	...	...	...	...	2	...
136	Dealers in opium	2	...	2	...	...	...	...
137	Dealers in ganja	1	1	...	...	...	...	...
	33. Trade in clothing and toilet articles ...	5	5	...	...	...	...	...
138	Trade in ready-made clothing and other articles of dress and the toilet (hats, umbrellas, socks, ready-made shoes, perfumes, etc.).	5	5	...	...	...	...	...
	34. Trade in furniture	...	...	...	...	...	...	...
140	Hardware, cooking utensils, porcelain, crockery, glassware, bottles, articles for gardening, etc.	...	...	...	...	...	...	...
	35. Trade in building materials ...	5	5	...	...	...	...	...
141	Trade in building materials (other than bricks, tiles and woody materials).	5	5	...	...	...	...	...
	36. Trade in means of transport ...	49	...	...	...	...	5	44
142	Dealers and hirers in mechanical transport, motors, cycles, etc.	...	...	...	...	...	...	...
143	Dealers and hirers in other carriages, carts, boats, etc.	...	...	...	...	...	...	...
144	Dealers and hirers of elephants, camels, horses, cattle, asses, mules, etc.	49	...	...	...	...	5	44
	37. Trade in fuel	310	87	110	18	67	22	6
145	Dealers in firewood, charcoal, coal, cowdung, etc.	310	87	110	18	67	22	6
	38. Trade in articles of luxury and those pertaining to letters and the arts and sciences.	221	151	23	13	10	22	2
146	Dealers in precious stones, jewellery (real and imitation), clocks, optical instruments, etc.	24	12	...	3	...	9	...
147	Dealers in common bangles, bead, necklaces, fans, small articles, toys, hunting and fishing tackle, flowers, etc.	196	138	23	10	10	13	2
148	Publishers, booksellers, stationers, dealers in music, pictures, musical instruments and curiosities.	1	1	...	...	...	...	...

Livelihood. *Part I.—District Details.—(contd.)*

SHEOPUR.							NARWAR.						
Total following occupation.	As principal occupation.		As working dependents.		As subsidiary to other occupation.		Total following occupation.	As principal occupation.		As working dependents.		As subsidiary to other occupation.	
	M.	F.	M.	F.	M.	F.		M.	F.	M.	F.	M.	F.
31	32	33	34	35	36	37	38	39	40	41	42	43	44
1,711	1,013	274	41	133	107	23	5,105	2,483	1,277	128	210	[illegible]	190
56	51	...	5	...	...	.	137	105	3	10	3	16	...
33	33	...	...	...	...	...	199	192	...	7	...	...	...
302	70	63	1	49	112	7	870	435	10	33	70	256	66
...		...	.	...	...	..	180	...	...	..	...	180	...
34	4	...	...	..	27	3	2,052	536	967	41	115	278	115
[illegible]	[illegible]	911	54	63	58	[illegible]	1,653	1,201	294	37	22	90	9
...	...	...	...	...	...	...	1	...	1	...	...	...	...
...	...	...	...	...	...	...	8	8	...	...	...	...	...
4	2		1	1	.	...	..	...	...	...	...	...	...
378	365	...	13	...	...	...	69	69	...	...	...	...	...
378	365	...	13	...	...	...	69	69	...	...	...	...	...
...	...	...	...	...	...	...	...	...	...	...	...	...	...
...	...	...	...	...	...	...	...	...	...	...	...	...	...
...	...	..	...	...	..	...	..	...	...	...	...	...	...
...	...	...	...	...	...	..	...	...	...	...	...	...	...
313	...	...	...	...	303	10	8	8	...	...	...	...	...
...	...	...	...	...	...	...	...	...	...	...	..	...	...
...	...	...	...	...	...	...	...	...	...	...	...	...	...
313	...	...	...	...	303	10	8	8	...	...	...	...	...
879	306	315	42	201	14	1	1,931	297	1,015	20	89	305	205
879	306	315	42	201	14	1	1,931	297	1,015	20	89	305	205
40	36	3	1	...	...	...	326	280	33	4	1	8	...
6	6	...	...	...	...	...	141	130	4	...	...	7	...
31	30	2	1	..	...	...	185	150	29	4	1	1	...
—	...	...	...	...	...	...	...	...	...	...	...	...	...

TABLE X.—Occupation or Means of

	Occupation.	ISAGARH.						
		Total following occupation.	As principal occupation.		As working dependents.		As subsidiary to other occupation.	
			Males.	Females.	Males.	Females.	Males.	Females.
	2	45	46	47	48	49	50	51
	B. Preparation and supply of material substances—(contd.)							
	V. Trade—(contd.)							
	32. Other trade in food stuffs ...	4,639	2,220	1,286	165	297	438	233
129	Grain and pulse dealers	244	223	7	7	1	...	6
130	Dealers in sweetmeats, sugar and spices ...	...	...	...	...	...	...	...
131	Dealers in dairy product, eggs and poultry ...	424	168	105	15	24	96	21
132	Dealers in animals for food	...	...	...	...	...	...	...
133	Dealers in fodder for animals	1,664	620	691	62	139	56	96
134	Dealers in other food stuffs	2,283	1,195	482	78	133	285	110
135	Dealers in tobacco	...	...	...	...	...	...	...
136	Dealers in opium	...	...	...	...	...	...	...
137	Dealers in ganja	24	10	1	3	...	1	...
	33. Trade in clothing and toilet articles...	...	...	...	...	...	...	...
138	Trade in ready-made clothing and other articles of dress and the toilet (hats, umbrellas, socks, ready-made shoes, perfumes, etc.)	...	...	...	...	...	...	...
	34. Trade in furniture	...	...	...	...	...	...	...
139	Hardware, cooking utensils, porcelain, crockery, glassware, bottles, articles for gardening, etc.	...	...	...	...	...	...	...
	35. Trade in building materials... ...	1	...	...	...	...	1	...
140	Trade in building materials (other than bricks, [illegible] materials).	1	...	...	...	...	1	...
	36. Trade in means of transport ...	...	...	...	...	...	...	...
141	[illegible] transport, [illegible]	...	...	...	...	...	...	...
142	[illegible]	...	...	...	...	...	...	...
143	[illegible]	...	...	...	...	...	...	...
	37. Trade in fuel ...	1,376	511	417	25	73	132	131
144	[illegible]	[illegible]	[illegible]	417	65	[illegible]	[illegible]	131
	38. Trade in articles of luxury and those pertaining to letters and the arts and sciences	241	161	17	2	1	12	...
145	[illegible]	[illegible]	[illegible]	...	...	...	...	...
146	[illegible]	[illegible]	[illegible]	17	[illegible]	[illegible]	11	...
147	[illegible]		...	...		...	...	...

Livelihood. *Part I.—District Details.—(contd.)*

[illegible]							UJJAIN.						
Total following occupation.	As principal occupation.		As working dependents.		As subsidiary to other occupations.		Total following occupation.	As principal occupation.		As working dependents.		As subsidiary to other occupation.	
	M.	F.	M.	F.	M.	F.		M.	F.	M.	F.	M.	F.
[illegible]	[illegible]	[illegible]	[illegible]	[illegible]	[illegible]	[illegible]	[illegible]	60	61	62	63	64	65
[illegible]	[illegible]	[illegible]	[illegible]	[illegible]	[illegible]	[illegible]	3,113	3,153	753	139	109	872	104
[illegible]	[illegible]	[illegible]	[illegible]	[illegible]	[illegible]	[illegible]	[illegible]	717	.	7	...	...	...
[illegible]	[illegible]	[illegible]	[illegible]	[illegible]	..	.		...	...	...	...	...	...
[illegible]	[illegible]	[illegible]	[illegible]	[illegible]	[illegible]	[illegible]	[illegible]	275	247	21	61	270	60
[illegible]		.			[illegible]	..		...	...	...	...	...	...
[illegible]	[illegible]	[illegible]	[illegible]	[illegible]	[illegible]	[illegible]	[illegible]	[illegible]	[illegible]	19	[illegible]	151	22
[illegible]	[illegible]	[illegible]	[illegible]	[illegible]	[illegible]	[illegible]	[illegible]	[illegible]	[illegible]	[illegible]	19	[illegible]	23
[illegible]	[illegible]		.	..	.		54	...	.	..	...	54	...
[illegible]		[illegible]	.		.				...	...	...	...	...
.	[illegible]	.			[illegible]	...	114	[illegible]	...	6	...	...	...
[illegible]	[illegible]	.			[illegible]	[illegible]	[illegible]	199	...	1	...	...	...
[illegible]	[illegible]			..	[illegible]	[illegible]	[illegible]	193	...	1	...	...	...
						..	...	..	...	...	...	...	...
..	..	.				..		...	...	...	...	...	...
.	.				.	...	...	...	...	..	...	...	...
..				.	..	.	.	...	...	...	...	...	...
25	25	..	...		.		44	37	...	7	..	...	...
...		..		..	..	...	...	...	...	...	...	...	...
1	1		.	...		..	...	..	...	...	...	...	...
[illegible]	[illegible]	...	..	..		...	44	37	...	7	...	...	...
612	[illegible]	[illegible]	16	46	122	58	158	259	87	3	17	...	122
612	[illegible]	[illegible]	10	46	122	[illegible]	498	259	87	3	17	...	131
[illegible]	[illegible]	24	1	1	3	..	521	378	409	4	31	...	...
27	[illegible]		...	...	1	...	...	...	...	...	...	...	...
[illegible]	[illegible]	24	1	1	1	...	[illegible]	[illegible]	409	4	33	...	...
5	4	...	...	...	1	...	15	15	...	...	...	...	...

TABLE X.—Occupation or Means of

Group No.	Occupation	MANDSAUR. Total following occupation.	As principal occupation. Males.	As principal occupation. Females.	As working dependents. Males.	As working dependents. Females.	As subsidiary to other occupation. Males.	As subsidiary to other occupation. Females.
1	1	66	67	68	69	70	71	72
	B. Preparation and supply of material substances.—(contd.).							
	V. Trade.—(contd.)							
	32. Other trade in food stuffs ...	2,856	1,923	355	101	33	291	130
129	Grain and pulse dealers	[illegible]	301	7	19	1	75	...
130	Dealers in sweetmeats, sugar and spices ...	51	50	1	...	...	...	...
131	Dealers in dairy product, eggs and poultry ...	[illegible]	[illegible]	[illegible]	27	6	119	12
132	Dealers in animals for food	...	...	...	...	...	...	...
133	Dealers in fodder for animals	207	85	40	8	1	4	68
134	Dealers in other food stuffs	1,610	1,193	242	50	43	94	48
135	Dealers in tobacco	21	7	1	...	2	9	2
136	Dealers in opium	...	...	...	...	...	...	...
137	Dealers in gania	12	12	...	...	...	...	...
	33. Trade in clothing and toilet articles ...	12	12	...	...	...	...	...
138	Trade in ready-made clothing and other articles of dress and the toilet (hats, umbrellas, socks, ready, made shoes, perfumes, etc.).	12	12	...	...	...	...	...
	34. Trade in furniture	3	1	2	...	...	...	...
140	Hardware, cooking utensils, porcelain, crockery, glassware, bottles, articles, articles for gardening, etc.	3	1	2	...	...	...	...
	35. Trade in building materials ...	3	1	...	...	2	...	...
141	Trade in building materials (other than bricks, tiles and woody materials).	3	1	...	...	2	...	...
	36. Trade in means of transport ...	397	379	...	18	...	...	...
142	Dealers and hirers in mechanical transport, motors, cycles, etc.	...	...	...	...	...	...	...
143	Dealers and hirers in other carriages, carts, boats, etc.	5	5	...	...	...	...	...
144	Dealers and hirers of elephants, camels, horses, cattle, asses, mules, etc.	392	374	...	18	...	...	...
	37. Trade in fuel	612	227	243	23		32	27
145	Dealers in fire wood, charcoal, coal, cowdung, etc.	612	227	248	23	60	32	27
	38 Trade in articles of luxury and those pertaining to letters and the arts and sciences.	306	126	57	10	113	...	...
146	Dealers in precious stones, jewellery (real and imitation), clocks, optical instruments, etc.	36	31	1	4	...	...	...
147	Dealers in common bangles, bead, necklaces, fans, small articles, toys, hunting and fishing tackle, flowers, etc.	269	94	56	6	113	...	...
148	Publishers, book-sellers, stationers, dealers in music, pictures, musical instruments and curiosities.	1	1	...	...	...	...	...

Livelihood. *Part 1.—District Details.—(contd.)*

SHAJAPUR.							AMJHERA.						
Total following occupation.	As principal occupation.		As working dependents.		As subsidiary to other occupation.		Total following occupation.	As principal occupation.		As working dependents.		As subsidiary to other occupation.	
	M.	F.	M.	F.	M.	F.		M.	F.	M.	F.	M.	F.
73	74	75	76	77	78	79	80	81	82	83	84	85	86
1,791	1,145	235	26	48	282	55	1,030	618	103	47	69	106	87
286	240	10	8	...	82	1	120	98	5	12	1	4	...
...	...	...	...	...	...	...	...	...	...	...	...	...	...
229	115	54	8	14	87	6	178	74	16	2	12	24	50
...	...	...	...	...	...	...	...	...	...	...	...	...	...
78	54	5	4	15	...	...	174	54	33	6	44	...	87
1,134	699	162	16	18	191	48	540	383	47	26	12	72	...
...	...	...	...	...	...	...	6	4	2	...	...	...	...
22	...	...	...	...	22	...	...	...	...	...	...	...	...
42	37	4	...	1	...	...	12	5	...	1	...	6	...
109	60	11	10	...	...	28	...	...	...	...	...	...	...
109	60	11	10	...	...	28	...	...	...	...	...	...	...
...	...	...	...	...	...	...	...	...	...	...	...	...	...
...	...	...	...	...	...	...	...	...	...	...	...	...	...
2	2	...	...	...	...	...	...	...	...	...	...	...	...
2	2	...	...	...	...	...	...	...	...	...	...	...	...
78	49	1	1	...	27	...	8	...	...	...	...	8	...
...	...	...	...	...	...	...	...	...	...	...	...	...	...
...	...	...	...	...	...	...	...	...	...	...	...	...	...
78	49	1	1	...	27	...	8	...	...	...	...	8	...
114	76	18	2	8	10	...	132	53	13	5	17	36	8
114	76	18	2	8	10	...	132	53	13	5	17	36	8
1,082	963	30	32	7	50	...	117	95	12	...	9	1	...
821	782	8	31	...	...	...	1	...	...	...	...	1	...
260	180	22	1	7	50	...	116	95	12	...	9	...	...
1	1	...	...	...	...	...	...	...	...	...	...	...	...

TABLE X.—Occupation or Means of

Group No.	Occupation.	GWALIOR STATE.						
		Total following occupation.	As principal occupation.		As working dependents.		As subsidiary to other occupation.	
			Males.	Females.	Males.	Famales.	Males.	Females.
	B. Preparation and supply of material substances.—(concld.)							
	V. Trade.—(concld.)							
	39. Trade of other sorts	26,180	19,143	1,790	927	437	3,481	402
149	Dealers in rags, stable refuse, etc.	79	...	2	...	...	77	...
150	General store-keepers and shop-keepers otherwise unspecified.	24,576	17,668	1,788	878	437	3,403	402
151	Itinerant traders, pedlars and hawkers (of other than food, etc.).	5	5	...	...	...	...	...
152	Other trades (including farmers of pounds, tools and markets).	1,520	1,470	...	49	...	1	...
	C. Public administration and Liberal Arts ...	*60,763*	*49,320*	*2,864*	*1,375*	*358*	*6,500*	*351*
	VI. Public Force...	*18,530*	*16,296*	...	*454*	...	*1,780*	...
	40. Army	9,342	9,024	...	281	...	37	...
153	Army (Imperial)	615	615	...	...	...	...	...
154	Army (Indian States)	8,727	8,409	...	281	...	37	...
	43. Police	9,188	7.272	...	173	...	1,743	...
157	Police	3,916	3,571	...	33	...	312	...
158	Village watchmen	5,272	3,701	...	140	...	1,431	...
	VII. Public Administration	*16,278*	*15,405*	*120*	*253*	*4*	*480*	*16*
	44. Public Administration	16,278	15,405	120	253	4	480	16
159	Service of the State	60	60	...	...	...	...	...
160	Service of Indian and Foreign State	15,891	15,088	103	228	1	477	4
161	Municipal and other local (not village) service ...	327	262	17	30	3	3	12
	VIII. Professions and Liberal Arts ...	*25,960*	*17,619*	*2,744*	*668*	*354*	*4,240*	*335*
	45. Religion	13,712	9,871	529	404	67	2,695	140
163	Priests, ministers, etc.	6,686	5,145	306	195	46	965	29
164	Monks, nuns, religious mendicants	6,355	4,094	222	182	21	1,719	117
165	Other religious workers	30	18	1	...	...	11	...
166	Servants in religious edifices, burial and burning grounds, pilgrim conductors, circumcisers, etc.	641	614	...	27	...	...	...
	46. Law	894	822	1	9	...	62	...
167	Lawyers of all kinds, including Qazis, Law agents and Mukhtiars.	370	344	1	3	...	22	...
168	Lawyers' clerks, petition writers, etc. ...	524	478	...	6	...	40	...
	47. Medicine	2,414	951	924	22	179	272	66
169	Registered medical practitioners including oculists.	150	128	3	13	...	6	...
170	Other persons practising the healing arts without being registered.	790	567	...	2	...	221	...
172	Midwives, vaccinators, compounders, nurses, masseurs, etc.	1,400	215	918	7	179	15	66
173	Veterinary surgeons	74	41	3	...	...	30	...

Livelihood. *Part I—District Details.—(contd.)*

GIRD.							BHIND.						
Total following occupation.	As principal occupation.		As working dependents.		As subsidiary to other occupation.		Total following occupation.	As principal occupation.		As working dependents.		As subsidiary to other occupation.	
	M.	F.	M.	F.	M.	F.		M.	F.	M.	F	M.	F.
4,260	3,224	291	105	100	491	49	2,487	1,471	160	72	31	705	48
72	...	...	...	...	72	...	...	...	...	...	...	...	...
4,181	8,917	291	105	100	419	49	2,487	1,471	160	72	31	705	48
5	5	...	...	...	...	...	...	...	...	...	...	...	...
2	2	...	...	...	...	...	...	...	...	...	...	...	...
17,354	15,764	600	374	70	513	33	4,257	2,843	329	49	56	943	37
8,265	7,954	...	242	...	69	...	881	657	...	25	...	199	...
7,024	6,775	...	229	...	20	...	62	62	...	...	...	...	...
...	...	...	...	...	...	...	...	...	...	...	...	...	...
7,024	6,775	...	229	...	20	...	62	62	...	...	...	...	...
1,241	1,179	...	13	...	49	...	819	595	...	25	...	199	...
927	901	...	10	...	16	...	184	177	...	...	...	7	...
314	278	...	3	...	33	...	635	418	...	25	...	192	...
5,335	5,240	54	30	1	10	...	662	651	...	...	...	11	...
5,335	5,240	54	30	1	10	...	662	651	...	...	...	11	...
10	10	...	...	...	...	...	...	...	...	...	...	...	...
5,265	5,174	50	30	1	10	...	629	620	...	...	...	9	...
60	56	4	...	...	...	...	33	31	...	...	...	2	...
3,754	2,570	546	102	69	434	33	2,714	1,535	329	24	56	733	37
1,877	1,382	161	67	34	225	8	1,522	914	55	19	7	515	12
1,404	1,120	128	65	33	58	5	1,027	483	38	8	2	489	7
216	7	33	...	1	172	3	495	431	17	11	5	26	5
...	...	...	...	...	...	...	...	...	...	...	...	...	...
257	255	...	2	...	...	...	...	...	...	...	...	...	...
270	236	...	6	...	28	...	100	93	...	...	...	7	...
114	96	...	2	...	16	...	14	12	...	...	...	2	...
156	140	...	4	...	12	...	86	81	...	...	...	5	...
580	249	174	1	29	109	18	310	64	160	...	41	35	10
88	86	1	1	...	...	...	2	...	...	...	...	2	...
297	125	...	...	...	102	...	62	50	...	...	...	12	...
226	8	178	...	29	...	18	217	6	160	...	41	...	10
87	80	...	...	...	7	...	29	8	...	...	...	21	...

TABLE X.—Occupation or Means of

Group No.	Occupation.	TONWARGHAR.						
		Total following occupation.	As principal occupation.		As working dependents.		As subsidiary to other occupation.	
			Males.	Females.	Males.	Females.	Males.	Females.
	B. Preparation and supply of material substances.—(concld.)							
	V. Trade.—(concld.)							
	39. Trade of other sorts	2,961	2,296	203	88	26	246	102
149	Dealers in rags, stable refuse, etc.	5	...	...	...	...	5	...
150	General store-keepers and shop-keepers otherwise unspecified.	2,955	2,296	203	88	26	240	102
151	Itinerant traders, pedlars and hawkers (of other than food, etc.).	...	...	...	...	...	...	...
152	Other trades (including farmers of pounds, tools and markets).	1	...	...	...	...	1	...
	C. Public Administration and Liberal Arts.	*4,881*	*3,452*	*242*	*184*	*14*	*961*	*23*
	VI. Public Force...	*1,091*	*901*	...	*41*	...	*149*	...
	40. Army	119	88	...	22	...	14	...
153	Army (Imperial)	...	...	...	...	...	...	...
154	Army (Indian States)	119	88	...	22	...	14	...
	43. Police	972	818	...	19	...	135	...
157	Police	537	522	...	...	...	15	...
158	Village watchmen	435	296	...	19	...	120	...
	VII. Public Administration	*1,140*	*1,002*	*9*	*21*	...	*108*	...
	44. Public Administration	1,140	1,002	9	21	...	108	...
159	Service of the State	...	...	...	...	...	...	...
160	Service of Indian and Foreign State	1,108	968	8	20	...	107	...
161	Municipal and other local (not village) service.	37	34	1	1	...	1	...
	VIII. Professions and Liberal Arts ...	*2,650*	*1,549*	*233*	*122*	*14*	*704*	*28*
	45. Religion	1,714	998	86	55	5	554	16
163	Priests, ministers, etc.	899	594	62	30	5	200	8
164	Monks, nuns, religious mendicants	414	39	24	...	...	343	8
165	Other religious workers	27	16	...	...	...	11	...
166	Servants in religious edifices, burial and burning grounds, pilgrim conductors, circumcisers, etc.	374	349	...	25	...	...	...
	46. Law	76	52	1	...	...	23	...
167	Lawyers of all kinds, including Qazis, Law Agents and Mukhtiars.	27	26	1	...	...	...	...
168	Lawyers' clerks, petition writers, etc. ...	49	26	...	...	...	23	...
	47. Medicine	186	69	62	12	6	32	5
169	Registered medical practitioners including oculists.	37	24	...	12	...	1	...
170	Other persons practising the healing arts without being registered.	72	48	...	...	...	20	...
172	Midwives, vaccinators, compounders, nurses, masseurs, etc.	73	...	62	...	6	...	5
173	Veterinary surgeons	4	2	...	...	...	2	...

Livelihood. *Part I.—District Details.—(contd.)*

SHEOPUR.							NARWAR.						
Total following occupation.	As principal occupation.		As working dependents.		As subsidiary to other occupation.		Total following occupation.	As principal occupation.		As working dependents.		As subsidiary to other occupation.	
	M.	F.	M.	F.	M.	F.		M.	F.	M.	F.	M.	F.
836	618	46	18	13	125	16	2,550	1,867	209	55	69	341	9
...	...	...	...	...	...	...	...	...	...	...	...	...	...
836	618	46	18	13	125	16	1,038	899	209	6	69	341	9
...	...	...	...	...	...	...	...	...	...	...	...	...	...
...	...	...	...	...	...	...	1,517	1,468	...	49	...	...	...
1,892	*1,554*	*81*	*59*	*20*	*173*	...	*4,305*	*3,733*	*193*	*61*	*18*	*299*	*1*
526	*458*	...	*6*	...	*62*	...	*904*	*826*	...	*24*	...	*54*	...
37	36	...	...	...	1	...	260	260	...	...	...	...	...
...	...	...	...	...	...	...	...	...	...	...	...	...	...
37	36	...	...	...	[illegible]	[illegible]	260	260	...	...	...	...	...
489	422	...	6	...	[illegible]	[illegible]	644	566	...	24	...	54	...
259	256	...	3	...	[illegible]	...	156	152	...	8	...	1	...
280	166	...	8	...	[illegible]	...	488	414	...	21	...	58	...
320	*294*	*9*	*14*	*3*	...	...	*1,531*	*1,400*	*6*	*5*	...	*120*	...
320	294	9	14	[illegible]	[illegible]	...	1,531	1,400	6	5	...	120	...
...	...	...	...	[illegible]	...	...	...	...	...	...	...	...	...
302	285	3	14	[illegible]	[illegible]	...	1,521	1,390	6	5	...	120	...
18	9	6	...	[illegible]	...	...	10	10	...	...	...	...	...
1,016	*802*	*72*	*39*	[illegible]	[illegible]	...	*1,870*	*1,507*	*187*	*32*	*13*	*125*	[illegible]
747	599	19	32	34	96	...	1,255	1,103	53	25	4	70	...
...	...	...	...	[illegible]	...	...	786	721	46	16	2	1	...
747	599	19	32	[illegible]	96	...	469	382	7	9	2	69	...
...	...	...	...	...	...	...	...	...	...	...	...	...	...
...	...	...	...	...	...	...	...	...	...	...	...	...	...
12	12	...	...	...	...	...	49	49	...	...	...	...	...
12	12	...	...	...	...	...	25	25	...	...	...	...	...
...	...	...	...	...	...	...	24	24	...	...	...	...	...
72	29	31	...	5	7	...	149	63	60	...	12	14	...
1	1	...	...	...	...	...	4	4	...	...	...	...	...
25	25	...	...	...	...	...	68	54	...	...	...	14	...
46	3	31	...	5	7	...	73	4	57	...	12	...	...
...	...	...	...	...	...	...	4	1	3	...	...	...	...

TABLE X.—Occupation or Means of

Group No.	Occupation.	ISAGARH. Total following occupation.	As principal occupation. Males.	As principal occupation. Females.	As working dependents. Males.	As working dependents. Females.	As subsidiary to other occupation. Males.	As subsidiary to other occupation. Females.
	B. Preparation and supply of materal substance.—(concld.)							
	V. Trade.—(concld.)							
	39. Trade of other sorts	3,061	2,346	339	98	72	190	16
149	Dealers in rags, stable refuse, etc.	...	...	...	...	...	...	...
150	General store-keepers and shop-keepers otherwise unspecified.	3,061	2,346	339	98	72	190	16
151	Itinerant traders, pedlars and hawkers (of other than food, etc).	...	...	...	...	...	...	...
152	Other trades (including farmers of pounds, tools and markets).	...	...	...	...	...	...	...
	C. Public Administration and Liberal Arts...	*6,983*	*5,887*	*270*	*157*	*6*	*635*	*28*
	VI. Public Force	*1,448*	*1,272*	...	*7*	...	*169*	...
	40. Army	391	389	...	...	...	2	...
153	Army (Imperial)	...	...	...	...	...	...	...
154	Army (Indian States)	391	389	...	...	...	2	...
	43. Police	[illegible]57	883	...	7	...	167	...
157	Police	53[illegible]	481	...	1	...	14	...
158	Village watchmen		402	...	6	...	158	...
	VII. Public Administration... ...	*[illegible],460*	*2,291*	*6*	*41*	...	*116*	*6*
	44. Public Administration	2,460	2,291	6	41	...	116	6
159	Service of the State		...	...	...	...	...	...
160	Service of Indian and Foreign State	2,417	261	...	40	...	116	...
161	Municipal and other local (not village) service ...	43	30	6	1	...	...	6
	VIII. Professions and Liberal Arts ...	*3,075*	*1,5[illegible]4*	*264*	*109*	*6*	*350*	*22*
	45. Religion	1,924	1,698	61	84	4	137	4
163	Priests, Ministers, etc.	1,199	1,0[illegible]4	27	54	4	34	1
164	Monks, nuns, religious mendicants	725	5[illegible]0	34	30	...	103	3
165	Other religious workers	...	...	...	...	...	...	...
166	Servants in religious edifices, burial and burning grounds, pilgrim conductors, circumcisers, etc.	...	...	...	...	...	...	...
	46. Law	30	30	..	...	...	...	...
167	Lawyers of all kinds, including Qazis, Law Agents and Mukhtiars.	23	23	...	...	...	...	...
168	Lawyers, clerks, petition writers, etc. ...	7	7	...	...	...	...	...
	47. Medicine	165	102	43	1	1	13	5
169	Registered medical practitioners including oculists.	...	...	...	...	...	...	...
170	Other persons practising the healing arts without being registered.	55	49	...	1	...	5	...
171	Midwives, vaccinators, compounders, nurses, masseurs, etc.	110	53	43	...	1	8	5
172	Veterinary surgeons	...	...	...	...	...	...	...

Livelihood. *Part I.—District Details.—(contd.)*

BHILSA.							UJJAIN.						
Total following occupation.	As principal occupation.		As working dependents.		As subsidiary to other occupation.		Total following occupation.	As principal occupation.		As working dependents.		As subsidiary to other occupation.	
	M.	F.	M.	F.	M.	F.		M.	F.	M.	F.	M.	F.
1,442	1,083	107	23	32	186	11	2,623	1,808	165	228	29	278	115
...	...	...	...	...	...	...	...	...	...	...	...	...	...
1,442	1,083	107	23	32	186	11	2,623	1,808	165	228	29	278	115
—	...	...	...	...	...	...	...	...	...	...	...	...	...
...	...	...	...	...	...	...	...	...	...	...	...	...	...
2,425	*1,811*	*151*	*61*	*23*	*349*	*31*	*7,433*	*5,850*	*419*	*216*	*78*	*806*	*64*
420	*366*	...	*5*	...	*49*	...	*1,461*	*1,158*	...	*40*	...	*266*	...
...	...	...	...	...	...	...	353	346	...	7	...	...	...
...	...	...	...	...	...	...	...	...	...	...	...	...	...
...	...	...	...	...	...	...	353	346	...	7	...	...	...
420	366	...	5	...	49	...	1,111	812	...	33	...	266	...
134	128	...	1	...	5	...	237	230	...	7	...	...	...
286	238	...	4	...	44	...	874	582	...	26	...	266	...
515	*487*	*8*	*5*	...	*9*	*6*	*2,371*	*2,260*	...	*111*	...	...	...
515	487	8	5	...	9	6	2,371	2,260	...	111	...	...	...
...	...	...	...	...	...	...	...	...	...	...	...	...	...
503	491	8	5	...	9	...	2,314	2,228	...	86	...	...	...
12	6	...	...	...	...	6	57	32	...	25	...	...	...
1,493	*958*	*143*	*51*	*25*	*291*	*25*	*3,598*	*2,432*	*419*	*63*	*78*	*540*	*64*
628	443	9	26	...	142	8	1,537	1,006	23	28	...	429	51
229	187	3	11	...	27	1	563	408	...	2	...	153	...
396	253	6	15	...	115	7	974	598	23	26	...	276	51
...	...	...	...	...	...	...	...	...	...	...	...	...	...
8	8	...	...	...	...	...	...	...	...	...	...	...	...
35	31	...	...	...	4	...	118	116	...	2	...	...	...
28	24	...	...	...	4	...	59	58	...	1	...	...	...
7	7	...	...	...	...	...	59	58	...	1	...	...	...
174	58	64	...	21	14	17	334	138	158	...	36	...	2
2	2	...	...	...	...	...	...	...	...	...	...	...	...
70	56	...	...	...	14	...	104	104	...	...	...	...	...
102	...	64	...	21	...	17	280	84	158	...	36	...	2
...	...	...	...	...	...	...	...	...	...	...	...	...	...

TABLE X:—Occupation or Means of

Group No.	Occupation.	MANDSAUR. Total following occupation.	As principal occupation. Males.	As principal occupation. Females.	As working dependents. Males.	As working dependents. Females.	As subsidiary to other occupation. Males.	As subsidiary to other occupation. Females.
	B. Preparation and supply of material substances.—(concld.)							
	V. Trade.—(concld.)							
	39. Trade of other sorts	3,445	2,446	126	213	20	618	22
149	Dealers in rags, stable refuse, etc.	2	...	2	...	...	...	...
150	General store-keepers and shop-keepers otherwise unspecified.	3,443	2,446	124	213	20	618	22
151	Itinerant traders, pedlars and hawkers (of other than food, etc.).	...	...	...	...	...	...	...
152	Other trades (including farmers of pounds, tools and markets).	...	...	...	...	...	...	...
	C. Public Administration and Liberal Arts ...	*5,018*	*3,779*	*290*	*129*	*49*	*709*	*62*
	VI. Public Force	*2,138*	*1,738*	...	*32*	...	*368*	...
	40. Army	1,018	1,007	...	11	...	...	...
153	Army (Imperial)	615	615	...	...	...	...	...
154	Army (Indian States)	403	392	...	11	...	...	...
	43. Police	1,120	731	...	21	...	368	...
157	Police	441	366	...	6	...	69	...
158	Village watchmen	679	365	...	15	...	299	...
	VII. Public Administration	*626*	*551*	*19*	*14*	...	*42*	...
	44. Public Administration	626	551	19	14	...	42	...
159	Service of the State	50	50	...	...	...	...	...
160	Service of Indian and Foreign State	550	475	19	14	...	42	...
161	Municipal and other local (not village) service ...	26	26	...	...	...	...	...
	VIII. Professions and Liberal Arts ...	*2,254*	*1,490*	*271*	*83*	*49*	*299*	*62*
	45. Religion	1,012	795	12	55	9	120	21
163	Priests, ministers, etc.	242	221	2	8	...	4	7
164	Monks, nuns, religious mendicants	760	565	9	47	9	116	14
165	Other religious workers	3	2	1	...	...	...	...
166	Servants in religious edifices, burial and burning grounds, pilgrim conductors, circumcisers, etc.	7	7	...	...	...	...	...
	46. Law	63	62	...	1	...	...	...
167	Lawyers of all kinds, including Qazis, Law Agents and Mukhtiars.	33	33	...	...	...	...	...
168	Lawyer's clerks, petition writers, etc. ...	30	29	...	1	...	...	...
	47. Medicine	247	28	152	1	23	34	9
169	Registered medical practitioners including oculists.	13	11	2	...	...	...	...
170	Other persons practising the healing arts without being registered.	44	9	...	1	...	34	...
172	Midwives, vaccinators, compounders, nurses, masseurs, etc.	190	8	150	...	23	...	9
173	Veterinary surgeons	...	...	...	...	...	...	...

Livelihood. *Part I.—District Details.—(contd.)*

SHAJAPUR.							AMJHERA.						
Total following occupation.	As principal occupation.		As working dependents.		As subsidiary to other occupation.		Total following occupation.	As principal occupation.		As working dependents.		As subsidiary to other occupation.	
	M.	F.	M.	F.	M.	F.		M.	F.	M.	F.	M.	F.
73	74	75	76	77	78	79	80	81	82	83	84	85	86
1,942	1,584	133	8	20	187	10	573	400	11	19	25	114	4
...	...	...	...	...	...	...	...	...	...	...	...	...	...
1,942	1,584	133	8	20	187	10	573	400	11	19	25	114	4
...	...	...	...	...	...	..	...	...	...	...	...	...	...
...	...	...	...	...	...	...	...	...	...	...	...	...	...
4,532	*3,449*	*240*	*67*	*12*	*709*	*55*	*1,635*	*1,198*	*49*	*18*	*10*	*398*	*12*
933	*684*	...	*27*	...	*222*	...	*460*	*282*	...	*5*	..	*173*	...
78	66	...	12	...	...	...	...	...	...	...	...	...	...
...	...	...	...	...	...	...	...	...	...	...	...	...	...
78	66	...	12	...	...	...	...	...	...	...	...	...	...
855	618	...	15	...	212	...	460	282	...	5	...	173	...
334	223	...	1	...	110	...	211	135	...	1	...	75	...
521	395	...	14	...	112	...	249	147	...	4	...	98	...
808	*750*	*9*	*7*	...	*40*	*2*	*510*	*479*	...	*5*	...	*24*	*2*
808	750	9	7	...	40	2	510	479	...	5	...	24	2
...	...	...	...	...	...	...	...	...	...	...	...	...	...
780	725	9	4	...	40	2	507	476	...	5	...	24	2
28	25	...	3	...	...	...	3	3	...	...	...	...	...
2,791	*2,015*	*231*	*33*	*12*	*437*	*53*	*715*	*437*	*49*	*8*	*10*	*201*	*10*
1,110	766	40	9	1	269	25	386	231	10	4	2	138	1
299	298	...	1	...	...	...	38	34	...	...	...	4	...
811	468	40	8	1	269	25	348	197	10	4	2	134	1
...	...	...	...	...	...	...	...	...	...	...	...	...	...
...	...	...	...	...	...	...	...	...	...	...	...	...	...
100	100	...	...	...	...	...	41	41	...	...	...	...	...
28	28	...	...	...	...	...	7	7	...	...	...	...	...
72	72	...	...	...	...	...	34	34	...	...	...	...	...
153	133	...	7	...	13	...	44	18	20	...	5	1	...
3	...	...	...	...	3	...	...	...	...	...	...	...	...
47	87	...	...	...	10	...	16	15	...	...	...	1	...
103	96	...	7	...	...	...	28	3	20	...	5	...	...
...	...	...	...	...	...	...	...	...	...	...	...	...	...

TABLE X.—Occupation or Means of

Group No.	Occupation.	GWALIOR STATE.						
		Total following occupation.	As principal occupation.		As working dependents.		As subsidiary to other occupation.	
			Males.	Females.	Males.	Females.	Males.	Females.
1	2	8	4	5	6	7	8	9
	C. Public Administration and Liberal Arts.-(concld.)							
	VIII. Professions and Liberal Arts.-(concld.)							
	48. Instruction	1,986	1,534	156	86	1	207	2
174	Professors and teachers of all kinds	1,978	1,529	156	86	1	204	2
175	Clerks and servants connected with education ...	8	5	...	...	...	3	...
	49. Letters, arts and sciences (other than 44).	6,954	4,441	1,134	147	107	1,004	121
177	Architects, surveyors, engineers and their employees (not being State servants).	78	71	...	...	...	2	...
178	Authors, editors, journalists and photographers ...	207	124	8	3	2	69	1
179	Artists, sculptors and image-makers	21	13	...	...	...	8	...
181	Horoscope casters, astrologers, fortune tellers, wizards, witches and mediums.	88	60	10	1	8	...	...
182	Musicians (composers and performers other than military), actors, dancers, etc.	5,868	3,520	1,064	135	99	925	120
183	Managers and employees of places of public entertainments, race courses, societies, clubs.	6	6	...	...	...	...	...
184	Conjurors, acrobats, reciters, exhibitors of curiosities and wild animals, etc.	701	647	43	3	8	...	...
	D. Miscellaneous	*203,366*	*100,922*	*51,035*	*8,452*	*12,858*	*22,627*	*7,412*
	IX. Persons Living on their Income ...	*1,739*	*786*	*405*	*33*	*26*	*454*	*35*
	50. Persons living principally on their income.	1,739	786	405	33	26	454	35
185	Proprietors (other than of agricultural land), fund and scholarship-holders and pensioners.	1,739	786	405	33	26	454	35
	X. Domestic Service	*31,732*	*21,279*	*5,736*	*673*	*1,068*	*1,942*	*1,034*
	51. Domestic service	31,732	21,279	5,736	673	1,068	1,942	1,034
186	Private motor-drivers and cleaners	714	689	2	20	...	3	...
187	Other domestic service	31,018	20,590	5,734	653	1,068	1,939	1,034
	XI. Insufficiently described Occupations ...	*143,599*	*64,060*	*40,719*	*5,140*	*10,810*	*16,957*	*5,913*
	52. General terms which do not indicate a definite occupation.	143,599	64,060	40,719	5,140	10,810	16,957	5,913
188	Manufacturers, businessmen and contractors otherwise unspecified.	4,844	3,016	740	65	366	636	15
189	Cashiers, accountants, bookkeepers, clerks and other employees in unspecified offices and warehouses and shops.	14,625	9,695	666	390	63	3,659	152
190	Mechanics otherwise unspecified	140	13	106	...	30	...	...
191	Labourers and workmen otherwise unspecified ...	123,981	51,336	39,201	4,685	10,351	12,662	5,746
	XII. Unproductive	*26,236*	*14,797*	*4,175*	*2,606*	*954*	*3,274*	*430*
	53. Inmates of jails, asylums and alms houses.	1,909	...	...	1,605	302	2	...
192	Inmates of jails, asylums and alms houses ...	1,909	...	...	1,605	302	2	...
	54. Beggars, vagrants, prostitutes ...	24,167	14,796	4,171	1,001	652	3,117	430
193	Beggars and vagrants	23,898	14,756	4,033	993	636	3,113	367
194	Procurers and prostitutes	269	40	138	8	16	4	63
	55. Other unclassified non productive industries.	160	1	4	...	...	155	...
195	Other unclassified non-productive industries ...	160	1	4	...	...	155	...

Livelihood. *Part I—District Details.—(contd.)*

GIRD.							BHIND.						
Total following occupation.	As principal occupation.		As working dependents.		As subsidiary to other occupation.		Total following occupation.	As principal occupation.		As working dependents.		As subsidiary to other occupation.	
	M.	F.	M.	F.	M.	F.		M.	F.	M.	F	M.	F.
10	11	12	13	14	15	16	17	18	19	20	21	22	23
444	351	57	4	...	32	...	150	129	2	...	...	19	...
436	346	57	4	...	29	...	150	129	2	...	...	19	...
8	5	...	...	...	8	...	...	...	...	...	...	...	...
583	352	154	24	6	40	7	632	335	112	5	8	157	15
6	6	...	...	...	...	...	9	9	...	...	...	...	...
9	8	1	...	...	...	...	38	25	...	1	...	12	...
6	6	...	...	...	...	...	...	...	...	...	...	...	...
6	6	...	...	...	...	...	...	...	...	...	...	...	...
521	294	150	24	6	40	7	585	301	112	4	8	145	15
6	6	...	...	...	...	...	...	...	...	...	...	...	...
29	26	3	...	...	...	...	...	...	...	...	...	...	...
29,992	*16,975*	*6,632*	*1,694*	*1,490*	*2,327*	*874*	*13,100*	*5,678*	*1,568*	*218*	*452*	*3,881*	*1,303*
669	*475*	*71*	*24*	*3*	*92*	*4*	*101*	*16*	*10*	*1*	*2*	*58*	*14*
669	475	71	24	3	92	4	101	16	10	1	2	58	14
669	475	71	24	3	92	4	101	16	10	1	2	58	14
8,200	*5,719*	*1,626*	*60*	*242*	*451*	*102*	*2,921*	*1,868*	*539*	*57*	*285*	*81*	*91*
8,200	5,719	1,626	60	242	451	102	2,921	1,868	539	57	285	81	91
179	175	...	2	...	2	...	9	9	...	...	...	...	...
8,021	5,544	1,626	58	242	449	102	2,912	1,859	539	57	285	81	91
17,821	*9,464*	*4,588*	*425*	*930*	*1,665*	*749*	*8,405*	*2,872*	*872*	*76*	*138*	*3,324*	*1,123*
17,821	9,464	4,588	425	930	1,665	749	8,405	2,872	872	76	138	3,324	1,123
817	388	29	3	2	395	...	471	427	12	11	3	17	1
2,138	1,815	3	3	...	293	24	850	...	...	...	...	840	10
...	...	...	...	...	...	...	...	...	...	...	...	...	...
14,866	7,261	4,556	419	928	977	725	7,075	2,445	860	65	125	2,467	1,103
3,302	*1,317*	*347*	*1,185*	*315*	*119*	*19*	*1,673*	*922*	*147*	*84*	*27*	*418*	*75*
1,389	...	...	1,126	261	2	...	61	...	...	61	...	...	...
1,389	...	...	1,126	261	2	...	61	...	...	61	...	...	...
1,912	1,316	347	59	54	117	19	1,461	922	147	23	27	267	75
1,897	1,316	337	59	54	117	14	1,425	922	140	23	27	[illegible]	[illegible]
15	...	10	...	...	...	5	[illegible]	...	7	...	...	...	[illegible]
1	1	...	...	...	...	...	151	...	...	...	...	151	...
1	1	...	...	...	...	...	151	...	...	...	...	151	...

TABLE X.—Occupation or Means of

Group No.	Occupation.	TONWARGHAR.						
		Total following occupation.	As principal occupation.		As working dependents.		As subsidiary to other occupation.	
			Males.	Females.	Males.	Females.	Males.	Females.
1	2	24	25	26	27	28	29	30
	C. Public Administration and Liberal Arts—(concld.)							
	VIII. Professions and Liberal Arts—(concld.)							
	48. Instruction	233	163	5	52	...	11	2
174	Professors and teachers of all kinds	233	163	5	52	...	11	2
[illegible]	Clerks and servants connected with education ...	...	...	...	...	...	...	...
	49. Letters, arts and sciences (other than 44)	441	267	79	3	3	84	5
177	Architects, surveyors, engineers and their employees (not being State servants).	13	13	...	...	...	...	...
[illegible]	Authors, editors, journalists and photographers...	36	25	...	...	...	10	1
[illegible]	Artists, sculptors and image-makers	5	5	...	...	...	...	...
[illegible]	Horoscope casters, astrologers, fortune-tellers, wizards, witches and mediums.	...	...	...	...	...	...	...
[illegible]	Musicians (composers and performers other than military), actors, dancers, etc.	360	197	79	3	3	74	4
[illegible]	Managers and employees of places of public entertainment, race courses, societies, clubs.	...	...	...	...	...	...	...
[illegible]	[illegible], exhibitors of [illegible] animals, etc.	27	27	...	...	...	...	...
	D. Miscellaneous	12,351	1,713	2,366	418	1,021	2,731	1,075
	IX. Persons living on their income ...	150	2[illegible]	11	...	1	107	2
	53. Persons living principally on their income.	150	29	11	...	1	107	2
[illegible]	Proprietors (other than of agricultural land), fund and scholarship holders and pensioners.	180	29	11	...	1	107	2
	X. Domestic service	2,31[illegible]	1,672	320	6[illegible]	11[illegible]	78	300
	54. Domestic service	2,319	1,672	320	65	114	78	300
[illegible]	Private grooms, coachmen, dog-boys, etc.	4	4	...	...	...	...	...
[illegible]	Other domestic service	2,315	1,6[illegible]	320	65	114	78	300
	XI. Insufficiently described occupations ...	7,72[illegible]	1,9[illegible]7	1,6[illegible]1	219	812	2,213	749
	55. General terms which do not indicate a definite occupation.	7,729	1,987	1,681	219	812	2,218	749
[illegible]	[illegible]	3[illegible]5	251	[illegible]	10	9	[illegible]0	...
[illegible]	[illegible]	5[illegible]7	...	[illegible]7	...	1	5[illegible]	6
[illegible]	[illegible]	1	1	...	...	...	...	...
[illegible]	[illegible]	[illegible]	1,7[illegible]	1,[illegible]	[illegible]	[illegible]	1,[illegible]	[illegible]
	[illegible]	[illegible]	[illegible]	[illegible]	[illegible]	[illegible]	[illegible]	2[illegible]
	56. Inmates of jails, asylums and almshouses.	41		–	36	4	...	
[illegible]	[illegible]	4[illegible]	...		[illegible]	4		
	57. Beggars, vagrants, prostitutes.	1,9[illegible]	1,6[illegible]	[illegible]	124	[illegible]	[illegible]	[illegible]
[illegible]	[illegible]	1,8[illegible]	[illegible]	[illegible]	[illegible]	[illegible]	[illegible]	[illegible]
[illegible]	[illegible]	[illegible]	[illegible]	[illegible]		7	1	
	58. [illegible]							
[illegible]	[illegible]					...	...	

Livelihood. *Part I.—District Details.—(contd.)*

SHEOPUR.							NARWAR.						
Total following occupation.	As principal occupation.		As working dependents.		As subsidiary to other occupation.		Total following occupation.	As principal occupation.		As working dependents.		As subsidiary to other occupation.	
	M.	F.	M.	F.	M.	F.		M.	F.	M.	F.	M.	F.
31	32	33	34	35	36	37	38	39	40	41	42	43	44
39	34	5	...	..	...	...	122	92	17	2	...	11	...
39	34	5	...	...	...	...	122	92	17	2	...	11	...
...	..	..	...	...	...	...	...	...	...	...	...	...	...
156	128	17	7	11	13	...	293	200	57	5	2	30	1
1	1	...	.	...	...	...	1	1	...	...	...	...	...
[illegible]	7	2	...	2	13	.	...	...	...	...	...	...	...
...	..	.	...	...	...	...	2	2	...	...	...	...	...
1	1	..	...	.	...	...	3	3	...	...	...	...	...
133	11[illegible]	15	7	8	...	...	278	183	57	5	2	30	1
...	...	..	...	...	...	..	...	...	...	...	...	—	...
24	23	...	..	1	...	...	11	11	...	...	...	...	...
[illegible]	*[illegible]*	*[illegible]*	*[illegible]*	*[illegible]*	*[illegible]*	*[illegible]*	*21,563*	*10,599*	*5,383*	*731*	*1,939*	*2,455*	*472*
25	*7*	*7*	...	...	*12*	...	*16*	*12*	*4*	...	...	...	...
25	8	5	..	.	12	...	16	12	4	...	...	...	...
25	8	5	...	...	12	...	16	12	4	...	...	...	...
[illegible]	*[illegible]*	*[illegible]*	*87*	*28*	*19*	*8*	*3,107*	*2,358*	*189*	*89*	*10*	*434*	*27*
1,013	655	243	87	28	19	8	3,107	2,358	189	89	10	434	27
47	14	...	3	...	..	...	22	22	...	...	...	...	...
[illegible]	641	243	84	28	19	8	3,095	2,336	189	89	10	434	27
7,376	*3,258*	*2,137*	*170*	*760*	*813*	*238*	*16,452*	*6,918*	*4,872*	*556*	*1,855*	*1,854*	*427*
7,376	3,258	2,137	170	760	813	238	16,452	6,918	4,672	556	1,853	1,854	427
142	111	17	...	...	12	2	1,919	416	400	...	313	...	...
[illegible]	[illegible]	7	6	...	101	3	758	481	...	100	...	177	...
...	...	...	...	...	...	...	...	...	...	...	...	...	...
[illegible]	2,267	2,113	115	760	700	203	14,505	6,021	4,089	456	1,549	1,677	427
[illegible]	*617*	*62*	*25*	*21*	*130*	*4*	*1,964*	*1,311*	*318*	*86*	*61*	*167*	*18*
...	...	...	...	...	...	...	...	...	...	...	...	...	...
...	...	...	...	...	...	...	...	...	...	...	...	...	...
911	637	62	25	23	130	4	1,964	1,311	318	86	64	167	18
901	637	62	25	23	130	4	1,953	1,311	311	86	64	167	14
...	...	...	...	...	...	...	11	...	7	...	...	...	4
...	...	...	...	...	...	...	...	...	...	...	...	...	...
...	...	...	...	...	...	...	...	...	...	...	...	...	...

TABLE X.—Occupation or Means of

Group No.	Occupation.	ISAGARH.						
		Total following occupation.	As principal occupation.		As working dependents.		As subsidiary to other occupation.	
			Males.	Females.	Males.	Females.	Males.	Females
1	2	45	46	47	48	49	50	51
	C. Public Administration and Liberal Arts.—(concld.)							
	VIII. Professions and Liberal Arts.—(concld.)							
	48. Instruction	168	151	6	1	...	10	...
174	Professors and teachers of all kinds ...	168	151	6	1	...	10	...
175	Clerks and servants connected with education ...	...	...	...	...	...	...	...
	49. Letters, arts and sciences (other than 44).	788	407	154	23	1	190	13
177	Architects, surveyors, engineers and their employees (not being State servants).	...	...	...	...	...	...	...
178	Authors, editors, journalists and photographers...	29	28	...	1	...	...	...
179	Artists, sculptors and image-makers ...	7	...	...	...	...	7	...
181	Horoscope casters, astrologers, fortune-tellers, wizards, witches and mediums.	4	4	...	...	...	...	...
182	Musicians (composers and performers other than military), actors, dancers, etc.	678	316	148	22	1	188	18
183	Managers and employees of places of public entertainments, race courses, societies, clubs.	...	...	...	...	...	...	...
184	Conjurors, acrobats, reciters, exhibitors of curiosities and wild animals, etc.	70	59	11	...	...	...	...
	D. Miscellaneous	*29,334*	*13,835*	*8,486*	*944*	*1,963*	*2,877*	*1,229*
	IX. Persons Living on their Income ...	*60*	*36*	*20*	...	*3*	*1*	...
	50. persons living Principally on their income.	60	36	20	...	3	1	...
185	Proprietors (other than of agricultural land), fund and scholarship-holders and pensioners.	60	36	20	...	3	1	...
	X. Domestic Service...	*2,788*	*1,069*	*1,016*	*62*	*149*	*277*	*215*
	51. Domestic service	2,788	1,069	1,016	62	149	277	215
186	Private motor-drivers and cleaners	27	22	...	5	...	...	...
187	Other domestic service	2,761	1,047	1,016	57	149	277	215
	XI. Insufficiently described Occupations ...	*23,523*	*10,834*	*6,947*	*767*	*1,764*	*2,254*	*957*
	52. General terms which do not indicate a definite occupation.	23,523	10,834	6,947	767	1,764	2,254	957
188	Manufacturers, businessmen and contractors otherwise unspecified.	775	502	184	4	87	98	...
189	Cashiers, accountants, bookkeepers, clerks and other employees in unspecified offices and warehouses and shops.	616	428	60	7	1	95	25
190	Mechanics otherwise unspecified	...	...	...	...	...	...	...
191	Labourers and workmen otherwise unspecified ...	22,132	9,904	6,758	756	1,726	2,061	982
	XII. Unproductive	*2,963*	*1,896*	*503*	*115*	*47*	*345*	*57*
	53. Inmates of jails, asylums and alms houses.	...	...	...	...	...	...	...
192	Inmates of jails, asylums and alms houses ...	...	...	...	...	...	...	...
	54 Beggars, vagrants, prostitutes ...	2,963	1,896	503	115	47	345	57
193	Beggars and vagrants	2,951	1,896	495	115	47	345	53
194	Procurers and prostitutes	12	...	8	...	...	...	4
	55. Other unclassified non-productive industries.	...	...	...	...	...	...	...
195	Other unclassified non-productive industries ...	...	...	...	...	...	...	...

Livelihood. *Part I.—District Details.—(contd.)*

BHILSA.							UJJAIN.						
Total following occupation.	As principal occupation.		As working dependents.		As subsidiary to other occupation.		Total following occupation.	As principal occupation.		As working dependents.		As subsidiary to other occupation.	
	M.	F.	M.	F.	M.	F.		M.	F.	M.	F.	M.	F.
52	53	54	55	56	57	58	59	60	61	62	63	64	65
142	108	14	9	...	11	...	147	143	1	3	...	...	...
142	108	14	9	...	11	...	147	148	1	8	...	...	...
...	...	...	...	...	...	...	..	...	...	...	...	...	...
514	318	56	16	4	120	...	1,462	1,029	237	32	42	111	11
5	5	...	...	...	...	...	21	21	...	...	...	...	...
8	8	...	...	...	...	...	81	9	...	...	...	22	...
...	...	...	...	...	...	...	...	...	...	...	...	...	...
...	...	...	...	...	...	...	...	...	...	...	...	...	...
437	251	47	15	4	120	...	1,164	753	237	27	42	89	11
...	...	...	...	...	..	...	...	...	...	...	...	...	...
69	59	9	1	...	...	...	246	241	...	5	...	...	...
17,497	10,387	3,847	644	856	1,454	309	27,300	13,174	9,239	1,208	1,306	1,599	774
51	24	5	...	...	21	1	407	99	180	2	4	111	11
51	24	5	...	...	21	1	407	99	180	2	4	111	11
51	24	5	...	...	21	1	407	99	180	2	4	111	11
1,807	1,268	294	40	25	152	28	5,346	3,765	1,131	87	148	141	74
1,807	1,268	294	40	25	152	28	5,346	3,765	1,131	87	148	141	74
8	8	...	...	...	...	...	308	299	...	9	...	...	...
1,804	1,265	294	40	25	152	28	5,038	3,466	1,131	78	148	141	74
12,955	7,376	3,208	480	792	857	242	16,790	6,891	6,936	532	939	907	585
12,955	7,376	3,208	480	792	857	242	16,799	6,891	6,936	532	939	907	585
77	59	2	1	...	15	...	432	399	...	19	...	14	...
1,559	1,257	53	48	4	194	3	866	309	48	21	5	457	26
140	4	106	...	30	...	...	..	...	...	...	...	...	...
11,179	6,056	3,047	481	758	648	239	15,492	6,183	6,868	492	984	406	559
2,684	1,719	340	124	39	421	38	4,757	2,419	992	587	215	440	104
...	...	...	...	...	...	...	419	...	...	352	37	...	...
...	...	...	...	...	...	...	419	...	...	382	37	...	...
2,680	1,719	336	124	39	424	38	4,338	2,419	992	205	178	440	104
2,677	1,718	336	124	39	424	36	4,257	2,386	973	202	169	440	87
3	1	...	...	...	...	2	81	33	19	3	9	...	17
4	...	4	...	...	...	...	...	...	...	...	...	...	...
4	...	4	...	...	...	...	...	...	...	...	...	...	...

TABLE X.—Occupation or Means of

Group No.	Occupation	MANDSAUR.						
		Total following occupation.	As principal occupation.		As working dependents.		As subsidiary to other occupation.	
			Males.	Females.	Males.	Females.	Males.	Females.
1	2	66	67	68	69	70	71	72
	C. Public Administration and Liberal Arts—(concld.)							
	VIII. Professions and Liberal Arts.—(concld.)							
	48 Instruction	297	169	29	12	1	86	...
174	Professors and teachers of all kinds	297	169	29	12	1	86	...
175	Clerks and servants connected with education ...	...	...	...	...	...	...	...
	49 Letters arts and sciences (other than 44)	635	436	78	14	16	59	32
177	Architects surveyors, engineers and their employees (not being State servants).	...	...	...	...	...	...	...
178	Authors, editors, journalists and photographers.	1	1	...	...	...	...	...
179	Artists, sculptors and image-makers	...	...	...	...	...	...	...
181	Horoscope casters, astrologers, fortune-tellers, wizards, witches and mediums	40	39	1	...	...	...	...
182	Musicians (composers and performers other than military), actors, dancers, etc.	580	382	77	14	16	59	32
183	Managers and employees of places of public entertainment, race courses, societies, clubs.	...	...	...	...	...	...	...
184	Conjurers, acrobats, reciters, exhibitors of curiosities and wild animals, etc.	14	14	...	...	...	...	...
	D. Miscellaneous	*21,573*	*9,691*	*5,183*	*1,382*	*1,816*	*2,535*	*726*
	IX. Persons Living on their Income ...	*169*	*40*	*72*	*5*	*12*	*31*	...
	50 Persons living principally on their income.	169	40	72	5	12	31	...
185	Proprietors (other than of agricultural land), fund and scholarship holders and pensioners.	169	40	72	5	12	31	...
	X. Domestic Service	*2,260*	*1,570*	*212*	*60*	*49*	*189*	*150*
	51. Domestic Service	2,260	1,570	212	60	49	189	150
186	Private motor drivers and cleaners	35	33	...	1	...	1	...
187	Other domestic service	2,225	1,537	212	59	49	188	150
	XI. Insufficiently described Occupations ...	*16,619*	*6,636*	*4,6[illegible]*	*1,184*	*1,691*	*1,[illegible]*	*525*
	52 General terms which do not indicate a definite occupation.	16,619	6,636	[illegible]	1,184	1,691	1,[illegible]	525
[illegible]	[illegible] and contractors [illegible]	[illegible]	151	9	16	...	1	...
[illegible]	[illegible] clerks [illegible] and [illegible]	2,[illegible]	1,45[illegible]	223	181	29	[illegible]	27
[illegible]	[illegible]	5	5	...	...	...	...	...
[illegible]	[illegible]	13,[illegible]	4,752	[illegible]	1,037	1,662	1,212	499
	[illegible]	2,[illegible]	[illegible]	[illegible]	[illegible]	[illegible]	41[illegible]	51
	53 Inmates of jails, asylums and alms houses.	...	...	...	...	...	...	...
[illegible]	[illegible]	...	...	...	...	...	...	...
	54 [illegible]	2,[illegible]	1,[illegible]	[illegible]	12[illegible]	91	415	51
[illegible]	[illegible]	2,[illegible]	1,[illegible]	[illegible]	[illegible]	[illegible]	415	51
[illegible]	[illegible]	...			...	...	...	...
	[illegible]	...	...	...	...	...	...	...
[illegible]	[illegible]	...		...	...		...	...

Livelihood. *Part I—District Details.—(concld.)*

SHAJAPUR.							AMJHERA.						
Total following occupation.	As principal occupation.		As working dependents.		As subsidiary to other occupation.		Total following occupation.	As principal occupation.		As working dependents.		As subsidiary to other occupation.	
	M.	F.	M.	F.	M.	F.		M.	F.	M.	F.	M.	F.
73	74	75	76	77	78	79	80	81	82	83	84	85	86
172	124	19	2	...	27	...	52	50	1	1	...	...	...
172	124	19	2	...	27	...	52	50	1	1	...	...	...
...	...	...	...	...	...	...	...	...	...	...	...	...	...
1,256	892	172	15	11	138	28	192	97	18	3	3	62	9
15	15	...	...	...	...	...	2	...	...	...	...	2	...
28	22	5	1	...	...	...	13	1	...	...	...	12	...
1	...	...	...	...	1	...	...	...	...	...	...	...	...
...	...	...	...	...	...	...	29	7	18	1	3	...	...
1,007	672	147	14	9	137	28	142	85	...	...	...	48	9
...	...	...	...	...	...	...	...	...	...	...	...	...	...
205	183	20	...	2	...	...	6	4	...	2	...	...	...
15,199	*7,914*	*4,398*	*444*	*686*	*1,386*	*371*	*6,046*	*3,458*	*1,166*	*457*	*498*	*408*	*59*
69	*20*	*27*	*1*	*1*	*20*	...	*31*	*27*	...	...	...	*1*	*3*
69	20	27	1	1	20	...	31	27	...	...	...	1	3
69	20	27	1	1	20	...	31	27	...	...	...	1	3
826	*543*	*100*	*15*	*9*	*120*	*39*	*888*	*792*	*36*	*51*	*9*	...	...
826	543	100	15	9	120	39	888	792	36	51	9	...	...
70	68	2	...	...	...	...	10	10	...	...	...	...	...
756	475	98	15	9	120	39	878	782	36	51	9	...	...
11,518	*5,713*	*3,739*	*360*	*627*	*785*	*294*	*4,381*	*2,081*	*1,053*	*371*	*462*	*360*	*54*
11,518	5,713	3,739	360	627	785	294	4,381	2,081	1,053	371	462	360	54
296	246	17	...	...	33	...	71	33	2	1	2	21	12
2,679	2,257	176	48	3	177	18	874	662	59	27	20	104	2
...	...	...	...	...	...	...	...	...	...	...	...	...	...
8,543	3,210	3,546	312	624	575	276	3,486	1,886	992	348	440	235	40
2,786	*1,638*	*532*	*68*	*49*	*461*	*38*	*746*	*558*	*77*	*35*	*27*	*47*	*2*
...	...	...	...	...	...	...	...	...	...	...	...	...	...
...	...	...	...	...	...	...	...	...	...	...	...	...	...
2,782	1,638	532	68	49	457	38	746	558	77	35	27	47	2
2,757	1,633	519	68	49	457	36	746	558	77	35	27	47	2
25	5	13	5	...	...	2	...	...	...	...	...	...	...
4	...	...	...	...	4	...	...	...	...	...	...	...	...
4	...	...	...	...	4	...	...	...	...	...	...	...	...

TABLE X.—Occupation or Means of Livelihood. Part II.—Cities.

Group No.	Occupation.	LASHKAR CITY. Total following occupation.	As principal occupation. M.	F.	As working dependents. M.	F.	As subsidiary to other occupation. M.	F.	UJJAIN CITY. Total following occupation.	As principal occupation. M.	F.	As working dependents. M.	F.	As subsidiary to other occupation. M.	F.
		Total Earners ... 35,930; Total Working Dependents ... 2,198; Total Non-Working Dependents ... 48,639; Total Population ... 86,767							Total Earners ... 26,641; Total Working Dependents ... 1,468; Total Non-Working Dependents ... 26,541; Total Population ... 54,650						
1	2	3	4	5	6	7	8	9	10	11	12	13	14	15	16
	Total ...	39,608	32,603	3,927	1,707	491	809	71	29,645	23,334	3,307	1,1	447	1,403	133
	A. Production of Raw Materials	*3,452*	*2,793*	*327*	*96*	*6*	*190*	*20*	*3,657*	*2,664*	*416*	*134*	*163*	*248*	*32*
	I. Exploitation of Animals and Vegetation ...	*2,510*	*1,982*	*277*	*85*	*6*	*158*	*2*	*3,657*	*2,664*	*416*	*134*	*163*	*248*	*32*
	1. Pasture and agriculture	2,500	1,979	275	85	6	154	1	3,653	2,662	416	134	163	246	32
	(a) Cultivation	*1,907*	*1,507*	*206*	*41*	*5*	*147*	*1*	*2,911*	*2,207*	*249*	*108*	*138*	*190*	*19*
1	Non-cultivating proprietors taking rent in money or kind.	1,203	967	123	9	1	108	...	586	548	17	11	5	5	...
5	Cultivating owners	108	60	21	10	...	17	...	186	142	18	2	2	22	...
6	Tenant cultivators	457	381	28	18	2	27	1	1,275	1,026	66	52	10	104	17
7	Agricultural labourers	139	99	84	4	2	..	...	864	491	148	43	121	59	2
	(b) Cultivation of special crops, fruit, etc. (planters, managers, clerks and labourers).	*134*	*121*	*11*	*2*	...	...	...	*110*	*104*	...	*2*	...	*4*	...
16	Market gardeners, flower and fruit growers ...	134	121	11	2	...	...	...	110	104	...	2	...	4	...
	(c) Forestry	*25*	*25*	...	...	...	...	...	*52*	*4*	*37*	...	*10*	*1*	...
17	Forest officers, rangers, guards, etc.... ...	23	23	...	...	...	...	...	...	...	...	...	...	...	...
18	Wood cutters and charcoal burners	2	2	...	...	...	...	...	...	...	...	...	...	...	...
19	Collectors of forest produce	...	...	...	...	...	...	...	52	4	37	...	10	1	...
	(d) Stock raising	*429*	*321*	*58*	*42*	*1*	*7*	...	*580*	*347*	*130*	*24*	*15*	*51*	*13*
21	Cattle and buffalo breeders and keepers ...	303	222	50	31	...	...	...	197	168	15	1	9	4	...
23	Herdsmen, shepherds & breeders of other animals	126	99	8	11	1	7	...	383	179	115	23	6	47	13
	(e) Raising of small animals and insects.	*5*	*5*	...	...	...	...	...	...	...	...	...	...	...	...
24	Birds, bees, etc.	5	5	...	...	...	...	...	...	...	...	...	...	...	...
	2. Fishing and hunting	10	3	2	...	...	4	1	4	2	...	...	...	2	...
27	Fishing and pearling	7	2	2	...	...	2	1	4	2	...	...	...	2	...
28	Hunting	3	1	...	...	...	2	...	...	...	...	...	...	...	...
	II. Exploitation of Minerals	*922*	*811*	*50*	*11*	...	*32*	*18*	...	...	...	...	...	...	...
	4. Non-metallic minerals	922	811	50	11	...	32	18	...	...	...	...	...	...	...
37	Building materials (including stone, materials for cement manufacture and clays).	922	811	50	11	...	32	18	...	...	...	...	...	...	...
	B. Preparation and Supply of Material Substances.	*15,660*	*12,916*	*1,873*	*289*	*216*	*346*	*20*	*14,176*	*11,766*	*1,385*	*354*	*127*	*505*	*39*
	III. Industry	*7,935*	*6,186*	*1,257*	*216*	*138*	*152*	*6*	*7,633*	*6,148*	*1,071*	*188*	*97*	*121*	*25*
	5. Textiles	1,668	1,434	156	29	17	30	2	2,933	2,641	251	16	17	2	6
42	Cotton ginning, cleaning and pressing ...	118	90	13	10	...	...	...	846	206	117	7	16	...	...
43	Cotton spinning, sizing and weaving ...	1,400	1,234	109	18	11	26	2	2,186	2,043	134	...	1	2	6
45	Rope, twine, string and other fibres ...	33	33	...	...	...	...	...	...	...	...	...	...	...	...
47	Wool carding, spinning and weaving ...	...	...	...	...	...	...	...	9	9	...	...	...	...	...
47	Dyeing, bleaching, printing, preparation and sponging of textiles.	104	68	26	1	6	3	...	392	383	...	9	...	...	...
50	Lace, crepe, embroideries, fringes, etc., and insufficiently described textile industries.	18	9	8	...	...	1	...	...	...	...	...	...	...	...

TABLE X.—Occupation or Means of Livelihood. *Part II.—Cities.—(contd.)*

Group No.	Occupation.	LASHKAR CITY. Total following occupation.	As principal occupation. M.	As principal occupation. F.	As working dependents. M.	As working dependents. F.	As subsidiary to other occupation. M.	As subsidiary to other occupation. F.	UJJAIN CITY. Total following occupation.	As principal occupation. M.	As principal occupation. F.	As working dependents. M.	As working dependents. F.	As subsidiary to other occupation. M.	As subsidiary to other occupation. F.
1	2	3	4	5	6	7	8	9	10	11	12	13	14	15	16
	B. Preparation and Supply of Material Substances.—(contd.)														
	III. Industry—(contd.)														
	6. Hides, skins and hard materials from the animal kingdom.	160	92	26	21	2	18	1	549	390	102	15	27	15	...
51	Working in leather	160	92	26	21	2	18	1	549	390	102	15	27	15	...
	7. Wood	475	356	97	10	7	5	...	647	425	143	45	3	22	9
55	Carpenters, turners and joiners, etc.... ...	303	286	10	3	...	4	...	294	231	...	45	...	10	8
56	Basket makers and other industries of woody materials, including leaves and thatchers and builders working with bamboo, reeds or similar materials.	172	70	87	7	7	1	...	358	194	148	...	3	12	1
	8. Metals	370	331	7	1	...	31	...	285	259	...	18	...	6	2
58	Makers of arms, guns, etc...	2	2	...	...	...	...	...	20	20	...	...	...	...	...
59	Blacksmiths, other workers in iron, makers of implements.	203	195	7	1	...	...	...	198	174	...	16	...	6	2
60	Workers in brass, copper and bell metal ...	148	117	...	...	...	31	...	44	42	...	2	...	...	...
61	Workers in other metals (except precious metals).	17	17	...	...	...	...	...	23	23	...	...	...	...	...
	9. Ceramics	505	327	158	10	9	...	1	293	212	58	7	6	10	...
63	Potters and makers of earthenware	503	325	158	10	9	...	1	208	162	28	6	2	10	...
64	Brick and tile makers	...	...	...	...	...	...	...	85	50	30	1	4	...	...
65	Other workers in ceramics	2	2	...	...	...	...	...	...	...	...	...	...	...	...
	10. Chemical products properly so-called and analogous.	324	294	29	...	...	1	...	254	202	3	2	...	47	...
66	Manufacture of matches, fireworks and other explosives.	50	50	...	...	...	...	...	41	...	...	...	...	41	...
67	Manufacture of aerated and mineral waters & ice.	30	30	...	...	...	...	...	30	22	3	...	...	5	...
68	Manufacture and refining of vegetable oils ...	241	211	29	...	...	1	...	183	180	...	2	...	1	...
70	Others	3	3	...	...	...	...	...	...	...	...	...	...	...	...
	11. Food Industries	739	623	102	4	5	3	2	549	367	171	6	4	...	1
71	Rice pounders and huskers and flour grinders ...	122	25	91	...	4	...	2	188	27	156	...	4	...	1
72	Grain parchers, etc.	72	61	11	...	...	...	...	45	42	3	...	...	...	...
73	Butchers	48	48	...	...	...	...	...	15	15	...	...	...	...	...
75	Sweetmeat and condiment makers	410	408	...	...	...	2	...	289	283	...	6	...	...	...
78	Manufacture of tobacco	13	11	...	...	1	1	...	12	...	12	...	...	...	...
81	Others	79	75	...	4	...	...	...	...	...	...	...	...	...	...
	12. Industries of dress and the toilet ...	1,389	1,018	238	84	45	4	...	1,151	911	153	46	17	17	7
82	Boot, shoe, sandal and clog makers	349	277	22	46	4	...	...	227	219	...	7	...	1	...
83	Tailors, milliners, dress makers and darners ...	374	279	74	6	12	3	...	274	189	50	15	12	1	7
84	Embroiderers, hat-makers and makers of other articles of wear.	2	2	...	...	...	...	...	...	...	...	...	...	...	...
85	Washing and cleaning	359	186	149	2	22	...	...	360	245	103	8	5	4	...
86	Barbers, hair-dressers and wig makers ...	305	274	...	30	...	1	...	290	258	...	21	...	11	...

TABLE X.—Occupation or Means of Livelihood. *Part II.—Cities.—(contd.)*

Group No.	Occupation.	LASHKAR CITY. Total following occupation.	As principal occupation. M.	As principal occupation. F.	As working dependents. M.	As working dependents. F.	As subsidiary to other occupation. M.	As subsidiary to other occupation. F.	UJJAIN CITY. Total following occupation.	As principal occupation. M.	As principal occupation. F.	As working dependents. M.	As working dependents. F.	As subsidiary to other occupation. M.	As subsidiary to other occupation. F.
1	2	3	4	5	6	7	8	9	10	11	12	13	14	15	16
	B *Preparation and Supply of Material Substances—(contd.)*														
	III. Industry—(concld.)														
	13. Furniture industries	77	64	...	1	...	12	...	21	5	...	14	...	2	...
88	Cabinet-makers, carriage painters, etc. ...	77	64	...	1	...	12	...	21	5	...	14	...	2	...
	14. Building industries	891	749	123	18	...	1	...	297	293	...	3	...	1	...
90	Lime burners, cement workers; Excavators and well sinkers; Stone cutters and dressers; Brick layers and masons; Builders (other than buildings made of bamboo or similar materials), painters, decorators of houses, tilers, plumbers, etc.	891	749	123	18	...	1	...	297	293	...	3	...	1	...
	16. Production and transmisson of physical force.	43	11	...	...	...	32	...	...	...	...	...	...	...	...
94	Heat, light, electricity, motive power, etc., Gas works and electric light and power.	43	11	...	...	...	32	...	...	...	...	...	...	...	..
	17. Miscellaneous and undefined industries.	1,294	887	301	38	53	15	...	674	443	190	16	23	2	...
95	Printers, engravers, book-binders, etc. ...	292	292	...	...	...	...	...	...	...	...	...	...	...	...
96	Makers of musical instruments	1	1	...	...	...	...	...	78	...	50	...	28	...	...
97	Makers of clocks and surgical or scientific instruments, etc.	4	4	...	...	...	...	...	3	3	...	...	...	...	...
98	Makers of jewellery and ornaments	337	233	40	37	20	7	...	140	137	...	3	...	...	...
99	Other miscellaneous and undefined industries (toy-making, taxidermy, etc.).	40	38	...	...	...	2	...	...	...	...	...	...	...	...
100	Scavenging	620	319	261	1	33	6	...	458	303	140	13	...	2	...
	IV. Transport	*815*	*813*	*1*	...	...	*1*	...	*548*	*546*	...	*1*	...	*1*	...
	20. Transport by road	490	488	1	...	...	1	...	316	314	...	1	...	1	...
105	Persons (other than labourers) employed on the construction and maintenance of roads and bridges.	25	25	..	...	...	...	...	...	...	...	...	...	...	...
106	Labourers employed on roads and bridges ...	31	31	...	...	...	...	...	41	41	...	...	...	...	...
108	Owners, managers and employees (excluding personal servants) connected with other vehicles.	414	412	1	...	...	1	...	275	273	...	1	...	1	...
109	Palki, etc., bearers and owners	20	20	...	...	...	...	...	...	...	...	...	...	...	...
	21. Transport by rail	205	205	...	...	...	...	...	174	174	...	...	...	...	...
112	Railway employees of all kinds other than coolies.	199	199	...	...	...	...	...	75	75	...	...	...	...	...
113	Labourers employed on railway construction and maintenance and coolies and porters employed on railway premises.	6	6	...	...	...	...	...	99	99	...	...	...	...	...
	22. Post Office, Telegraph and Telephone services.	120	120	...	...	...	...	...	58	58	...	...	...	...	...
114	Post Office, Telegraph and Telephone services ...	120	120	...	...	...	...	...	58	58	...	...	...	...	...
	V. Trade	*6,910*	*5,917*	*635*	*73*	*78*	*193*	*14*	*5,975*	*5,072*	*314*	*165*	*30*	*380*	*14*
	23. Banks, establishments of credit, exchange and insurance.	118	87	22	7	...	2	...	560	251	...	9	...	292	8
115	Bank managers, money lenders, exchange and insurance agents, money changers and brokers and their employees.	118	87	22	7	...	2	...	560	251	...	9	...	292	8
	24. Brokerage commission and export ...	96	75	...	...	...	20	1	177	169	...	8	...	...	...
116	Brokers, commission agents, commercial travellers, warehouse owners and employees.	96	75	...	...	...	20	1	177	169	...	8	...	...	...

TABLE X.—Occupation or Means of Livelihood. *Part II.—Cities.*—(*contd.*)

Group No.	Occupation.	LASHKAR CITY. Total following occupation.	As principal occupation. M.	As principal occupation. F.	As working dependents. M.	As working dependents. F.	As subsidiary to other occupation. M.	As subsidiary to other occupation. F.	UJJAIN CITY. Total following occupation.	As principal occupation. M.	As principal occupation. F.	As working dependents. M.	As working dependents. F.	As subsidiary to other occupation. M.	As subsidiary to other occupation. F.
1	2	3	4	5	6	7	8	9	10	11	12	13	14	15	16
	B. Preparation and Supply of Material Substances—(*contd.*)														
	V. *Trade.*—(*contd.*).														
	25. Trade in textiles	196	182	9	1	3	1	...	163	155	...	8	...	...	...
117	Trade in piece-goods, wool, cotton, silk, hair and other textiles.	196	182	9	1	3	1	...	163	155	...	8	...	...	...
	27. Trade in wood	65	63	...	2	...	...	...	...	...	...	...	...	...	...
119	Trade in wood (not fire-wood)	65	63	...	2	...	...	...	...	...	...	...	...	...	...
	28. Trade in metals	33	33	...	...	...	...	...	...	...	...	...	...	...	...
123	Trade in metals, machinery, knives, tools, etc. ...	33	33	...	...	...	...	...	...	...	...	...	...	...	...
	30. Trade in chemical products ...	31	31	...	...	...	...	...	24	23	...	1	...	...	...
125	Drugs, dyes, paints, petroleum, explosives, etc.	31	31	...	...	...	...	...	24	23	...	1	...	...	...
	31. Hotels, cafes, restaurants, etc. ...	189	161	24	1	...	3	...	62	48	9	4	...	1	...
126	Vendors of wine, liquors, aerated waters and ice.	36	29	3	1	...	3	...	27	15	9	2	...	1	...
127	Owners and managers of hotels, cook shops, sarais, etc. (and employees).	69	69	...	...	...	...	...	3	3	...	...	...	...	...
128	Hawkers of drink and food stuffs	81	63	21	...	...	...	...	32	30	...	2	...	...	...
	32. Other trade in food stuffs... ...	2,654	2,184	369	16	56	23	6	2,399	2,111	138	51	15	78	6
129	Grain and pulse dealers	90	82	1	1	...	6	...	202	195	...	7	...	...	...
130	Dealers in sweetmeats, sugar and spices ...	239	211	22	...	...	6	...	...	...	...	...	...	...	...
131	Dealers in dairy product, eggs and poultry ...	298	203	72	11	7	4	1	167	61	34	20	9	42	1
133	Dealers in fodder for animals	67	23	30	...	14	...	...	490	370	88	6	8	18	5
134	Dealers in other food stuffs	1,935	1,640	244	4	35	7	5	1,522	1,478	16	18	3	7	...
135	Dealers in tobacco	25	25	...	...	...	...	...	11	...	...	...	...	11	...
137	Dealers in ganja	...	...	...	...	...	...	...	7	7	...	...	...	...	...
	33. Trade in clothing and toilet articles ...	577	573	...	3	...	1	...	178	178	...	...	...	...	...
138	Trade in ready-made clothing and other articles of dress and the toilet (hats, umbrellas, socks, ready-made shoes, perfumes, etc.).	577	573	...	3	...	1	...	178	178	...	...	...	...	...
	34. Trade in furniture	3	3	...	...	...	...	...	...	...	...	...	...	...	...
140	Hardware, cooking utensils, porcelain, crockery, glassware, bottles, articles for gardening, etc.	3	3	...	...	...	...	...	...	...	...	...	...	...	...
	35. Trade in building materials ...	4	4	...	...	...	...	...	...	...	...	...	...	...	...
141	Trade in building materials (other than bricks, tiles and woody materials).	4	4	...	...	...	...	...	...	...	...	...	...	...	...
	36. Trade in means of transport ...	45	...	...	...	...	45	...	6	4	...	2	...	...	...
142	Dealers and hirers in mechanical transport, motors, cycles, etc.	4	...	...	...	...	4	...	...	...	...	...	...	...	...
143	Dealers and hirers in other carriages, carts, boats, etc.	1	...	...	...	...	1	...	...	...	...	...	...	...	...
144	Dealers and hirers of elephants, camels, horses, cattle, asses, mules, etc.	40	...	...	...	...	40	...	6	4	...	2	...	...	...
	37. Trade in fuel	121	20	81	...	16	4	...	235	194	34	1	6	...	...
145	Dealers in firewood, charcoal, coal, cowdung, etc.	121	20	81	...	16	4	...	235	194	34	1	6	...	...

TABLE X.—Occupation or Means of Livelihood. *Part II.—Cities.—(contd.)*

Group No.	Occupation.	LASHKAR CITY. Total following occupation.	As principal occupation M.	As principal occupation F.	As working dependents. M.	As working dependents. F.	As subsidiary to other occupation. M.	As subsidiary to other occupation. F.	UJJAIN CITY. Total following occupation.	As principal occupation M.	As principal occupation F.	As working dependents. M.	As working dependents. F.	As subsidiary to other occupation. M.	As subsidiary to other occupation. F.
1	2	3	4	5	6	7	8	9	10	11	12	13	14	15	16
	B. Preparation and Supply of Material Substances—(concld.) *V. Trade.—(concld.)*														
	38. Trade in articles of luxury and those pertaining to letters and the arts and sciences.	156	124	26	5	...	1	...	259	158	99	...	2	...	...
146	Dealers in precious stones, jewellery (real and imitation), clocks, optical instruments, etc.	17	17	...	...	...	...	...	...	...	...	...	...	...	...
147	Dealers in common bangles, bead, necklaces, fans, small articles, toys, hunting and fishing tackle, flowers, etc.	128	96	26	5	...	1	...	248	147	99	...	2	...	...
148	Publishers, booksellers, stationers, dealers in music, pictures, musical instruments and curiosities.	11	11	...	...	...	...	...	11	11	...	...	...	...	...
	39. Trade of other sorts	2,502	2,257	104	38	3	93	7	1,912	1,781	34	81	7	9	...
149	Dealers in rags, stable refuse, etc.	71	...	...	...	...	71	...	...	...	...	...	...	...	...
150	General store-keepers and shop-keepers otherwise unspecified.	2,424	2,250	104	38	3	22	7	1,912	1,781	34	81	7	9	...
151	Itinerant traders, pedlars and hawkers (of other than food, etc.).	5	5	...	...	...	...	...	...	...	...	...	...	...	...
152	Other trades (including farmers of pounds, tolls and markets).	2	2	...	...	...	...	...	...	...	...	...	...	...	...
	C. Public Administration and Liberal Arts.	*8,277*	*7,910*	*238*	*76*	*1*	*15*	*4*	*3,363*	*3,067*	*112*	*101*	*46*	*30*	*7*
	VI. Public Force...	*2,841*	*2,810*	...	*31*	...	...	...	*510*	*481*	...	*20*	...	*9*	...
	40. Army	2,190	2,165	...	25	...	...	...	292	285	...	7	...	...	...
[illegible]	Army (Indian States)	2,190	2,165	...	25	...	...	...	292	285	...	7	...	...	...
	41. Police	651	645	...	6	...	...	...	218	196	...	13	...	9	...
[illegible]	[illegible]	601	599	...	6	...	...	...	116	114	...	2	...	...	...
[illegible]	[illegible]	47	47	...	...	...	...	...	102	82	...	11	...	9	...
	VII. Public Administration ...	[illegible]	*3,566*	*17*	*21*	*1*	...	...	*1,605*	*1,547*	...	*58*	...	...	...
	44. Public Administration	3,605	3,566	17	21	1	...	...	1,605	1,547	...	58	...	...	...
[illegible]	[illegible]	10	10		...	...	...	...	...	...	...	...	...	...	...
[illegible]	[illegible]	[illegible]	[illegible]	13	21	1	...	...	1,283	1,528	...	55	...	...	...
[illegible]	[illegible]	44	40	4	...	...	...	...	22	19	...	3	...	...	...
	[illegible]	[illegible]	*1,281*	*221*	*21*	[illegible]	*15*	*1*	[illegible]	[illegible]	*112*	*21*	*16*	*21*	*7*
	45. Religion	[illegible]	[illegible]	[illegible]	11	...	2	2	442	422	...	8	...	12	...
[illegible]	[illegible]	[illegible]	[illegible]		[illegible]		1	2	[illegible]	[illegible]	...	2	...	11	...
[illegible]	[illegible]	[illegible]	[illegible]	[illegible]			1		[illegible]	[illegible]	...	[illegible]	...	1	...
[illegible]	[illegible]	[illegible]	[illegible]	...	[illegible]	...	...		...		...	...	...	...	...
	[illegible]	[illegible]	[illegible]	.	2	...	[illegible]	.	[illegible]	99	...	1	...	...	...
[illegible]	[illegible]	[illegible]	[illegible]		2		6	...	41	41		...	...	...	...
[illegible]	[illegible]	[illegible]	[illegible]						85	[illegible]	...	1	...	...	

TABLE X.—Occupation or Means of Livelihood. *Part II.—Cities.—(concld.)*

Group No.	Occupation.	LASHKAR CITY. Total following occupation.	As principal occupation. M.	As principal occupation. F.	As working dependents. M.	As working dependents. F.	As subsidiary to other occupation. M.	As subsidiary to other occupation. F.	UJJAIN CITY. Total following occupation.	As principal occupation. M.	As principal occupation. F.	As working dependents. M.	As working dependents. F.	As subsidiary to other occupation. M.	As subsidiary to other occupation. F.
1	2	3	4	5	6	7	8	9	10	11	12	13	14	15	16
	C. *Public Administration & Liberal Arts—(concld.)* VIII. *Professions and Liberal Arts.—(concld.)*														
	47. Medicine	192	126	55	1	1	7	2	151	112	21	...	17	...	1
169	Registered medical practitioners including oculists.	55	54	...	1	...	...	...	...	...	...	...	...	...	...
170	Other persons practising the healing arts without being registered.	44	44	...	...	...	...	...	94	94	...	...	...	...	...
172	Midwives, vaccinators, compounders, nurses, masseurs, etc.	66	8	55	...	1	...	2	57	18	21	...	17	...	1
173	Veterinary surgeons	27	20	...	...	...	7	...	...	...	...	...	...	...	...
	48. Instruction	221	175	45	—	...	1	...	83	79	1	3	...	...	...
174	Professors and teachers of all kinds	218	173	45	...	...	1	...	83	79	1	3	...	...	...
175	Clerks and servants connected with education ...	3	3	...	...	...	...	...	...	...	...	...	...	...	...
	49. Letters, arts and sciences (other than 44)	241	130	99	10	2	...	...	472	327	90	11	29	9	6
177	Architects, surveyors, engineers and their employees (not being State servants).	6	6	...	...	...	...	...	17	17	...	...	...	...	...
178	Authors, editors, journalists and photographers.	7	6	1	...	...	...	...	10	4	...	...	...	6	...
179	Artists, sculptors and image-makers	6	6	...	...	...	...	...	...	...	...	...	...	...	...
181	Horoscope casters, astrologers, fortune-tellers, wizards, witches and mediums.	6	6	...	...	...	...	...	...	...	...	...	...	...	...
182	Musicians (composers and performers other than military), actors, dancers, etc.	204	97	95	10	2	...	...	268	129	90	6	29	8	6
183	Managers and employees of places of public entertainments, race courses, societies, clubs.	6	6	...	...	...	...	...	...	...	...	...	...	...	...
184	Conjurors, acrobats, reciters, exhibitors of curiosities and wild animals, etc.	6	3	3	...	...	...	...	182	177	...	5	...	...	...
	D. Miscellaneous	*11,639*	*8,354*	*1,439*	*1,216*	*265*	*258*	*27*	*8,449*	*5,837*	*1,394*	*432*	*171*	*620*	*55*
	IX. Persons Living on their Income ...	*480*	*317*	*66*	*71*	*3*	*22*	*1*	*284*	*67*	*125*	*2*	*1*	*87*	*2*
	50. Persons living principally on their income.	480	317	66	71	3	22	1	284	67	125	2	1	87	2
185	Proprietors (other than of agricultural land), fund and scholarship-holders and pensioners.	480	317	66	71	3	22	1	284	67	125	2	1	87	2
	X. Domestic Service	*4,934*	*4,166*	*678*	*34*	*19*	*34*	*3*	*2,606*	*1,994*	*527*	*31*	*34*	*5*	*15*
	51. Domestic service	4,934	4,166	678	34	19	34	3	2,606	1,994	527	31	34	5	15
186	Private motor-drivers and cleaners	124	123	...	...	...	1	...	134	132	...	2	...	...	...
187	Other domestic service	4,810	4,043	678	34	19	33	3	2,472	1,862	527	29	34	5	15
	XI. Insufficiently Described Occupations ...	*4,356*	*3,416*	*622*	*32*	*72*	*192*	*22*	*4,364*	*3,056*	*696*	*61*	*34*	*500*	*17*
	52. General terms which do not indicate a definite occupation.	4,356	3,416	622	32	72	192	22	4,364	3,056	696	61	34	500	17
188	Manufacturers, businessmen and contractors otherwise unspecified.	270	221	12	...	...	37	...	180	180	...	...	...	...	...
189	Cashiers, accountants, bookkeepers, clerks and other employees in unspecified offices and warehouses and shops.	1,356	1,223	...	...	...	120	13	650	203	9	9	3	422	4
190	Mechanics otherwise unspecified	...	...	...	...	...	...	...	...	...	...	...	...	...	...
191	Labourers and workmen otherwise unspecified ...	2,730	1,972	610	32	72	35	9	3,534	2,723	687	52	31	78	13
	XII. Unproductive	*1,869*	*455*	*125*	*1,109*	*171*	*10*	*1*	*1,195*	*720*	*46*	*338*	*42*	*28*	*21*
	53. Inmates of jails, asylums and alms houses.	1,247	...	...	1,099	148	...	...	322	...	...	297	25	...	...
192	Inmates of jails, asylums and alms houses ...	1,247	...	...	1,099	148	...	...	322	...	...	297	25	...	...
	54. Beggars, vagrants, prostitutes ...	621	454	123	10	23	10	1	873	720	46	41	17	28	21
193	Beggars and vagrants	619	454	121	10	23	10	1	827	701	36	39	17	28	6
194	Procurers and prostitutes	2	...	2	...	...	...	...	46	19	10	2	...	...	15
	55. Other unclassified non-productive industries.	1	1	...	...	...	...	...	...	...	...	...	...	...	...
195	Other unclassified non-productive industries ...	1	1	...	...	...	...	...	...	...	...	...	...	...	...

TABLE XI.

Occupation by Caste, Tribe or Race.

Part A.-Occupation of Selected Castes, Tribes or Races.

NOTE 1.— This Table is divided into two parts. Part B (Distribution of Earners and Working dependents in certain groups of occupation by Caste, Tribe or Race) has not been compiled.

NOTE 2.—The occupations of Europeans and Allied Races and Anglo-Indians have been shown at the end of this Table.

TABLE XI.—Occupation by

Part A.—Occupations of Selected

Caste, Tribe or Race.	Traditional Occupation.	Population dealt with. Earners. M.	Earners. F.	Working dependents. M.	Working dependents. F.	Non-working dependents. Both sexes.	Number of earners whose traditional caste occupation was returned as their Principal means of livelihood. M.	Principal means of livelihood. F.	Subsidiary means of livelihood. M.	Subsidiary means of livelihood. F.
1	2	3	4	5	6	7	8	9	10	11
Hindu.										
1 Badhai ...	Carpenters	9,715	2,208	472	1,188	18,481	2,962	605	276	191
2 Balai ...	Field Labourers	33,190	15,920	1,784	3,780	43,154	13,250	9,879	446	935
3 Banjara ...	Carriers by pack animals ...	7,528	2,032	683	1,161	8,838	1,240	447	166	16
4 Bania ...	Traders	30,281	3,048	2,407	1,760	50,259	13,873	1,481	1,186	236
5 Beragi ...	Beggars	9,567	2,078	673	897	15,993	2,335	698	467	56
6 Bhangi ...	Scavengers	9,602	3,477	697	2,639	10,990	4,859	2,417	337	178
7 Bhat ...	Legend Singers	2,221	992	490	582	3,131	464	299	73	46
8 Bhil ...	Labourers	28,473	6,755	3,766	7,799	35,977	8,185	1,996	1,271	116
9 Bhilala ...	Labourers	10,115	1,040	2,837	5,245	16,899	646	383	1,069	1
10 Brahmin...	Priests	100,423	12,502	3,457	8,003	171,657	18,956	2,318	2,502	279
11 Chamar ...	Field Labourers and Leather workers.	143,423	48,044	10,807	21,849	193,328	35,551	25,544	5,053	2,747
12 Chhipa ...	Dyers	3,081	1,264	211	341	5,559	1,046	620	68	43
13 Darzi ...	Tailors	7,924	1,751	454	710	9,425	4,131	1,172	139	99
14 Dhobi ...	Washermen	14,089	4,876	1,237	1,976	18,407	6,548	3,485	1,001	209
15 Gadaria ...	Shepherds and Herdsmen ...	31,832	13,555	1,567	2,312	33,475	12,068	6,007	1,344	166
16 Ghosi ...	Cattle keepers and Milkmen ...	3,095	790	157	418	4,156	897	522	47	15
17 Gosain ...	Beggars	4,693	1,001	387	581	6,838	1,414	323	254	81
18 Gujar ...	Agriculturists	40,765	9,070	2,238	4,862	62,879	16,914	3,871	1,579	218
19 Jogi ...	Beggars	2,584	573	310	147	3,618	927	298	185	32
20 Joshi ...	Astrologers and Beggars ...	1,705	606	320	227	3,473	1,101	389	130	30
21 Kayastha.	Writers	11,170	885	709	520	20,642	3,151	311	241	35
22 Khati ...	Carpenters	6,124	1,809	550	413	7,696	2,067	251	165	13
23 Koli ...	Weavers	27,782	8,132	1,567	3,516	34,854	8,241	3,259	1,063	429
24 Kumhar.	Potters	20,693	6,816	1,545	2,833	30,598	9,650	3,732	890	297
25 Lodhi ...	Agriculturists	36,798	7,275	1,374	4,557	41,769	18,975	3,691	513	160
26 Lohar ...	Blacksmiths	10,559	2,270	1,003	1,484	14,830	4,179	606	491	61
27 Mali ...	Gardeners	10,251	3,418	1,061	1,008	16,135	987	817	96	249
28 Maratha...	Military	4,875	1,215	226	372	7,463	988	...	39	...
29 Mirdha ...	Village watchmen ...	4,910	1,205	588	985	5,465	1,003	...	225	...
30 Nai ...	Barbers and Hair-dressers ...	19,862	4,225	1,791	2,230	26,235	11,069	1,061	1,226	84
31 Rajput ...	Military	143,609	12,362	3,003	7,613	225,589	9,639	...	1,742	...
32 Saharia ...	Hunters and collectors of jungle produce.	26,600	14,094	2,013	3,473	27,322	2,961	4,186	184	277
33 Sonar ...	Goldsmiths	9,316	1,119	514	654	10,561	5,213	454	231	51
34 Teli ...	Oil pressers and sellers ...	20,299	5,823	1,631	2,602	25,425	7,233	3,195	1,217	266
Muslim.										
35 [illegible] ...	Traders	3,017	655	74	673	4,565	2,283	486	23	20
36 [illegible] ...	Beggars	4,003	891	212	365	5,707	2,493	299	173	2
37 [illegible] ...	Weavers	233	123	7	41	973	192	77	16	...
38 [illegible] ...	[illegible]	7	...	...	...	...	1	...	...	...

Caste, Tribe or Race.

Castes, Tribes or Races.

Number of working dependents following the traditional occupation of their caste.		Number of earners returning their traditional occupation as their principal means of livelihood who had some subsidiary occupation.		RECORDED PRINCIPAL OCCUPATION OF EARNERS OTHER THAN TRADITIONAL OCCUPATION OF THE CASTE (BY SUB-CLASSES).											
				Income from rent of land.		Cultivators of all kinds.		Agents and managers of landed estates, planters forest officers and their clerks, rent collectors, etc.		Field labourers, wood cutters, etc.		Raisers of live stock, milkmen and herdsmen.		Fishing and hunting.	
M.	F.	M.	F.	M.	F.	M.	F.	M.	F.	M.	F.	M.	F.	M.	F.
12	13	14	15	16	17	18	19	20	21	22	23	24	25	26	27
159	90	633	182	353	42	4,961	366	...	...	545*	746*	181	27	...	...
607	1,989	2,703	1,830	965	115	18,106	3,019	...	...	1,3.3	798	755	104	...	...
107	105	263	185	199	3	4,077	343	...	...	716	678	275	137	10	...
890	403	2,590	284	771	116	11,545	458	...	...	434	196	55	33	...	...
190	100	463	172	463	66	4,065	358	...	...	470	461	216	10	...	...
290	552	1,099	547	...	...	2,798	482	...	...	189	156	101	13	6	...
152	120	118	96	110	33	533	99	...	...	378	227	46	44	...	...
1,986	1,063	259	202	565	84	15,909	1,388	...	...	1,934	2,602	576	50	11	1
761	354	60	35	58	2	9,158	471	...	...	100	159	50	3	...	...
2,366	839	4,830	669	5,024	772	56,231	3,921	84	...	2,157*	1,496*	819	186	...	...
4,573	7,928	7,321	4,145	2,035	219	67,773	7,921	...	...	3,921	3,726	2,891	541	...	...
86	158	245	115	350	7	969	249	...	...	161	144	43	66	...	...
137	288	681	255	164	49	2,820	153	...	...	298	193	88	11	...	...
416	798	2,322	864	248	43	5,826	622	...	...	573	407	269	40	...	...
1,205	250	2,541	1,393	112	61	18,768	5,447	...	...	557	1,587	...	...	...	...
29	92	147	179	85	14	844	28	...	...	407	103	...	...	...	...
119	61	891	91	227	15	2,248	174	...	...	262	179	77	13	...	...
951	813	3,341	789	2,726	899	...	...	...	...	15,790	2,806	3,069	708	...	...
76	48	240	96	34	16	1,194	16	...	...	79	46	14	3	...	...
81	79	281	107	37	16	300	34	...	...	53	50	10	...	...	...
207	41	607	88	342	59	4,723	175	15	...	281	78	33	40	...	...
112	35	749	67	188	22	3,410	278	...	...	218	360	44	28	...	...
859	970	2,583	1,031	922	39	11,228	1,550	...	...	2,185	1,405	371	30	11	1
567	1,063	2,589	847	384	120	7,494	891	...	...	948	891	308	99	...	...
967	1,284	1,444	421	1,732	264	...	...	...	...	13,244	2,069	608	137	9	...
251	144	1,215	151	273	37	3,999*	432*	...	...	487	680	224	33	...	...
155	163	235	106	1,042	117	5,059	526	...	...	1,423	1,184	323	52	...	...
68	...	133	...	175	87	968	295	18	...	118	285	64	10	...	...
86	...	321	...	186	21	2,557	814	8	...	514	328	131	45	...	...
549	243	3,529	231	211	163	6,873	581	...	...	453	654	166	97	...	...
899	...	2,220	...	14,808	880	97,969	3,693	14	...	6,707	4,921	2,471	247	...	...
141	511	677	377	921	81	9,295	1,261	1	...	5,889	4,479	983	68	...	...
226	180	899	130	222	37	2,806	153	...	...	177	155	44	7	...	...
571	509	2,605	910	681	141	9,054	887	...	...	1,028	847	289	52	...	...
47	25	63	25	17	4	148	56	...	...	4	6	50	7	...	...
50	50	300	81	139	12	486	184	...	...	185	111	47	71	...	...
6	34	23	9	5	...	18	2	...	...	22	12	2	...	...	...
...	...	...	...	...	...	1	...	...	...	...	...	...	...	...	...

*Exclusive of the number shown in columns 8 and 9 as following the traditional occupation of the caste.

TABLE XI.—Occupation by

Part A.—Occupations of Selected

	Caste, Tribe or Race.	Traditional Occupation.	RECORDED PRINCIPAL OCCUPATION OF EARNERS OTHER THAN													
			Extraction of Minerals.				Industries.				Transport.				Trade.	
			Owners, managers, clerks, etc.		Labourers.		Owners, managers, clerks, etc.		Artisans and other workmen.		Owners, managers, ships' officers, etc.		Labourers, boatmen, carters, palki bearers, etc.			
			M.	F.	M.	F.	M.	F.	M.	F.	M.	F.	M.	F.	M.	F.
	1	2	28	29	30	31	32	33	34	35	36	37	38	39	40	41
	Hindu.															
1	Badhai ...	Carpenters	...	...	10	6	3	...	*262	*52	...	...	23	5	123	47
2	Balai ...	Field Labourers ..	...	...	12	14	...	...	686	56	...	...	104	5	278	62
3	Banjara ...	Carriers by pack animals...	...	...	28	1	...	...	39	20	...	...	*48	*35	167	72
4	Bania ...	Traders	...	...	27	24	20	...	158	98	18	...	37	5	...	...
5	Beragi ...	Beggars	...	...	27	10	...	...	165	104	...	...	35	5	120	28
6	Bhangi ...	Scavengers	...	...	36	22	...	...	*86	*27	...	...	158	9	65	14
7	Bhat ...	Legend Singers ...	...	...	1	10	...	...	14	23	...	...	17	8	35	12
8	Bhil ...	Labourers	...	...	31	...	...	..	60	4	...	...	30	17	104	122
9	Bhilala ...	Labourers	...	...	...	...	1	...	12	8	...	...	8	...	9	1
10	Brahmin...	Priests	8	...	15	...	40	3	415	221	101	...	319	66	3,500	623
11	Chamar ...	Field Labourers and Leather workers.	...	...	338	126	7	...	*11,888	*1,236	23	...	770	43	2,882	909
12	Chhipa ...	Dyers	...	...	57	4	1	...	*87	*16	...	...	4	5	134	41
13	Darzi ...	Tailors	...	...	12	...	...	...	*87	*39	...	...	2	...	52	4
14	Dhobi ...	Washermen	...	...	40	42	...	...	*24	*36	...	...	26	9	50	7
15	Gadaria ...	Shepherds and Herdsmen.	...	...	8	6	...	...	35	20	...	...	19	...	21	17
16	Ghosi ...	Cattlekeepers and Milkmen.	...	...	2	...	...	...	23	...	1	...	18	...	61	5
17	Gosain ...	Beggars	...	...	...	27	...	...	23	4	...	...	28	5	40	25
18	Gujar ...	Agriculturists	...	...	98	69	...	...	26	66	3	...	185	22	393	285
19	Jogi ...	Beggars	...	...	...	...	1	...	18	2	...	...	5	8	121	65
20	Joshi ...	Astrologers and Beggars ...	...	...	...	1	1	...	3	6	...	...	2	...	30	14
21	Kayastha.	Writers	...	...	29	8	6	1	548	24	17	...	26	12	317	27
	Khati ...	Carpenters	...	...	10	1	...	...	*85	*96	...	...	...	2	77	22
	Koli ...	Weavers	5	...	131	59	...	...	*490	*166	...	...	162	13	775	135
	Kumbhar.	Potters	...	...	158	107	...	...	*884	*115	...	...	112	19	225	208
	Lodhi ...	Agriculturists	...	...	...	...	...	...	285	163	2	...	218	5	188	20
	Luhar ...	Blacksmiths	...	...	59	15	...	...	865	68	...	...	54	1	282	10
27	Mali ...	Gardeners	...	...	83	180	...	...	91	88	1	...	125	12	204	176
28	Maratha...	Military	...	...	5	2	2	...	34	9	30	...	60	5	159	22
29	Mirdha ...	Village watchmen ...	...	...	22	14	...	...	22	8	1	...	24	16	26	98
30	Nai ...	Barbers and Hair-dressers.	...	...	44	65	...	...	*88	*359	...	...	11	...	119	203
31	Rajput ...	Military	...	...	...	...	11	...	1,956	195	70	3	482	10	1,557	182
32	Sahariya.	Hunters and collectors of Jungle produce.	...	...	64	...	...	...	504	266	9	...	203	14	600	278
33	Sonar ...	Goldsmiths	...	...	8	...	...	...	*179	*68	...	...	18	...	261	49
34	Teli ...	Oil manufacturers ...	...	...	...	...	...	...	*221	*48	...	...	125	2	617	160
	Muslim.															
35	Bohra ...	Traders	...	...	...	...	...	...	104	15	...	...	70	9	...	...
36	Faqir ...	Beggars	...	...	...	...	...	...	78	44	...	...	52	3	105	40
37	Momin ...	Weavers	...	...	...	...	...	...	*22	*4	...	...	1	...	14	4
38	Mulla ...	Priests	...	...	...	...	...	...	...	...	...	...	...	...	2	...

*Exclusive of the number shown in columns 8 and 9 as following the traditional occupation of the caste

Caste, Tribe or Race.

Castes, Tribes or Races—(concld.)

TRADITIONAL OCCUPATION OF THE CASTE (BY SUB-CLASSES).

Public Force.				Public Administration.				Arts and Professions.						Persons living on their income.		Domestic service.		Contractors, clerks, cashiers, etc., otherwise unspecified.		Labourers unspecified.		Beggars, prostitutes, etc.	
Commissioned and Gazetted officers.		Others.		Gazetted officers.		Others.		Religious.		Lawyers, doctors and teachers.		Others.											
M.	F.	M.	F.	M.	F.	M.	F.	M.	F.	M.	F.	M.	F.	M.	F.	M.	F.	M.	F.	M.	F.	M.	F.
42	43	44	45	46	47	48	49	50	51	52	53	54	55	56	57	58	59	60	61	62	63	64	65
...	...	21	...	...	...	15	...	20	1	1	...	14	5	1	...	68	15	21	1	124	240	7	50
...	...	107	...	...	...	165	...	26	1	...	...	151	131	20	2	181	83	225	62	1,720	1,618	116	26
...	...	2	...	...	...	170	...	2	...	3	...	40	...	8	...	25	20	16	4	437	258	26	19
2	...	50	...	41	...	448	...	56	7	133	15	346	50	143	41	1,840	199	311	17	808	240	105	68
...	...	39	...	...	...	74	2	759	35	37	8	74	3	9	4	150	14	25	2	504	270	...	...
...	...	96	...	...	...	324	3	60	10	...	...	137	44	...	...	305	68	81	22	270	164	86	31
...	...	14	...	1	...	28	...	37	13	2	...	*44	*2	13	2	31	41	25	32	162	53	271	94
...	...	93	...	...	...	109	...	19	4	1	...	39	104	2	...	595	297	60	55	...	...	100	31
1	...	3	...	...	...	1	...	3	...	...	...	...	...	10	...	34	18	19	...	...	...	2	...
53	...	1828	...	163	2	2,595	61	*1,034	*160	925	49	366	158	115	61	3,628	495	525	59	2,058	940	3,921	959
...	...	144	...	...	...	338	...	275	20	4	...	2,324	362	13	7	2,564	199	748	83	3,691	6,994	307	114
...	...	11	...	...	...	25	...	...	...	2	1	12	12	1	1	88	7	9	...	73	81	8	10
...	...	7	...	...	...	10	...	...	...	8	...	23	8	9	1	90	19	7	8	101	92	10	2
...	...	9	...	...	...	38	...	4	10	...	...	8	4	4	1	129	12	27	15	237	189	39	4
1	...	10	...	...	...	11	...	3	1	...	...	8	33	2	2	38	24	6	...	161	203	4	7
...	...	33	...	...	...	8	...	4	...	...	...	23	5	...	...	216	10	4	...	421	69	48	4
...	...	18	...	...	...	17	6	70	5	32	...	15	6	10	...	40	14	29	1	142	204	...	...
3	...	222	...	...	...	170	...	39	...	4	1	92	15	17	11	431	82	10	51	524	662	93	27
...	...	...	...	...	...	21	...	12	...	...	...	13	2	1	4	13	1	3	2	128	110	...	...
...	...	9	...	...	...	2	...	11	...	10	...	*50	*12	...	...	51	4	9	7	26	73	...	...
3	...	92	...	...	...	...	...	27	...	170	16	79	8	60	8	852	32	171	2	202	61	26	23
...	...	10	...	...	...	5	4	8	...	...	...	1	...	12	3	21	3	12	2	65	259	1	5
...	...	103	...	...	...	183	3	30	...	4	...	158	65	15	7	672	136	100	14	1,909	1,056	182	194
...	...	37	...	...	...	56	7	21	...	2	...	56	65	12	3	215	18	36	87	570	426	30	28
...	...	101	...	...	...	92	...	5	1	5	...	58	18	2	...	330	23	72	...	928	675	49	11
...	...	15	...	...	...	64	...	10	...	7	...	65	23	4	1	182	42	45	26	205	525	26	16
...	...	198	...	1	...	53	1	18	1	19	...	41	15	4	...	206	18	45	2	312	215	21	13
...	...	...	...	50	...	937	3	55	8	26	20	113	31	52	89	828	160	45	45	137	169	11	25
...	...	32	...	...	...	47	...	...	5	...	...	1	...	2	...	188	15	13	3	175	330	13	8
1	...	24	...	1	...	88	...	4	27	2	...	40	249	4	4	287	109	30	24	387	615	41	14
...	...	...	...	82	...	1,691	...	274	16	261	12	257	103	44	17	2,615	314	882	98	1,928	1,457	321	64
...	...	4	...	...	...	77	...	30	2	1	...	117	48	...	...	502	64	152	68	4,129	3,215	[illegible]	29
...	...	25	...	—	...	85	...	8	1	34	1	20	8	12	1	79	11	12	15	187	278	11	17
...	...	22	...	...	...	50	...	—	1	21	...	67	24	19	5	260	38	20	9	575	477	45	22
2	...	25	...	...	...	103	...	13	1	13	4	31	8	27	4	30	9	16	58	2	[illegible]	10	10
...	...	25	...	...	...	70	2	20	...	47	2	53	24	11	4	101	16	19	15	54	[illegible]	...	...
...	...	1	...	...	...	6	—	1	...	1	...	8	3	4	...	12	10	8	3	15	8	1	...
...	...	...	...	...	...	...	...	...	...	...	...	...	...	...	...	3	...	...	...	...	...	...	...

*Exclusive of the number shown in columns 8 and 9 as following the traditional occupation of the caste.

TABLE XI.—Occupation by Caste, Tribe or Race.

Part A.—Occupation of Selected Castes, Tribes or Races.

Europeans and Anglo-Indians.

Total Number of Earners and Working dependents.		Total Number of Non-working dependents.	Sub-class III Industry.		Sub-class IV Transport.		Sub-class V Trade.		Sub-class VI Public Force.		Sub-class VII Public Administration.		Sub-class VIII Professions and Liberal Arts.		Sub-class IX Persons living on their income.		Sub-class X Domestic Service.		Sub-class XI Insufficiently described occupations.	
M.	F.	Both Sexes.	M.	F.	M.	F.	M.	F.	M.	F.	M.	F.	M.	F.	M.	F.	M.	F.	M.	F.
1	2	3	4	5	6	7	8	9	10	11	12	13	14	15	16	17	18	19	20	21
(a) Europeans and Allied Races.																				
41	10	60	6	...	18	...	1	...	10	...	2	...	4	9	2	...	2	1	1	...
(b) Anglo-Indians.																				
47	13	71	8	...	14	...	2	...	2	...	2	...	2	5	1	...	4	4	12	4

TABLE XIII.

Literacy by Religion and Age.

NOTE 1.—This Table is divided into three parts. Part I shows literacy by age and religion for the State as a whole. Part II gives similar details for each district and for certain selected religions in each district. Part III gives similar details for the cities of Lashkar and Ujjain.

NOTE 2.—The following statement shows literacy among Christians:—

Age.	POPULATION.									Literate in English.		
	TOTAL.			LITERATE.			ILLITERATE.					
	P.	M.	F.	P.	M.	F.	P.	M.	F.	P.	M.	F.
1	2	3	4	5	6	7	8	9	10	11	12	13
Christians ...	1,198	592	606	672	329	343	526	263	263	417	203	214
0—5	169	82	107	...	...	...	169	82	107	...	...	...
5—10	146	65	81	89	35	54	57	30	27	45	20	25
10—15	131	59	72	87	32	55	44	27	17	42	14	28
15—20	112	42	70	80	33	47	32	9	23	57	19	38
20 and Over.	620	344	276	416	229	187	204	115	89	273	150	123
Indian Christians ...	956	465	491	463	220	243	493	245	248	208	94	114
0—5	156	64	92	...	...	...	156	64	92	...	...	—
5—10	136	61	75	79	31	48	57	30	27	35	16	19
10—15	107	49	58	68	22	41	44	27	17	18	4	14
15—20	97	33	64	65	24	41	32	9	23	42	10	32
20 and Over.	460	258	202	256	143	113	204	115	89	113	64	49
Others	242	127	115	209	109	100	33	18	15	209	109	100
0—5	33	18	15	...	...	...	33	18	15	...	...	...
5—10	10	4	6	10	4	6	...	...	...	10	4	6
10—15	24	10	14	24	10	14	...	...	...	24	10	14
15—20	15	9	6	15	9	6	...	...	...	15	9	6
20 and Over.	160	86	74	160	86	74	...	...	...	160	86	74

TABLE XIII.—Literacy by Religion and Age. *Part I.—State Summary.*

Religion and Age.	POPULATION.											
	TOTAL.			LITERATE.			ILLITERATE.			LITERATE IN ENGLISH		
	Persons.	Males.	Females.	Persons.	Males.	Females.	Persons.	Males.	Females.	P.	M.	F.
1	2	3	4	5	6	7	8	9	10	11	12	13
All Religions ...	3,523,070	1,867,031	1,656,039	141,342	126,147	15,195	3,381,728	1,740,884	1,640,844	13,614	12,717	897
0—5	509,014	255,623	253,391	...	...	...	509,014	255,623	253,391	...	...	...
5—10	448,541	239,108	209,433	8,884	7,420	1,414	439,707	231,688	208,019	453	400	53
10—15	431,207	233,911	197,296	14,697	12,671	2,026	416,510	221,240	195,270	1,073	971	102
15—20	352,988	186,671	166,312	19,033	16,723	2,360	333,900	169,948	163,952	2,044	1,899	145
20 and Over.	1,781,325	951,718	829,607	98,728	89,333	9,395	1,682,597	862,885	820,212	10,044	9,447	597
Hindu (Brahmanic)	3,255,977	1,724,311	1,531,666	113,380	102,072	11,308	3,142,597	1,622,239	1,520,358	10,628	10,146	482
0—5	470,141	236,280	233,861	...	...	...	470,141	236,280	233,861	...	...	
5—10	415,505	221,727	193,778	7,002	5,965	1,037	408,503	215,762	192,741	320	302	18
10—15	399,955	217,222	182,733	12,080	10,492	1,588	387,925	206,730	181,195	844	784	60
15—20	327,036	172,984	154,052	15,551	13,764	1,787	311,485	159,220	152,265	1,646	1,567	79
20 and Over.	1,643,840	876,098	767,242	78,797	71,851	6,946	1,564,543	804,247	760,296	7,818	7,493	325
Arya	1,308	688	620	279	235	44	1,029	453	576	60	50	10
0—5	208	87	121	...	...	...	208	87	121	...		...
5—10	168	88	80	32	21	11	136	67	69	5	2	3
10—15	167	92	75	37	28	9	130	64	66	5	4	1
15—20	131	66	65	31	23	8	100	43	57	10	9	1
20 and Over.	634	355	279	179	163	16	455	192	263	40	35	5
Hinduized Tribal ...	14,291	7,248	7,043	94	88	6	14,197	7,160	7,037	...	...	...
0—5	2,682	1,319	1,363	...	...	...	2,682	1,319	1,363	...	...	...
5—10	2,074	1,042	1,032	20	19	1	2,054	1,023	1,031	...	...	...
10—15	1,919	965	954	13	12	1	1,906	953	953	...	...	...
15—20	1,399	705	694	18	17	1	1,381	688	693	...	...	...
20 and Over.	6,217	3,217	3,000	43	40	3	6,174	3,177	2,997	...	...	...
Muslim	204,297	109,412	94,885	16,927	14,716	2,211	187,370	94,696	92,674	1,800	1,676	124
0—5	29,839	14,861	14,978	...	...	...	29,839	14,861	14,978	...	...	...
5—10	25,459	13,430	12,029	971	789	182	24,488	12,641	11,847	48	43	5
10—15	23,920	12,769	11,151	1,585	1,275	260	22,335	11,494	10,891	112	103	9
15—20	20,078	10,613	9,465	2,164	1,845	319	17,914	8,768	9,146	221	204	17
20 and Over.	105,001	57,739	47,262	12,257	10,807	1,450	92,744	46,932	45,812	1,419	1,326	93
Jain	45,079	24,238	20,841	9,627	8,480	1,147	35,452	15,758	19,694	558	535	23
0—5	5,327	2,930	2,897	...	...	...	5,327	2,930	2,897	...	...	...
5—10	5,099	2,695	2,404	694	576	118	4,405	2,119	2,286	31	30	1
10—15	5,022	2,746	2,276	962	812	150	4,060	1,934	2,126	59	58	1
15—20	4,147	2,225	1,922	1,204	1,022	182	2,943	1,203	1,740	93	91	2
20 and Over.	24,984	13,642	11,342	6,767	6,070	697	18,217	7,572	10,645	375	356	19
Christian ...	1,198	592	606	672	329	343	526	263	263	417	203	214
0—5	189	82	107	...	...		189	82	107	...	...	...
5—10	146	65	81	89	35	54	57	30	27	45	20	25
10—15	131	59	72	87	32	55	44	27	17	42	14	28
15—20	112	42	70	80	33	47	32	9	23	57	19	38
20 and Over.	620	344	276	416	229	187	204	115	89	273	150	123
Zoroastrian ...	239	96	143	199	86	113	40	10	30	116	76	40
0—5	28	6	22		...	...	28	6	22	...	...	...
5—10	19	8	11	13	6	7	6	2	4	2	2	...
10—15	15	7	11	13	5	8	5	2	3	7	4	3
15—20	19	5	14	18	5	13	1	...	1	13	5	8
20 and Over.	155	70	85	155	70	85	...	...	...	94	65	29
Sikh	681	446	235	164	141	23	517	305	212	35	31	4
0—5	100	58	42	...	...	...	100	58	42	...	...	...
5—10	71	53	18	13	9	4	58	44	14	2	1	1
10—15	75	51	24	20	15	5	55	36	19	4	4	...
15—20	61	31	30	17	14	3	44	17	27	4	4	...
20 and Over.	374	253	121	114	103	11	260	150	110	25	22	3

TABLE XIII.—Literacy by Religion and Age. *Part II.—District Details.*

Religion and Age.	POPULATION.									LITERATE IN ENGLISH.		
	TOTAL.			LITERATE.			ILLITERATE.					
	Persons.	Males.	Females.	Persons.	Males.	Females.	Persons.	Males.	Females.	P.	M.	F.
1	2	3	4	5	6	7	8	9	10	11	12	13
District Gird.												
All Religions ...	364,806	197,935	166,871	27,798	24,480	3,318	337,008	173,455	163,553	4,945	4,631	314
0—5	47,903	23,337	24,566	...	...	...	47,903	23,337	24,566	...	...	...
5—10	42,068	22,622	19,446	1,588	1,278	310	40,480	21,344	19,136	168	143	25
10—15	42,167	23,301	18,862	2,588	2,102	486	39,578	21,202	18,376	388	335	53
15—20	37,887	20,527	17,360	3,904	3,327	577	33,983	17,200	16,783	796	735	61
20 and Over	194,782	108,145	86,637	19,718	17,773	1,945	175,064	90,372	84,692	3,593	3,418	175
Hindu (Brahmanic) ..	322,345	174,591	147,754	22,511	20,053	2,488	299,834	154,538	145,266	3,895	3,685	210
0—5	42,278	20,570	21,708	...	...	...	42,278	20,570	21,708	...	...	...
5—10	37,290	20,033	17,257	1,286	1,043	243	36,004	18,990	17,014	123	108	15
10—15	37,574	20,799	16,775	2,127	1,747	380	35,447	19,052	16,395	300	259	41
15—20	33,530	18,210	15,320	3,265	2,814	451	30,274	15,405	14,869	646	598	48
20 and Over.	171,061	94,970	76,091	15,863	14,449	1,414	155,801	80,521	75,280	2,826	2,720	106
Muslim ...	39,232	21,575	17,657	4,174	3,602	572	35,058	17,973	17,085	766	731	35
0—5	5,264	2,593	2,671	...	...	...	5,264	2,593	2,671	...	...	...
5—10	4,489	2,433	2,058	229	186	43	4,260	2,250	2,010	29	26	3
10—15	4,276	2,340	1,936	362	288	74	3,914	2,052	1,862	65	60	5
15—20	4,012	2,140	1,872	503	416	87	3,509	1,724	1,785	113	107	6
20 and Over.	21,191	12,066	9,125	3,080	2,712	368	18,111	9,354	8,757	559	538	21
Jain	2,569	1,405	1,161	714	587	127	1,855	818	1,037	82	77	5
0—5	279	141	138	...	...	...	279	141	138	...	...	...
5—10	236	128	103	43	31	12	193	97	96	3	3	...
10—15	261	137	124	67	48	19	194	79	105	8	7	1
15—20	260	131	129	91	69	22	169	62	107	14	14	...
20 and Over.	1,533	868	665	513	439	74	1,02	429	591	57	53	4
District Bhind.												
All Religions ...	418,224	228,214	190,010	13,306	12,316	990	404,918	215,898	189,020	631	628	3
0—5	59,724	31,004	28,720	...	...	...	59,724	31,004	28,720	...	...	...
5—10	52,380	28,962	23,418	895	774	121	51,485	28,188	23,297	21	21	...
10—15	49,307	27,870	21,437	1,441	1,291	150	47,866	26,579	21,287	50	49	1
15—20	40,163	21,799	18,364	1,778	1,594	184	38,385	20,205	18,180	92	91	1
20 and Over	216,650	118,579	98,071	9,192	8,657	535	207,458	109,922	97,536	468	467	1
Hindu (Brahmanic)...	398,110	217,360	180,750	11,335	10,522	813	386,775	206,838	179,937	558	556	2
0—5	56,848	29,591	27,257	...	...	...	56,848	29,591	27,257	...	...	...
5—10	49,934	27,625	22,309	743	650	93	49,191	26,975	22,216	20	20	...
10—15	46,979	26,528	20,451	1,201	1,085	116	45,778	25,443	20,335	44	44	...
15—20	38,177	20,721	17,456	1,510	1,354	156	36,667	19,367	17,300	84	83	1
20 and Over	206,172	112,895	93,277	7,881	7,433	448	198,291	105,462	92,829	410	409	1
Muslim ...	12,689	6,887	5,802	804	750	54	11,885	6,137	5,748	57	57	...
0—5	1,840	920	920	...	...	...	1,840	920	920	...	...	...
5—10	1,590	879	711	51	45	6	1,539	834	705	...	...	...
10—15	1,549	901	648	104	96	8	1,445	805	640	2	2	...
15—20	1,329	740	589	131	121	10	1,198	619	579	4	4	...
20 and Over	6,381	3,447	2,934	518	488	30	5,863	2,959	2,904	51	51	...
Jain ...	6,551	3,442	3,112	1,094	972	122	5,460	2,470	2,990	13	13	...
0—5	904	418	486	...	...	...	904	418	486	...	...	...
5—10	759	405	354	93	71	22	666	334	332	1	1	...
10—15	698	398	300	130	104	26	568	294	274	3	3	...
15—20	592	308	284	133	115	18	459	193	266	3	3	...
20 and Over	3,601	1,913	1,688	738	682	56	2,863	1,231	1,632	6	6	...

TABLE XIII.—Literacy by Religion and Age. *Part II.—District Details.—(contd.)*

Religion and Age	POPULATION. Total. Persons	Males	Females	Literate. Persons	Males	Females	Illiterate. Persons	Males	Females	Literate in English. P.	M.	F.
1	2	3	4	5	6	7	8	9	10	11	12	13
District Narwar.												
All Religions ...	[illegible]	211,555	190,031	7,443	6,935	508	394,143	204,620	189,523	557	548	9
0—5	[illegible]	29,437	29,071	...	...	...	58,508	29,437	29,071	...	...	...
5—10	[illegible]	[illegible]	[illegible]	461	425	36	52,601	27,851	24,750	25	25	...
10—15	[illegible]	[illegible]	23,047	[illegible]	707	63	49,642	26,678	22,964	54	53	1
15—20	[illegible]	[illegible]	[illegible]	[illegible]	[illegible]	93	39,750	20,997	18,758	82	81	1
20 and Over	[illegible]	[illegible]	[illegible]	[illegible]	4,916	276	193,442	99,457	93,985	396	389	7
Hindu (Brahmanic) ...	[illegible]	204,258	183,816	6,099	5,685	414	381,975	198,573	183,402	448	442	6
0—5	[illegible]	[illegible]	28,114	...	...	...	56,582	28,468	28,114	...	...	...
5—10	[illegible]	[illegible]	[illegible]	[illegible]	[illegible]	48	51,052	27,043	24,009	20	20	...
10—15	[illegible]	[illegible]	[illegible]	[illegible]	574	[illegible]	48,436	26,141	22,295	43	42	1
15—20	[illegible]	[illegible]	[illegible]	793	718	72	[illegible]	20,421	18,191	58	57	1
20 and Over	[illegible]	103,847	91,019	4,273	4,047	226	187,293	95,600	90,793	327	323	4
Muslim ...	9,237	5,031	4,236	752	682	70	8,485	4,319	4,166	52	51	1
0—5	[illegible]	[illegible]	[illegible]	...	...	...	1,294	648	646	...	...	...
5—10	[illegible]	[illegible]	[illegible]	[illegible]	34	4	1,096	567	519	3	3	...
10—15	[illegible]	[illegible]	[illegible]	[illegible]	[illegible]	10	951	527	454	3	3	...
15—20	[illegible]	[illegible]	[illegible]	104	[illegible]	17	798	419	379	6	6	...
20 and Over	[illegible]	[illegible]	2,237	[illegible]	[illegible]	[illegible]	4,320	2,159	2,168	40	39	1
Jain ...	3,610	1,937	1,673	574	553	21	3,036	1,384	1,652	51	51	...
0—5	[illegible]	[illegible]	249	...	...	...	505	256	249	...	...	...
5—10	417	[illegible]	187	47	45	4	368	185	183	2	2	...
10—15	411	234	177	[illegible]	78	4	329	156	173	8	8	...
15—20	[illegible]	159	151	43	79	4	257	110	147	17	17	...
20 and Over	1,937	[illegible]	920	[illegible]	251	9	1,577	677	900	24	24	...
District Isagarh.												
All Religions ...	421,311	221,556	199,755	12,689	11,657	1,032	408,622	209,899	198,723	845	812	33
0—5	62,651	31,185	31,666	...	...	...	62,651	31,185	31,666	...	...	...
5—10	[illegible]	[illegible]	[illegible]	1,097	936	161	56,268	29,368	26,900	47	45	2
10—15	[illegible]	[illegible]	25,467	1,711	1,541	170	54,149	28,852	25,297	106	101	5
15—20	[illegible]	22,822	20,877	2,011	1,865	146	41,198	20,967	20,231	134	128	6
20 and Over	[illegible]	[illegible]	95,184	7,890	7,335	555	194,156	99,527	94,629	558	538	20
Hindu (Brahmanic) ..	397,936	209,130	188,826	10,386	9,539	847	387,570	199,591	187,979	683	661	22
0—5	59,380	29,475	29,905	...	...	...	59,380	29,475	29,905	...	...	...
5—10	54,331	28,716	25,615	914	780	134	53,417	27,936	25,481	82	80	2
10—15	53,040	28,851	24,189	1,468	1,322	146	51,572	27,529	24,048	88	83	5
15—20	40,963	21,699	19,264	1,673	1,557	116	39,290	20,042	19,248	114	109	5
20 and Over.	190,242	100,489	89,753	6,331	5,880	451	183,911	94,609	89,302	449	439	10
Muslim	15,864	8,355	7,509	1,057	981	76	14,807	7,374	7,433	81	76	5
0—5	2,379	1,141	1,238	...	...	...	2,379	1,141	1,238	...	...	...
5—10	2,045	1,059	986	66	59	7	1,979	1,000	979	2	2	...
10—15	1,892	1,018	874	120	113	7	1,772	905	867	8	8	...
15—20	1,548	863	685	168	157	11	1,380	706	674	11	11	...
20 and Over.	8,000	4,274	3,726	703	652	51	7,297	3,622	3,675	60	55	5
Jain	6,512	3,554	2,958	1,117	1,023	94	5,395	2,531	2,864	53	53	...
0—5	894	473	421	...	...	...	894	473	421	...	...	...
5—10	852	457	395	92	78	14	760	379	381	11	11	...
10—15	802	450	352	109	93	16	693	357	336	8	8	...
15—20	600	315	285	145	127	18	455	188	267	6	6	...
20 and Over.	3,364	1,859	1,505	771	725	46	2,593	1,134	1,459	28	28	...

TABLE XIII.—Literacy by Religion and Age. *Part II.—District Details.—(contd.)*

Religion and Age.	POPULATION.									LITERATE IN ENGLISH.		
	TOTAL.			LITERATE.			ILLITERATE.					
	Persons.	Males.	Females.	Persons.	Males.	Females.	Persons.	Males.	Females.	P.	M.	F.
1	2	3	4	5	6	7	8	9	10	11	12	13
District Bhilsa.												
All Religions ...	235,288	123,084	112.204	7,496	6,790	706	227,792	116,294	111,498	598	587	11
0–5	35,860	17,717	18,143	...	...	...	35,860	17,717	18,143	...	...	...
5–10	30,670	16,201	14,400	492	389	103	30,178	15,872	14,806	15	15	...
10–15	29,188	15,817	13,371	694	592	102	28,494	15,225	13,269	44	43	1
15–20	24,908	12 746	12,162	867	700	97	24,041	11,976	12,065	81	79	2
20 and Over.	114,662	60,543	54,119	5,443	5,039	404	109,219	55.504	53.715	458	450	8
Hindu (Brahmanic) ...	219,968	114,901	105,067	6.178	5,588	590	213,790	109.313	104,477	501	493	8
0–5	33,438	16,556	16,882	...	...	...	33.438	16,556	16,882	...	..	...
5–10	28,708	15,228	13,480	410	321	89	28,298	14,907	13,391	11	11	...
10–15	27.408	14,753	12,555	587	503	84	26,821	14 350	12,471	33	32	1
15–20	23,447	11,996	11,451	688	611	77	22,759	11,385	11,374	68	66	2
20 and Over	106,967	56,268	50.699	4,493	4,153	340	102,474	52,115	50,859	389	384	5
Muslim ...	12.422	6,651	5,771	790	739	51	11.632	5.912	5,720	50	50	...
0–5	2,012	952	1,060	...	...	...	2,012	952	1,060	...	...	...
5–10	1,048	807	776	85	80	5	1,008	837	771	1	1	...
10–15	1,458	780	672	67	60	7	1,391	726	665	2	2	...
15–20	1,170	592	578	111	101	10	1,059	491	568	6	6	...
20 and Over.	6,139	3,454	2,685	577	548	29	5,562	2.906	2,656	41	41	...
Jain	2,489	1,329	1,160	499	444	55	1,990	885	1.105	33	32	1
0–5	355	119	176	...	...	...	355	179	176	...	...	...
5–10	277	143	134	44	35	9	233	108	125	2	2	...
10–15	277	153	124	32	24	8	245	129	116	6	6	...
15–20	245	138	107	65	58	7	180	80	100	7	7	...
20 and Over.	1,335	716	619	358	327	31	977	389	588	18	17	1
District Ujjain.												
All Religions ...	405,961	211,274	194,687	23,489	19,828	3,661	382,472	191,446	191,026	2,721	2,401	320
0–5	57,419	28,688	28,781	...	...	...	57,419	28,638	28,781	...	...	...
5–10	48,937	25,468	23.469	1,152	958	194	47,785	24,510	23,275	74	64	10
10–15	47,202	24,866	22,836	2,008	1,681	322	45,199	22,685	22,514	185	173	12
15–20	41,350	21,239	20,111	2,874	2,381	493	38,476	18,858	19,618	408	373	35
20 and Over.	211,053	111,563	99,490	17,460	14,808	2,652	193,593	96,755	96,838	2,054	1,791	263
Hindu (Brahmanic)...	357,911	185,638	172,273	17,146	14,772	2,374	340,765	170,866	169,899	1,966	1,774	192
0–5	50,745	25,240	25,505	...	...	...	50,745	25,240	25,505	...	...	...
5–10	43,208	22,489	20,719	770	660	110	42,438	21,829	20,609	49	49	...
10–15	41,727	21,519	20,208	1,445	1,238	207	40,282	20,281	20,001	148	141	7
15–20	36,643	18,785	17,858	2,155	1,834	321	34,488	16,951	17,537	322	303	19
20 and Over.	185,568	97,605	87,983	12,776	11,040	1,786	172,812	86,565	86,247	1,447	1,281	166
Muslim	40,346	21,426	18,920	4,302	3,461	841	36,044	17,965	18,079	470	393	77
5–0	5,785	2,940	2,845	...	...	...	5,785	2,940	2,845	...	...	...
5–10	4,887	2,535	2,352	228	179	49	4,659	2,856	2.303	4	2	2
10–15	4,552	2,361	2,191	358	284	74	4,194	2.077	2,117	14	10	4
15–20	3,959	2,040	1,899	480	372	108	3,459	1,668	1,791	44	36	8
20 and Over.	21,188	11,550	9,633	3,236	2,626	610	17,947	8,924	9,023	408	345	63
Jain	6.149	3,398	2,751	1,810	1,446	364	4,339	1,952	2,387	186	169	17
5–0	672	355	317	...	...	...	672	355	317	...	...	...
5–10	638	330	308	115	96	19	523	234	289	6	5	1
10–15	686	351	335	169	136	33	517	215	302	14	14	...
15–20	594	326	268	207	155	52	387	171	216	27	25	2
20 and Over.	3,559	2,036	1,523	1,319	1,059	260	2,240	977	1,263	189	125	14

TABLE XIII.—Literacy by Religion and Age. *Part II.—District Details.—(contd.)*

Religion and Age.	POPULATION.									LITERATE IN ENGLISH.		
	TOTAL.			LITERATE.			ILLITERATE.					
	Persons.	Males.	Females.	Persons.	Males.	Females.	Persons.	Males.	Females.	P.	M.	F.
1	2	3	4	5	6	7	8	9	10	11	12	13
District Mandsaur.												
All Religions ...	272.166	140,333	131,833	17.591	15.448	2,143	254,575	124,885	129,690	1,625	1,435	190
0—5	39,589	19,715	19,874	...	...	...	39,589	19,715	19.874	...	...	...
5—10	34,291	17,684	16,607	1 102	873	229	33,189	16,811	16,378	47	32	15
10—15	33,103	17,336	15,767	1,726	1,414	312	31,377	15,922	15,455	119	92	27
15—25	28,374	14,488	13,886	2,246	1,920	326	26,128	12,568	13,560	225	190	35
20 and Over.	136,809	71,110	65,699	12,517	11,241	1,276	124,292	59,869	64,423	1,234	1,121	118
Hindu (Brahmanic)...	237,040	122,062	114,978	12,926	11,401	1,525	224,114	110,661	113,453	1,132	1,101	31
0—5	34,385	17,118	17,267	...	...	...	34,385	17,118	17,267	...	...	...
5—10	29,878	15,425	14,453	778	626	152	29 100	14,799	14,301	17	17	...
10—15	28,914	15,145	13,769	1,279	1,061	218	27,635	14,084	13,551	76	74	2
15—20	24,986	12,778	12,208	1,079	1,445	234	23,807	11,833	11,974	159	157	2
20 and Over.	118,877	61,596	57,281	9,190	8,269	921	109,687	53,327	56,360	880	853	27
Muslim	24,525	12,800	11,725	2,055	1.883	172	22.470	10,917	11,553	145	143	2
0—5	3,710	1,855	1,855	...	...	...	3.710	1,855	1,855	...	...	...
5—10	3,190	1,638	1,552	116	98	18	3,074	1,540	1,534	2	2	...
10—15	3,006	1,593	1,413	160	139	21	2 846	1,454	1,392	3	3	...
15—20	2,429	1,231	1,198	227	202	25	2,202	1,029	1,173	14	13	1
20 and Over.	12,190	6,483	5.707	1.552	1,444	108	10,638	5,089	5,599	126	125	1
Jain	8,139	4,297	3,842	2,122	1,946	176	6,017	2,351	3,666	90	90	...
0—5	1,090	550	540	...	...	...	1,090	550	540	...	...	...
5—10	904	472	432	152	133	19	752	339	413	5	5	...
10—15	866	460	406	219	196	23	647	264	383	12	12	...
15—20	715	373	342	287	256	31	428	117	311	14	14	...
20 and Over.	4,564	2,442	2,122	1,464	1,361	103	3,100	1,081	2,019	59	59	...
Christian ...	510	215	295	322	126	196	188	89	99	194	70	124
0—5	94	38	56	...	...	...	94	38	56	...	...	...
5—10	67	21	46	42	9	33	25	12	13	23	8	15
10—15	65	16	49	55	10	45	10	6	4	28	3	25
15—20	49	14	35	41	12	29	8	2	6	31	4	27
20 and Over.	235	126	109	184	95	89	51	31	20	112	55	57
District Shajapur.												
All Religions ...	336,980	174,985	161,995	11,474	10,372	1,102	325,506	164,613	160,893	454	450	4
0—5	46,561	22,912	23,649	...	...	...	46,561	22,912	23,649	...	...	...
5—10	40,829	21,118	19,711	756	662	94	40,073	20,456	19,617	18	17	1
10—15	38,994	20,523	18,471	1,252	1,116	136	37,742	19,407	18,335	27	26	1
15—20	32,008	16,394	15,614	1,476	1.321	155	30,532	15,073	15,459	56	56	...
20 and Over.	178,588	94,038	84,550	7,990	7,273	717	170,598	86,765	83,833	353	351	2
Hindu (Brahmanic)...	304,304	157,723	146,581	9,453	8,638	815	294,851	149,085	145,766	368	364	4
0—5	41,610	20,436	21,174	...	...	...	41,610	20,436	21,174	...	...	...
5—10	36,550	18,905	17,645	639	575	64	35,911	18,330	17,581	15	14	1
10—15	34,948	18,429	16,519	1,086	986	100	33,862	17,443	16,419	22	21	1
15—20	29,111	14,824	14,287	1,237	1,123	114	27,874	13,701	14,173	44	44	...
20 and Over.	162,085	85,129	76,956	6,491	5,954	537	155,594	79,175	76,419	287	285	2
Muslim	27,005	14.276	12,729	1.204	1.023	181	25,801	13,253	12,548	64	64	...
0—5	4,197	2,094	2,103	...	...	...	4,197	2,094	2,103	...	...	...
5—10	3,631	1,860	1 771	67	42	25	3,564	1,818	1,746	3	3	...
10—15	3,413	1,740	1,673	96	68	28	3,317	1,672	1,645	5	5	...
15—20	2,431	1,325	1,106	168	134	24	2,278	1,191	1,082	9	9	...
20 and Over.	13,333	7,257	6,076	883	779	104	12,450	6,478	5,972	47	47	...
Jain	4,831	2,579	2,252	785	686	99	4,046	1,893	2,153	17	17	...
0—5	614	316	298	...	...	...	614	316	298	...	...	...
5—10	547	298	249	47	44	3	500	254	246	...	...	...
10—15	539	301	238	68	60	8	471	241	230	...	...	...
15—20	382	205	177	76	61	15	306	144	162	2	2	...
20 and Over.	2,749	1,459	1,290	594	521	73	2,155	938	1,217	15	15	...

TABLE XIII.—Literacy by Religion and Age. *Part II.—District Details.—(concld.)*

Religion and Age.	POPULATION.									LITERATE IN ENGLISH.		
	TOTAL.			LITERATE.			ILLITERATE.					
	Persons.	Males.	Females.	Persons.	Males.	Females.	Persons.	Males.	Females.	P.	M.	F.
1	2	3	4	5	6	7	8	9	10	11	12	13
District Amjhera.												
All Religions. ...	160,066	80,411	79,655	4,808	4,315	493	155,258	76,096	79,162	350	345	5
0—5	27,030	13,325	13,705	...	...	...	27,030	13,325	13,705	...	...	...
5—10	22,435	11,415	11,020	250	206		22,185	11,209	10,976	7	7	...
10—15	20,684	10,872	10,812	508	422	86	20,176	9,950	10,226	20	19	1
15—20	15,576	7,647	7,929	710	617	93	14,866	7,030	7,836	56	54	2
20 and Over.	74,341	37,652	36,689	3,340	3,070	270	71,001	34,582	36,410	267	265	2
Hindu (Brahmanic)...	143,170	71,624	71,546	3,653	3,291	362	139,517	68,333	71,184	312	309	3
0—5	24,049	11,879	12,170	...	...	...	24,049	11,879	12,170	...	...	...
5—10	20,120	10,233	9,887	181	153	28	19,939	10,080	9,859	7	7	...
10—15	18,523	9,297	9,226	410	342	68	18,113	8,955	9,158	18	17	1
15—20	13,908	6,819	7,089	558	483	75	13,350	6,336	7,014	51	50	1
20 and Over.	66,570	33,396	33,174	2,504	2,313	191	64,066	31,083	32,983	286	285	1
Hinduised Tribal ...	8,443	4,292	4,151	10	9	1	8,433	4,283	4,150	...	...	...
0—5	1,694	824	870	...	...	...	1,694	824	870	...	...	...
5—10	1,827	662	665	1	1	...	1,826	661	665	...	...	...
10—15	1,160	581	579	3	3	...	1,157	578	579	...	...	...
15—20	763	390	373	2	2	...	761	388	373	...	...	...
20 and Over.	3,499	1,835	1,664	4	3	1	3,495	1,832	1,663	...	...	...
Muslim	6,480	3,428	3,052	605	517	88	5,875	2,911	2,964	21	19	2
0—5	1,047	508	539	...	...	...	1,047	508	539	...	...	...
5—10	785	413	372	34	27	7	751	386	365	...	...	...
10—15	796	380	416	53	40	13	743	340	403	2	2	...
15—20	697	324	373	85	73	12	612	251	361	4	3	1
20 and Over.	3,155	1,803	1,352	433	377	56	2,722	1,426	1,296	15	14	1
Jain	1,907	1,038	869	540	498	42	1,367	540	827	17	17	...
0—5	235	112	123	...	...	...	235	112	123	...	...	...
5—10	197	104	93	34	25	9	163	79	84	...	...	...
10—15	198	112	86	42	37	5	156	75	81	...	...	...
15—20	199	112	87	65	59	6	134	53	81	1	1	...
20 and Over.	1,078	598	480	399	377	22	679	221	458	16	16	...

TABLE XIII.—Literacy by Religion and Age. *Part III.—Cities.*

Religion and Age.	POPULATION.									LITERATE IN ENGLISH.		
	TOTAL.			LITERATE.			ILLITERATE.					
	Persons.	Males.	Females.	Persons.	Males.	Females.	Persons.	Males.	Females.	P.	M.	F.
1	2	3	4	5	6	7	8	9	10	11	12	13
Lashkar City.												
All Religions ...	86,767	47,358	39,409	14,836	12,871	1,965	71,931	34,487	37,444	3,687	3,455	232
0—5	10,567	5,299	5,168	...	...	...	10,567	5,899	5,168	...	...	...
5—10	8,824	4,868	3,961	948	760	183	7,881	4,108	3,778	187	117	20
10—15	8,917	4,818	4,104	1,437	1,143	294	7,480	3,670	3,810	299	264	35
15—20	8,945	4,729	4,216	1,955	1,687	318	6,990	3,092	3,898	605	560	45
20 & Over.	49,514	27,554	21,960	10,501	9,331	1,170	39,018	18,228	20,790	2,646	2,514	132
Hindu (Brahmanic)...	64,399	35'147	29,252	11,682	10,231	1,451	52,717	24,916	27,801	2,997	2,846	151
0—5	7,522	3,931	3,591	...	...	...	7,522	3,931	3,591	...	...	...
5—10	6,461	3,522	2,939	743	604	139	5,718	2,918	2,800	98	87	11
10—15	6,519	3,531	2,988	1,151	923	228	5,368	2,608	2,760	234	207	27
15—20	6,686	3 552	3,134	1,582	1,339	243	5,104	2,213	2,891	501	467	34
20 & Over.	37,211	20,611	16,600	8,206	7,365	841	29,005	13,246	15,759	2,164	2,085	79
Muslim	20,729	11,278	9,451	2,497	2,152	345	18,232	9,126	9,106	478	454	24
0—5	2,886	1,885	1 501	...	...	...	2 886	1,885	1,501	...	...	...
5—10	2,243	1,278	970	155	125	30	2,088	1,148	940	24	22	2
10—15	2,260	1,207	1,053	234	185	49	2,026	1,022	1,004	50	45	5
15—20	2,103	1,092	1,011	296	246	50	1,807	846	961	78	73	5
20 and Over.	11,237	6,321	4,916	1,812	1,596	216	9,425	4,725	4,700	326	314	12
Jain	1,220	699	521	395	321	74	825	378	447	63	61	2
0—5	114	64	50	...	...	...	114	64	50	...	...	...
5—10	92	52	40	21	16	5	71	36	35	3	3	...
10—15	110	61	49	33	24	9	77	37	40	6	6	...
15—20	116	64	52	48	35	13	68	29	39	11	11	...
20 and Over.	788	458	330	293	246	47	495	212	283	43	41	2
Christian	196	104	92	142	85	57	54	19	35	103	61	42
0—5	18	9	9	...	...	...	18	9	9	...	...	...
5—10	9	6	3	7	5	2	2	1	1	7	3	4
10—15	9	3	6	6	3	3	3	...	3	4	3	1
15—20	13	7	6	11	6	5	2	1	1	8	4	4
20 and Over.	147	79	68	118	71	47	29	8	21	84	51	33
Others	223	130	93	120	82	38	103	48	55	46	33	13
0—5	27	10	17	...	...	...	27	10	17	...	...	...
5—10	19	10	9	17	10	7	2	...	2	5	2	3
10—15	19	11	8	13	8	5	6	3	3	5	3	2
15—20	27	14	13	18	11	7	9	3	6	7	5	2
20 and Over.	131	85	46	72	53	19	59	32	27	29	23	6
Ujjain City.												
All Religions ...	54,650	30,597	24,053	12,086	9,550	2,536	42,564	21,047	21,517	1,725	1,447	278
0—5	7,056	3,809	3,247	...	...	...	7,056	3,809	3,247	...	...	...
5—10	5,199	2,772	2,427	664	564	100	4,535	2,208	2,327	39	34	5
10—15	6,025	3,107	2,918	1,009	815	194	5,016	2,292	2,724	112	99	13
15—20	6,083	3,489	2,594	1,639	1,288	351	4,444	2,201	2,243	232	203	29
20 and Over.	30,287	17,420	12,867	8,774	6,883	1,891	21,513	10,537	10,976	1,342	1,111	231
Hindu (Brahmanic)...	37,115	21,024	16,091	8 386	6,840	1,546	28,729	14,184	14,545	1,177	1,001	176
0—5	4,691	2,577	2,114	...	...	...	4,691	2 577	2,114	...	...	...
5—10	3,446	1 884	1,562	496	446	50	2,950	1,438	1,512	28	28	...
10—15	4,140	2,173	1,967	706	592	114	3,434	1,581	1,853	84	78	6
15—20	4,261	2 502	1,759	1,252	1,031	221	3 009	1,471	1,538	172	157	15
20 and Over.	20,577	11,888	8,689	5,932	4,771	1,161	14,645	7,117	7,528	693	738	155
Muslim ...	15,397	8,351	7,046	2,982	2,247	735	12,415	6,104	6,311	376	302	74
0—5	2,146	1,118	1.028	...	...	...	2,146	1,118	1,028	...	...	...
5—10	1,555	800	755	182	93	89	1,423	707	716	4	2	2
10—15	1,647	831	816	235	175	60	1,412	656	756	13	8	5
15—20	1,593	875	728	295	200	95	1,308	675	628	35	26	9
20 & Over.	8,451	4,727	3,724	2,320	1,779	541	6,131	2,948	3,183	324	266	58

TABLE XIII.—Literacy by Religion and Age. *Part III—Cities.—(concld.)*

Ujjain City.—(*concld.*)

Religion and Age.	POPULATION.									LITERATE IN ENGLISH.		
	TOTAL.			LITERATE.			ILLITERATE.					
	Persons.	Males.	Females.	Persons.	Males.	Females.	Persons.	Males.	Females.	P.	M.	F.
1	2	3	4	5	6	7	8	9	10	11	12	13
Jain	1,906	1,080	826	605	390	215	1,301	690	611	131	115	16
0—5	179	93	86	...	...	...	179	93	86	...	...	...
5—10	167	71	96	23	17	6	144	54	90	2	1	1
10—15	208	86	122	51	37	14	157	49	108	10	10	...
15—20	206	99	107	81	49	32	125	50	75	19	17	2
20 and Over	1,146	731	415	450	287	163	696	444	252	100	87	13
Christian ...	85	50	35	62	36	26	23	14	9	30	20	10
0—5	12	7	5	...	...	...	12	7	5	...	...	...
5—10	12	8	4	7	4	3	5	4	1	3	2	1
10—15	12	7	5	10	5	5	2	2	...	4	2	2
15—20	6	4	2	5	3	2	1	1	...	5	3	2
20 and Over.	43	24	19	40	24	16	3	...	3	18	13	5
Others	135	87	48	51	37	14	84	50	34	11	9	2
0—5	26	13	13	...	...	...	26	13	13	...	...	...
5—10	16	8	8	6	4	2	10	4	6	2	1	1
10—15	15	9	5	7	6	1	8	3	5	1	1	...
15—20	12	9	3	6	5	1	6	4	2	1	...	1
20 and Over.	66	48	18	32	22	10	34	26	8	7	7	...
Hinduised Tribal ...	12	5	7	...	...	...	12	5	7	...	...	...
0—5	2	1	1	...	...	...	2	1	1	...	...	...
5—10	3	1	2	...	...	...	3	1	2	...	...	...
10—15	3	1	2	...	...	...	3	1	2	...	...	...
20 and Over.	4	2	2	...	...	...	4	2	2	...	...	...

TABLE XIV.

Literacy by Selected Castes, Tribes or Races.

NOTE.—This Table does not deal with the whole population but with certain selected castes only.

TABLE XIV.—Literacy by Selected

Caste, Tribe or Race.	Locality.	POPULATION.		
		TOTAL.		
		Persons.	Males.	Females.
1	2	3	4	5
1 Ahir	Narwar and Isagarh	105,336	57,161	48,175
2 Balai	Ujjain and Shajapur	78,835	40,431	38,404
3 Bania	Gird and Ujjain	73,542	41,028	32,514
4 Beragi	Ujjain and Mandsaur	24,691	13,272	11,419
5 Bhil	Amjhera	61,530	32,282	29,248
6 Bhilala	Amjhera	28,231	14,877	13,354
7 Brahman (except Dakshini)...	State...	233,994	133,890	100,104
8 Brahman Dakshini ...	Gird and Ujjain	10,991	5,889	5,102
9 Chamar	Isagarh and Narwar	329,871	172,338	157 533
10 Gadariya	Bhind and Narwar	69,671	37,723	31,948
11 Gujar	Tonwarghar and Shajapur	95,398	50,130	45,268
12 Kachhi	Gird and Bhind	135,588	74,444	61,144
13 Kayastha	Gird and Shajapur	27,831	15,949	11,882
14 Kirar	Tonwarghar and Narwar...	60,894	33,430	27,464
15 Koli	Gird and Tonwarghar	61,002	34,015	26,987
16 Kumbhar	Gird and Ujjain	49,185	26,427	22,758
17 Lodhi	Narwar and Isagarh	74,320	40,026	34,294
18 Maratha	Gird and Ujjain	11,984	6,790	5,194
19 Mina	Sheopur and Isagarh	54,195	28,732	25,463
20 Mirdha	Gird and Bhilsa	10,410	5,662	4,748
21 Nai	State	44,891	24,055	20,836
22 Rajput Bhadauriya ...	Bhind	15,666	9,541	6,125
23 Rajput Chauhan	Bhind and Ujjain	21,988	11,842	10,146
24 Rajput Kachhawaha ...	Bhind and Tonwarghar	13,399	7,970	5,429
25 Rajput Raghubansi ...	Isagarh and Bhilsa	18,259	9,584	8,675
26 Rajput Tonwar	Tonwarghar	26,678	16,326	10,352
27 Sahariya	Narwar and Isagarh	55,560	28,895	26,665
28 Sondhia	Ujjain and Shajapur	20,309	10,430	9,879
29 Teli	Bhind and Isagarh	44,877	24,399	20,478

Castes, Tribes or Races.

(7 YEARS AND OVER).						Literate in English (7 years and over).		
LITERATE.			ILLITERATE.					
Persons.	Males.	Females.	Persons.	Males.	Females.	Persons.	Males.	Females
6	7	8	9	10	11	12	13	14
1,066	1,015	51	104,270	56,146	48,124	33	33	...
148	139	9	78,687	40,292	38,395	1	1	...
12,781	10,809	1,972	60,761	30,219	30,542	1,000	961	39
908	839	69	23,783	12,433	11,350	27	27	...
152	147	5	61,378	32,135	29,243	2	2	...
193	192	1	28,038	14,685	13,353	...	...	...
25,784	22,019	3,765	208,210	111,841	96,369	2,244	2,143	101
6,721	5,423	1,298	4,260	466	3,794	2,655	2,580	75
906	817	89	328,965	171,521	157,444	13	12	1
257	232	25	69,414	37,491	31,923	16	16	...
652	602	50	94,741	49,528	45,213	33	29	4
1,925	1,852	73	133,663	72,592	61,071	32	28	4
11,588	10,071	1,517	16,243	5,878	10,365	1,549	1,418	131
453	442	11	60,441	32,988	27,453	24	22	2
524	480	44	60,478	33,535	26,913	13	13	...
264	229	35	48,921	26,198	22,723	9	9	...
576	560	16	73,744	39,466	34,278	37	36	1
4,027	3,452	545	7,957	3,308	4,649	805	769	36
286	280	6	53,909	28,452	25,457	5	5	...
110	101	6	10,300	5,558	4,742	23	23	...
1,039	993	46	43,352	23,062	20,290	50	48	2
1,640	1,585	55	14,026	7,956	6,070	42	42	...
2,045	1,932	113	19,913	9,910	10,033	109	107	2
782	663	70	12,667	7,308	5,359	51	47	4
895	794	101	17,364	8,790	8,574	30	29	1
2,068	2,008	60	24,590	14,318	10,272	62	60	2
16	15	1	55,544	28,880	26,664	...	...	...
44	42	2	20,265	10,388	9,877	4	4	...
856	718	148	44,021	23,686	20,335	27	25	2

TABLE XV.

Part I.—Language.

Part II.—Bi-lingualism.

NOTE 1.— The Table is divided into two parts. Part I shows the number of persons speaking (A) Vernaculars of India, (B) Vernaculars of other Asiatic countries and (C) European Languages. The Vernaculars of India have been divided into (1) Vernaculars proper to the State and (2) Vernaculars not proper to the State. The different Languages and Dialects in the above groups have been classified in accordance with the revised scheme. This part has been further divided into two sub-parts. Part (A) gives the Statistics of the State as a whole and of each District. Part (B) gives the Statistics for the Cities of Lashkar and Ujjain.

NOTE 2.— Part II gives by districts the number of persons who speak subsidiary languages besides their mother-tongue. The figures for the Mandsaur District in this part do not include those for the Nimach Cantonment.

Part I—Languages. *A. District Details.*

BHIND.			TONWARGHAR.			SHEOPUR.			NARWAR.		
Persons.	Males.	Females.	Persons.	Males.	Females.	Persons.	Males.	Females.	Persons.	Males.	Females.
8	9	10	11	12	13	14	15	16	17	18	19
[illegible]	[illegible]	[illegible]	[illegible]	[illegible]	[illegible]	[illegible]	72,925	64,109	401,586	211,555	190,031
[illegible]	[illegible]	[illegible]	[illegible]	[illegible]	[illegible]	[illegible]	72,923	64,109	401,584	211,555	190,029
[illegible]	[illegible]	[illegible]	[illegible]	[illegible]	[illegible]	[illegible]	71,418	62,954	400,573	210,941	189,631
[illegible]	[illegible]	[illegible]	[illegible]	[illegible]	[illegible]	[illegible]	[illegible]	[illegible]	[illegible]	*210,941*	[illegible]
...			...	...			...	...	[illegible]	27	31
			...		...	...		...	[illegible]	27	37
					...	...		...	...	...	...
	...	...				...		...	...	...	...
[illegible]	[illegible]	[illegible]	[illegible]	[illegible]	[illegible]	[illegible]	[illegible]	[illegible]	307	170	137
		...	[illegible]			[illegible]	[illegible]	27	[illegible]	53	53
...			...				...		...	...	...
[illegible]	[illegible]	[illegible]	[illegible]	[illegible]	[illegible]			...	201	117	84
...		...					...	...	...	...	...
...	...		...	...			...		...	...	...
	...	...	[illegible]	...		[illegible]	[illegible]	[illegible]	...	...	...
[illegible]	[illegible]	[illegible]	[illegible]	[illegible]	[illegible]	[illegible]	[illegible]	[illegible]	[illegible]	[illegible]	[illegible]
[illegible]	[illegible]	[illegible]	[illegible]	[illegible]	[illegible]	[illegible]	[illegible]	[illegible]	[illegible]	[illegible]	63,416
[illegible]	[illegible]	[illegible]	[illegible]	[illegible]	[illegible]	...			7	4	3
[illegible]	[illegible]	[illegible]	[illegible]	[illegible]		...		...	...	...	...
[illegible]	[illegible]	[illegible]	[illegible]	[illegible]	[illegible]	[illegible]	[illegible]	[illegible]	[illegible]	[illegible]	125,568
		...	...		...	...		...	...	...	...
[illegible]	[illegible]	[illegible]			...	[illegible]	[illegible]	[illegible]	59	30	29
[illegible]	[illegible]	[illegible]	[illegible]	[illegible]	[illegible]	[illegible]	[illegible]	10	1	1	...
[illegible]	[illegible]	[illegible]	[illegible]	[illegible]	[illegible]	[illegible]	[illegible]	17	16	12	4
[illegible]	[illegible]	[illegible]	[illegible]	[illegible]	[illegible]	[illegible]	[illegible]	141	1,046	610	436
...	...	...			...	...	...	...	...	...	...
...	...	...	...	...		...	...	...	...	...	...
...	...	...	...	...		...	...	...	...	...	...
6,863	3,414	3,449	2,751	1,106	1,645	2,630	1,475	1,155	1,009	614	395
6,863	*3,414*	*3,449*	*2,751*	*1,106*	*1,645*	*2,630*	*1,475*	*1,155*	*1,007*	*612*	*395*
...	...	...	4	...	3	...	...	...	21	12	12
3,659	1,630	2,029	842	114	728	295	108	187	31	9	22
3,659	1,630	2,029	842	114	729	295	108	187	31	9	22
9	6	3	16	14	2	359	211	148	2	1	1
9	6	3	16	14	2	359	211	148	2	1	1
...	...	...	...	...	...	...	...	...	...	...	...
...	...	...	...	...	...	...	...	...	...	...	...

TABLE XV.—

Languages and Dialects.	ISAGARH.			BHILSA.		
	Persons.	Males.	Females.	Persons.	Males.	Females.
1	2	3	4	5	6	7
Gwalior State	421,311	221,556	199,755	235,288	123,084	112,204
A. Languages of India	421,264	221,523	199,741	2 35,276	123,078	112,198
(1) Languages Proper to State ...	415,027	217,929	197,098	233,102	121,873	111,229
Indo-European Family ...	*414,974*	*217,893*	*197,081*	*232,976*	*121,778*	*111,198*
Bhil Dialects	4,158	2,347	1,806	...	...	...
Bhili	4,158	2,347	1,806	...	...	...
Bhilali	...	...	...	...	...	...
Rathvi	...	...	...	...	...	...
Rajasthani	82,828	48,838	38,990	73,715	41,442	32,273
Banjari	1,811	987	824	265	171	94
Khichiwadi	76,567	40,466	36,101	...	...	...
Malvi	4,421	2,376	2,045	73,450	41,271	32,179
Nimadi	...	...	...	...	...	...
Sondhi	29	9	20	...	...	...
Sipari	...	...	...	...	...	...
Western Hindi	327,993	171,708	156,285	159,261	80,336	78,925
Bundelkhandi	18,139	8,850	9,289	4,775	2,749	2,026
Bhadauri	170	147	23	166	102	64
Kachwahi	...	...	...	2	2	...
Hindi	306,578	161,044	145,531	152,149	76,205	75,944
Hindustani	...	...	...	...	...	...
Jatwari	...	...	...	...	...	...
Sikarwari	89	52	37	176	119	57
Tonwarghari	65	37	28	135	54	81
Urdu	2,952	1,578	1,374	1,858	1,105	753
Dravadian Family	*53*	*36*	*17*	*126*	*95*	*31*
Burgandi	...	...	...	...	...	...
Gondi	53	36	17	126	95	31
(2) Languages not proper to State ...	6,237	3,594	2,643	2,174	1,205	969
Indo-European Family	*6,237*	*3,591*	*2,643*	*2,174*	*1,205*	*969*
Bengali	41	26	15	6	5	1
Eastern Hindi	131	92	39	47	29	18
Purbi	131	92	39	47	29	18
Gujrati	21	10	11	314	177	137
Gujrati	21	10	11	314	177	137
Kathiawari	...	...	...	...	...	...
Kashmiri	...	...	...	...	...	...

Part I.—Languages. *A. District Details.—(contd.)*

UJJAIN.			MANDSAUR.			SHAJAPUR.			AMJHERA.		
Persons.	Males.	Females.	Persons.	Males.	Females.	Persons.	Males.	Females.	Persons.	Males.	Females.
8	9	10	11	12	13	14	15	16	17	18	19
405,961	211,274	194,687	272,166	140,333	131,833	336,980	174,985	161,995	160,066	80,411	79,655
[illegible]	[illegible]	194,623	272,037	140,246	131,791	336,974	174,982	161,992	160,054	80,399	79,655
369,381	[illegible]	[illegible]	175,023	89,088	85,935	330,026	170,886	159,140	149,694	74,219	75,475
[illegible]	[illegible]	[illegible]	[illegible]	[illegible]	[illegible]	[illegible]	[illegible]	[illegible]	[illegible]	*74,215*	*75,472*
165	[illegible]	107	1,215	422	793	3	3	...	69,842	23,932	25,910
[illegible]	57	[illegible]	...	...	...	5	5	...	24,768	12,615	12,153
...	..	...	1,215	422	793	...	...	...	44,963	21,247	23,716
...		..	...	...	...	...	...	...	109	70	39
[illegible]	[illegible]	[illegible]	[illegible]	[illegible]	[illegible]	[illegible]	[illegible]	[illegible]	[illegible]	[illegible]	29,501
[illegible]	[illegible]	[illegible]	[illegible]	[illegible]	[illegible]	[illegible]	[illegible]	279	[illegible]	184	179
..	...	.	...	..	...	[illegible]	[illegible]	...	...	...	...
[illegible]	[illegible]	[illegible]	[illegible]	[illegible]	[illegible]	[illegible]	[illegible]	[illegible]	[illegible]	[illegible]	24,136
...	-	...	1	1	..	1	...	1	10,742	5,214	5,528
[illegible]	[illegible]	[illegible]	[illegible]	[illegible]	[illegible]	[illegible]	[illegible]	[illegible]	[illegible]	72	58
3	...	[illegible]	[illegible]	[illegible]	...	...	...	...	...	...	...
[illegible]	[illegible]	[illegible]	[illegible]	[illegible]	[illegible]	[illegible]	[illegible]	17,414	[illegible]	[illegible]	[illegible]
[illegible]	157	[illegible]	[illegible]	[illegible]	159	[illegible]	574	416	452	253	199
[illegible]	445	[illegible]	[illegible]	[illegible]		[illegible]	[illegible]	58	4	1	3
[illegible]	[illegible]	..	...	..	...	1	...	1	...	...	...
[illegible]	[illegible]	[illegible]	[illegible]	14,077	11,411	[illegible]	[illegible]	15,129	18,163	[illegible]	8,775
...	...	...	[illegible]	1,497	1,473	...	...	...	...	...	...
.	..	...	...	...	...	...	...	...	...	...	...
[illegible]	5	...	[illegible]	[illegible]	317	9	4	5	3	3	...
[illegible]	[illegible]	156	...	..	...	674	315	359	...	...	...
[illegible]	[illegible]	5,105	[illegible]	[illegible]	1,933	[illegible]	1,486	1,466	1,426	742	684
[illegible]	*237*	*161*	*135*	*44*	*91*	[illegible]	*46*	*44*	*7*	*4*	*3*
[illegible]	276	161	135	44	91	[illegible]	45	44	7	4	8
9	9	...	...	...	...	1	1	...	...	...	...
[illegible]	20,078	16,230	97,016	51,161	45,855	6,948	4,096	2,852	10,360	6,180	4,180
36,266	[illegible]	*16,228*	[illegible]	*50,978*	[illegible]	*6,948*	*4,096*	*2,852*	*10,360*	*6,180*	*4,180*
23	16	7	8	7	1	...	...	...	1	1	...
605	305	300	722	360	362	503	263	240	162	121	41
605	305	300	722	360	362	503	263	240	162	121	41
18,603	11,274	7,329	3,143	1,735	1,408	1,192	622	470	4,814	2,843	1,971
18,596	11,269	7,327	3,142	1,734	1,408	1,092	622	470	4,346	2,621	1,725
7	5	2	1	1	...	...	...	...	468	222	246
4	2	2	...	...	...	...	...	...	...	...	...

TABLE. XV.—

Languages and Dialects.	GWALIOR STATE.			GIRD.		
	Persons.	Males.	Females.	Persons.	Males.	Females.
1	2	3	4	5	6	7
Marathi	21,585	12,060	9,475	10,876	6,044	4,882
Eastern Pahadi	53	39	14	34	21	13
Nepali	53	39	14	34	21	13
Western Pahadi	245	142	103	287	184	103
Pashtoo	560	359	201	8	6	2
Punjabi	3,810	1,939	1,871	210	146	64
Punjabi	3,808	1,937	1,871	210	146	64
Narnoli	2	2	...	...	...	...
Rajasthani	121,156	64,047	57,109	1,895	1,198	697
Gujari	750	479	271	9	9	...
Hadauti	2,439	1,438	1,001	...	...	...
Jaipuri	5,095	2,533	2,562	83	62	21
Marwari	93,492	48,216	45,276	1,732	1,089	643
Mewari	9,207	3,884	5,323	62	34	28
Mewati	9,988	7,423	2,565	9	4	5
Rajasthani	61	5	56	...	...	...
Shekhawati	124	69	55	...	...	...
Western Hindi	2,794	1,445	1,349	88	59	29
Ahirwadi	135	65	70	...	...	...
Antarvedi	788	347	441	63	47	16
Brij-Bhasha	1,871	1,033	838	25	12	13
Sanskrit...	95	81	14	...	...	...
Sindhi	65	33	32	38	22	16
Sindhi	43	24	19	38	22	16
Kachchhi	22	9	13	...	...	...
Dravadian Family	*349*	*309*	*40*	*22*	*14*	*8*
Tamil	279	252	27	11	7	4
Telegu	70	57	13	11	7	4
B. Languages of other Asiatic Countries.	445	340	105	101	93	8
Indo-European Family	*190*	*152*	*38*	*62*	*57*	*5*
Persian	190	152	38	62	57	5
Semitic Family	*255*	*188*	*67*	*39*	*36*	*3*
Arabic	255	188	67	39	36	3
C. European Languages	244	165	79	75	42	33
Indo-European Family ...	*244*	*165*	*79*	*75*	*42*	*33*
English	228	151	77	75	42	33
German	2	...	2	...	...	...
Portuguese	14	14	...	...	...	...

Part I.—Languages. *A. District Details.—(contd.)*

BHIND.			TONWARGHAR.			SHEOPUR.			NARWAR.		
Persons.	Males.	Females.	Persons.	Males.	Females.	Persons.	Males.	Females.	Persons.	Males.	Females.
8	9	10	11	12	13	14	15	16	17	18	19
[illegible]	[illegible]	[illegible]	[illegible]	[illegible]	276	409	222	187	359	187	172
[illegible]	7	...	[illegible]	2	1	...	...	...	...	...	...
[illegible]	7	...	[illegible]	2	1	...	...	...	...	...	...
...	...	...	...	...	...	6	6	...	2	2	...
[illegible]	[illegible]	1	...	...	...	...	...	...	33	33	...
[illegible]	[illegible]	[illegible]	[illegible]	[illegible]	21	43	19	24	34	23	11
[illegible]	[illegible]	[illegible]	[illegible]	[illegible]	21	43	19	24	34	23	11
...	...	...	...	...	...	...	...	...	...	...	...
[illegible]	[illegible]	[illegible]	[illegible]	[illegible]	[illegible]	[illegible]	[illegible]	[illegible]	516	343	173
...		...	...	...	...	...	...	...	...	...	...
...		...	...	...	...	[illegible]	[illegible]	187	...	...	...
[illegible]	[illegible]	[illegible]	[illegible]	[illegible]	6	[illegible]	[illegible]	[illegible]	...	...	...
[illegible]	[illegible]	[illegible]	[illegible]	[illegible]	211	[illegible]	[illegible]	[illegible]	515	342	173
...	...	...	[illegible]	[illegible]	[illegible]	218	[illegible]	[illegible]	...	...	...
...		...	1	1	...	...	...	...	1	1	...
...	...	...	[illegible]	[illegible]	[illegible]	...	...	...	...	...	...
...	...	...	...	...	...	...	...	...	...	...	...
[illegible]	[illegible]	[illegible]	[illegible]	[illegible]	[illegible]	...	...	...	3	1	2
...	...	...	...	...	...	...	...	...	...	...	...
[illegible]	[illegible]	[illegible]	[illegible]	[illegible]	[illegible]	...	...	...	3	1	2
[illegible]	[illegible]	[illegible]	...	...	...	...	...	...	...	...	...
[illegible]	[illegible]	...	1	1	...	...	...	...	...	...	...
2	2	...	...		...	...	...	...	3	1	2
...		...	...	...	...	...	...	...	3	1	2
2	2	...	...	...	...	...	...	...	...	...	...
...		...	...	...	...	2	2	...	...	...	...
...	...	...	...	...	...	...	...	...	...	...	...
...	...	...	...	...	...	2	...	2	...	...	...
19	12	7	9	5	4	2	2	...	...	...	...
12	9	3	9	5	4	...	...	...	...	...	...
12	9	3	9	5	4	...	...	...	...	...	...
7	3	4	...	...	...	2	2	...	...	...	...
7	3	4	...	...	...	2	2	...	...	...	...
...	...	...	2	2	...	...	...	...	2	...	2
...	...	...	2	2	...	...	...	...	2	...	2
...	...	...	2	2	...	...	...	...	...	...	...
...	...	...	...	...	...	...	...	...	2	...	2
...	...	...	...	...	...	...	...	...	...	...	...

TABLE XV.—

Languages and Dialects.	ISAGARH.			BHILSA.		
	Persons.	Males.	Females.	Persons	Males.	Females.
1	2	3	4	5	6	7
Marathi...	514	310	204	724	408	321
Eastern Pahadi	...	...	...	...	...	...
Nepali	...	...	...	...	...	...
Western Pahadi	...	...	...	...	...	...
Pashtoo ...	30	10	20	1	1	...
Punjabi ...	546	282	264	54	35	19
Punjabi	545	281	264	54	35	19
Narnoli	1	1	...	...	...	...
Rajasthani	4,819	2,799	2,020	1,002	542	460
Gujari	540	361	179	46	...	46
Hadauti	1,762	1,025	737	...	...	...
Jaipuri	826	451	375	59	34	25
Marwari	1,617	930	687	495	286	209
Mewari	...	...	...	166	129	37
Mewati	74	32	42	236	93	143
Rajasthani	...	...	...	...	...	...
Shekhawati	...	...	...	...	...	...
Western Hindi	135	65	70	10	6	4
Ahirwadi	135	65	70	...	...	...
Antarvedi	...	...	...	...	...	...
Brij-Bhasha	...	...	...	10	6	4
Sanskrit...	...	...	...	...	...	...
Sindhi ...	...	...	...	16	7	9
Sindhi	...	...	...	...	...	...
Kachchhi	...	...	...	16	7	9
Dravadian Family	...	...	...	...	...	...
Tamil ...	...	...	...	...	...	...
Telegu ...	...	...	...	...	...	...
B. Languages of other Asiatic Countries.	5	5	...	12	6	6
Indo-European Family ...	*5*	*5*	...	*12*	*6*	*6*
Persian ...	5	5	...	12	6	6
Semitic Family	...	...	...	...	...	...
Arabic ...	...	...	...	...	...	...
C. European Languages ...	42	28	14	...	...	...
Indo-European Family ..	*42*	*28*	*14*	...	...	...
English ...	42	28	14	...	...	...
German ...	...	...	...	...	...	...
Portuguese	...	...	...	...	...	...

Part.—I Languages. *A. District Details.—(concld.)*

UJJAIN.			MANDSAUR.			SHAJAPUR.			AMJHERA.		
Persons.	Males.	Females.	Persons.	Males.	Females.	Persons.	Males.	Females.	Persons.	Males.	Females.
8	9	10	11	12	13	14	15	16	17	18	19
4,07[illegible]	2,168	1,871	1,090	1,061	609	1,4[illegible]	79[illegible]	672	505	25[illegible]	150
2	2	...	3	3	...	4	4	...	...	...	...
2	2	...	3	3	...	4	4	...	...	...	...
...	...	...	...	...	...	...	...	...	...	...	...
[illegible]	[illegible]	[illegible]	122	91	31	227	[illegible]	[illegible]	[illegible]	24	4
177	[illegible]	48	1,13[illegible]	563	573	198	169	29	9	8	1
177	129	48	1,13[illegible]	563	573	198	169	29	9	8	1
...	...	...	1	1	...	...	...	...	...	...	...
12,[illegible]	[illegible]	[illegible]	[illegible]	[illegible]	42,75[illegible]	2,[illegible]	1,821	1,071	[illegible]	[illegible]	2,012
149	10[illegible]	[illegible]	...	...	...	6	6	...	...	...	...
[illegible]	2	[illegible]	...	...	...	[illegible]	[illegible]	[illegible]	10	5	5
2,316	1,0[illegible]	1,2[illegible]	[illegible]	[illegible]	[illegible]	[illegible]	[illegible]	141	16	[illegible]	6
9,[illegible]	4,54[illegible]	5,011	[illegible]	[illegible]	[illegible]	[illegible]	1,0[illegible]	[illegible]	[illegible]	[illegible]	1,5[illegible]
474	211	[illegible]	[illegible]	[illegible]	4,077	[illegible]	[illegible]	125	[illegible]	[illegible]	414
6	...	[illegible]	[illegible]	[illegible]	3,15[illegible]	[illegible]	[illegible]	[illegible]	[illegible]	[illegible]	14
[illegible]	...	[illegible]	...	...	...	21	4	17			...
...	...	...	124	[illegible]	55	...	...		...	...	...
[illegible]	[illegible]	...	[illegible]	[illegible]	[illegible]	[illegible]	[illegible]	254	2	2	...
...	...		...	...		...	...	...	...	...	...
...	...	...		...					...	...	...
[illegible]	[illegible]	...	[illegible]	[illegible]	[illegible]	[illegible]	[illegible]	[illegible]	2	2	...
...	...	...		...		[illegible]	14	14	...	...	...
1	...	1	2	1	1	[illegible]	...	[illegible]	...	...	...
...	...	...	2	1	1	...			...	...	...
1	...	1	...	...	...	[illegible]	...	[illegible]	...	...	...
[illegible]	[illegible]	2	[illegible]	213	[illegible]	...	...		...		...
1	1	...	[illegible]	244	[illegible]	...	...		...		...
41	[illegible]	2	16	9	7	...	...	...	...	...	...
225	161	64	54	41	13	6	3	3	12	12	...
[illegible]	15	5	[illegible]	41	13	[illegible]	[illegible]	2	12	12	...
20	15	5	54	[illegible]	13	4	2	2	12	12	...
[illegible]	116	59	...	...	...	2	1	1	...	...	...
205	116	[illegible]	...	...	...	2	1	1	...	...	...
47	47	...	76	[illegible]	[illegible]			...	...	...	...
47	47	...	76	[illegible]	[illegible]	...	...	...	...	...	...
17	17	...	63	[illegible]	[illegible]	[illegible]	...	...	...	...	...
...	...	...	...	...	...	...	...	...	...	...	...
...	...	...	11	11	...	...	...	...	...	...	...

TABLE XV.—Part I—Languages. B.—Cities

Languages and Dialects.	LASHKAR CITY. Persons.	LASHKAR CITY. Males.	LASHKAR CITY. Females.	UJJAIN CITY. Persons.	UJJAIN CITY. Males.	UJJAIN CITY. Females.
1	2	3	4	5	6	7
Total ...	86,767	47,358	39,409	54,650	30,597	24,053
A. Languages of India	86,682	47,304	39,378	54,396	30,407	23,989
(1) Languages proper to State ...	74,587	40,276	34,311	43,343	24,162	19,181
Indo-European Family	*74,587*	*40,276*	*34,311*	*43,341*	*24,160*	*19,181*
Bhil Dialects—Bhili	...	...	...	4	...	4
Rajasthani	9	...	9	10,866	5,407	4,959
Banjari	3	...	3	...	...	...
Malvi	6	...	6	10,866	5,407	4,959
Western Hindi	74,578	40,276	34,302	32,971	18,758	14,218
Bundelkhandi	218	145	68	598	340	258
Bhadauri	131	112	19	351	228	123
Kachwahi	41	35	6	3	3	...
Hindi	61,669	32,425	29,244	23,062	12,549	10,513
Sikarwari	117	111	6	9	9	...
Tonwarghari	30	7	23	150	131	19
Urdoo	12,377	7,441	4,936	8,803	5,493	3,310
Dravadian Family.—Burgandi ...	...	...	...	2	2	...
2. Languages not proper to State ...	12,095	7,028	5,067	11,053	6,245	4,808
Indo-European Family	*12,077*	*7,016*	*5,061*	*11,042*	*6,236*	*4,806*
Bengali	83	54	29	17	12	5
Eastern Hindi—Purbi ...	248	173	75	...	...	...
Gujrati	197	153	44	5,655	3 075	2,580
Gujrati	197	153	44	5,648	3,070	2,578
Kathiawadi	...	...	...	7	5	2
Kashmiri	23	18	5	4	2	2
Marathi	9,817	5,491	4,326	2,998	1,823	1,175
Eastern Pahadi—Nepali ...	21	14	7	...	...	...
Pastoo	2	...	2	17	8	9
Punjabi	77	56	21	74	57	17
Rajasthani	1,518	996	522	2,275	1,258	1,017
Gujari	...	...	...	3	3	...
Jaipuri	62	54	8	406	242	164
Marwari	1,445	936	509	1,771	962	809
Mewari	11	6	5	95	51	41
Western Hindi	53	39	14	1	1	...
Antarvedi	45	32	13	...	...	...
Brij-Bhasha	8	7	1	1	1	...
[illegible]	38	22	16	1	...	1
[illegible]	38	22	16	...	...	...
[illegible]	...	...	...	1	...	1
[illegible] Family ...	*18*	*12*	*6*	*11*	*9*	*2*
[illegible]	7	5	2	...	...	...
[illegible]	11	7	4	11	9	2
B. Languages of other Asiatic Countries	24	22	2	211	147	61
[illegible] ...	13	11	2	14	9	5
[illegible] ...	11	11	...	197	138	59
C. European Languages	61	32	29	43	43	—
[illegible] ...	61	32	29	43	43	—

TABLE XV.—Part II.—Bi-lingualism.

District.	Mother-tongue.	NUMBER OF PERSONS SPEAKING MOTHER-TONGUE.			NUMBER OF PERSONS SPEAKING SUBSIDIARY LANGUAGES.									
					Bhil Dialects.		Rajasthani.		Western Hindi.		Gujrati.		Marathi.	
		Persons.	Males.	Females.	M.	F.	Males.	Females	Males.	F.	M.	F.	M.	F.
1	2	3	4	5	6	7	8	9	10	11	12	13	14	15
Gwalior State.	Total ...	3,508,865	1,859,296	1,649,569	491	757	23,582	21,093	54,989	50,004	2,942	900	2,414	1,897
	Bhil Dialects ...	75,469	37,200	38,269	...	...	1,821	1,741	1,332	2,414	—	...	...	...
	Rajasthani ...	1,082,132	558,770	523,362	188	160	...	...	45,609	41,017	1,561	691	100	318
	Western Hindi ...	2,301,068	1,234,178	1,066,895	302	597	17,995	18,205	...	...	1,365	197	2,318	1,579
	Gujrati ...	28,661	17,093	11,568	1	...	2,998	1,840	3,016	2,190	...	...	1	...
	Marathi ...	21,535	12,060	9,475	...	...	768	807	5,032	4,383	16	12	—	...
Gird District	Total ...	363,270	196,861	166,409	...	...	161	37	3,346	3,144	24	22	904	728
	Bhil Dialects ...	32	12	20	...	...	...	...	10	19	...	...	...	...
	Rajasthani ...	2,147	1,367	780	...	...	...	...	461	395	...	...	1	...
	Western Hindi...	349,927	189,288	160,639	...	...	161	37	...	...	24	22	903	728
	Gujrati ...	288	200	88	...	...	...	...	127	5	...	...	...	...
	Marathi ...	10,876	6,044	4,832	...	...	...	...	2,748	2,725	...	...	...	...
Bhind District	Total ...	413,650	225,985	187,665	...	...	333	168	421	256	410	...	476	73
	Rajasthani ...	1,671	1,019	652	...	...	...	...	348	198	...	...	9	2
	Western Hindi...	411,575	224,746	186,829	...	..	333	168	...	...	410	...	467	71
	Gujrati ...	9	6	3	...	...	...	...	6	1	...	...	...	...
	Marathi ...	395	214	181	...	...	...	...	67	57	...	...	...	...
Tonwarghar District.	Total ...	368,709	204,578	164,131	...	...	1	7	536	283	...	1	10	10
	Rajasthani ...	823	469	354	...	...	...	...	348	100	...	...	...	...
	Western Hindi...	367,315	203,816	163,499	...	...	1	7	...	...	...	1	10	10
	Gujrati ...	16	14	2	...	...	...	...	11	2	...	...	...	...
	Marathi ...	555	279	276	...	...	...	...	177	181	...	...	...	...
Sheopur District.	Total ...	136,678	72,730	63,948	...	...	21	67	851	1,648	2	..	9	2
	Rajasthani ...	53,625	27,706	25,919	...	...	...	...	588	1,532	...	...	...	...
	Western Hindi...	82,285	44,591	37,694	...	...	10	57	...	...	...	...	9	2
	Gujrati. ...	359	211	148	...	...	10	10	101	96	...	...	...	...
	Marathi ...	409	222	187	...	...	1	...	162	20	2	...	...	...
Narwar District.	Total ...	401,455	211,473	189,982	...	...	220	204	302	266	38	12	13	1
	Bhil Dialects ...	58	27	31	...	...	...	...	23	19	...	...	...	...
	Rajasthani ...	823	513	310	...	...	...	...	153	143	15	...	3	1
	Wetern Hindi ...	400,213	210,745	189,468	...	...	220	204	...	...	23	12	10	...
	Gujrati ...	2	1	1	...	...	...	...	1	1	...	...	...	...
	Marathi ...	359	187	172	...	...	...	...	125	108	...	...	...	...

TABLE XV.—Part II.—Bi-lingualism.—(concld.)

District.	Mother-tongue.	NUMBER OF PERSONS SPEAKING MOTHER-TONGUE.			NUMBER OF PERSONS SPEAKING SUBSIDIARY LANGUAGES.									
					BHIL DIALECTS.		RAJASTHANI.		WESTERN HINDI.		GUJRATI.		MARATHI.	
		Persons.	Males.	Females.	M.	F.	Males.	Females	M.	F.	M.	F.	M.	F.
1	2	3	4	5	6	7	8	9	10	11	12	13	14	15
Isagarh District.	Total ...	420,463	221,077	199,386	178	435	1,444	1,212	758	796	13	3	326	161
	Bhil Dialects ...	4,153	2,347	1,806	...	...	...	...	2	...	...	...	...	...
	Rajasthani ...	87,647	46,637	41,010	...	...	...	...	545	710	...	1	...	1
	Western Hindi...	328,128	171,773	156,355	178	435	1,443	1,212	...	...	13	2	326	160
	Gujrati ...	21	10	11	...	...	1	...	6	8	...	...	...	...
	Marathi ...	514	310	204	...	...	...	...	205	78	...	...	...	...
Bhilsa District.	Total ..	235,026	122,906	112,120	6	48	422	349	11,175	4,974	369	4	27	13
	Rajasthani ...	74,717	41,934	32,783	...	34	...	...	10,940	4,761	9	...	...	3
	Western Hindi...	159,271	80,342	78,929	6	14	412	338	...	...	360	4	27	10
	Gujrati ...	314	177	137	...	...	6	...	119	105	...	...	...	...
	Marathi ...	724	403	321	...	...	4	11	116	108	...	...	...	...
Ujjain District.	Total ...	404,231	210,173	194,058	19	3	8,472	8,828	13,821	12,797	1,442	209	414	637
	Bhil Dialects ...	166	57	109	...	...	11	...	4	...	...	...	...	...
	Rajasthani ...	273,775	139,748	134,027	15	3	...	...	11,770	11,032	1,152	107	37	115
	Western Hindi ...	107,648	56,926	50,722	3	...	6,113	7,760	...	...	277	90	376	522
	Gujrati ...	18,003	11,274	7,829	1	...	1,927	1,019	1,552	1,271	...	...	1	...
	Marathi ...	4,039	2,168	1,871	...	...	421	49	495	494	13	12	...	...
Mandsaur District.	Total ...	269,625	138,924	130,701	...	17	2,988	2,230	4,860	2,772	12	20	29	1
	Bhil Dialects ...	1,215	822	393	...	...	74	...	25	...	...	...	...	...
	Rajasthani ...	229,803	116,893	112,910	...	17	...	...	3,817	2,234	10	18	3	1
	Western Hindi...	33,774	18,393	15,381	...	...	2,714	2,125	...	...	1	2	26	...
	Gujrati ...	3,143	1,735	1,408	...	...	156	104	663	312	...	...	...	...
	Marathi ...	1,690	1,081	609	...	...	44	1	355	226	1	...	...	...
Shajapur District.	Total ...	335,911	174,348	161,563	29	8	6,117	5,665	15,279	17,429	291	473	80	208
	Bhil Dialects ...	8	8	...	...	...	8	...	...	...	...	...	...	...
	Rajasthani ...	292,466	149,713	142,753	26	8	...	...	14,579	16,853	244	411	44	132
	Western Hindi ...	40,852	23,214	17,638	3	...	5,042	5,557	...	...	47	62	36	76
	Gujrati ...	1,092	622	470	...	...	186	81	252	234	...	...	...	...
	Marathi ...	1,468	796	672	...	...	286	224	448	342	...	...	...	...
Amjhera District.	Total ...	159,847	80,231	79,616	220	246	3,4[illegible]3	2,126	3,640	5,639	321	156	126	3
	[illegible] ...	[illegible]	33,932	35,910	...	...	1,733	1,711	1,208	2,376	...	...	...	...
	[illegible] ...	64,435	[illegible]	31,914	147	94	...	...	2,060	2,059	131	154	3	3
	[illegible] ...	[illegible]	[illegible]	9,071	112	119	[illegible]	740	...	...	100	2	123	...
	[illegible] ...	[illegible]	[illegible]	1,971	...	...	712	623	178	155	...	...	...	...
	[illegible] ...	[illegible]	233	150	...	...	12	22	131	4[illegible]	...	...	...	...

TABLE XVI.

Religion.

NOTE 1.—The Sub-head "Hinduized Tribal" includes those of primitive and forest Tribes whose tribal names were entered in lieu of religion in column 4 of the General Schedule. The remainder of these Tribes returned themselves as Hindus. The details of each Tribe have been shown in Table XVIII under the headings "Bhil," "Bhilala," "Mina," "Saharya," etc., etc.

NOTE 2.—The details of Christians are given below :—

Sect.	Persons.	Males.	Females.
Roman Catholics	450	362	188
Romo-Syrians	...	...	...
Other Syrians	...	...	...
Others	748	330	418

TABLE XVI.—Religion.

[illegible]	Population.			Hindu. Brahmanic.			Arya.			Hinduized Tribal.			Total Hindus.		
	Persons.	Males.	Females.	Persons.	Males.	Females.	P.	M.	F.	P.	M.	F.	Persons.	Males.	Females.
1	2	3	4	5	6	7	8	9	10	11	12	13	14	15	16
[illegible] State	[illegible]	1,587,631	[illegible]	3,255,977	1,724,311	1,531,666	[illegible]	658	620	14,291	7,248	7,043	3,271,376	1,732,247	1,539,329
[illegible]	[illegible]	[illegible]	[illegible]	[illegible]	174,591	147,751	112	72	40	19	11	8	322,476	174,674	147,802
[illegible]	[illegible]	[illegible]	[illegible]	[illegible]	217,360	180,750	129	80	49	583	342	241	[illegible]	217,782	181,010
[illegible]	[illegible]	[illegible]	[illegible]	[illegible]	197,628	[illegible]	30	12	18	52	29	23	356,803	197,669	159,134
[illegible]	[illegible]	[illegible]	64,109	130,378	69,396	60,982	46	24	22	601	299	302	131,025	69,719	61,306
[illegible]	[illegible]	[illegible]	[illegible]	[illegible]	201,258	183,816	37	30	7	617	324	293	385,728	201,612	184,116
[illegible]	[illegible]	[illegible]	[illegible]	[illegible]	[illegible]	188,826	231	116	115	517	252	265	398,701	209,498	189,206
[illegible]	[illegible]	[illegible]	112,331	[illegible]	114,901	105,067	25	11	14	332	166	166	220,325	115,078	105,247
[illegible]	[illegible]	[illegible]	[illegible]	357,911	[illegible]	172,273	421	212	209	723	357	366	359,055	186,207	172,848
[illegible]	[illegible]	[illegible]	[illegible]	[illegible]	122,062	114,978	76	41	35	1,727	846	881	[illegible]	122,949	115,894
[illegible]	[illegible]	[illegible]	[illegible]	[illegible]	157,723	146,581	135	61	74	677	330	347	305,116	158,114	147,002
[illegible]	[illegible]	[illegible]	[illegible]	[illegible]	71,624	71,546	66	29	37	8,443	4,292	4,151	151,679	76,045	75,734

[illegible]	Sikh.			Jain.			Zoroastrian.			Muslim.			Christian.		
	P.	M.	F.	P.	M.	F.	P.	M.	F.	P.	M.	F.	P.	M.	F.
1	17	18	19	20	21	22	23	24	25	26	27	28	29	30	31
[illegible] State	631	[illegible]	215	[illegible]	[illegible]	[illegible]	[illegible]	96	[illegible]	[illegible]	169,412	91,885	1,198	592	[illegible]
[illegible]	[illegible]	[illegible]	[illegible]	[illegible]	[illegible]	[illegible]	105	43	62	[illegible]	31,575	17,657	[illegible]	113	125
[illegible]	[illegible]	[illegible]	[illegible]	[illegible]	[illegible]	[illegible]	...	...	...	[illegible]	[illegible]	[illegible]	5	3	2
[illegible]	[illegible]	[illegible]	[illegible]	[illegible]	[illegible]	[illegible]	...	...		[illegible]	[illegible]	[illegible]	24	13	11
[illegible]	[illegible]	[illegible]	[illegible]	[illegible]	[illegible]	[illegible]	...		...	[illegible]	[illegible]	[illegible]	...	...	...
[illegible]	[illegible]	[illegible]	[illegible]	[illegible]	[illegible]	[illegible]		...	...	[illegible]	[illegible]	[illegible]	[illegible]	[illegible]	[illegible]
[illegible]	[illegible]	[illegible]	[illegible]	[illegible]	[illegible]	[illegible]	[illegible]	[illegible]	...	[illegible]	[illegible]	[illegible]	[illegible]	[illegible]	[illegible]
[illegible]	[illegible]	[illegible]	[illegible]	[illegible]	[illegible]	[illegible]	[illegible]	[illegible]	[illegible]	[illegible]	[illegible]	[illegible]	[illegible]	[illegible]	[illegible]
[illegible]	[illegible]	[illegible]	[illegible]	[illegible]	[illegible]	[illegible]	[illegible]	[illegible]	[illegible]	[illegible]	[illegible]	[illegible]	[illegible]	[illegible]	[illegible]
[illegible]	[illegible]	[illegible]	[illegible]	[illegible]	[illegible]	[illegible]	[illegible]	[illegible]	[illegible]	[illegible]	[illegible]	[illegible]	[illegible]	[illegible]	[illegible]
[illegible]	[illegible]	[illegible]	[illegible]	[illegible]	[illegible]	[illegible]	[illegible]	[illegible]	[illegible]	[illegible]	[illegible]	[illegible]	[illegible]	[illegible]	[illegible]
[illegible]	[illegible]	[illegible]	[illegible]	[illegible]	[illegible]	[illegible]	[illegible]	[illegible]	[illegible]	[illegible]	[illegible]	[illegible]	[illegible]	[illegible]	[illegible]

TABLE XVII.

Race, Tribe or Caste

TABLE XVII.—

Caste and Religion.	GWALIOR STATE. Persons.	Males.	Females.	GIRD. Persons.	Males.	Females.
1	2	3	4	5	6	7
Gwalior State	3,523,070	1,867,031	1,656,039	364,806	197,935	166,871
Hindu-Brahmanic	3,255,977	1,724,311	1,531,666	322,315	174,591	147,724
1 Aghori	110	82	28	...	...	...
2 Ahir	130,682	70,208	60,474	15,774	9,327	6,447
3 Ajna	9,778	5,095	4,683	...	...	...
4 Atit (Sanyasi)	1,103	1,044	59	2	2	...
5 Badhai	32,059	16,806	15,253	2,799	1,491	1,317
6 Bahrupi	17	13	4	12	8	4
7 Bagri	23,209	11,698	11,511	...	...	...
8 Balai	97,828	49,031	48,797	26	11	15
9 Banjara	19,731	10,716	9,015	99	61	38
10 Barai	149	96	53	105	74	31
11 Barar	1,384	772	612	...	...	...
12 Bargunda	1,931	960	971	...	...	...
13 Bari	3,225	1,730	1,495	53	31	2[illegible]
14 Basor	13,052	6,394	6,658	1,005	498	5[illegible]
15 Bania	87,750	48,011	39,739	14,637	7,706	6,93[illegible]
1 Agarwal	26,952	14,754	12,198	4,537	2,437	2,100
2 Bhalera	31	31	...	...	...	...
3 Bijabargi	641	369	272	54	29	25
4 Deswal	124	86	38	...	...	...
5 Dhusar	442	241	201	...	...	...
6 Gahoi	7,550	4,043	3,507	2,159	1,191	968
7 Jaiswal	1,431	667	764	73	37	36
8 Khandelwal	828	493	335	67	39	28
9 Maheshri	6,699	3,291	3,408	75	41	34
10 Mahur	637	341	296	138	76	62
11 Mod	510	316	194	...	...	...
12 Oswal	2,071	1,208	863	151	90	61
13 Porwal	2,526	1,325	1,201	1	1	...
14 Palliwal	11	10	1	4	4	...
15 Saraogi	326	157	169	19	9	10
16 Others and unspecified ...	36,971	20,679	16,292	7,359	3,752	3,607
16 Beria	5,807	3,051	2,756	...	...	...
17 Behna	2	2	...	...	...	...
18 Beldar	476	269	207	...	...	...
19 Beragi	30,203	16,177	14,026	96	73	23
20 Bhami	2,798	1,387	1,411	...	...	...
21 Bhand	549	316	233	...	...	...
22 Bhangi	27,405	14,732	12,673	3,717	2,069	1,648
23 Bharbhunja	939	514	425	91	45	46
24 Bharud	364	184	180	...	...	...
25 Bhat	7,425	4,205	3,220	294	212	82
26 Bhil	77,770	39,430	38,340	...	...	...
27 Bhilala	36,136	18,205	17,931	...	...	...
28 Bhoi	13,229	7,092	6,137	3,846	2,247	1,599
29 Bidur	162	71	91	...	...	...
30 Brahman	296,049	166,237	129,812	42,774	24,197	18,577
1 Ad-Gaur	1,338	785	553	...	...	...
2 Ametha	110	74	36	...	...	...
3 Audich	4,308	2,105	2,203	4	2	2
4 Audumber	26	18	8	...	...	...
5 Bengali	142	89	53	108	66	42
6 Bhadauria	504	286	218	...	...	...
7 Bhagor	14,967	8,466	6,501	4,999	2,840	2,159
8 Chaturvedi	1,485	801	684	76	56	20
9 Dakshini	13,151	6,826	6,325	6,028	3,075	2,953
10 Dayma	496	239	257	10	5	5
11 Gaur	13,548	7,157	6,391	1,350	821	529
12 Gujrati	1,758	883	875	119	71	48
13 Jijhotia	5,423	3,111	2,312	835	402	433
14 Kanya-kubja	10,261	6,220	4,041	1,907	1,429	478
15 Kashmiri	220	138	82	153	95	58
16 Nagar	3,394	1,759	1,635	45	19	26
17 Ojha	133	52	81	119	41	78
18 Rikhisur	8,452	4,188	4,264	2	...	2
19 Sanadhya	114,086	66,711	47,375	15,352	8,276	7,076
20 Sarwariya	3,395	1,839	1,556	...	...	...
21 Saraswat	959	497	462	104	76	28
22 Shenwai	281	141	140	96	61	35
23 Shrigaur	543	301	242	...	...	...
24 Shrimali	1,334	709	625	...	...	...
25 Telang	8	5	3	...	...	...
26 Others and unspecified ...	95,727	52,837	42,890	11,467	6,862	4,605

Race, Tribe or Caste. *Part I.—District Details.*

Bhind.			Tonwarghar.			Sheopur.			Narwar.		
Persons.	Males.	Females.	Persons.	Males.	Females.	Persons.	Males.	Females.	Persons.	Males.	Females.
8	9	10	11	12	13	14	15	16	17	18	19
418,224	225,214	193,010	369,648	204,759	164,889	137,031	72,925	64,109	401,586	211,555	190,031
398,110	217,362	180,750	356,721	197,628	159,093	133,378	69,396	63,982	358,074	204,258	153,816
...	...	...	...	...	...	...	...	...	...	...	...
15,165	8,981	[illegible]	[illegible]	[illegible]	1,213	3,448	1,723	1,725	26,505	14,331	12,171
...	...	...	...	...	...	...	...	...	...	...	...
57	25	11	31	10	21	...	...	...	4	1	3
4,243	2,167	2,075	5,155	[illegible]	2,265	241	76	173	[illegible]	1,010	866
...	...	...	..	..	..	...	...	...	...	...	...
...	...	...	..	...	...	...	...	...	...	...	...
21	10	21	..	..	...	521	249	272	33	20	18
158	73	75	212	178	71	[illegible]	415	523	538	313	225
...	...	...	.	...	...	...	...	...	...	...	...
1,325	718	607	..	...		...	...	...	13	8	5
...	...	...	...	...	...	...	...	...	...	...	...
[illegible]	472	257	232	124	51	...	...	...	15	...	15
29	12	22	72	41	31	16	6	6	[illegible]	768	825
1,875	4,012	[illegible]	12,250	[illegible]	[illegible]	4,410	2,394	2,016	6,825	[illegible]	4,026
[illegible]	654	[illegible]	[illegible]	[illegible]	[illegible]	2,113	1,671	1,442	3,250	1,609	1,641
...	...	...	..	..	..	24	16	8	12	4	8
...	...	.	..		...	...	...	...	...	...	...
...	...	..	.	..	.	...	...	..	...	...	...
...	...	...	...	..	...	...	..	...	...	...	...
[illegible]	1,002	[illegible]		...	..		...	...	3,155	1,710	1,445
...	...	...	..	...	...	...	...	...	51	27	24
...	...	...	31	17	13	[illegible]	42	46	28	18	10
...	...	...	466	[illegible]	246	[illegible]	26	15	[illegible]	25	24
49	47	22	...	...	..	...	..	...	...	...	...
...	...	...	...	...	...	...	...	...	...	...	...
40	25	15	...	.	..	18	14	4	4	4	...
[illegible]	61	[illegible]	..	...		[illegible]	[illegible]	245	...	...	...
...	...	...	.	...	...	...	..	...	...	...	...
29	20	...	...	..	...	...	...	...	...	...	...
5,021	[illegible]	2,163	[illegible]	[illegible]	[illegible]	511	255	256	2,156	1,182	974
1	...	1	[illegible]	312	[illegible]	...	...	...	41	...	41
...	...	...	..	..	...	...	...	...	2	2	...
...	...	...	...	...	...	...	...	...	18	8	10
755	441	317	814	[illegible]	371	[illegible]	[illegible]	[illegible]	838	419	419
...	..	...	...	..	...	16	7	9	...	...	...
411	251	163	...	...	..	[illegible]	24	8	...	...	...
[illegible]	[illegible]	[illegible]	[illegible]	[illegible]	1,159	1,172	[illegible]	547	2,194	1,502	1,102
515	235	[illegible]	[illegible]	6	11	10	4	6	15	6	9
...	...	...	...	...	...	...	...	...	109	60	49
645	435	[illegible]	[illegible]	[illegible]	117	[illegible]	[illegible]	79	265	117	148
2	..	2	...	...	...	56	41	15	460	201	259
319	119	121	1,016	546	470	[illegible]	126	246	...	...	...
[illegible]	[illegible]	[illegible]	[illegible]	[illegible]	[illegible]	14,144	7,468	6,676	20,139	11,225	8,914
...	...	...	152	91	[illegible]	10	8	2	94	71	23
...	...	...	...	...	...	...	...	...	...	...	...
...	...	...	...	...	...	...	...	...	...	...	...
...	...	...	...	...	...	...	...	...	1	1	...
...	...	...	197	147	49	...	...	...	...	...	...
[illegible]	254	275	421	205	216	53	28	23	5,914	3,385	2,529
37	27	10	[illegible]	[illegible]	[illegible]	23	18	4	...	...	...
610	245	[illegible]	411	194	217	196	120	76	204	94	110
2,082	969	1,113	1,149	644	505	1,145	637	511	351	205	146
24	12	12	...	...	...	151	72	82	1	1	...
4	3	1	167	109	58	...	...	...	116	84	32
4,614	2,636	1,978	656	464	[illegible]	77	46	31	132	81	51
...	...	...	31	23	11	...	...	..	8	4	4
...	...	...	...	...	...	229	114	115	380	200	180
...	...	...	8	5	3	...	...	...	..	...	...
3,421	1,521	1,900	5,026	2,667	2,359	...	...	...	...	...	...
38,840	23,223	15,617	30,168	18,636	11,532	6,637	3,656	2,981	6,842	3,775	3,067
18	15	3	53	25	28	2,785	1,507	1,278	...	...	...
...	...	...	...	...	...	89	55	34	3	3	...
12	5	7	...	...	...	...	...	...	...	...	...
...	...	...	...	...	...	...	...	...	...	...	...
1,079	588	491	...	...	...	...	...	...	...	...	...
16,556	9,572	6,984	12,509	7,053	5,456	2,741	1,307	1,434	6,093	3,321	2,772

TABLE XVII.—

Caste and Religion.	ISAGARH.			BHILSA.		
	Persons.	Males.	Females.	Persons.	Males.	Females.
1	2	3	4	5	6	7
Gwalior State	421,311	221,556	199,755	235,288	123,084	112,204
Hindu-Brahmanic	397,956	209,130	188,826	219,968	114,901	105,067
1 Aghori	...	...	...	...	...	...
2 Ahir	37,373	19,748	17,625	10,563	5,340	5,223
3 Ajna	...	...	...	...	...	...
4 Atit (Sanyasi)	18	14	4	...	...	...
5 Badhai	4,679	2,199	2,480	96	49	47
6 Bahrupi	...	...	...	...	...	...
7 Bagri	...	...	...	...	...	...
8 Balai	555	334	221	17	17	...
9 Banjara	6,844	3,572	3,272	1,041	390	651
10 Barai	9	7	2	...	...	...
11 Barar	...	...	...	46	46	...
12 Bargunda	...	...	...	...	...	...
13 Bari	1	1	...	...	...	...
14 Basor	2,433	1,300	1,133	2,471	1,384	1,087
15 Bania	4,908	2,675	2,233	2,369	1,145	1,224
1 Agarwal	1,285	700	585	684	355	329
2 Bhatera	31	31	...	...	...	...
3 Bijabargi	52	28	24	...	...	...
4 Deswal	...	...	...	...	...	...
5 Dhusar	...	...	...	...	...	...
6 Gahoi...	220	123	97	30	15	15
7 Jaiswal	51	35	16	394	145	249
8 Khandelwal	108	54	54	118	56	62
9 Maheshri	453	267	186	24	18	6
10 Mahur	218	112	106	...	...	...
11 Mod	...	...	...	...	...	...
12 Oswal...	2	2	..	361	208	153
13 Porwal	415	243	172	37	21	16
14 Palliwal	7	6	1	...	...	...
15 Saraogi	15	7	8	...	...	...
16 Others and unspecified ...	2,051	1,067	984	721	327	394
16 Beria	740	311	429	1,850	902	948
17 Behna	...	...	...	...	...	...
18 Beldar	22	11	11	...	...	...
19 Beragi	2,497	1,453	1,044	1,868	890	978
20 Bhami	...	...	...	...	...	...
21 Bhand	...	...	...	...	...	...
22 Bhangi	3,769	1,810	1,959	2,425	1,258	1,167
23 Bharbhunja	93	49	44	6	2	4
24 Bharud	...	...	...	...	...	...
25 Bhat	316	214	102	76	40	36
26 Bhil	7,986	3,924	4,062	1,850	853	997
27 Bhilala	10	10	...	...	...	...
28 Bhoi	105	54	51	2,313	1,125	1,188
29 Bilar	...	...	...	...	...	...
30 Brahman	20,656	11,297	9,359	17,692	9,507	8,395
1 Ad-Gaur	8	8	...	69	46	23
2 Ametha	...	...	...	...	...	...
3 Audich	...	...	...	...	...	...
4 [illegible]	...	...	...	...	...	...
5 Bengali	11	8	3	...	...	...
6 [illegible]	15	15	...	...	...	...
7 [illegible]	1,326	[illegible]	449	1,253	557	696
8 [illegible]	2	1	1	53	31	22
9 [illegible]	718	303	415	452	200	252
10 [illegible]	...	...	...	...	...	...
11 [illegible]	[illegible]	[illegible]	221	713	[illegible]	346
12 [illegible]	52	40	41	[illegible]	[illegible]	67
13 [illegible]	[illegible]	[illegible]	[illegible]	1,524	811	713
14 [illegible]	[illegible]	[illegible]	77	[illegible]	671	[illegible]
15 [illegible]	[illegible]	13	9	...	...	...
16 [illegible]	6	6	...	...	...	...
17 [illegible]	...	...	...	...	...	...
18 [illegible]	[illegible]	[illegible]	[illegible]	[illegible]	[illegible]	[illegible]
19 [illegible]	...	...	...	...	...	...
20 [illegible]	[illegible]	[illegible]	4	4	2	3
21 [illegible]	...	...	...	...	...	...
22 [illegible]	...	...	...	...	...	...
23 [illegible]	...	...	...	6	[illegible]	3
24 [illegible]	[illegible]	11,[illegible]	[illegible]	[illegible]	[illegible]	[illegible]
[illegible] ...						

Race, Tribe or Caste. *Part I.—District Details.—(contd.)*

UJJAIN.			MANDSAUR.			SHAJAPUR.			AMJHERA.		
Persons.	Males.	Females.	Persons.	Males.	Females.	Persons.	Males.	Females.	Persons.	Males.	Females.
8	9	10	11	12	13	14	15	16	17	18	19
405.961	211,274	194,687	272,166	140,333	131,833	336,980	174,985	161,995	160,066	80,411	79,655
357,911	185,638	172,273	237,040	122,062	114,978	304,304	157,723	146,581	143,170	71,624	71,546
...	...	...	...	...	...	...	...	...	110	82	28
9,881	4,422	5,459	1,711	930	781	7,051	3,516	3,535	304	191	113
6,898	3,828	3,070	1,685	881	804	1,690	876	814	...	...	...
11	8	3	976	974	2	4	4	...	...	...	...
3,935	2,042	1,893	3,187	1,631	1,556	4,907	2,667	2,240	601	261	340
5	5	...	...	...	...	...	...	...	...	...	...
13,202	6,783	6,419	5,238	2,538	2,700	4,724	2,333	2,391	50	49	1
29,479	15,062	14,417	10,282	5,102	5,180	36,788	18,962	17,826	19,993	9,161	10,832
4,957	2,912	2,045	2,878	1,808	1,070	1,644	744	900	1,153	751	402
...	...	...	35	15	20	...	...	...	...	...	...
...	...	...	...	...	...	...	...	...	...	...	...
1,342	626	716	266	124	142	328	210	118	...	...	...
1,375	720	655	500	269	231	259	143	116	...	...	...
3,275	1,118	2,157	45	45	...	2,391	1,215	1,176	...	...	...
15,326	8,756	6,570	8,824	4,999	3,825	5,221	2,765	2,456	2,001	1,100	901
1,535	923	612	2,386	1,262	1,124	792	485	307	120	75	45
...	...	...	...	...	...	...	...	...	...	...	...
365	212	153	15	15	...	119	65	54	...	...	...
...	...	...	...	...	...	9	9	...	115	77	38
...	—	...	...	...	...	3	3	...	439	238	201
2	2	...	...	...	...	...	...	...	...	...	...
554	305	249	...	...	...	307	118	189	1	...	1
207	143	64	61	38	23	69	33	36	8	8	...
2,899	1,261	1,638	1,941	983	958	762	401	361	...	...	...
192	100	92	5	5	...	4	1	3	...	...	...
...	...	...	...	...	...	510	316	194	...	...	...
598	333	265	369	243	126	533	294	239	...	...	...
194	89	105	1,156	582	574	84	38	46	...	...	...
...	...	...	...	...	...	...	...	...	...	...	...
...	...	...	...	...	...	259	112	147	4	...	4
8,785	5,393	3,392	2,891	1,871	1,020	1,770	890	880	1,314	702	612
2,420	1,458	962	42	41	1	23	...	23	...	...	...
...	...	...	...	...	...	...	...	...	...	...	...
4	4	...	28	15	13	404	231	173	...	...	...
6,028	3,140	2,888	9,302	4,824	4,478	5,488	3,169	2,319	869	452	417
1,211	651	560	971	422	549	490	257	233	110	50	60
47	11	36	15	9	6	44	21	23	...	...	...
2,257	1,140	1,117	2,109	1,119	990	1,927	1,002	925	345	197	148
78	48	30	10	10	...	49	20	29	20	7	13
...	...	...	...	...	...	...	...	...	255	124	131
2,667	1,498	1,169	966	457	509	1,002	562	440	754	464	290
5,261	2,767	2,494	11,105	5,674	5,431	8,867	4,590	4,277	42,183	21,380	20,803
...	...	...	...	...	...	...	...	...	36,126	18,195	17,931
3,560	1,857	1,703	516	282	234	1,182	573	609	200	94	106
...	...	...	161	70	91	1	1	...	...	...	...
27,566	14,961	12,605	13,265	6,960	6,305	14.788	7,942	6,846	4,321	2,343	1,978
80	57	23	380	189	191	463	280	183	55	35	20
...	...	...	23	23	...	87	51	36	...	...	...
3,089	1,491	1,598	522	292	230	693	320	373	...	...	...
26	18	8	...	...	...	...	...	...	...	...	...
3	3	...	...	...	...	19	11	8	...	...	...
246	101	145	7	2	5	40	21	19	...	...	...
316	185	131	26	18	8	14	6	8	...	...	...
57	48	9	42	16	26	...	...	...	...	...	...
2,547	1,497	1,050	1,247	720	527	650	322	328	88	56	32
15	10	5	200	75	125	271	149	122	...	...	...
2,305	1,307	998	1,128	535	593	2,587	1,304	1,283	346	150	196
577	247	330	60	34	26	581	315	266	24	14	10
64	64	...	20	17	3	62	46	16	...	...	...
369	210	159	93	59	34	333	174	159	...	...	...
3	3	...	...	...	...	...	...	...	...	...	...
1,350	699	651	237	145	92	1,147	576	571	...	...	...
6	6	...	...	...	...	...	...	...	...	...	...
...	...	...	...	...	...	3	...	3	...	...	...
952	528	424	256	174	82	1,167	636	531	73	34	39
...	...	...	9	7	2	526	281	245	4	4	...
28	19	9	699	330	369	25	7	18	...	...	...
167	72	95	...	...	...	2	1	1	...	...	...
60	30	30	12	3	9	471	268	203	...	...	...
...	...	...	103	54	49	152	67	85	...	...	...
2	2	...	...	...	...	...	...	...	...	...	...
15,304	8,364	6,940	8,201	4,267	3,934	5,545	3,107	2,438	3,781	[illegible]	1,631

TABLE XVII.—

Caste and Religion.	GWALIOR STATE.			GIRD.		
	Persons.	Males.	Females.	Persons.	Males.	Females.
1	2	3	4	5	6	7
31 Chamar	415,950	212,626	203,324	50,263	25,586	24,677
32 Charan	994	408	586	...	...	...
33 Chhipa	10,486	5,558	4,928	1,743	874	869
34 Chidar	8,876	4,517	4,359	...	...	...
35 Chudigar	4	3	1	3	3	...
36 Darzi	20,264	10,683	9,581	1,523	800	723
37 Dhakad	30,945	15,453	15,492	1	1	...
38 Dhangar	514	276	238	...	...	...
39 Dhanuk	3,358	1,776	1 582	506	324	182
40 Dhimar	25,447	13,226	12,221	3,393	1,834	1,559
41 Dhobi	40,585	21,418	19,167	3,979	2,252	1,727
42 Dholi	5,277	2,645	2,632	2	...	2
43 Gadaria	87,741	45,433	42,308	13,115	6,382	6,733
44 Gaoli	343	159	184	...	...	...
45 Goley	3,105	1,617	1,488	977	499	478
46 Ghosi	8,616	4,366	4,250	2,516	1,289	1,227
47 Gond	843	446	397	...	...	...
48 Gosain	12,999	7,417	5,582	914	404	420
49 Gujar	119,314	60,816	58,498	13,278	6,766	6,512
50 Halwai	7	5	2	7	5	2
51 Jat	23,491	11,930	11,561	5,100	2,817	2,288
52 Jingar	16	11	5	1	1	...
53 Jogi	7,232	3,915	3,317	1,294	619	675
54 Joshi	6,330	3,415	2,915	837	430	398
55 Kachera	124	107	17	...	...	...
56 Kachhi	171,614	91,891	79,723	20,678	15,918	18,760
57 Kadera	9,263	4,978	4,285	1,903	1,030	873
58 Kahar	4,793	2,461	2,332	663	187	476
59 Kalamant	5,945	2,826	3,119	...	...	...
60 Kalbelia	1,053	566	487	—	...	...
61 Kanjar	402	292	110	11	11	...
62 Kalal	15,225	7,989	7,236	1,940	955	985
63 Kasera	1,051	552	499	88	34	54
64 Kayastha	33,926	18,866	15,060	6,092	3,394	2,698
65 Khangar	17,100	9,024	8,076	2,951	1,610	1,341
66 Kharol	1,846	1,108	738	...	...	...
67 Khati	16,101	8,611	7,490	150	88	67
68 Khatik	15,800	8,960	6,840	2,994	1,980	1,014
69 Khatri	2,049	1,150	899	482	206	226
70 Kherwa	1,395	660	735	...	...	...
71 Kir	2,574	1,471	1,103	...	...	...
72 Kirar	75,897	40,981	34,916	7,266	4,010	3,256
73 Koli	75,351	41,043	34,308	16,744	8,654	8,090
74 Koshti	3,560	2,110	1,450	...	...	...
75 Kumbhar	62,485	32,836	29,649	6,806	3,744	3,062
76 Kurmi	47,577	23,885	23,692	778	401	372
77 Lakhera	2,230	1,290	940	387	252	135
78 Lodhi	91,778	48,908	42,870	1,905	1,011	864
79 Luhar	30,146	16,146	14,000	3,130	1,797	1,312
80 Mahar	949	542	407	...	...	...
81 Mali	31,903	16,813	15,090	420	230	190
82 Mallah	3,853	2,142	1,711	11	7	4
83 Manibar	189	107	82	88	36	52
84 Maratha	14 151	7,823	6,328	5,957	3,212	2,745
85 Maru	2,186	1,054	1,132	...	...	...
86 Mina	67,125	34,376	32,749	21	91	...
87 Mirasi	25	24	1	...	...	...
88 Mirdha	13,153	6,869	6,281	3,084	1,697	1,387
89 Mochi	2,402	1,181	1,221	229	108	121
90 Moghia	2,846	1,805	1,041	7	6	2
91 Naga	2	2	...	...	...	...
92 Nai	51,373	28,677	25,496	5,494	2,826	2,659
93 Nat	3,567	1,801	1,766	177	94	83
94 Nath	3,819	2,233	1,586	96	60	16
95 Nayak	3,270	1,716	1,554	...	...	...
96 Par[illegible]	2,366	1,253	1,113	90	53	31
97 Pasi	225	128	97	15	3	12
98 Patwa	1,595	868	727	72	30	11
99 Pinjara	1,412	767	675	...	...	...
100 Pra[illegible]	187	101	83	112	67	15
101 Rai	1,639	[illegible]	674	131	66	65

Race, Tribe or Caste. *Part I —District Details.—(contd.)*

BHIND.			TONWARGHAR.			SHEOPUR.			NARWAR.		
Persons.	Males.	Females.	Persons.	Males.	Females.	Persons.	Males.	Females.	Persons.	Males.	Females.
8	9	10	11	12	13	14	15	16	17	18	19
58,646	30,389	28,257	52,714	26,672	26,042	11,411	6,184	5,227	73,190	36,565	36,625
...	...	...	...	...	...	...	...	...	1	1	...
3,443	1,909	1,534	291	193	98	288	124	114	921	500	421
30	30	...	6	5	1	171	73	98	2,035	987	1,046
1	...	1	...	...	...	...	...	...	...	...	...
2,193	1,844	349	1,178	691	487	149	76	73	1,156	555	601
52	26	26	103	53	50	1,516	770	746	133	74	59
...	...	...	...	...	...	...	...	...	...	...	...
1,235	507	728	756	416	340	162	99	63	151	84	67
1,669	904	765	2,854	1,509	1,345	370	286	184	7,009	3,644	3,365
6,318	3,316	3,002	5,312	3,062	2,250	1,202	720	482	5,806	3,093	2,713
...	...	...	...	...	...	...	...	...	...	...	...
29,930	15,524	14,406	10,080	5,750	4,330	690	402	288	16,026	7,892	8,134
...	...	...	...	...	...	...	...	...	...	...	...
...	...	...	1,054	556	498	...	...	...	92	36	56
601	239	362	54	52	2	...	...	...	498	203	295
...	...	...	...	...	...	...	...	...	...	...	...
328	268	60	1,638	1,135	503	279	215	64	2 204	1,142	1,062
9,606	5,223	4,383	27,162	13,555	13,606	7,197	4,122	3,075	10,835	5,940	4,895
...	...	...	...	...	...	...	...	...	...	...	...
845	445	400	96	53	43	2,405	1,260	1,125	549	309	240
...	...	...	...	...	...	...	...	...	...	...	...
987	569	418	196	122	74	41	40	1	878	483	395
1,283	776	507	1,146	661	485	231	107	124	1,109	632	477
...	...	...	63	56	7	...	...	...	27	27	...
33,256	17,629	15,627	26,169	13,714	12,455	4,559	2,434	2,125	27,039	14 361	12,678
2,486	1,332	1,054	2,143	1,133	1 010	435	247	188	1,036	535	501
519	282	237	428	257	171	925	469	456	17	...	17
...	...	...	...	...	...	...	...	...	...	...	...
...	...	...	95	31	64	...	...	...	6	...	6
48	26	22	8	8	...	...	...	...	15	15	...
1,095	612	483	831	484	347	681	372	309	3,579	1,877	1,702
...	...	...	78	45	33	...	...	...	62	35	27
4,867	2,746	2,121	2,597	1,466	1,181	495	311	184	2 304	1,248	1,056
1,577	827	750	...	...	...	18	18	...	8,751	4,592	4 159
...	...	...	...	...	...	...	...	...	...	...	...
...	...	...	24	15	9	763	377	386	755	434	321
3,095	1,680	1,415	2,225	1,333	892	654	311	343	1,013	501	512
137	119	18	407	274	133	43	25	18	51	22	29
37	16	21	...	...	...	384	202	182	...	...	...
...	...	...	...	...	...	...	...	...	...	...	...
28	18	10	19,253	10,532	8,721	4,443	2,265	2 178	24 728	12,954	11,774
11,753	6,494	5,259	11,977	7,104	4,873	3,789	1,712	2,077	9,970	5,810	4,160
22	12	10	...	..	...	...	...	...	...	...	...
7,166	3,797	3,369	5,803	3,042	2,761	2,250	1,195	1 055	5,939	2,907	3,032
226	114	112	589	338	201	569	267	302	210	116	94
367	206	161	132	89	43	63	35	28	260	140	120
13,432	6,655	6,777	1,881	1,025	856	45	22	23	34,184	19,834	14,350
4,059	2,224	1,835	1,292	546	746	1,197	726	471	4,638	2,481	2,157
...	...	...	389	246	143	31	18	13	...	...	...
385	152	233	45	19	26	6,320	3,316	3,004	502	176	326
1,283	591	692	2,290	1,411	879	47	22	25	...	...	...
6	4	2	89	61	28	...	...	...	3	3	...
331	174	157	218	136	82	29	16	13	216	180	36
...	...	...	...	...	...	...	...	...	32	16	16
...	...	...	5,947	2,782	3,165	19,595	10,811	8,784	17	7	10
...	...	...	...	...	...	...	...	...	...	...	...
2,468	1,139	1,329	487	303	184	...	...	...	849	459	390
3	1	2	33	20	13	111	51	60	43	20	23
...	...	...	...	...	...	...	...	...	...	...	...
...	...	...	...	...	...	...	...	...	...	...	...
7,985	4,542	3,443	6,838	3,665	3 223	1,660	917	743	5,986	3,151	2,835
169	89	80	334	169	165	116	66	50	145	76	69
5	2	3	406	357	49	544	326	218	69	33	36
...	...	...	...	...	...	177	96	81	...	...	...
9	4	5	25	4	21	6	3	3	58	35	23
...	...	...	...	...	...	...	...	...	...	...	...
45	24	21	541	347	194	80	64	16	73	20	53
281	149	132	23	18	5	...	...	...	...	...	...
...	...	...	...	...	...	12	4	8	...	...	...
...	...	...	166	126	40	425	220	205	813	453	360

TABLE XVII.—

Caste and Religion.	ISAGARH.			BHILSA.		
	Persons.	Males.	Females.	Persons.	Males.	Females.
1	2	3	4	5	6	7
31 Chamar	61,572	30,889	30,783	36,334	18,163	18,171
32 Charan	...	...	...	...	...	...
33 Chhipa	362	181	181	678	314	364
34 Chidar	5,300	2,802	2,498	1,270	580	690
35 Chudigar	...	...	...	...	...	...
36 Darzi	1,979	1,041	938	2,400	1,200	1,200
37 Dhakad	573	331	242	844	442	402
38 Dhangar	...	...	...	...	...	...
39 Dhanuk	33	14	19	112	70	42
40 Dhimar	7,748	3,893	3,855	2,114	1,021	1,093
41 Dholi	4,665	2,248	2,417	5,690	2,882	2,808
42 Dholi	...	...	...	...	...	...
43 Gadaria	6,269	3,419	2,850	2,299	1,275	1,024
44 Gaoli	...	...	...	...	...	...
45 Goley	...	...	...	...	...	...
46 Ghosi	749	360	389	2,330	1,194	1,136
47 Gond	8	8	...	...	...	...
48 Gosain	1,171	668	503	869	476	393
49 Gujar	9,218	5,097	4,121	3,988	2,120	1,868
50 Halwai	...	...	...	...	...	...
51 Jat	1,199	653	546	837	398	439
52 Jingar	15	10	5	...	...	...
53 Jogi	1,214	659	555	443	201	242
54 Joshi	446	177	269	261	119	142
55 Kachera	...	...	...	...	...	...
56 Kachhi	22,818	12,592	10,226	19,207	11,004	8,203
57 Kadera	803	354	449	439	246	193
58 Kahar	364	182	182	418	220	198
59 Kalamant	...	...	...	...	...	...
60 Kalbelia	24	24	...	...	...	...
61 Kanjar	37	37	...	...	...	...
62 Kaval	2,189	1,346	843	759	362	397
63 Kasera	87	28	14	...	...	...
64 Kayastha	3,167	1,612	1,555	2,395	1,270	1,125
65 Khangar	1,769	964	805	947	588	409
66 Kharol	372	372	...	...	...	...
67 Khati	2,881	1,662	1,219	118	68	50
68 Khatik	1,408	879	529	283	130	103
69 Khatri	32	18	14	115	68	47
70 Kherwa	821	362	459	153	80	73
71 Kir	...	...	...	...	...	...
72 Kirar	12,937	6,938	5,999	5,368	3,209	2,159
73 Koli	7,725	4,065	3,660	7,939	4,528	3,411
74 Koshti	2	2	...	44	36	8
75 Kumbhar	6,240	3,191	3,049	6,444	3,790	2,654
76 Kurmi	567	257	310	2,651	1,467	1,184
77 Lakhera	97	46	51	19	11	8
78 Lodhi	27,520	14,273	13,247	7,904	4,015	3,889
79 Luhar	3,756	2,223	1,533	2,732	1,421	1,311
80 Mahar	262	135	127	13	13	...
81 Mali	3,118	1,688	1,430	525	289	236
82 Mallah	...	...	...	118	60	58
83 Manihar	3	3	...	...	...	...
84 Maratha	703	385	318	340	196	144
85 Maru	82	40	42	...	...	...
86 Mina	19,416	10,107	9,309	8,155	3,960	4,195
87 Mirasi	...	...	...	...	...	...
88 Mirdha	1,256	635	621	2,589	1,425	1,164
89 Mochi	33	19	14	70	28	32
90 Moghia	571	317	254	...	...	...
91 Naga	...	...	...	...	...	...
92 Nai	7,861	3,925	3,436	3,629	1,764	1,865
93 Nat	244	128	116	275	162	113
94 Nath	207	136	71	357	152	205
95 Nayak	88	41	47	...	...	...
96 Pardhi	475	269	206	129	95	84
97 Pasi	...	...	...	...	...	...
98 Patwa	105	68	97	244	134	110
99 Pinjara	123	83	40	94	50	44
100 Prabhu	31	10	21	...	...	...
101 Rai	...	...	...	...	...	...

Race, Tribe or Caste, *Part I.—District Details.—(contd.)*

UJJAIN.			MANDSAUR.			SHAJAPUR.			AMJHERA.		
Persons.	Males.	Females.	Persons.	Males.	Females.	Persons.	Males.	Females.	Persons.	Males.	Females.
8	9	10	11	12	13	14	15	16	17	18	19
21,446	11,030	10,416	18,070	9,285	8,785	27,998	15,792	12,206	4,306	2,121	2,185
1	1	...	451	208	243	3	...	3	538	198	340
731	362	369	1,273	627	646	726	429	297	80	45	35
47	26	21	...	...	...	17	14	3	...	...	...
...	...	...	...	...	...	...	...	...	...	...	...
3,558	1,828	1,730	2,854	1,625	1,229	2,806	1,297	1,509	468	226	242
8,130	3,908	4,222	16,357	8,037	8,320	1,288	838	450	1,953	978	975
31	18	13	153	79	74	...	...	...	330	179	151
26	10	16	177	119	58	200	133	67	...	...	...
78	38	40	87	87	...	125	60	65	...	...	...
3,443	1,720	1,723	1,518	814	704	2,121	1,042	1,079	531	269	262
2,379	1,195	1,184	1,547	825	722	1,221	562	659	128	63	65
2,695	1,468	1,227	4,494	2,287	2,207	2,047	999	1,048	96	35	61
...	...	...	343	159	184	...	...	...	...	...	...
128	111	17	716	310	406	118	94	24	20	11	9
516	312	204	243	141	102	1,075	559	516	34	17	17
20	13	7	541	273	268	274	152	122	...	...	...
1,776	1,070	706	1,238	619	619	2,377	1,219	1,158	205	111	94
10,686	5,577	5,109	12,766	5,914	6,852	13,886	6,147	7,739	692	354	338
...	...	...	—	...	...	...	...	...	...	...	...
6,190	2,648	3,542	4,067	2,076	1,991	1,399	855	544	804	396	408
...	...	...	...	...	...	...	...	...	...	...	...
675	416	259	223	114	109	1,235	671	564	46	21	25
845	391	454	53	26	27	64	34	30	55	53	2
10	...	10	24	24	...	...	...	...	...	...	...
5,430	2,750	2,680	594	428	166	2,592	902	1,690	272	159	113
26	23	3	33	22	11	...	...	—	9	6	3
802	472	330	79	34	45	290	206	84	293	152	141
...	...	...	5,945	2,826	3,119	...	...	...	...	...	...
176	78	98	538	368	170	201	65	136	18	...	13
39	17	22	180	114	66	64	64	...	...	...	...
1,749	905	844	648	330	318	1,181	468	713	578	278	295
330	154	176	102	48	54	352	211	141	2	2	...
3,247	1,639	1,608	966	552	414	7,203	4,367	2,836	593	261	332
807	332	475	275	141	134	2	2	...	3	...	3
632	213	419	614	352	262	124	124	...	104	47	57
4,669	2,733	1,936	596	339	257	4,967	2,342	2,625	1,188	568	620
1,671	843	828	1,702	816	886	774	467	307	31	20	11
325	157	168	116	86	30	374	167	207	17	8	9
...	...	...	...	...	...	...	...	...	...	...	...
943	523	420	584	305	279	880	583	297	217	110	107
986	577	409	109	81	28	599	301	298	180	96	84
2,888	1,326	1,562	618	293	325	833	457	376	1,115	600	515
...	...	...	7	7	...	3,485	2,053	1,432	...	...	...
7,986	4,133	3,853	6,381	2,833	3,548	5,605	3,192	2,413	1,865	1,012	853
10,352	5,591	4,761	13,372	6,708	6,664	14,435	6,819	7,616	3,883	1,807	2,076
358	176	182	342	207	135	143	94	49	62	34	28
1,023	631	392	458	204	254	2,047	502	1,545	1,374	701	673
3,318	1,674	1,644	2,858	1,825	1,033	2,647	1,264	1,383	1,010	485	545
230	117	113	24	13	11	...	...	...	...	...	...
9,786	5,344	4,442	6,847	3,592	3,255	3,538	1,812	1,726	418	191	222
...	...	...	4	4	...	105	47	58	...	...	...
3,969	2,056	1,913	1,081	729	352	946	570	376	361	219	142
...	...	...	98	54	44	1	1	...	1,973	943	1,030
5,515	2,515	3,000	4,707	2,353	2,354	3,752	1,820	1,932	...	...	...
...	...	...	25	24	1	...	...	...	...	...	...
2,196	1,104	1,092	71	33	38	153	74	79	...	...	...
861	429	432	499	234	265	243	131	112	277	130	147
888	440	448	880	543	337	...	...	...	...	...	...
...	...	...	...	...	...	2	2	...	...	...	...
4,968	2,603	2,365	3,921	2,014	1,907	5,334	2,867	2,467	1,147	593	554
517	294	223	193	111	82	1,397	612	785	...	...	...
685	373	312	528	326	202	918	477	441	4	1	3
1,049	523	526	1,677	887	790	59	45	14	220	124	96
754	395	359	86	34	52	728	353	375	6	3	3
155	100	55	44	14	30	11	11	...	...	...	...
...	...	...	4	...	4	4	4	...	367	177	190
18	11	7	54	42	12	250	116	134	599	298	301
20	15	5	...	...	...	12	8	4	...	...	...
...	...	...	...	...	...	...	...	...	4	...	4

TABLE XVII.—

Caste and Religion.	GWALIOR STATE.			GIRD.		
	Persons.	Males.	Females.	Persons.	Males.	Females.
1	2	3	4	5	6	7
102 Rajput	393,076	213,136	179,940	14,969	9,262	5,707
1 Baghele	3,070	1,709	1,361	194	106	88
2 Bais	1,155	686	469	72	48	24
3 Bhadauria	18,596	11,379	7,217	1,546	1,033	513
4 Bundela	2,757	1,474	1,283	540	301	239
5 Chandel	2,845	1,567	1,278	18	11	7
6 Chandrabansi	20	14	6	20	14	6
7 Chandrawat	861	462	399	...	...	...
8 Chauhan	25,660	13,843	11,817	1,321	850	471
9 Dangi	16,184	8,695	7,489	502	396	106
10 Deora	3,995	1,764	2,231	...	...	...
11 Dhandera	521	290	231	1	1	...
12 Gaharbar	305	188	117	...	...	...
13 Gahlot	5,140	2,944	2,196	35	26	9
14 Gautam	383	246	137	...	...	...
15 Gole	464	242	222	52	34	18
16 Gond	3,653	1,900	1,753	...	...	...
17 Jadho	11,313	6,298	5,015	376	209	167
18 Kachhawaha	15,436	9,011	6,425	1,290	769	521
19 Khichi	1,041	642	399	...	...	...
20 Nandbansi	851	508	343	102	54	48
21 Parihar	3,766	1,990	1,776	97	49	48
22 Parmar	8,232	3,926	4,306	...	...	...
23 Pawayya	1,728	933	705	199	105	94
24 Ponwar	15,230	8,488	6,742	582	232	350
25 Raghubansi	23,063	11,869	11,194	160	105	55
26 Rathor	14,213	7,995	6,218	196	129	67
27 Rawat	31,341	15,114	16,227	380	136	244
28 Sendho	2,560	1,268	1,292	...	...	...
29 Sengar	1,016	601	415	167	112	55
30 Sikarwar	10,899	6,707	4,192	526	382	144
31 Sisodia	4,807	2,875	1,932	41	21	20
32 Solanki	3,220	1,598	1,622	25	25	...
33 Suryabansi	50	43	7	50	43	7
34 Tonwar	32,726	20,172	12,554	1,770	1,107	663
35 Others and unspecified ...	126,445	66,165	60,280	4,707	2,964	1,743
103 Rangrez	1,347	655	692	82	57	25
104 Rawat	16,397	8,859	7,538	7,542	4,520	3,022
105 Sadhu	136	123	13	26	25	1
106 Saharia	73,537	37,204	36,333	3,793	1,876	1,917
107 Sansi	1,731	855	876	20	20	...
108 Sikligar	1,439	856	583	...	...	...
109 Silawat	2,486	1,319	1,167	...	...	...
110 Sisgar	11	3	8	...	...	...
111 Sondhia	25,518	12,786	12,732	10	10	...
112 Sunar	22,215	12,251	9,964	2,920	1,630	1,290
113 Sutar	50	27	23	...	...	...
114 Tamboli	7,422	3,754	3,668	3,105	1,560	1,545
115 Teli	55,779	29,867	25,912	5,305	2,750	2,555
116 Thathera	112	38	74	57	18	39
117 Others	720	382	338	...	...	...
Hindu-Arya	1,308	688	620	112	72	40
Hinduized Tribal	14,291	7,248	7,043	19	11	8
1 Bhil	8,801	4,252	4,549	...	...	...
2 Bhilala	2,319	1,226	1,093	...	...	...
3 Gond	320	171	149	...	...	...
4 Kirar	99	29	70	...	...	...
5 Kol	2	...	2	...	...	...
6 Mina	77	38	39	...	...	...
7 Saharia	2,682	1,541	1,141	19	11	8
Sikh	651	416	235	156	95	61

Race, Tribe or Caste. *Part I.—District Details.—(contd.).*

BHIND.			TONWARGHAR.			SHEOPUR.			NARWAR.		
Persons.	Males.	Females.	Persons.	Males.	Females.	Persons.	Males.	Females.	Persons.	Males.	Females.
8	9	10	11	12	13	14	15	16	17	18	19
66,176	36,975	29,201	61,204	36,609	24,585	2,421	1,333	1,088	32,528	16,484	16,089
69	37	32	284	166	118	...	...	...	23	10	13
182	98	84	...	...	...	...	...	...	67	34	33
11,286	7,274	3,962	3,958	2,049	1,904	62	36	26	2	2	...
...	...	...	...	...	...	7	3	4	38	18	20
294	167	127	...	...	...	...	...	...	1	1	...
...	...	...	...	...	...	...	...	...	...	...	...
32	15	17	...	...	...	...	...	...	...	...	...
7,454	3,831	3,623	4,594	2,678	1,916	256	154	102	470	309	161
...	...	...	...	...	...	...	...	...	674	370	304
...	...	...	...	...	...	...	...	...	...	...	...
...	...	...	...	...	...	...	...	...	...	...	...
...	...	...	...	...	...	...	...	...	...	...	...
...	...	...	...	...	...	...	...	...	...	...	...
...	...	...	...	...	...	...	...	...	...	...	...
...	...	...	...	...	...	...	...	...	...	...	...
214	90	124	...	...	...	...	...	...	45	42	8
148	93	56	4,399	2,544	1,855	494	302	192	494	271	228
9,035	5,502	3,533	3,086	1,646	1,440	76	41	35	105	66	39
...	...	...	...	...	...	114	78	41	...	...	...
...	...	...	...	...	...	...	...	...	70	57	18
837	469	368	1,090	621	469	...	...	...	7	...	7
68	68	...	...	...	...	27	14	18	28	16	7
...	...	...	...	...	...	...	...	...	33	28	10
1,720	863	857	1,821	831	990	...	...	...	1,586	966	570
168	103	65	...	...	...	...	...	...	1,788	792	991
587	264	328	2,532	1,448	1,084	...	...	...	20	5	15
9	9	...	...	...	...	335	178	157	19,642	9,325	10,317
2	2	...	520	305	215	46	33	13	...	...	...
...	...	...	...	...	...	...	...	...	...	...	...
26	6	20	8,351	5,158	3,198	154	95	59	10	10	...
...	...	...	...	...	...	...	...	...	9	6	3
...	...	...	1,189	689	500	28	12	16	7	...	7
...	...	...	...	...	...	...	...	...	...	...	...
5,420	2,810	2,610	22,496	14,625	7,871	52	25	27	422	165	257
28,680	15,280	13,400	6,989	3,964	2,975	770	367	403	7,042	3,946	3,096
1	...	1	...	...	...	...	...	...	28	10	18
...	...	...	8,487	4,114	4,373	...	...	...	...	...	...
...	...	...	...	...	...	...	...	...	...	...	...
...	...	...	304	204	100	1,6265	8,171	8,094	28,357	14,386	13,971
...	...	...	...	...	...	1,402	717	685	...	...	...
39	39	...	51	20	31	1	1	...	9	4	5
...	...	...	...	...	...	20	4	16	...	...	...
11	3	8	...	...	...	...	...	...	...	...	...
...	...	...	...	...	...	4,411	2,243	2,168	...	...	...
2,259	1,354	905	1,291	742	549	623	363	260	1,339	1,019	320
754	333	421	311	201	110	72	41	31	417	190	227
8,841	4,633	4,208	7,204	4,040	3,164	1,549	842	707	5,392	2,904	2,488
50	15	35	...	...	...	...	...	...	...	...	...
...	...	...	...	...	...	...	...	...	...	...	...
129	80	49	30	12	18	46	24	22	37	30	7
583	342	241	52	29	23	601	299	302	617	324	293
45	30	15	...	...	...	...	...	...	230	77	153
32	9	23	...	...	...	...	...	...	...	...	...
...	...	...	...	...	...	...	...	...	179	107	72
...	...	...	...	...	...	...	...	...	...	...	...
...	...	...	...	...	...	...	...	...	...	...	...
...	...	...	29	18	11	1	...	1	2	2	...
506	303	203	23	11	12	600	299	301	206	136	68
154	100	54	8	6	2	6	5	1	9	5	4

TABLE XVII.—

Caste and Religion.	ISAGARH.			BHILSA.		
	Persons.	Males.	Females.	Persons.	Males	Females.
1	2	3	4	5	6	7
102 Rajput	39,083	20,495	18,588	30,437	15,826	14,611
1 Baghele	240	101	139	...	...	...
2 Bais	44	25	19	197	116	81
3 Bhadauria	111	39	72	861	461	400
4 Bundela	340	100	159	590	485	155
5 Chandel	26	12	14	453	284	219
6 Chandrabansi	...	...	...	...	...	...
7 Chandrawat	...	...	...	...	...	...
8 Chauhan	623	289	334	1,317	644	678
9 Dangi...	2,102	1,137	965	7,203	3,591	3,612
10 Deora...	2	2	...	...	...	...
11 Dhandera	...	...	...	...	...	...
12 Gaharbar	...	...	...	...	...	...
13 Gahlot	47	25	22	...	...	...
14 Gautam	...	...	...	...	...	...
15 Gole	...	...	...	412	208	204
16 Gond	132	41	91	...	...	...
17 Jadho	1,368	716	652	709	310	399
18 Kachhwaha	449	242	207	201	102	102
19 Khichi	297	209	88	...	...	...
20 Nandbansi	434	245	189	...	...	...
21 Parihar	34	27	7	40	34	6
22 Parmar	363	149	214	1,015	560	485
23 Pawayya	3	2	...	...	...	...
24 Ponwar	452	227	225	...	...	...
25 Raghubansi	11,077	5,673	5,404	6,892	3,759	3,133
26 Rathor	971	634	337	227	112	115
27 Rawat	8,885	4,345	4,540	1,808	914	894
28 Sendho	301	173	128	...	...	...
29 Sengar	50	11	39	205	134	71
30 Sikarwar	173	50	123	260	167	93
31 Sisodia	29	10	19	...	...	...
32 Solanki	92	62	30	146	69	77
33 Suryabansi	...	...	...	...	...	...
34 Tonwar	439	268	171	285	149	136
35 Others and unspecified ...	9,991	5,591	4,400	7,583	3,827	3,756
103 Rangrez	37	21	16	...	...	...
104 Rawat	...	...	...	...	...	...
105 Sadhu	...	...	...	...	...	...
106 Saharia	20,490	10.302	10,188	3,908	2,026	1,882
107 Sansi	...	...	...	...	...	...
108 Sikligar	12	12	...	...	...	...
109 Silawat	1,841	1,013	828	131	60	71
110 Sisgar	...	...	...	...	...	...
111 Sondhia	10	10	...	...	...	...
112 Sunar	2,349	1,281	1,068	1,170	613	557
113 Sutar	...	...	...	...	...	...
114 Tamboli	810	438	372	590	253	337
115 Teli	8,085	4,764	3,321	3,972	1,924	2,048
116 Thathera	5	5	...	...	...	...
117 Others	...	...	...	...	...	...
Hindu—Arya	231	116	115	25	11	14
Hinduized Tribal	517	252	265	332	166	166
1 Bhil	3	1	2	11	4	7
2 Bhilala	...	...	...	141	64	77
3 Gond	...	...	...	...	...	...
4 Kirar	...	...	...	...	...	...
5 Korku	...	...	...	...	...	...
6 Mina	10	...	10	...	...	...
7 Sahariya	504	251	253	180	98	82
Sikh	190	126	64	33	17	16

Race, Tribe or Caste. *Part I.—District Details—(contd.)*

UJJAIN.			MANDSAUR.			SHAJAPUR.			AMJHERA.		
Persons.	Males.	Females.	Persons.	Males.	Females.	Persons.	Males.	Females.	Persons.	Males.	Females.
8	9	10	11	12	13	14	15	16	17	18	19
59,597	30,853	28,744	23,606	12,610	10,996	60,188	31,267	28,921	2,872	1,412	1,460
132	85	47	51	28	23	2,077	1,176	901	...	...	...
176	98	78	...	...	...	417	267	150	...	...	...
208	155	53	24	19	5	593	311	282	...	...	...
444	246	198	...	...	...	788	281	507	1	...	1
1,547	780	767	215	125	90	291	237	54	...	...	...
...	...	...	...	...	...	...	...	...	...	...	...
36	35	1	468	236	232	325	176	149	...	...	...
4,896	2,639	2,257	747	329	418	3,736	1,995	1,741	246	125	121
1,832	1,032	800	1,096	643	453	2,676	1,477	1,199	99	49	50
480	192	288	2,460	1,012	1,448	1,053	558	495	...	...	...
153	75	78	216	116	100	151	98	53	...	...	...
...	...	...	19	17	2	286	171	115	...	...	...
1	...	1	297	149	148	4,789	2,783	2,006	21	11	10
1	1	...	20	20	...	362	225	137	...	...	...
...	...	...	...	...	...	...	...	...	...	...	...
1,809	922	887	196	75	121	1,257	730	527	...	...	...
1,253	729	524	43	36	7	2,029	1,089	940	...	...	...
719	356	363	239	189	50	218	104	114	45	24	21
532	294	238	27	18	9	71	43	28	...	...	...
243	150	93	2	2	...	...	...	...	...	...	...
245	91	154	436	276	160	980	423	557	...	...	...
2,073	1,094	979	104	38	66	4,534	1,992	2,542	...	...	...
...	...	...	103	53	50	1,391	750	641	...	...	...
2,628	1,448	1,180	1,446	880	566	5,088	3,087	2,001	12	9	3
1,305	627	678	48	29	19	587	299	288	1,043	482	561
4,622	2,512	2,110	818	460	358	3,286	1,936	1,350	959	495	464
282	207	75	...	...	...	...	...	...	...	...	...
1,671	735	936	20	20	...	...	...	...	...	...	...
2	...	2	353	201	152	239	143	96	...	...	...
583	372	211	730	419	311	86	53	33	...	...	...
635	403	232	1,447	887	560	2,146	1,048	1,098	...	...	...
625	278	347	383	210	173	732	289	443	43	14	29
...	...	...	...	...	...	...	...	...	...	...	...
1,551	922	629	288	101	187	...	...	...	3	...	3
28,918	14,380	14,538	11,315	6,022	5,293	20,100	9,621	10,479	400	203	197
268	97	171	470	189	281	461	281	180	...	...	...
...	...	...	...	...	...	368	225	143	...	...	...
...	...	...	110	98	12	...	...	...	...	...	...
411	230	181	8	8	...	...	...	...	1	1	...
188	64	124	85	33	52	...	...	...	36	21	15
668	395	273	94	64	30	529	305	224	36	16	20
164	108	56	321	131	190	6	...	6	8	8	...
...	...	...	...	...	...	...	...	...	...	...	...
5,930	3,196	2,734	4,756	2,247	2,509	10,401	5,080	5,321	...	...	...
2,717	1,496	1,221	3,147	1,668	1,479	2,842	1,569	1,273	1,058	516	542
...	...	...	50	27	23	...	...	...	...	...	...
515	248	267	221	130	91	432	263	169	195	97	98
4,389	2,231	2,158	5,290	2,711	2,579	4,634	2,488	2,146	1,118	580	538
...	...	...	...	...	...	...	...	...	...	...	...
...	...	...	720	382	338	...	...	...	...	...	...
421	212	209	76	41	35	135	61	74	66	29	37
723	357	366	1,727	846	881	677	330	347	8,443	4,292	4,151
447	151	296	1,357	607	750	552	307	245	6,156	3,075	3,081
...	...	...	...	...	...	...	...	...	2,287	1,217	1,070
...	...	...	...	...	...	...	...	...	...	...	...
...	...	...	...	...	...	90	20	70	...	...	...
2	...	2	...	...	...	...	...	...	...	...	...
2	...	2	33	18	15	...	...	...	...	...	...
272	206	66	337	221	116	35	3	32	...	...	...
78	56	22	36	28	8	11	8	3	...	...	...

TABLE XVII.—

Caste and Religion.	GWALIOR STATE.			GIRD.		
	Persons.	Males.	Females.	Persons.	Males.	Females.
1	2	3	4	5	6	7
Jain	45,079	24,238	20,841	2,569	1,405	1,164
1 Agarwal	1,973	998	975	247	134	113
2 Gole	999	528	471	...	...	...
3 Jaiswal	1,793	1 008	785	256	163	93
4 Jati	34	24	10	...	...	...
5 Khandelwal	542	297	245	103	53	50
6 Nima	52	34	18	...	...	...
7 Oswal	13,974	7,552	6,422	298	182	116
8 Palliwal	449	233	216	...	...	...
9 Parwar	2,297	1,456	841	...	...	...
10 Porwal	2 364	1,242	1,122	5	5	...
11 Saraogi	3,474	1,881	1,593	227	121	106
12 Others and unspecified ...	17,123	8,990	8,133	1,433	747	686
Zoroastrian	239	96	143	105	43	62
Muslim	204,297	109,412	94,885	39,232	21,575	17,657
1 Bhand	328	187	141	17	13	4
2 Bhangi	1,122	561	561	124	64	60
3 Bharbhunja	730	398	332	63	36	27
4 Bhatiyara	123	77	46	65	45	20
5 Bhishti	2,416	1,261	1,155	960	477	483
6 Bilochi	24	13	11	...	...	...
7 Bohra	8,944	4,412	4,532	83	57	26
8 Chhipa	1,477	875	602	3	3	...
9 Darzi	21	3	18	...	...	...
10 Dhobi	392	207	185	169	102	87
11 Dholi	18	16	2	...	...	...
12 Faqir	11,178	5,977	5,201	678	388	290
13 Hammal	409	229	180	160	70	90
14 Julaha	782	430	352	82	43	39
15 Kunjada	2,081	1,153	928	330	161	169
16 Hijda	48	48	...	4	4	...
17 Lakhera	416	231	185	1	...	1
18 Luhar	503	312	191	7	7	...
19 Manihar	632	345	287	6	2	4
20 Mewati	8,820	4,747	4,073	1,205	670	535
21 Mirasi	644	391	253	22	15	7
22 Mochi	1,099	597	502	12	8	4
23 Mogal	2,972	1,530	1,442	782	473	309
24 Momin	1,480	749	731	7	7	...
25 Mulla	7	7	...	2	2	...
26 Nai	446	258	188	102	59	43
27 Narigar	6	3	3	...	...	...
28 Naita	916	448	468	1	...	1
29 Nat	1,896	1,042	854	185	98	87
30 Pathan	57,628	31,614	26,014	14,768	8,162	6,601
31 Pinjara	12,166	6,017	6,149	92	49	43
32 Qassab	1,505	828	677	274	174	100
33 Qari	195	137	58	83	83	...
34 Rangrez	3,221	1,739	1,482	315	166	149
35 Sayyad	10,780	6,449	4,331	4,026	2,560	1,446
36 Sheikh	45,850	24,810	21,040	11,499	6,305	5,194
37 Sikligar	327	252	75	25	14	11
38 Tawaif	501	118	383	46	1	45
39 Teli	1,454	810	644	272	151	121
40 Others and unspecified... ...	20,740	10,126	10,614	2,797	1,136	1,661
Christian	1,198	592	606	268	143	125
1 Anglo-Indian	131	69	62	23	13	10
2 European and Allied Races ...	111	58	53	21	11	10
3 Indian	956	465	491	224	119	105

Race, Tribe or Caste. II *Part I.—District Details.*—(*contd.*)

BHIND.			TONWARGHAR			SHIVPURI.			NARWAR		
Persons.	Males.	Females.	Persons.	Males.	Females.	Persons.	Males.	Females.	Persons.	Males.	Females.
8	9	10	11	12	13	14	15	16	17	18	19
6,554	3,442	3,112	2,691	1,132	959	239	137	101	3,613	1,937	1,673
112	58	54	32	22	10	10	2	1	434	[illegible]	[illegible]
915	490	425	...	...	...	...	...	...	64	35	29
108	58	50	491	246	245	...	...	...	432	[illegible]	[illegible]
...	...	...	...	...	...	...	...	...	...	...	...
35	26	9	15	6	9	33	16	17	4	...	4
...	...	...	...	...	...	...	...	...	...	...	...
144	77	67	19	15	4	33	18	15	125	78	47
...	...	...	91	41	50	...	...	...	...	...	...
4	3	1	...	...	...	...	...	...	...	...	...
...	...	...	...	...	...	...	...	...	17	7	10
1,319	662	657	51	36	15	45	27	18	12	7	5
3,917	2,039	1,878	1,272	696	576	110	67	43	3,249	[illegible]	[illegible]
...	...	...	...	...	...	...	...	...	...	...	...
12,659	6,857	5,802	10,732	5,949	4,783	5,765	[illegible]	2,721	9,257	5,021	4,236
31	8	23	84	42	36	...	...	...	11	7	4
43	27	16	...	...	...	...	...	...	22	17	5
469	247	223	99	63	36	11	5	6	...	...	...
17	10	7	13	8	5	...	...	...	57	34	23
74	34	40	291	139	152	129	72	57	45	22	23
...	...	...	2	...	2	...	...	...	...	...	...
...	...	...	...	...	...	178	95	83	...	...	...
...	...	...	19	14	5	...	...	...	...	...	...
...	...	...	...	...	...	...	...	...	...	...	...
6	5	1	...	...	...	...	...	...	...	...	...
514	290	224	605	318	287	[illegible]	211	[illegible]	[illegible]	[illegible]	[illegible]
6	3	3	...	...	...	[illegible]	27	13	170	[illegible]	[illegible]
49	31	18	27	12	15	[illegible]	23	6	[illegible]	37	31
165	94	72	42	22	20	9	2	...	[illegible]	[illegible]	[illegible]
...	...	...	...	...	...	...	...	...	3	2	
1	1	...	92	45	47	...	...	...	...	...	
3	1	2	...	...	...	[illegible]	[illegible]	11	[illegible]	2	
165	[illegible]	[illegible]	[illegible]	[illegible]	[illegible]	...	...	...	[illegible]	[illegible]	...
172	76	[illegible]	314	[illegible]	155	[illegible]	[illegible]	[illegible]	[illegible]	[illegible]	[illegible]
[illegible]	[illegible]	[illegible]	24	[illegible]	[illegible]	...	...	...	...	...	...
[illegible]	[illegible]	...	[illegible]	2	[illegible]	...	...	...	[illegible]	[illegible]	[illegible]
218	[illegible]	132	[illegible]	[illegible]	[illegible]	[illegible]	[illegible]	[illegible]	[illegible]	[illegible]	[illegible]
[illegible]	[illegible]	[illegible]	[illegible]	[illegible]	[illegible]	[illegible]	[illegible]	[illegible]	[illegible]	[illegible]	[illegible]
[illegible]	[illegible]	[illegible]	[illegible]	[illegible]	[illegible]	[illegible]	[illegible]	[illegible]	[illegible]	[illegible]	[illegible]
[illegible]	[illegible]	[illegible]	[illegible]	[illegible]	[illegible]	[illegible]	[illegible]	[illegible]	[illegible]	[illegible]	[illegible]
[illegible]	[illegible]	[illegible]	[illegible]	[illegible]	[illegible]	[illegible]	[illegible]	[illegible]	[illegible]	[illegible]	[illegible]
[illegible]	[illegible]	[illegible]	[illegible]	[illegible]	[illegible]	[illegible]	[illegible]	[illegible]	[illegible]	[illegible]	[illegible]
[illegible]	[illegible]	[illegible]	[illegible]	[illegible]	[illegible]	[illegible]	[illegible]	[illegible]	[illegible]	[illegible]	[illegible]
[illegible]	[illegible]	[illegible]	[illegible]	[illegible]	[illegible]	[illegible]	[illegible]	[illegible]	[illegible]	[illegible]	[illegible]
[illegible]	[illegible]	[illegible]	[illegible]	[illegible]	[illegible]	[illegible]	[illegible]	[illegible]	[illegible]	[illegible]	[illegible]

TABLE XVII.—

Caste and Religion.	ISAGARH. Persons.	ISAGARH. Males.	ISAGARH. Females.	BHILSA. Persons.	BHILSA. Males.	BHILSA. Females.
1	2	3	4	5	6	7
Jain	6,512	3,554	2,958	2,489	1,329	1,160
1 Agarwal	119	47	72	300	151	149
2 Gole	20	4	16	...	...	...
3 Jaiswal	197	107	90	89	58	31
4 Jati	...	...	...	8	8	...
5 Khandelwal	110	57	53	23	16	7
6 Nima	...	...	...	...	...	...
7 Oswal	189	79	110	460	253	207
8 Palliwal	...	...	...	358	192	166
9 Parwar	2,293	1,453	840	...	...	...
10 Porwal	505	273	232	...	...	...
11 Saraogi	40	27	13	337	210	127
12 Others and unspecified	3,039	1,507	1,532	914	441	473
Zoroastrian	2	2	...	9	[illegible]	6
Muslim	15,864	8,355	7,509	12,422	6,651	5,771
1 Bhand	9	9	...	20	14	6
2 Bhangi	41	20	21	96	44	52
3 Bharbhunja	14	10	4	...	...	...
4 Bhatiyara	2	...	2	...	...	...
5 Bhishti	30	17	13	122	68	54
6 Bilochi	...	...	...	22	13	9
7 Bohra	18	9	9	122	73	49
8 Chhipa	54	24	30	...	...	...
9 Darzi	...	...	...	...	...	...
10 Dhobi	63	36	27	15	9	6
11 Dholi	...	...	...	...	...	...
12 Faqir	645	391	254	810	420	390
13 Hammal	...	...	...	...	...	...
14 Julaha	194	99	95	22	16	6
15 Kunjda	417	242	175	248	121	127
16 Hijda	42	42	...	...	...	...
17 Lakhera	81	47	34	...	...	...
18 Lohar	5	3	2	77	49	28
19 Manihar	21	11	10	98	57	41
20 Mewati	646	327	319	945	462	483
21 Mirasi	5	2	3	63	48	15
22 Mochi	460	249	211	114	71	43
23 Mogal	169	55	181	186	98	89
24 Momin	492	261	231	...	...	...
25 Mulla	4	4	...	...	...	...
26 Nai	1	1	...	76	52	24
27 Narigar	...	...	...	...	...	...
28 Naita	1	...	1	...	...	...
29 Nat	161	94	67	310	148	162
30 Pathan	5,355	2,955	2,400	2,407	1,203	1,204
31 Pinjara	510	275	235	1,437	675	762
32 Qassab	13	10	3	142	83	59
33 Qazi	35	8	27	62	61	1
34 [illegible]	166	94	72	348	169	160
35 [illegible]	518	[illegible]	230	1,070	491	579
36 [illegible]	3,117	1,591	1,526	1,947	1,310	637
37 [illegible]	...	...	...	130	125	5
38 [illegible]	4	2	2	17	...	17
39 [illegible]	...	...	...	99	43	56
40 [illegible]	2,552	1,179	1,373	1,468	760	708
Christian	[illegible]	21	[illegible]	10	6	4
1 [illegible]	...	...	...	8	5	3
2 [illegible]	2	1	1	...	...	...
3 [illegible]	27	[illegible]	17	2	1	1

Race, Tribe or Caste. *Part I.—District Details.—(concld.)*

UJJAIN.			MANDSAUR.			SHAJAPUR.			AMJHERA.		
Persons.	Males.	Females.	Persons.	Males.	Females.	Persons.	Males.	Females.	Persons.	Males.	Females.
8	9	10	11	12	13	14	15	16	17	18	19
6,149	3,398	2,751	8,139	4,297	3,842	4,831	2,579	2,252	1,907	1,038	869
80	26	54	419	289	180	168	104	59	1	...	1
...	...	...	..	...	...	...	...	...	...	...	...
13	5	8	19	16	3	23	12	11	...	...	...
...	...	...	17	10	7	9	6	8	...	...	...
94	57	37	64	28	36	12	2	10	49	36	13
52	34	18	...	...	...	...	...	...	...	...	...
2,856	1,581	1,275	6,695	3509	3,186	1,911	1,045	866	1,254	718	536
...	...	...	...	...	...	...	...	...	...	...	...
...	...	...	...	...	...	...	...	...	...	...	...
118	84	34	292	134	158	798	433	365	516	242	274
849	438	411	390	240	150	116	51	55	87	42	45
2,037	1,178	914	248	121	122	1,799	926	873	—	...	...
10	4	6	113	44	69	...	...	...	...	...	...
40,346	21,426	18,920	24,525	12,800	11,725	27,005	14,276	12,729	6,480	3,428	3,052
...	...	...	1	1	...	155	92	68	...	...	...
491	213	278	127	81	46	159	93	66	17	6	11
8	4	4	51	31	20	4	4	...	...	...	...
...	...	...	...	...	...	...	...	...	...	...	...
257	144	113	488	288	205	42	23	19	20	10	10
...	...	...	...	...	...	...	...	...	...	...	...
4,278	1,911	2,367	2,642	1,348	1,294	643	313	330	980	606	374
950	561	389	845	215	130	4	3	1	102	55	47
...	...	...	21	8	18	...	..	...	...	...	...
84	40	44	27	10	17	8	5	3	...	...	...
...	...	...	18	16	2	...	...	...	...	...	...
2,248	1,190	1,058	1,972	1,076	896	2,557	1,304	1,253	274	145	129
84	54	30	26	18	8	...	...	...	...	...	...
147	78	69	58	35	23	108	48	60	9	8	1
302	191	108	186	112	74	100	52	48	26	18	8
...	...	...	...	...	...	...	...	...	...	...	...
2	...	2	87	48	44	122	82	40	30	18	17
188	73	65	143	95	48	27	18	14	41	29	12
28	10	18	67	47	20	57	25	32	76	36	40
1,551	868	684	1,786	907	879	1,526	853	673	303	143	145
149	95	54	199	189	60	93	35	58	11	4	7
407	201	206	86	59	27	6	...	6	...	...	...
833	369	514	114	81	33	225	114	111	58	48	15
185	77	58	185	76	59	345	150	195	2	...	2
1	1	...	...	...	...	...	...	...	...	...	...
61	39	22	80	14	16	84	33	46	...	...	...
...	...	...	6	3	3	...	...	...	...	...	...
918	447	466	...	...	...	1	1	...	...	...	...
...	—	...	...	...	...	27	13	14	...	...	...
7,440	3,978	3,462	5,904	2,962	2,942	6,760	3,407	3,853	1,526	971	555
3,301	1,743	1,558	2,607	1,377	1,230	3 385	1,565	1,820	633	252	431
169	92	77	559	289	270	157	66	91	56	41	15
...	...	...	...	...	...	...	...	...	...	...	...
293	156	142	781	463	318	59	21	33	25	21	4
1,855	1,175	680	871	580	291	932	490	493	246	138	118
9,728	5,350	4,378	4,251	1,906	2,345	4,937	3,1[illegible]8	1,819	1,488	751	687
...	...	...	...	...	...	...	...	...	...	...	...
59	1	58	...	—	...	—	...	...	...	...	...
475	259	216	37	31	6	420	227	193	...	...	...
3,903	2,108	1,805	950	549	401	3,962	2,071	1,891	557	133	419
323	183	140	510	215	295	17	8	9	...	...	...
6	5	1	94	46	48	...	...	...	...	...	...
14	7	7	67	35	32	...	...	...	...	...	...
303	171	132	349	184	215	17	8	9	...	...	...

TABLE XVII.—Race, Tribe or Caste. *Part II.—Cities.*

Caste and Religion.	LASHKAR CITY.			UJJAIN CITY.		
	Persons.	Males.	Females.	Persons.	Males.	Females.
1	2	3	4	5	6	7
Total	86,767	47,358	39,409	54,650	30,597	24,053
Hindu (Brahmanic)	64,399	35,147	29,252	37,115	21,024	16,091
1 Ahir	331	190	141	737	363	374
2 Badhai	396	211	185	...	...	...
3 Balai	25	10	15	1,375	753	622
4 Banjara	12	5	7	2,014	1,048	966
5 Basor	141	99	42	43	28	15
6 Bania	5,894	3,015	2,879	2,905	1,998	907
1 Agarwal	2,644	1,440	1,204	357	226	131
2 Gahoi	327	188	139	2	2	...
3 Khandelwal	45	37	8	164	121	43
4 Others and unspecified ...	2,878	1,850	1,028	2,442	1,649	793
7 Beragi	49	32	17	454	281	173
8 Bhangi	1,481	743	738	361	193	168
9 Bhoi	1,782	861	921	497	239	258
10 Brahman	15,878	8,622	7,256	6,990	4,251	2,739
1 Audich	2	...	2	812	460	352
2 Bhadauria	372	222	150	...	...	...
3 Bhagor	396	194	202	285	166	119
4 Dakshini	5,339	2,551	2,788	975	607	368
5 Gaur	920	491	429	1,002	657	345
6 Kanyakubja	1,037	787	250	139	107	32
7 Sanadhya	2,236	1,289	947	322	252	70
8 Others and unspecified ...	5,576	3,088	2,488	3,455	2,002	1,453
11 Chamar	3,743	1,930	1,813	2,682	1,525	1,157
12 Chhipa	850	417	433	161	68	93
13 Darzi	376	203	173	309	164	145
14 Dhanuk	217	130	87	...	...	...
15 Dhobi	671	329	342	579	398	181
16 Ghosi	1,921	1,015	906	4	4	...
17 Gosain	109	56	53	181	95	86
18 Gujar	222	150	72	305	150	155
19 Jat	111	64	47	147	50	97
20 Jogi	70	35	35	128	45	83
21 Joshi	217	105	112	253	150	103
22 Kachhi	4,675	2,447	2,228	681	342	339
23 Kalal	386	191	195	126	38	88
24 Kasera	156	95	61	105	38	67
25 [illegible]	2,687	1,589	1,098	718	403	315
26 Khangar	15	11	4	110	58	52
27 Khatik	618	304	314	75	49	26
28 Kirar	286	149	137	296	182	114
29 [illegible]	304	178	126	10	10	...
30 [illegible]	4,650	2,535	2,115	449	235	214
31 [illegible]	1,201	612	589	[illegible]	460	[illegible]
32 [illegible]	[illegible]	[illegible]	290	...	...	...
33 Mali	284	142	142	1,643	[illegible]	[illegible]
34 Maratha	4,505	2,510	[illegible]	1,251	[illegible]	[illegible]
35 [illegible]	...	...	...	[illegible]	[illegible]	[illegible]
36 [illegible]	107	44	63	[illegible]	[illegible]	[illegible]
37 [illegible]	1,477	774	703	725	[illegible]	[illegible]

TABLE XVII.—Race, Tribe or Caste. *Part II.—Cities—(concld.)*

Caste and Religion.	LASHKAR CITY.			UJJAIN CITY.		
	Persons.	Males.	Females.	Persons.	Males.	Females.
1	2	3	4	5	6	7
38 Rajput	4,577	3,071	1,506	4,596	3,024	1,572
1 Bhadauria	334	234	100	144	118	26
2 Chauhan	371	236	135	570	352	218
3 Jadho	142	89	53	22	11	11
4 Kachhwaha	347	234	113	161	107	54
5 Parmar	151	98	53	69	39	30
6 Raghubansi	112	57	55	185	109	76
7 Rathor	88	54	34	130	75	55
8 Sengar	81	52	29	136	123	13
9 Sikarwar	291	204	87	32	30	2
10 Tonwar	523	344	179	147	119	28
11 Others and unspecified ...	2,137	1,469	668	3,000	1,941	1,059
39 Sunar	1,134	592	542	716	360	356
40 Sutar	...	...	...	418	280	138
41 Tamboli	242	127	115	183	95	88
42 Teli	882	463	419	481	193	288
43 Others	1,184	753	431	2,343	1,216	1,127
Hindu-Arya	43	38	5	86	54	32
Hinduized Tribal	...	...	...	12	5	7
Sikh	96	60	36	40	30	10
Jain	1,220	699	521	1,906	1,080	826
1 Agarwal	109	59	50	42	12	30
2 Oswal	255	148	107	907	489	418
3 Saraogi	94	53	41	225	120	105
4 Others and unspecified ...	762	439	323	732	459	273
Zoroastrian	84	32	52	9	3	6
Muslim	20,729	11,278	9,451	15,397	8,351	7,046
1 Bhangi	109	59	50	177	85	92
2 Bhishti	534	267	267	112	90	22
3 Bohra	63	37	26	3,213	1,388	1,825
4 Faqir	151	86	65	207	111	96
5 Hammal	164	75	89	84	54	30
6 Kunjda	272	146	126	87	49	38
7 Mewati	165	113	52	250	136	114
8 Mirasi	5	5	...	101	37	64
9 Mogal	480	314	166	116	76	40
10 Pathan	7,805	4,274	3,531	3,254	1,859	1,395
11 Pinjara	51	18	33	114	25	89
12 Rangrez	137	67	70	232	179	53
13 Sayyad	2,510	1,277	1,233	862	562	300
14 Sheikh	7,248	3,975	3,273	5,027	2,858	2,169
15 Tawaif	22	1	21	58	...	58
16 Teli	272	151	121	13	5	8
17 Others and unspecified ...	751	423	328	1,470	817	653
Christian	196	104	92	85	50	35

TABLE XVIII.

Variation of Population of Selected Tribes.

TABLE XVIII.—Variation of Population of Selected Tribes.

Tribe and Locality.	Persons. 1931	1921	1911	1901	Variation Increase + Decrease —. 1921 to 1931.	1911 to 1921.	1901 to 1911.	Net variation 1901 to 1931. Increase + Decrease —.
1	2	3	4	5	6	7	8	9
Bhil.								
Gwalior State	86,571	71,295	53,299	41,248	+15,276	+17,996	+12,051	+45,323
Hindu	77,770	2,463	10,478	...	+75,307	— 8,015	+10,478	+77,770
Hinduized Tribal	8,801	...	...	...	+ 8,801	...	...	+ 8,801
Tribal	...	68,832	42,821	41,248	—68,832	+26,011	+ 1,578	—41,248
Bhilala.								
Gwalior State	38,455	26,482	1,563	17,145	+11,973	+24,919	—15,582	+21,310
Hindu	36,186	...	...	...	+36,186	...	...	+36,186
Hinduized Tribal	2,819	...	...	...	+ 2,819	...	...	+ 2,819
Tribal	...	26,482	1,563	17,145	—26,482	+24,919	—15,582	—17,145
Kirar.								
Gwalior State	75,987	66,886	51,740	62,397	+ 9,101	+15,146	—10,657	+13,590
Hindu	75,897	66,877	50,975	...	+ 9,020	+15,902	+50,975	+75,897
Hinduized Tribal	90	...	...	...	+ 90	...	...	+ 90
Tribal	...	9	765	62,397	— 9	— 756	—61,632	—62,397
Mina.								
Gwalior State	67,202	65,304	47,525	61,274	+ 1,898	+17,779	—13,749	+ 5,928
Hindu	67,125	60,128	46,943	...	+ 6,997	+13,185	+46,943	+67,125
Hinduized Tribal	77	...	...	...	+ 77	...	...	+ 77
Tribal	...	5,176	582	61,274	— 5,176	+ 4,594	—60,692	—61,274
Sahariya.								
Gwalior State	76,219	58,380	55,428	35,525	+17,839	+ 2,952	+19,903	+40,694
Hindu	73,537	1,897	42,448	...	+71,640	—40,551	+42,448	+73,537
Hinduized Tribal	2,682	...	...	...	+ 2,682	...	...	+ 2,682
Tribal	...	56,483	12,980	35,525	—56,483	+43,503	—22,545	—35,525

	Males. 1931	1921	1911	1901	Females. 1931	1921	1911	1901
	10	11	12	13	14	15	16	17
Bhil—	43,682	36,329	26,538	21,514	42,889	34,966	26,761	19,734
	39,430	1,319	5,570	...	38,340	1,144	4,908	...
	4,252	...	...	...	4,549	...	...	...
	...	35,010	20,968	21,514	...	33,822	21,853	19,734
Bhilala—	19,431	13,300	858	9,309	19,024	13,182	705	7,836
	18,205	...	...	...	17,981	...	...	...
	1,226	...	...	...	1,093	...	...	...
	...	13,300	858	9,309	...	13,182	705	7,836
Kirar—	41,001	37,264	28,099	33,169	34,986	29,622	23,641	29,228
	40,981	37,258	27,666	...	34,916	29,619	23,309	...
	20	...	...	...	70	...	...	...
	...	6	433	33,169	...	3	332	29,228
Mina—	34,414	35,704	24,585	30,613	32,788	29,600	22,940	30,661
	34,376	33,040	24,255	...	32,749	27,088	22,688	...
	38	...	...	...	39	...	...	...
	...	2,664	330	30,613	...	2,512	252	30,661
Sahariya—	38,745	29,708	28,749	20,455	37,474	28,672	26,679	15,070
	37,204	1,168	21,945	...	36,333	729	20,503	...
	1,541	...	...	...	1,141	...	...	...
	...	28,540	6,804	20,455	...	27,943	6,176	15,070

TABLE XIX.

European and Allied Races and Anglo-Indians

By

Race and Age.

Armenians—Nil.

TABLE XIX.—European and Allied Races and Anglo-Indians by Race and Age.

	Districts.	TOTAL.			A.—EUROPEAN AND ALLIED RACES (INCLUDING ARMENIANS). (a) British Subjects. All Ages.			0—13		14—16		17—23		24—33		34—43		44—53		54 and over.		(b) Others. All Ages.			0—13		14—16		17—23		24—33		34—43	
		P.	M.	F.	P.	M.	F.	M.	F.	M.	F.	M.	F.	M.	F.	M.	F.	M.	F.	M.	F.	P.	M.	F.	M.	F.	M.	F.	M.	F.	M.	F.	M.	F.
	1	2	3	4	5	6	7	8	9	10	11	12	13	14	15	16	17	18	19	20	21	22	23	24	25	26	27	28	29	30	31	32	33	34
	Gwalior State ...	242	127	115	101	54	47	7	7	3	2	5	7	12	5	10	10	11	9	6	7	10	4	6	...	...	...	...	1	...	...	1	2	2
1	Gird District ...	44	24	20	17	9	8	...	...	...	...	1	2	3	1	1	2	2	2	2	1	4	2	2	...	...	...	...	...	...	...	...	2	...
2	Bhind District ...	1	1	...	...	...	...	...	...	...	...	...	...	...	...	...	...	...	...	...	...	1	1	...	...	...	...	...	...	...	...	...	...	...
3	Tonwarghar Dist.	4	3	1	4	3	1	...	...	1	...	...	...	...	...	...	1	1	...	1	...	...	...	...	...	...	...	...	...	...	...	...	...	...
4	Narwar District.	2	...	2	...	...	...	...	...	...	...	...	...	...	...	...	...	...	...	...	...	2	...	2	...	...	...	...	...	...	...	...	...	1
5	Isagarh District ...	2	1	1	2	1	1	...	...	...	...	...	...	...	...	1	...	...	1	...	...	...	...	...	...	...	...	...	...	...	...	...	...	...
6	Bhilsa District ...	8	5	3	...	...	...	...	...	...	...	...	...	...	...	...	...	...	...	...	...	...	...	...	...	...	...	...	...	...	...	...	...	...
7	Ujjain District ...	20	12	8	12	6	6	1	1	1	...	...	...	2	1	1	...	1	...	...	4	2	1	1	...	...	...	...	1	...	...	1	...	...
8	Mandsaur District	161	81	80	66	35	31	6	6	1	2	4	5	7	3	7	7	7	6	3	2	1	...	1	...	...	...	...	...	...	...	...	...	1

	45—53		54 and over.		B. ANGLO-INDIANS. All Ages.			0—3		4—6		7—13		14—16		17—19		20—29		30—39		40—49		50—59		60—69		70 and over.	
	M.	F.	M.	F.	P.	M.	F.	M.	F.	M.	F.	M.	F.	M.	F.	M.	F.	M.	F.	M.	F.	M.	F.	M.	F.	M.	F.	M.	F.
	35	36	37	38	39	40	41	42	43	44	45	46	47	48	49	50	51	52	53	54	55	56	57	58	59	60	61	62	63
	...	1	1	2	131	69	62	8	8	9	10	7	10	2	...	...	3	9	7	17	11	8	4	5	4	2	1	2	4
1	...	...	...	2	23	13	10	...	...	1	1	...	1	...	...	...	...	1	1	3	1	2	2	3	2	2	...	1	2
2	...	...	1	...	...	...	...	...	...	...	...	...	...	...	...	...	...	...	...	...	...	...	...	...	...	...	...	...	...
3	...	...	...	...	...	...	...	...	...	...	...	...	...	...	...	...	...	...	...	...	...	...	...	...	...	...	...	...	...
4	...	1	...	...	...	...	...	...	...	...	...	...	...	...	...	...	...	...	...	...	...	...	...	...	...	...	...	...	...
5	...	...	...	...	...	...	...	...	...	...	...	...	...	...	...	...	...	...	...	...	...	...	...	...	...	...	...	...	...
6	...	...	...	...	8	5	3	2	...	...	...	...	...	...	...	...	1	1	2	2	...	...	...	...	...	...	...	...	...
7	...	...	...	...	6	5	1	...	...	1	...	...	1	...	...	...	...	1	...	1	...	2	...	...	...	...	...	...	...
8	...	...	...	...	94	46	48	6	8	7	9	7	8	2	...	...	2	6	4	11	10	4	2	2	2	...	1	1	2

TABLE XX.

Summary Figures for Districts.

TABLE XX.—Summary Figures for Districts.

Serial Number.	DISTRICT.	Area in Square Miles.	POPULATION.			Population 1921.	Percentage of Variation	
			Persons.	Males.	Females.		1921-1931	1911-1921
1	2	3	4	5	6	7	8	9
	Gwalior State ...	26,367	3,523,070	1,867,031	1,656,039	3,193,176	+10·3	—1·3
1	Gird District ...	1,712	364,806	197,935	166,871	326,466	+11·7	+4·5
2	Bhind District ...	1,718	418,224	228,214	190,010	382,179	+9·4	—4·5
3	Tonwarghar District...	2,004	369,648	204,759	164,889	336,660	+9 8	—11·2
4	Sheopur District ...	2,366	137,034	72,925	64,109	124,865	+9·7	—0·7
5	Narwar District ...	3 876	401,586	211,555	190,031	376,715	+6·6	—9·1
6	Isagarh District ...	4,477	421,311	221,556	199,755	377,000	+11·8	—3·5
7	Bhilsa District ...	1,905	235,288	123,084	112,204	244,263	—3·7	+27·1
8	Ujjain District ...	2,741	405,961	211,274	194,687	343,870	+18·2	—0·3
9	Mandsaur District ...	1,777	272,166	140,333	131,833	237,745	+14·5	+0·3
10	Shajapur District ...	2,460	336,930	174,935	161,995	307,293	+9·6	—1·9
11	Amjhera District ...	1,231	160,066	80,411	79,655	136,520	+17·2	+8·5

Serial Number.	DISTRICT.	Number of Persons per Square Mile in		DISTRIBUTION BY RELIGION.									
				HINDU.		MUSLIM.		JAIN.		CHRISTIAN.		OTHERS.	
		1931.	1921.	Males.	Females.	Males.	Females.	Males.	Females.	M.	F.	M.	F.
1	2	10	11	12	13	14	15	16	17	18	19	20	21
	Gwalior State ...	134	121	1,732,247	1,539,329	109,412	94,885	24,238	20,841	592	606	542	378
1	Grid District ...	218	190	174,674	147,802	21,575	17,657	1,405	1,164	143	125	138	123
2	Bhind Distrct ...	248	222	217,782	181,040	6,887	5,802	3,442	3,112	8	2	100	54
3	Tonwarghar District ...	184	167	197,669	159,184	5,949	4,783	1,122	959	13	11	6	2
4	Sheopur District ...	58	53	69,219	61,806	3,064	2,701	137	101	...	...	5	1
5	Narwar District ...	104	98	204,612	184,116	5,001	4,236	1,937	1,678	...	2	5	4
6	Isagarh District ...	94	83	209,498	189,206	8,855	7,509	3,554	2,958	21	18	128	64
7	Bhilsa District ...	124	128	115,078	105,247	6,651	5,771	1,329	1,160	6	4	20	22
8	Ujjain District ...	148	125	186,207	172,848	21,426	18,920	3,398	2,751	183	140	90	23
9	Mandsaur District ...	153	133	122,949	115,894	12,800	11,725	4,297	3,842	215	295	72	77
10	Shajapur District ...	137	124	158,114	147,002	14,276	12,729	2,579	2,252	8	9	8	3
11	Amjhera District ...	120	108	75,945	75,734	3,428	3,052	1,038	869	...	...	...	...

STATE TABLE I.

Area and Population of Tehsils and Districts.

STATE TABLE I.—Area and Population of Tehsils and Districts.

Serial Number.	District and Tehsil.	Area in Square Miles.	NUMBER OF Towns.	NUMBER OF Villages.	Number of Occupied Houses.	POPULATION. 1981 Persons.	POPULATION. 1981 Males.	POPULATION. 1981 Females.	POPULATION. 1921. Both Sexes.	PERCENTAGE OF VARIATION. 1921 to 1981	PERCENTAGE OF VARIATION. 1911 to 1921	Number of persons per square mile in 1981.
1	2	3	4	5	6	7	8	9	10	11	12	184
	Gwalior State ...	26,367	43	10,852	767,£30	3,523,070	1,867,031	1,656,039	3,193,176	+10·3	— 1·3	184
I	**Gird District ...**	1,712	6	783	83,150	364,806	197,935	166,871	326,466	+11·7	+ 4·5	213
	1. Gird ...	440	5	217	44,575	184,911	103,046	81,865	161,858	+14·6	+16·2	412
	2. Pichhore ...	622	...	257	16,317	81,179	42,555	38,624	67,088	+20·1	— 7·5	130
	3. Mastura ...	420	...	186	11,948	53,332	28,720	24,612	53,866	— 0·1	— 1·7	127
	4. Bhander ...	221	1	123	10,815	45,384	23,614	21,770	44,159	+ 2·8	— 4·8	205
I	**Bhind District ...**	1,718	2	879	86,214	418,224	228,214	190,010	382,179	+ 9·4	— 4·5	243
	5. Bhind ...	569	1	278	30,650	152,688	84,046	68,592	139,046	+ 9·8	— 7·4	268
	6. Mehgaon ...	368	...	199	16,787	80,082	43,485	36,597	74,972	+ 6·8	+ 1·7	218
	7. Lahar ...	397	...	229	21,144	99,664	53,232	46,432	89,968	+10·8	— 6·7	251
	8. Gohad ...	384	1	173	17,688	85,840	47,451	38,389	78,191	+ 9·8	— 2·2	224
III	**Tonwarghar District**	2,004	4	784	74,107	369,648	204,759	164,889	336,660	+ 9·8	—11·2	184
	9. Joura ...	452	1	183	17,003	84,042	46,688	37,359	77,170	+ 8·9	—21·2	186
	10. Ambah ...	393	1	142	20,092	107,754	60,127	47,627	98,541	+ 9·3	—13·2	274
	11. Nurabad ...	627	1	175	17,129	83,975	46,925	37,050	75,759	+10·8	— 7·2	134
	12. Sabalgarh ...	532	1	284	19,883	93,877	51,024	42,853	85,190	+10·2	— 0·9	176
IV	**Sheopur District...**	2,366	1	566	30,888	137,034	72,925	64,109	124,865	+ 9·7	— 0·7	58
	13. Sheopur ...	1,506	1	371	19,097	86,972	45,730	41,242	76,402	+13·8	— 0·7	56
	14. Bijeypur ...	860	...	195	11,191	50,062	27,195	22,867	48,463	+ 3·3	— 0·8	58
V	**Narwar District ...**	3,876	5	1,300	88,161	401,586	211,555	190,031	370,715	+ 6·6	— 9·1	104
	15. Shivpuri ...	1,677	1	445	28,080	121,061	63,629	57,432	117,868	+ 2·7	— 4·5	72
	16. Karera ...	637	3	264	19,050	98,151	49,792	48,359	87,728	+ 6·2	— 8·4	146
	17. Pichhore ...	554	...	288	23,293	104,000	54,944	49,056	97,101	+ 7·1	— 8·7	188
	18. Kolaras ...	1,008	1	303	17,738	83,374	43,190	40,184	74,018	+12·6	—16·7	83
VI	**Isagarh District ...**	4,477	6	1,902	89,942	421,311	221,556	199,755	377,000	+11·8	— 3·5	94
	19. Bajrangarh...	1,946	2	801	33,748	152,699	80,447	72,252	143,807	+ 6·2	— 2·1	78
	20. Pachhar ...	830	2	345	19,022	92,065	48,125	43,940	80,021	+15·1	+ 8·7	111
	21. Mungaoli ...	1,057	2	377	20,057	95,706	49,788	45,928	81,367	+17·6	— 6·7	90
	22. Kumbhraj ...	644	...	379	17,120	80,841	43,201	37,640	71,805	+12·6	—13·5	124
VII	**Bhilsa District ...**	1,905	2	899	50,628	235,288	123,084	112,204	244,263	— 3·7	+27·1	124
	23. Bhilsa ...	730	1	399	22,883	103,548	53,945	49,598	119,911	—13·7	+40·6	142
	24. Basoda ...	1,175	1	500	27,745	131,745	69,139	62,606	124,352	+ 5·9	+16.0	112
VIII	**Ujjain District ...**	2,741	6	1,133	93,233	405,961	211,274	194,687	343,370	+18·2	— 0·3	148
	25. Ujjain ...	587	2	303	32,450	135,929	72,675	63,254	107,985	+25·9	+ 2·7	232
	26. Barnagar ...	445	1	188	15,775	67,744	34,098	33,046	68,048	+ 7·4	+ 9·8	152
	27. Khachraud ...	490	2	221	29,850	72,111	37,244	34,867	60,100	+20·0	+ 0·1	147
	28. Sonkach ...	1,219	1	421	15,658	130,177	66,657	63,520	110,287	+16·0	— 8·0	107
IX	**Mandsaur District.**	1,777	5	947	62,010	272,166	140,333	131,833	237,745	+14·5	+ 0·3	153
	29. Mandsaur ...	555	1	263	28,456	103,476	53,728	49,748	81,816	+26·5	— 4·7	186
	30. Suvasra ...	225	...	188	8,835	39,451	20,228	19,223	42,300	— 6·8	+ 5·4	175
	31. Nimach ...	672	2	261	15,265	65,973	34,122	31,851	57,661	+14·4	+ 1·0	98
	32. Jawad ...	299	1	276	12,129	52,872	26,829	26,043	46,558	+13·6	+ 3·9	177
	33. Gangapur ...	26	1	9	2,325	10,394	5,426	4,968	9,401	+10·6	+ 2·2	399
X	**Shajapur District.**	2,460	3	1,064	77,740	336,930	174,935	161,995	307,393	+ 9·	— 1·9	137
	34 Shajapur ...	592	1	316	22,247	95,535	49,206	46,329	86,741	+10·1	— 4·7	162
	25 Agar ...	703	1	275	17,811	76,395	39,807	36,588	68,784	+11·1	— 5·9	109
	S5 Susner ...	499	...	225	15,302	66,597	34,729	31,868	61,794	+ 7·8	+ 1·8	133
	37 Shujalpur ...	CCG	1	248	22,880	98,458	51,248	47,210	90,074	+ 9·3	+ 2·0	148
XI	**Amjhera District.**	1,331	3	595	31,757	160,066	80,411	79,655	136,520	+17·2	+ 8·5	120
	28. Amjhera ...	730	2	289	17,132	76,554	38,584	37,970	69,002	+10·9	— 2·5	105
	29. Babaner ...	601	1	306	14,625	83,512	41,827	41,685	67,518	+23·7	+2 28.	139

STATE TABLE II.

Population of Districts and Tehsils by Religion and Literacy.

NOTE 1.—Classification of Hindus as Brahmans, Other Hindus and Depressed Classes has not been given as the education by caste for Table XIV has been sorted for some selected castes only.

2.—In columns 26 to 33 literacy has been given in age groups 0-13, 14-16, 17-23 and 24 and over instead of 0-15, 15-20 and 20 and over for the reason that figures have not been smoothed by Tehsils.

3.—Unsmoothed figures for Nimach Cantonment being not available the figures of literacy by religion and age against Mandsaur District and Gwalior State fall short of Nimach Cantonment figures which are as follows:—

	Hindu.		Jain.		Muslim.		Christian.		Others.		0-15		15-20		20 & over.		Literate in English.	
	M.	F.	M.	F	M.	F.	M.	F.	M	F.	M.	F.	M.	F.	M.	F.	M.	F.
Nimach Cantonment	1,253	83	53	3	357	24	33	147	44	61	104	94	246	48	1,440	176	291	140

STATE TABLE II.—Population of Districts and

Serial Number.	District and Tehsil.	HINDU. Brahmanic. Number of Persons. Males.	Females.	Number of Literates. Males.	Females.	Hinduized Tribal. Number of Persons. Males.	Females.	No. of Literates. Males.	Fem.	JAIN. Number of Persons. Males.	Females.	Number of Literates. Males.	Females.	MUSLIM. Number of Persons. Males.	Females.	Number of Literates. Males.	Females.
	1	2	3	4	5	6	7	8	9	10	11	12	13	14	15	16	17
	Gwalior State ...	**1,724,311**	**1,531,666**	**100,819**	**11,225**	**7,248**	**7,043**	**88**	**6**	**24,238**	**20,841**	**8,427**	**1,144**	**109,412**	**94,885**	**14,359**	**2,187**
I	**Gird District ...**	**174,591**	**147,754**	**20,053**	**2,488**	**11**	**8**	...	...	**1,405**	**1,164**	**587**	**127**	**21,575**	**17,657**	**3,602**	**572**
	1 Gird ...	82,757	65,498	14,670	2,089	..	...	...	...	1,048	810	465	98	18,897	15,271	3,275	498
	2 Pichhore ...	41,023	37,827	1,962	381	3	...	...	...	109	106	55	17	1,416	1,189	151	68
	3 Mastura ...	27,746	22,760	1,585	79	8	8	...	...	251	248	65	18	715	601	82	3
	4 Bhander ...	23,065	21,169	1,836	39	...	...	...	...	2	5	2	4	547	596	94	8
II	**Bhind District ...**	**217,360**	**180,750**	**10,522**	**813**	**342**	**241**	**3**	...	**3,442**	**3,112**	**972**	**122**	**6,887**	**5,802**	**750**	**54**
	5 Bhind ...	79,819	64,501	8,843	430	46	47	3	...	2,047	1,822	718	108	2,622	2,219	238	37
	6 Mehgaon ...	41,046	34,941	991	120	2	4	...	...	719	689	118	...	1,118	968	134	5
	7 Labar ...	51,744	45,053	3,114	111	...	...	...	...	88	96	1	...	1,400	1,288	269	12
	8 Gohad ...	44,651	36,255	2,574	152	294	190	...	...	588	505	145	14	1,747	1,337	109	...
III	**Tonwarghar District**	**197,628**	**159,093**	**9,098**	**660**	**29**	**23**	...	...	**1,122**	**959**	**261**	**28**	**5,949**	**4,783**	**741**	**71**
	9 Joura ...	44,756	35,848	1,884	145	14	14	...	...	211	179	68	4	1,702	1,328	325	30
	10 Ambah ...	58,379	46,276	2,426	162	...	...	...	...	680	529	112	7	1,064	822	168	22
	11 Nurabad ...	44,720	35,214	3,327	195	15	9	...	...	201	211	64	17	1,963	1,585	137	12
	12 Sabalgarh ...	49,773	41,760	1,901	158	...	...	...	...	30	40	17	...	1,220	1,053	116	7
IV	**Sheopur District**	**69,396**	**60,982**	**3,485**	**420**	**299**	**302**	...	...	**137**	**101**	**64**	**19**	**3,064**	**2,701**	**337**	**35**
	13 Sheopur ...	42,623	39,447	2,029	263	299	302	...	...	100	74	49	17	2,687	2,899	243	32
	14 Bijaypur ...	26,773	21,535	1,456	157	...	...	...	..	37	27	15	2	377	302	94	3
V	**Narwar District.**	**204,258**	**183,816**	**5,685**	**414**	**324**	**293**	**2**	...	**1,937**	**1,673**	**553**	**21**	**5,001**	**4,236**	**682**	**70**
	15 Shivpuri ...	60,671	55,034	2,202	191	148	135	2	...	898	289	183	6	2,381	1,961	359	45
	16 Karera ...	48,197	41,948	1,193	83	3	3	...	...	481	445	121	3	1,111	963	161	7
	17 Pichhore ...	53 691	48,021	949	74	173	155	...	...	565	496	79	5	512	384	65	10
	18 Kolaras ...	41,096	38 813	1,341	66	...	...	...	...	493	443	170	7	997	928	97	8
VI	**Isagarh District.**	**209,130**	**188,625**	**9,539**	**847**	**252**	**265**	**55**	...	**3,554**	**2,958**	**1,023**	**94**	**8,353**	**7,509**	**981**	**76**
	19 Bajrangarh.	76,154	68,319	2,971	279	137	140	...	...	1,154	892	255	9	2,956	2,888	302	26
	20 Pachhar ...	45,188	41,450	2,712	214	68	70	...	...	1,014	783	366	29	1,723	1,468	283	18
	21 Mungaoli ...	46,030	42,634	2,331	253	47	55	55	...	1,155	1,113	315	48	2,475	2,077	336	30
	22 Kumbhraj ...	41,754	36,374	1,522	101	...	...	...	...	231	170	87	13	1,201	1,081	60	2
V	**Bhilsa District...**	**114,901**	**105,067**	**5,538**	**590**	**166**	**166**	...	...	**1,329**	**1,160**	**444**	**55**	**6,651**	**5,771**	**739**	**51**
	23 Bhilsa ...	49,815	46,028	3,742	427	156	158	...	...	680	596	268	47	3,272	2,786	492	36
	24 Basoda ...	65,086	59,039	1,846	163	10	8	...	...	649	564	176	8	3,379	2,985	247	15
III	**Ujjain District...**	**185,638**	**172,273**	**14,772**	**2,374**	**357**	**366**	**5**	...	**3,398**	**2,751**	**1,446**	**364**	**21,426**	**18,920**	**3,461**	**841**
	25 Ujjain ...	59,882	52,519	8,256	1,809	8	8	4	...	1,354	1,062	547	249	11 210	9,515	2,523	756
	26 Barnagar...	30,844	29,591	2,364	246	195	208	...	...	630	540	391	67	2,851	2,529	352	32
	27 Khachraud.	33,684	31,620	1,606	134	154	150	...	...	883	715	368	26	2,490	2,865	264	10
	28 Sonkach ...	61,228	58,543	2,546	185	...	...	1	...	531	434	145	22	4,875	4,511	322	48
IX	**Mandsaur District.**	**122,062**	**114,978**	**10,148**	**1,442**	**846**	**881**	**13**	**4**	**4,297**	**3,842**	**1,893**	**173**	**12,800**	**11,725**	**1,526**	**148**
	29 Mandsaur.	45,522	42,320	4,008	890	498	495	...	...	1,875	1,627	800	81	5,810	5,288	847	110
	30 Suvasra ...	18,968	18,027	1,492	107	...	...	...	...	262	287	85	2	997	955	134	1
	31 Nimach ...	29,171	27,260	1,607	230	138	123	6	1	959	875	382	24	3,567	3,216	193	24
	32 Jawad ...	23,610	22,971	2,227	194	168	226	7	3	922	859	470	45	2,120	1,982	201	13
	33 Gangapur...	4,791	4,409	814	21	47	87	...	...	279	244	156	21	306	284	61	...
X	**Shajapur District.**	**137,723**	**140,581**	**8,633**	**815**	**330**	**347**	**1**	**1**	**2,579**	**2,252**	**686**	**59**	**14,276**	**12,729**	**1,023**	**181**
	34 Shajapur ...	44,378	41,672	2,062	303	160	153	1	1	462	375	75	14	4,191	4,116	451	100
	35 Agar ...	36,478	33,617	1,865	220	...	...	...	...	811	650	247	19	2,496	2,272	192	20
	36 [illegible] ...	32,161	29,341	1,709	112	185	179	...	...	653	614	134	58	1,771	1,725	99	45
	37 [illegible] ...	44,706	41,951	2,102	180	89	15	...	...	653	613	230	8	5,818	4,616	281	16
XI	**Amjhera District.**	**71,621**	**71,546**	**3,291**	**362**	**4,292**	**4,151**	**9**	**1**	**1,038**	**869**	**498**	**42**	**3,428**	**3,052**	**517**	**88**
	38 [illegible] ...	32,664	32,562	2,214	210	3,144	2,982	9	1	805	689	387	28	1,956	1,714	238	78
	39 [illegible] ...	38,959	38,984	1,077	152	1,148	1,169	...	...	233	180	111	14	1,472	1,338	279	10

Tehsils by Religion and Literacy.

CHRISTIAN.				OTHERS.				NUMBER OF LITERATES.								LITERATE IN ENGLISH.		
Number of Persons.		Number of Literates.		Number of Persons.		Number of Literates.		Aged 0—13.		Aged 14—16.		Aged 17—23.		Aged 24 and over.				
M.	F.	M.	F.	M.	F.	M.	F.	M.	F.	M.	F.	M.	F.	M.	F.	M.	F.	
18	19	20	21	22	23	24	25	26	27	28	29	30	31	32	33	34	35	
592	606	246	196	1,230	998	418	119	13,851	2,420	12,236	1,856	20,724	2,771	77,546	7,830	12,426	757	
143	125	97	66	210	163	141	65	2,445	567	1,868	455	4.785	701	15,382	1,595	4,631	314	I
140	193	95	65	209	168	140	65	1,845	480	1,286	847	8,602	564	11,912	1,864	4,482	299	
8	2	2	1	1	...	1	...	258	59	185	76	881	108	1,847	179	58	11	
...	...	...	...	...	...	...	...	185	18	146	25	484	28	967	24	80	...	
...	...	...	...	...	...	...	...	157	10	251	7	868	6	1,156	28	66	4	
3	2	3	1	180	103	66	...	1,478	205	1,172	131	2,013	238	7,653	416	628	3	I
8	2	8	1	9	1	8	...	626	115	488	69	888	145	2,901	247	266	8	
...	...	...	...	...	...	...	...	168	86	188	21	221	14	716	54	44	...	
...	...	...	...	...	...	...	...	889	16	292	25	404	84	2 299	48	180	...	
...	...	...	...	171	102	68	...	800	88	804	16	550	45	1,787	67	188	...	
13	11	3	1	18	20	2	...	1,320	121	1,424	107	1,636	119	5,725	413	572	2	III
...	...	...	...	...	...	...	...	155	46	249	22	312	82	1,061	79	98	...	
...	...	...	...	4	...	1	...	589	24	477	29	480	28	1,256	110	118	...	
12	11	2	1	14	20	1	...	430	34	469	83	592	82	2,020	126	202	1	
1	...	1	...	...	...	...	...	196	17	209	23	302	27	1,888	98	159	1	
...	...	...	...	29	23	15	8	455	55	469	99	575	72	2.402	256	308	6	IV
...	...	...	...	21	20	18	6	251	85	235	63	810	44	1,588	176	268	8	
...	...	...	...	8	3	2	2	204	20	284	86	265	28	864	80	40	8	
...	2	...	2	35	11	13	1	805	100	653	77	1,121	108	4,356	223	548	9	V
...	2	...	2	81	11	9	1	266	57	214	27	451	56	1,824	105	843	9	
...	...	...	...	...	...	...	...	196	19	120	18	258	20	901	36	157	...	
...	...	..	...	...	...	...	...	115	12	185	18	208	16	685	48	28	...	
...	...	...	...	4	...	4	...	228	12	184	14	204	16	996	39	20	...	
21	18	10	8	244	179	49	7	1,665	263	1,620	135	2,090	154	6,282	480	812	33	VI
7	2	4	2	89	16	10	...	513	71	540	40	824	50	1,605	155	262	16	
8	2	2	2	184	118	21	...	462	75	424	46	591	32	1,907	110	268	10	
6	9	2	2	61	85	18	7	518	101	491	35	898	46	1,663	153	201	7	
5	5	2	2	10	10	...	...	177	16	165	14	282	26	1,047	62	81	...	
6	4	4	2	31	36	15	8	705	162	546	79	1,001	116	4,538	349	587	11	V
8	8	2	1	19	27	14	7	523	111	877	59	578	89	3,046	259	453	5	
8	1	2	1	12	9	1	1	188	51	169	20	428	27	1,492	90	134	8	
183	140	86	67	272	237	58	15	1,792	350	1,692	330	3,070	655	13,274	2.326	2,401	320	VIII
128	93	70	49	93	57	89	14	910	210	950	288	1,600	493	7,979	1,986	1,784	290	
9	5	2	1	169	178	13	1	880	69	189	44	555	71	1,998	168	202	10	
27	13	7	..	6	4	4	...	218	86	288	17	414	38	1 884	79	261	8	
19	29	7	17	4	8	2	...	289	85	820	81	501	58	1,918	148	204	12	
215	295	43	49	113	112	35	9	1,535	347	1,289	223	2,061	334	8,773	921	1,144	50	IX
11	9	8	1	17	9	14	5	620	192	465	161	972	212	3,615	522	582	17	
1	4	...	...	...	...	...	...	252	12	195	13	245	27	1.039	58	250	...	
199	279	40	48	88	98	18	4	810	103	186	17	351	45	1,399	166	219	38	
4	3	...	...	5	2	3	...	272	85	375	25	368	48	1,988	147	79	...	
...	...	...	...	8	3	...	...	101	5	68	7	130	2	732	28	34	...	
8	9	...	...	69	77	24	6	1,258	170	1,040	120	1,603	189	6,474	623	450	4	X
...	...	...	...	19	13	7	1	522	74	471	44	529	70	1,974	231	213	2	
...	...	...	...	22	49	12	4	278	52	200	14	267	29	1,576	168	57	...	
8	9	..	...	1	...	...	...	159	18	200	31	336	36	1,247	130	18	...	
...	...	...	...	27	15	5	1	304	26	169	31	468	54	1,677	94	162	2	
...	...	...	...	29	37	...	...	393	80	463	100	772	85	2,687	228	345	5	XI
...	...	...	...	15	28	...	...	259	49	291	61	511	49	1,787	158	309	3	
...	...	...	...	14	14	...	...	184	31	172	39	261	36	900	70	36	2	